CW01309708

The War Against the Working Class

The War Against the Working Class

WILL PODMORE

Copyright © 2015 by Will Podmore.

Library of Congress Control Number: 2015905304
ISBN: Hardcover 978-1-5035-3109-3
        Softcover 978-1-5035-3111-6
        eBook 978-1-5035-3110-9

All rights reserved. No part of this book may be reproduced or transmitted in any form or by any means, electronic or mechanical, including photocopying, recording, or by any information storage and retrieval system, without permission in writing from the copyright owner.

Any people depicted in stock imagery provided by Thinkstock are models, and such images are being used for illustrative purposes only.
Certain stock imagery © Thinkstock.

Print information available on the last page.

Rev. date: 05/28/2015

To order additional copies of this book, contact:
Xlibris
1-888-795-4274
www.Xlibris.com
Orders@Xlibris.com
698969

Contents

Introduction vii
Acknowledgements xi

Chapter 1   Russia, to 1927 1
Chapter 2   The Soviet Union from 1927 to 1933 20
Chapter 3   Towards world war 41
Chapter 4   World War Two 59
Chapter 5   Stalingrad and victory 70
Chapter 6   The Soviet Union from 1945 to 1986 88
Chapter 7   Eastern Europe from 1945 to 1989 104
Chapter 8   China 115
Chapter 9   Korea 139
Chapter 10 Vietnam and South-East Asia 148
Chapter 11 Cuba, to 1990 164
Chapter 12 The Soviet Union - counter-revolution and
            catastroika 177
Chapter 13 Eastern Europe – counter-revolution and war 194
Chapter 14 Cuba, the Special Period – workers in control 216

Notes 239
Bibliography 303
Index 309

Introduction

Is history any use? Why should we look back into the past? In particular, why read a book on the history of the Soviet Union and the other socialist countries? Surely all we need to know is that they tried and failed to create an alternative to the free market economy? This book will present evidence that the attempts achieved real progress.

Human beings have created successively freer, more democratic and more prosperous societies. Archaeological evidence has shown that there was never a time of 'primitive communism'. Even hunter-gatherer societies competed for scarce resources. Societies developed from slavery, to feudalism, then to capitalism. In the 20th century, workers attempted the biggest change of all, creating socialism, the first form of classless society, in which the majority ruled, not the minority.

Reg Birch, the first chairman of the Communist Party of Britain Marxist-Leninist, said, "The Bolshevik Revolution upon which the Soviet Union is established owes its place in history to being the only change in class power from bourgeois to proletariat, the only change of relation of production from capitalist to socialist in the world. This revolutionary development has dictated the role of the Soviet Union in the world irrespective of individual leaders, for it is the relations of production that determines the political superstructure – hence the domestic and international line. ... The Bolshevik Revolution still is the most truly historic change in class forces. It represents the power to do by a working class. It is the example and hope for all other workers' aspiration. It did because of that great historic change accelerate the course of history in the world. Because of it, the Bolshevik Revolution, others were strengthened, invigorated and inspired. As in China, Vietnam, Cuba, Albania and so on."[1]

That is why the rulers feared and smeared the Soviet Union. Their hatred of socialism led to more than a century of wars and to grotesque outcomes. From 1947 to 1987, the US Department of Defense spent $7.62 trillion (in 1982 dollars). In 1985, the US Department of Commerce valued US plant, equipment and infrastructure at just over $7.29 trillion. So the USA spent more on destroying things than on making things.

Workers achieved the 20th-century's revolutions in the most backward pre-industrial societies, largely feudal, and suffering foreign rule and exploitation. Wherever a working class seized power, the capitalist states at once attacked it with every weapon, including war, terrorism and blockade. The ruling classes did all they could to add to the costs of revolution.

So workers had to build their new states when under attack, amid the ruin of war and under constant threat of new war. In so doing, they achieved much, but also, as was bound to happen, they got many things wrong. These first attempts to build socialist societies mostly failed in the end. To create is always harder than not to create. But we can learn from them. The answer to bad decisions is not 'no decisions' but better decisions. The answer to bad planning is not 'no planning' but better planning.

Societies which had revolutions - Britain in the 1640s, the USA in 1776, France in 1789, Russia in 1917, China in 1949 and Cuba in 1959 - were very different from societies which had not. For example, China's wealth, power and independence vastly surpassed its pre-revolutionary past and outstripped other countries in similar circumstances. Revolutions had costs, but the costs of not having a revolution were greater. And some pioneers, like Cuba, still survived against huge odds and remained true to the highest ideals that humanity had created.

These working classes built independent economies and societies. They created wealth through their own labour, without plundering other countries. They played major roles in ending wars, defeating fascism, freeing the colonies and keeping the peace in Europe from 1945 to 1990. By presenting a practical alternative to unrestrained capital, they aided the working classes of other countries to make gains, especially after 1945.

We can learn from the efforts and the errors of the pioneers, even though as pre-industrial colonised societies they were very different from Britain today. The hope is that this book will provoke thought about what the working class needs to do, not to copy but to create.

Acknowledgements

Thanks to the staffs at John Harvard Library, Borough High Street, Southwark, especially to Luke, at Park Road Library, Aldersbrook, especially to Matt, at University College London Library, and at the Library of the UCL School of Slavonic and East European Studies. Thanks to Nick Bateson and Gill Wrobel for their invaluable advice.

Chapter 1
Russia, to 1927

Tsarist Russia

Russia had worse farmland and a worse climate than the USA or Western Europe, so its agricultural productivity was lower than theirs under any system of farming. Only 1.4 per cent of land suitable for cereal cultivation was in an area with the best combination of temperature and moisture, compared to 56 per cent in the USA. 80 per cent of Russia's cropland lay in a zone of risky agriculture, compared to 20 per cent in the USA. Russia's growing season was nowhere more than 200 days a year, far less than Western Europe's 260 to 300 days.[1]

There were famines throughout Russia's history, usually every other year. Between 1800 and 1854, crops failed 35 times. Between 1891 and 1910, there were 13 poor harvests, three famine years and only four good harvests.

Before the revolution, 80 per cent of Russia's people were peasants, at the mercy of landlords and kulaks. A contemporary observer wrote, "this type of man was commonly termed a Koolak, or fist, to symbolize his utter callousness to pity or ruth. And of all the human monsters I have ever met in my travels, I cannot recall any so malignant and odious as the Russian Koolak."[2]

Tsarist Russia was the most backward, least industrialised and poorest of all the European powers. Tsar Nicholas II, a feudal autocrat, ruled. He supported the anti-Semitic Black Hundred terrorist gangs; he wore their badge on state occasions and called them a 'shining example of justice and order to all men'. The Russian Orthodox Church's "cathedrals and churches dominated the built landscape, its holy days shaped the calendar, its teaching was embedded in education, and its priests controlled the registration of births, deaths and marriages. Its ethos permeated family law, custom and a patriarchal order in which the status of women depended on that of their menfolk, and in which women were subordinate to men in terms of power, property, employment, pay and access to education."[3]

Labour productivity was 20-25 per cent of the USA's. In 1913, industrial production per head was 7 per cent of the USA's. Wages were between a third and a quarter of Western Europe's average. Russia relied on imports for all its iron and steel, for all complex electrical and optical equipment, for many types of machine tools and textile machinery, and for half its agricultural machinery.

But the Russian working class started to organise in the industries that they were building. They created their trade unions at first locally, then regionally and then, in September 1905, held the first all-Russian conference of trade unions. Workers had a growing sense of class unity and a growing belief that they could solve their problems.

World War One

In 1914, the ruling classes of the great powers wanted war. A British officer wrote, "A good big war just now might do a lot of good in killing Socialist nonsense and would probably put a stop to all this labour unrest."[4] The *Daily Telegraph* enthused, "This war provides our businessmen with such an opportunity as has never come their way before ... There is no reason why we should not permanently seize for this country a large proportion of Germany's export trade."[5]

In 1914, in Imperial Russia, only 15 per cent could vote, in France, 29 per cent, in Britain, 18 per cent. Only 22 per cent of Germany's people could vote, in Austria-Hungary, 21 per cent. None of them was a democracy. There was no democracy in their empires either. The British Empire had 350 million people in its colonies: none could vote. The French Empire numbered 54 million: none could vote. In Germany's colonies, none could vote. So the war was not a war for democracy.

In July 1914, Russia intervened unnecessarily in a Balkan conflict. France decided to back Russia. Britain followed France's lead. None of these three allies was attacked or even threatened.[6] So the war was not a war of national defence.

All the socialist parties of the Second International had pledged in 1910 to vote against war credits in the event of war. But on 4 August 1914, the German Social-Democrats in the Reichstag voted for the credits. So did the vast majority of Social-Democrats in all Europe's countries. Workers chose to reject the democratic ideas of 1789 – liberty, equality and fraternity.

Only the Bolshevik party in Russia kept its word and voted against war credits. It opposed this war between rival empires, this war against the peoples of the world, and called on the Russian working class and peasantry to turn the imperialist war into a civil war, to overthrow tsarism and end the war.

The leader of the Bolshevik party, Vladimir Ilyich Lenin, launched the idea that the working class of every country could make its own revolution, overthrow the government, stop the war and then build socialism in its country. He stated in 1915, "Uneven economic and political development is an absolute law of capitalism. Hence the victory of socialism is possible first in several or even in one capitalist country taken separately. The victorious proletariat of that country, having expropriated the capitalists and organised its own socialist production, would stand up against the rest of the world, the capitalist world."[7] He confirmed in 1916, "The development of capitalism proceeds extremely unevenly in the various countries. It cannot be otherwise under the commodity production system. From this it follows irrefutably that

Socialism cannot achieve victory simultaneously *in all* countries. It will achieve victory first in one or several countries, while the others will remain bourgeois or prebourgeois for some time."[8]

As he said after the revolution, "I know that there are, of course, sages who think they are very clever and even call themselves Socialists, who assert that power should not have been seized until the revolution had broken out in all countries. They do not suspect that by speaking in this way they are deserting the revolution and going over to the side of the bourgeoisie. To wait until the toiling classes bring about a revolution on an international scale means that everybody should stand stock-still in expectation. That is nonsense."[9]

In April 1917, the Russian state organised pogroms against the Bolsheviks. The new head of the army, General Lavr Kornilov, said, "It is time to put an end to all this. It is time to hang the German agents and spies, with Lenin at their head …"[10] In July 1917, the British Ambassador Sir George Buchanan "contacted the Foreign Minister to ask that the government should take advantage of the situation to crush the Bolsheviks once and for all." He told the Foreign Office, "normal conditions cannot be restored without bloodshed and the sooner we get it over the better."[11]

The British and French governments and the 'socialist' Alexander Kerensky all backed Kornilov's attempted coup in August, which aimed to set up a military dictatorship. Buchanan wrote later, "All my sympathies were with Kornilov."[12] British officers, tanks and armoured cars took part in the coup. US Colonel Raymond Robins told a Senate Committee, "English officers had been put in Russian uniforms in some of the English tanks to follow up the Kornilov advance."[13] But the Russian working class defeated Kornilov and his allies.

A popular revolution

The Bolsheviks had massive popular support. As the British government's Committee to Collect Information on Russia acknowledged, "Alone among this babel of dissentient voices the cries of the Bolsheviks 'Down with the War', 'Peace and the Land' and 'The Victory of the Exploited over the Exploiters' sounded a clear and certain note which went straight to the heart of the people."[14]

At the 2nd All-Russian Congress of Soviets in October 1917, the Bolsheviks had 65-70 per cent of the votes. They won 90 per cent majorities in the elections to the workers' Soviets, 60-70 per cent majorities in the Soldiers' Soviets, majorities in the Peasants' Soviets and majorities in the Soviets of Moscow, Petrograd and many other cities. They had the majority of delegates to the First All-Russian Conference of Factory Committees.

Recent historians have confirmed how much support the Bolsheviks had won. Donald Raleigh noted, "In Saratov, as in Petrograd, Moscow, and Baku, the Bolshevik platform of land, peace, and bread and the slogan 'All Power to the Soviets' appealed increasingly to common people …"[15] The Bolsheviks in Saratov won more than half the votes in elections to city soviets in September 1917. Evan Mawdsley affirmed, "Without doubt the Bolsheviks' early promises were a basic reason why they were able to seize and consolidate power in 1917-18: their program of Soviet power, peace, land reform, and workers' control was widely popular."[16] Alexander Statiev agreed, "The Decree on Land ordered the nationalization of all arable land, its confiscation from landlords and the church, and its distribution among peasants in equal parcels per person as a free lease. This agrarian reform proffered immediate and substantial benefits to many at the expense of few. It secured the consent of most peasants and generated vigorous support among the poorest ones."[17]

Ronald Suny agreed, "the Bolsheviks came to power in 1917 with considerable popular support in the largest cities of the empire – a case, as Terence Emmons puts it, that is 'incontrovertible'."[18] Suny also wrote, "The Bolsheviks came to power not because they were superior manipulators or cynical opportunists but because their policies as formulated by Lenin in April and shaped by the events of the following months placed them at the head of a genuinely popular movement."[19] Hugh Phillips noted, "in Tver, the party gained power peacefully and with the support of the majority of both the citizens and the local garrison."[20] He concluded, "the once-common notion that the Bolsheviks came to power because they duped a politically unsophisticated populace through a Machiavellian conspiracy simply does not wash when one looks at Tver."[21] John Wheeler-Bennett wrote that in March 1917, "There can be little doubt that the Petrograd Soviet represented the feelings of the great masses of the organized wage-earners far more than did the Provisional Government, or that it was trusted in a far greater degree by workers and peasants alike."[22] Robert Service agreed, "There could be no lasting possession of power unless the party had secured widespread popular support."[23] Raleigh summed up, "By the fall of 1917 the wide strata of workers, soldiers, and peasants had concluded that only an all-soviet government could solve the country's problems."[24]

As Rex Wade noted, "Workers moved quickly to create institutions to advance their interests. The Petrograd and other city soviets were especially important as institutions through which the workers could and did pursue their aspirations. The soviets had enormous popular support because they were class-based organs that pursued unabashedly class objectives. The soviets also were the primary institutions where working-class activism interacted with the socialist political parties. Here, parties put forth their respective programs for approval and competed for worker support, while workers influenced the political process by supporting this or that party. The allegiance of the workers (and soldiers) to the soviets, in turn, made the latter the most powerful political institutions in Russia."[25] The soviets won support because, as American historian Karel Berkhoff observed, they respected 'the self-esteem, independence, and trustworthiness of ordinary people'.[26]

The October revolution was a democratic act, not the work of a minority. It was not a conspiracy or a coup. In the revolutionary days of 24-26 October, fewer than 15 people were killed. But on 28 October, there was a massacre – counter-revolutionary Cadet forces killed 500 unarmed soldiers of the captured Kremlin garrison. After the revolution, the Bolshevik forces swiftly defeated the counter-revolution. American historian Frederick Schuman judged, "[C]ontrary to the impression which soon became current in the West, the Soviet Government between November and June, 1917-18, established itself and pursued its program with less violence and with far fewer victims than any other social revolutionary regime in human annals."[27] There was no civil war until May 1918 when the Czech Legion, 60,000 POWs freed by the Soviet government, attacked Soviet forces.

If the Bolsheviks had not taken power, a parliamentary democracy would not have resulted. The class forces that backed Kornilov and the other counter-revolutionary generals would have reimposed absolutism. In the regions that the White generals governed, power moved fast from non-Bolshevik Soviets to anti-Soviet socialist régimes, then to socialist-liberal coalitions, then to the forces of counter-revolution. If the White generals had won, they would have enforced a dictatorship, just as General Francisco Franco did after the 1936-39 war in Spain.

By late 1917, the two alliances of rival empires had killed at least 10 million people and wounded 20 million. So when the Bolsheviks took Russia out of the war a year early, they saved millions of lives, as well as helping to end the war. Even so, Russia had lost two million killed, five million wounded and 2.5 million POWs – more than any other belligerent and more than the other Allies' total losses.

In the famous peace decree of 8 November 1917, a year and three days before the general armistice, the Soviet government "proposes to all belligerent nations and their governments to commence immediately negotiations for an equitable and democratic peace."[28] But the British and French governments refused to send representatives to the peace conference at Brest-Litovsk held in January and February 1918.

At the peace talks, Leon Trotsky, Commissar of Foreign Affairs, disobeyed the Soviet government's order to sign the peace agreement. He 'refused to listen' to the warning from Major-General Max Hoffmann, the Chief of the General Staff of the Commander-in-Chief of the East, that Germany would resume the war.[29] Trotsky said, "They [the Germans] will be unable to make an offensive against us. If they attack us, our position will be no worse than now …"[30] Even Trotsky's biographer Isaac Deutscher commented, "Not without reason, he was blamed for having lulled the party into false security by his repeated assurances that the Germans would not dare to attack."[31] Trotsky told the German and Austrian generals, "We are issuing an order for the full demobilisation of our army."[32] As Lenin told him, "If there is war, we should not have demobilised. ... History will say that you have delivered the revolution [to the enemy]. We could have signed a peace that was not at all dangerous to the revolution."[33] Trotsky later admitted that "his plan had been to disrupt the negotiations and thus provoke a German offensive."[34] His actions were clearly treachery.[35]

The Soviet government promptly sacked Trotsky, but the damage was done. German and Austrian armies seized 1,267,000 square miles of land (equal in size to Germany and France combined), including all Ukraine, all the Caucasus, the Baltic provinces, southern Russia, a third of Russia's crop area, three-quarters of her coal and iron, and over half her industrial plants. When they occupied Ukraine, they restored land to the landlords, seized food, military and industrial supplies, and imposed martial law, all the while promising not to interfere in Ukraine's internal affairs. They aided the coup by General Skoropadsky, the leader of the Ukrainian Landowners' Party, which killed 50,000 Ukrainians.[36]

But the German army became over-extended on this Eastern front and the Bolshevik party's peace efforts undermined German soldiers' morale. In October, the German General Staff decided not to move its 27 divisions on the Eastern front to the Western front. As Hoffmann explained, "Immediately after conquering those Bolsheviks, we were conquered by them. Our victorious army on the Eastern Front became rotten with Bolshevism. We got to the point where we did not dare to transfer certain of our eastern divisions to the West."[37] These 27 divisions might have prolonged the World War for months, but, as American journalist Louis Fischer commented, "sinister Communist propaganda spared the world this additional slaughter."[38]

The war of intervention, 1918-21

In March, British troops occupied Murmansk. In April, British and Japanese troops occupied Vladivostok. Also in April, the British government sent troops to Central Asia to fight alongside Turkmen tribesmen against the Soviet government. (A year later, the British government withdrew these troops, although it continued to arm the rebels, who were only finally defeated in 1929.) In May, the Czech Legion started the war by attacking Soviet government forces.

Also in May, the Right Social Revolutionary party conference agreed to try to overthrow the Soviet government and set up a government willing to continue the world war. In July, SRs killed the German Ambassador, tried to seize power in Moscow and organised revolts in Yaroslavl, Murom, Nizhny Novgorod, Ekaterinburg, Penza and Vyatka. Fanny Kaplan, a member of the SRs, shot and wounded Lenin on 30 August. Robert Bruce Lockhart, a British government representative in Moscow, kept Foreign Secretary Lord Curzon informed about his plot with Boris Savinkov: "Savinkov's proposals for counter-revolution. Plan is how, on Allied intervention, Bolshevik barons will be murdered and military dictatorship formed."[39] Curzon replied, "Savinkoff's methods are drastic, though if successful probably effective, but we cannot say or do anything until intervention has been definitely decided upon."

From 1918 to 1921, fourteen states, led by the British, French and US governments, attacked Russia, backing Admiral Kolchak, General Denikin and General Yudenich. This was not a civil war, as the huge scale of foreign intervention proved. Sir Henry Wilson, Chief of the Imperial General Staff in 1918, observed, "In St James's Palace is sitting the League of Nations, their principal business being the limitation of armaments. In Downing Street is sitting the Allied Conference of Lloyd George, Millerand, Nitti and a Japanese, who are feverishly arming Finland, Baltic States, Poland, Romania, Georgia, Azerbaijan, Armenia, Persia, etc."[40] War Minister Winston Churchill later asked, "Were they [the Allies] at war with Soviet Russia? Certainly not; but they shot Soviet Russians at sight. They stood as invaders on Russian soil. They armed the enemies of the Soviet Government. They blockaded its ports, and sunk its battleships. They earnestly desired and schemed its downfall. But war - shocking! Interference - shame! It was, they repeated, a matter of indifference to them how Russians settled their own internal affairs. They were impartial - Bang!"[41]

The Lloyd George government organised the intervention, armed the invading forces and led the drive to cut Russia off from all trade. This blockade, like all blockades, targeted civilians. The Allies' wartime blockade of Germany, maintained until mid-1919, caused an estimated 500,000 famine-related deaths. The War of Intervention caused 7-10 million deaths, mostly civilians, largely through famine and disease.

Between October 1918 and October 1919, the Lloyd George government spent £94,830,000 on intervening in Russia.[42] It sent Kolchak's forces in the east 97,000 tons of supplies, including 600,000 rifles, 346 million rounds of small-arms ammunition, 6,831 machine guns, 192 field guns, and clothing and equipment for 200,500 men. Alfred Knox, a military attaché at the British embassy in Russia from 1911 to 1918, wrote, "Since about the middle of December [1918] every round of rifle ammunition fired on the front has been of British manufacture, conveyed to Vladivostok in British ships and delivered at Omsk by British guards."[43] As Churchill told the House of Commons, "In the main these armies are equipped by British munitions and British rifles, and a certain portion of the troops are actually wearing British uniforms."[44] Kolchak had 90,000 Russian soldiers and 116,800 foreign troops, including 1,600 British, 7,500 American, 55,000 Czechoslovakian, 10,000 Polish and 28,000 Japanese. The Middlesex battalion escorted Kolchak everywhere and he always wore a British military greatcoat. Knox attended Kolchak's state banquets where 'God save the King' was always sung straight after the Russian national anthem, 'God save the Tsar'.

The British state also backed and funded Denikin's army in south Russia. The British Military Mission to South Russia reported that the White recovery under Denikin after March 1919 'was due almost entirely to British assistance'. During 1919, the British government sent

Denikin 198,000 rifles, 500 million rounds of small-arms ammunition, 6,200 machine guns, 1,121 artillery pieces, 1.9 million shells, 60 tanks, 168 aircraft, 460,000 greatcoats and 645,000 pairs of boots. The British government let Denikin use three RAF flights, British planes flown by RAF pilots, which used mustard gas bombs. Churchill urged the use of chemical weapons, calling them, 'The right medicine for the Bolshevist'.[45]

General Bridges, who oversaw the Military Mission's withdrawal from Novorossisk, summed up the effects of Britain's war of intervention, "From time immemorial the classic penalty for mixing in family quarrel had been a thick ear, and our ill-staged interference in the Russian civil war cost us some thousands of British soldiers' lives and £100,000,000 in money, while we earned the bitter enmity of the Russian people for at least a decade … On the credit side I can think of nothing."[46]

Polish forces attacked Russia in January 1919. *The Times* claimed, "The Bolsheviki have forced the Poles to take up arms by their advance into Polish territory. … The Bolsheviki are advancing toward Vilna." But Vilna was in Soviet Lithuania, not in Poland. There had been no Russian 'advance into Polish territory'. As American journalists Walter Lippmann and Charles Merz commented on the press, "in the guise of news they picture Russia, and not Poland, as the aggressor."[47] In April, Polish troops seized Vilna and in August they occupied Minsk, deep inside Russia. By 2 December, Polish armies were more than 180 miles inside Russian territory. On 21 January 1920, *The Times* stated as fact this fiction: "The strategy of the Bolshevist military campaign during the coming Spring contemplates a massed attack against Poland, as the first step in a projected Red invasion of Europe and a military diversion through Turkestan and Afghanistan toward India."[48] On 29 January, the Soviet government, with Polish forces still 180 miles inside its borders, invited the Polish government to enter peace talks.

From 1917 to 1920, the *New York Times* headlined 18 times that Lenin had been overthrown, six times that he had fled, three times that he had been arrested and twice that he had been killed; Petrograd had been taken by the Whites ten times and burnt to the ground twice, its inhabitants had been massacred twice, starved to death constantly and revolted against the Bolsheviks ten times.[49] On 28 December 1918, the *New York Times*' headline was, 'Ludendorf Chief of Soviet Army'.[50] "[N]inety-one times was it stated that the Soviets were nearing their rope's end, or actually had reached it."[51] The *New York Times* carried fourteen dispatches in January 1920 warning of Red Peril to India, Poland, Europe, Azerbaijan, Persia, Georgia and Mesopotamia.[52] The dispatches were from 'British military authorities', 'diplomatic circles', 'government sources', 'official quarters', 'expert military opinion' and 'well-informed diplomats'. But there followed no such invasions. Lippmann and Merz summed up, "From the point of view of professional journalism the reporting of the Russian Revolution is nothing short of a disaster. On the essential questions the net effect was almost always misleading, and misleading news is worse than none at all."[53]

In 1920, the French government supplied Poland with huge amounts of military aid. Polish forces attacked Russia again in April in an attempt to annex parts of Ukraine, Belorussia and Lithuania, in coordination with General Wrangel's offensive in the Crimea. Ex-Prime Minister Herbert Asquith said, "it was a purely aggressive adventure … It was a wanton enterprise."[54] British warships supported the Polish attack by shelling Black Sea towns. British and French leaders, who had refused to feed Soviet Russia unless she stopped defending herself against attack, sent food to Poland without any effort to stop its government's aggression. 80,000-85,000 Soviet soldiers were taken prisoner and held in POW camps. At least 16,000 Soviet POWs died from brutal treatment, hunger, disease and executions.

The White generals' regimes had no economic basis for independent existence. The Soviet government kept control of Russia's good farm land, factories and arsenals. Only aid from the intervening powers kept the White armies going for so long. The White Army of the North lasted only four months after the British government withdrew its support. Nor did the White armies have any political base. As the British government's Committee to Collect Information on Russia acknowledged, "the political, administrative and moral bankruptcy of the White Russians gained for the Reds the active or tacit support of the majority of the Russian people in the civil war."[55] Sir Paul Dukes, formerly chief of the British Secret Intelligence Service in Soviet Russia, wrote, "The complete absence of an acceptable programme alternative to Bolshevism, the audibly whispered threats of landlords that in the event of a White victory the land seized by the peasants would be restored to its former owners, and the lamentable failure to understand that in the anti-Bolshevist war politics and not military strategy must play the dominant role, were the chief causes of the White defeats."[56] Major General William Graves, the US commander-in-chief in Siberia, said, "At no time while I was in Siberia was there enough popular support behind Kolchak in eastern Siberia for him to have lasted one month if all allied support had been removed."[57] British General Edmund Ironsides admitted, "the majority of the population is in sympathy with the Bolsheviki."[58] One Russian White fighter later noted, "Our rear was a cesspool. We lost this war because we were a minority fighting with foreign help against the majority."[59] General Sir Brian Horrocks admitted, "the only reason that the Reds were victorious was that they did have the backing of the people."[60]

Recent scholars agreed. Statiev pointed out, "After the Bolshevik government gave land to the peasants, the Red Army was always larger than the forces of all its opponents taken together, which shows that even during War Communism, most politically active peasants sided with the Bolsheviks."[61] Michael Hughes wrote that the Whites lost 'because no individual or group among them managed to attract any genuine measure of popular support'.[62] Clifford Kinvig noted, "the Reds also enjoyed more popular support than their opponents."[63] Edward Acton summed up that the Whites "were never able to mobilize more than a fraction of the number of men who fought for the Reds. Indeed, in a sense the Bolsheviks were saved by the preference of the vast majority of the population, including most of their socialist critics, for the Reds over the Whites. ... any chance the Whites would attract popular support was ruled out by the social policies they adopted. Kolchak's government smashed workers' organizations and attempted to halt and reverse peasant land seizures offering no more than vague intimations of subsequent land reform."[64]

Without popular support, the White forces resorted to terror. From the start, the generals waged a brutal war. General Wrangel boasted, "I ordered three hundred and seventy of the Bolsheviks to line up. They were all officers and non-commissioned officers, and I had them shot on the spot."[65] Kornilov also took no prisoners.[66] The US commander-in-chief in Siberia said, "I am well on the side of safety when I say that the anti-Bolsheviks killed a hundred people in eastern Siberia to every one killed by the Bolsheviks."[67]

A representative of the Czech Legion said of Kolchak's regime, "our army has been forced against its convictions to support a state of absolute despotism and unlawfulness which had had its beginnings here under defense of the Czech arms. The military authorities of the Government of Omsk are permitting criminal actions that will stagger the entire world. The burning of villages, the murder of masses of peaceful inhabitants and the shooting of hundreds of persons of democratic convictions and also those only suspected of political disloyalty occurs daily."[68]

General Rozanov, Kolchak's commander in Krasnoyarsk, western Siberia, ordered, "Burn down villages that offer armed resistance to government troops; shoot all adult males; confiscate all property, horses, carts, grain and so forth for the treasury."[69] General Budberg, who served in Kolchak's war ministry, wrote in his diary, "The lads do not seem to realize that if they rape, flog, rob, torture and kill indiscriminately and without restraint, they are thereby instilling such hatred for the government they represent that the swine in Moscow must be delighted at having such diligent, valuable and beneficial collaborators …"[70] Ralph Albertson, a British soldier, admitted, "night after night the firing squad took out its batches of victims."[71] The British Military Mission admitted that Kolchak's troops 'had undoubtedly been guilty of atrocities'.[72]

Schuman summed up, "The injuries inflicted upon Russia by the Western democracies between 1918 and 1921 not only exposed innocent millions to hideous suffering but disfigured the whole face of world politics for decades to come."[73]

Socialism in one country

After the Soviet working class defeated the intervention, it had to build socialism in a ruined and backward country, isolated by the failure of the working classes of more advanced countries to make their own revolutions. It could rely only on its own resources: there was no chance of aid from the West.

Lenin urged, "Socialism is no longer a matter of the distant future, or an abstract picture, or an icon. We still retain our old bad opinion of icons. We have dragged socialism into everyday life, and here we must find our way. ... we shall all - not in one day, but in the course of several years - all of us together fulfill it whatever happens so that NEP [New Economic Policy] Russia will become socialist Russia."[74] He also wrote, "As a matter of fact, state power over all large-scale means of production, state power in the hands of the proletariat, the alliance of this proletariat with the many millions of small and very small peasants, the assured leadership of the peasantry by the proletariat, etc. - is not this all that is necessary for building a complete socialist society ...?"[75] As the British historian E. H. Carr commented, "Socialism in one country was a declaration of independence of the west ... It was a declaration of faith in the capacities and in the destiny of the Russian people."[76]

The Soviet government at once started to reform Russian life. The government disestablished Russian Orthodoxy and secularised education, marriage and family law. Women got equal rights. It allowed divorce (virtually unobtainable before the revolution). In 1920, it legalised hospital abortion. Labour protection laws and efforts to provide maternity and nursery care assisted women into work. It ended the Pale of Settlement – areas of permitted residence for Jews. It ended Russification policies in regions inhabited by non-Russians and encouraged linguistic and cultural autonomy. The Central Asian Republics banned child marriage and marriage by purchase or barter.

In 1920 and 1921, war-ravaged and blockaded Russia suffered an unprecedentedly severe drought. When famine swept the country, killing five million people, the League of Nations rejected calls for famine relief. Huge surpluses of breadstuffs were allowed to rot, rather than be sent 'to aid Bolshevism'. Russia had the gold and goods to buy the food and medicines it needed, but it could not buy them because of the blockade.

The British, French and US governments, in particular, never ceased their attacks on the Soviet Union. White Russian officers in France, Czechoslovakia and Bulgaria trained terrorists who were then sent to the Soviet Union. These officers kept in touch with the British, French and US intelligence services. Throughout the 1920s and 1930s, MI6 sent terrorists into the Soviet Union to assassinate communist officials.[77] The Soviet Union's People's Commissariat for Internal Affairs, the NKVD, did not respond by sending terrorists into Britain.

Modern historians have acknowledged that the Soviet Union was defending itself against Western aggression, not vice versa. As Stephen Dorril commented, the NKVD was "an essentially defensive 'vigilant' organisation, primarily concerned with security and threats, both external and internal, against the USSR."[78] Gabriel Gorodetsky pointed out, "Given the reality of capitalist encirclement and fears of renewed intervention, defence against the external threat was a prerequisite for the achievement of 'Socialism in One Country'."[79] As Dorril observed, the British and US governments were "guilty of all the sins of subversion and interference, disregard for national sovereignty and war-mongering, of which they always accused their Cold War enemy, the Soviet Union."[80] US diplomat Raymond Garthoff stressed, "we were, for example, in fact going beyond what the adversary was doing in paramilitary and covert operations violating sovereignty and challenging the legitimacy of the Soviet Union."[81]

MI6 forged documents to whip up hatred of the Soviet Union. In 1921, Foreign Secretary Curzon, on the basis of such reports, protested against alleged Soviet intervention in Ireland and India. The Soviet government calmly exposed the documents as 'elementary fabrications', much to Curzon's embarrassment. The British government used the forged 'Zinoviev letter' to wreck negotiations for loans to the Soviet Union. The Secret Intelligence Service claimed, "the authenticity of the document is undoubted."[82] For more than 50 years, the Foreign Office continued to claim that it was genuine.

Isolated and threatened, the Soviet Union had to work out how to survive alone, an unprecedented task. In 1920, it drew up a plan for electrifying the whole country, which meant building 30 central power stations with a total capacity of 1.5 million kilowatts. It was achieved by 1930. By 1922, the government had set up a central bank (Gosbank) which started to stabilise the currency. The government had to defeat the 'swing to the left' that began to gather strength from 1922. This leftism pushed the notions that money would be quickly abolished and that finance would not exist in a socialist society. The party's slogans were "Use industry against capitalism. Use money against capitalism." In the 1920s, the government formed Industrial Banks and Agricultural Banks, with branches across the country. The Bolsheviks proved that you could have industry, money and banks, without capitalism.

By 1927, industrial and agricultural production regained their pre-war level. In the mid-1920s, industry grew faster and more steadily than in the capitalist countries, impressive achievements given that the Soviet Union had suffered more war damage than any other country. But under the New Economic Policy (1922-26), more than a tenth of workers were unemployed and private agriculture was not productive enough to support the industrial growth needed to keep the Soviet Union safe. NEP was blocking the necessary industrialisation of the country. NEP also increased the powers of a kulak class which believed that it should continue to be the master of all Russia's farmland.[83]

Carr summed up the progressive moves from market to plan: "The development both of agriculture and of industry stimulated by NEP followed capitalist rather than socialist lines. In agriculture it meant the encouragement of the *kulak*. In industry, it favoured the growth of light industries working with limited capital for the consumer market and earning quick profits rather than of the heavy industries which were, by common consent, the basis of a future socialist order, but required an initial volume of long-term capital investment; for this contingency the principles and practices of NEP made no provision. Hence the struggle in agricultural policy against the predominance of the *kulak*, which began in 1924 and remained acute throughout 1925, was matched at the same period by a similar struggle in industrial policy centring on the requirements of heavy industry. ... with the fourteenth party congress in December 1925, the expansion of heavy industry became the predominant aim of economic policy."[84] The Soviet Union increased industrial production and investment by 10-15 per cent a year from 1925 to 1929.

Threats of war

In May 1926, Marshal Josef Pilsudski seized power in Poland and imposed a military dictatorship. The British government backed the coup. In August, the Soviet government offered Poland a neutrality and non-aggression pact, which Poland rejected. Under British and French influence, the Polish and Romanian governments signed a military convention. Throughout the 1920s and 1930s, the Polish government sent armed Poles and White Russians on raids into Ukraine and Byelorussia to murder officials and destroy infrastructure.[85]

In early 1927, Chiang Kai-Shek crushed the Chinese revolution. The British government was aiding Tsarist forces still based in China. In India, the government was building air bases, forts and a military railroad through the Khyber Pass to the Afghan frontier. The British press increased its anti-Soviet propaganda. There were more terrorist acts than ever before in the Soviet Union and there were raids on Soviet embassies and trade missions in Berlin, Peking, Shanghai and Tientsin.

The British government sought a pretext for breaking off the diplomatic and trade relations established in 1924. Under the Official Secrets Act, possessing a secret Signals Training manual from the Aldershot military base was an offence. MI5 claimed that ARCOS [the All-Russian Cooperative Society] had a copy. So it got Prime Minister

Stanley Baldwin's permission to raid ARCOS (which was protected by diplomatic immunity) to get the evidence.[86] But no manual was found, nor any evidence of Soviet espionage.[87] As *The Observer* noted at the time, "The raid by itself was a fiasco. ... But this being so, Parliamentary considerations forced a total breach in order to defend the raid."[88]

So, on 26 May, the British government broke relations with the Soviet Union. As a result, Soviet imports from Britain fell sharply, which was a blow to British exporters and manufacturers when they were trying to increase exports. The break sabotaged a £10 million credit agreed on 11 May to assist the Soviet Union to buy British textile machinery. The break also led other governments to break off relations.

In June, a White Russian *emigré* named Koverda assassinated the Soviet Ambassador to Poland. The murderer was a member of an anti-Bolshevik body operating in Poland. Before the assassination, the Soviet government had warned the Polish government that this body was planning terrorist acts, but the Polish government did nothing to hinder its activities.

The British government continued to fund and arm counter-revolutionary terrorist groups in Ukraine, Belorussia, Georgia, and anti-Soviet forces in Turkey, Persia, Afghanistan and China. Britain, France, the Balkan states, Romania, Poland, the Baltic states and Finland had all given refuge to hundreds of thousands of White soldiers who had fled at the end of the War of Intervention, and these states had kept these soldiers in arms and ready for war. Senior British military officers often met their Eastern European counterparts. All these diplomatic and military ties were part of preparations for a new attack on the Soviet Union.[89]

Chapter 2
The Soviet Union from 1927 to 1933

The need to collectivise

All these acts increased the threat of war against the Soviet Union and brought new urgency to the tasks of industrialisation and collectivisation. Collectivisation was needed not just to fund industrialisation but also to end Russia's regular famines. The only alternative to collectivisation was to allow famines to continue every two to three years. Between 1918 and 1927, there were five poor harvests, two famine years and only three good harvests. Continuing the NEP would have led to more famines. If the Soviet Union had not collectivised agriculture, it would have caused millions of deaths.

To survive, the Soviet Union needed advanced industry as a basis for defence. To expand industry, it needed grain to feed the towns, and also for export, to finance imports of industrial equipment. Finance was needed to industrialise, but industry could not provide it quickly enough. Foreign investment was not likely. So investment could only come from larger agricultural yields, which meant that agriculture had to be mechanised. Therefore it was necessary to replace unproductive peasant smallholdings with modern large-scale farms, to collectivise agriculture.

The 15th Party Congress in December 1927 decided, "The way out is in the passing of small disintegrated peasant farms into large-scale amalgamated farms, on the basis of communal tillage of the soil; in passing to collective tillage of the soil on the basis of the new higher technique. The way out is to amalgamate the petty and tiny peasant farms gradually but steadily, not by means of pressure but by example and conviction, into large-scale undertakings on the basis of communal, fraternal collective tillage of the soil, supplying agricultural machinery and tractors, applying scientific methods for the intensification of agriculture. *There is no other way out.*"[1] General Secretary Joseph Stalin inserted a clause on the importance of industrialisation for defence.[2] He wrote, "to slow down the rate of development of industry means to weaken the working class."[3] As he warned in 1931, "we are fifty or a hundred years behind the advanced countries. We must make good this distance in ten years. Either we do it, or they crush us."

The capitalist states waged permanent blockades (which are acts of war) against the Soviet Union (as they did later against every other country trying to defend its sovereignty). These states knew that international trade helped developing countries to get better technologies, enabling them to increase their productivity, and that to import technologies, developing countries needed to export and earn universally accepted currencies like the dollar. So the capitalist states did all they could to stifle Soviet trade and therefore development. The Soviet Union had to industrialise as swiftly as possible to become self-sufficient before the capitalist powers could combine to attack it.

The kulaks profited from Russia's regular famines by buying and hoarding foodstuffs. In 1928, they stopped selling their grain to the cities, causing food shortages which forced workers out of the factories. Kulaks and monks fought collectivisation, damning tractors as 'devil-machines', 'the work of anti-Christ'. The government had to act against the kulaks to prevent a famine.

As the late Moshe Lewin advised, "In order to understand this process of wholesale dekulakization, it is also essential to bear in mind the misery in which millions of bednyaks lived. All too often they went hungry; they had neither shoes nor shirts, nor any other 'luxury items'. The tension which had built up in the countryside, and the eagerness to dispossess the kulaks, were in large measure contributed to by the wretchedness of the bednyaks' conditions, and the hatred which they were capable of feeling on occasion for their more fortunate neighbours, who exploited them pitilessly whenever they had the chance to do so."[4]

In 1928-29, the Soviet Union started to collectivise the farms. Agricultural cooperatives helped to mechanise farming. In 1924, Russia had only 2,560 tractors. As late as 1928, tractors ploughed less than one per cent of the land and hand labour did three quarters of the spring sowing. By 1929, there were 34,000 tractors. The party called for 25,000 workers to assist in collectivisation – more than 70,000 volunteered.

In September 1930, the government decided to concentrate all tractors owned by collective farms into state-owned Machine Tractor Stations. Shevchenko Machine Tractor Station, for example, comprised a central machine shop with 200 tractors and all necessary supporting machinery, servicing the surrounding peasants on 150,000 acres. It ran a school for village tractor drivers, giving peasants their first education in the use of tractors and other machines. It rented machines for a percentage of the crop and required peasants who wished to use them to adopt crop rotation in consultation with the station's experts. The peasants still lived in the ancient village they had always known. Yet their fields were knit with other fields beyond the horizon into one great factory system, producing not cloth or iron but grain. Credits, travelling libraries and health exhibits entered the countryside. In December 1929, there was only one such station in the whole Soviet Union; by 1934 there were 3,500, servicing two-thirds of all Soviet farming.[5]

The collective farms, based on traditional rural settlements or villages, were a form of socialist economy, because their main instruments of production were socialised, the land belonged to the state and there were no exploiting or exploited classes within them. The collective farms were more advanced than the individual peasant economies which surrounded them. Their fields were not divided into strips, so yields and incomes were higher than on comparable lands cultivated by individual peasants. As Thomas Campbell, who farmed a 95,000-acre wheat farm in Montana, noted in 1932, "Because of the increased area of holdings and higher yields in the collectives, as a result of the greater use of tractors and modern implements and production methods, the income per household on the average collectivized farm has increased at least 150 per cent as a nation-wide average, and by more than 200 per cent in numerous localities."[6]

Collectivisation converted the Soviet Union from a backward to a progressive agricultural nation. Before collectivisation, grain harvests averaged 70.4 million tons in 1928-32. After collectivisation, they averaged 77.1 million tons in 1934-40.[7] American historian Mark Tauger recently summed up, "collectivisation brought substantial modernisation to traditional agriculture in the Soviet Union, and laid the basis for relatively high food production and consumption by the 1970s and 1980s. ... collectivisation allowed the mobilisation and distribution of resources, like tractors, seed aid, and food relief, to enable farmers to produce a large harvest during a serious famine, which was unprecedented in Russian history and almost so in Soviet history. By implication, therefore, this research shows that collectivisation, whatever its disruptive effects on agriculture, did in fact function as a means to modernise and aid Soviet agriculture."[8]

In response to collectivisation, the kulaks destroyed food stores, seed and farm animals, killing 44 per cent of the Soviet Union's cattle, 65 per cent of its sheep and goats and 50 per cent of its horses. In 1930 alone, there were 13,800 terrorist attacks, which killed 1,197 Soviet officials and hundreds of teachers. There were armed rebellions in Chechnya, Fergana, Kazakhstan, Azerbaijan, Karachai-Cherkesa, Ingushieta and Dagestan. Kulaks 'openly toasted the forthcoming liquidation of all communists'.[9]

So the Soviet Union had to defeat the kulaks. It also had to defeat those who denied the needs to collectivise and industrialise. The Right Opposition, led by Nikolai Bukharin, favoured agriculture over industry, the market over the state, the private sector over the public sector and private investment over public investment. Bukharin said that the impetus for progress could only come from the peasantry as a whole, including the kulaks. He proposed, "We shall move ahead by tiny, tiny steps, pulling behind us our large peasant cart." Trotsky advocated a long period of collaboration with capitalism: "By introducing the New Economic Policy ... we created a certain space for capitalist relations in our country, and for a prolonged period ahead we must recognize them as inevitable."[10] In April 1930, Trotsky's *Bulletin of the Opposition* said, "Put a stop to 'mass collectivisation'. ... Put a stop to the hurdle race of industrialisation. ... Abandon the 'ideals' of self-contained economy. Draw up a new variant of a plan providing for the widest possible intercourse with the world market."

The First Five-Year Plan (1928-33)

Through central planning, the country built up its industry and became self-sufficient, independent of the capitalist world. The First Five-Year Plan proposed that 47 per cent of investment should be in new factories, especially steel and chemical plants. Building large, new capital-intensive factories using the newest technology became government policy. The 1929 Fifth Union Congress of Soviets' resolution on the plan recognised 'the full utilisation of the recent achievements of world science and technology' as one of the 'indispensable conditions of the successful realisation of the five-year plan'. New industries produced capital equipment, especially machine tools, the core industry that produced the machines needed to make all other types of machinery. In 1914, Russia barely had a machine tool industry; by 1939, it was producing 58,000 different types of machine tools. The expansion of industry based on the production of the means of production created a self-reliant socialist economy. Whole new industries produced caterpillar tractors, cotton pickers, chemicals, airplanes, blooming mills, lathes, precision instruments, linotypes, turbines, generators, locomotives and electric cars.

Work started in 1927 on Dnieperstroy, the great hydro-electric dam project in the Ukraine, then the world's biggest dam, and it was finished in 1932, two years ahead of schedule. 1930 saw the completion of three major projects - the Turkish railway, the agricultural machinery factory at Rostov-on-Don and the Stalingrad tractor factory. At the Uralmashzavod heavy engineering factory in Sverdlovsk, work started on building the main production shops of the greatly expanded project. After many difficulties, construction was started at both ends of the great Ural-Kuznetsk combine.

American journalist Anna Louise Strong wrote in 1935, "The Five-Year Plan was Soviet Russia's 'War for Independence' from the exploiting capitalist world. Men died in that war, but they won it. They changed their country from a land of backward industry and medieval farming, defended only by grim will, to a land of modern industry, farming and defence. From an agrarian country of small peasant holdings farmed in the manner of the Middle Ages, the Soviet Union became a predominantly industrial country. Twenty million tiny farms became two hundred thousand large farms, collectively owned and partly mechanized. A country once illiterate became a land of compulsory education covered by a net-work of schools and universities. New branches of industry arose: machine tools, automotive, tractor, chemical, aviation, high-grade steel, powerful turbines, nitrates, synthetic rubber, artificial fibers. Thousands of new industrial plants were built; thousands of old ones remodelled. The Soviet Union emerged from the Five-Year Plan a powerful, modern nation, whose word has weight in the councils of the world. To this end millions of men fought and endured as in battle."[11] The Chinese, the Koreans, the Cubans and the peoples of Eastern Europe later used the Five-Year Plan model.

More recently, British historian R. W. Davies commented, "The outstanding achievement was the astonishing expansion in industrial investment, which was in 1929/30 more than 90 per cent above the level of the previous year, and several times as large as in 1913. ... The vast construction programme which began the transformation of the USSR into a great industrial power was under way."[12] American historian David Granick concluded, "If, as the Russians of that era did, we define modern production methods as consisting of those of mass production and continuous flow, then it must be admitted that Soviet machinebuilding achieved a massive shift towards modernity. Judged by these criteria, Soviet machinebuilding by 1932 had probably caught up with its American and surpassed its west European counterpart in its level of technological organization."[13]

Social progress

This industrial progress brought social progress too. Public services included free education (up through higher education), free health care, guaranteed pensions, low-cost child care, very low rents and cheap holidays. Between 1917 and 1931, half a million people were rehoused in central Moscow. Between 1926 and 1931, the Soviet Union built 30 million square metres of new housing space. By 1928, there were 63,219 doctors, up from the pre-war number of 19,785. There were 225,000 hospital beds, up from 175,000, and 256,000 nursery places, up from 11,000. By the end of the First Five-Year Plan, there were 76,000 doctors, more than 330,000 hospital beds and 5,750,000 nursery places. By 1938, there were 4,384 child and maternity welfare centres; in tsarist Russia, there had been only nine. Fourteen new medical colleges were founded and 133 new secondary medical schools. By 1937, there were 132,000 doctors. In Azerbaijan for example, there were 2,500 doctors, where before the revolution there had been only 291. The Soviet public health budget in 1937 was about 75 times that of Russia in 1913.

In 1914, half all peasant children had died before the age of five and the infant mortality rate was 273/1,000. By 1935, it was 77/1,000. By 1971, only 22.9 of every 1,000 infants died before the age of one. From 1917 to the mid-1960s, life expectancy for men rose from 31 years to 66 and for women from 33 to 74. Life expectancy was the best indicator of a country's health status. Sir Arthur Newsholme, former General Medical Officer of the Local Government Board, London, and Dr J. A. Kingston, summed up their 1933 survey, "Our observations of soviet arrangements for the medical and hygienic care of mothers and their children have filled us with admiration, and with wonder that such good work, scientific and advanced work, should be undertaken and successfully accomplished in the period when the finances of the country are at a low ebb. The maternity and child-welfare institutions and arrangements seen by us gave us the impression that they were nowhere being stinted or restricted because of financial stress."[14] Better living conditions improved peoples' health. In World War One, 30 per cent of Russians called up had been unfit for service; in World War Two, just 5 per cent were unfit for service.

The Soviet Union was the first country to introduce equal pay for equal work. The proportion of women in institutions of higher education rose from 31 per cent in 1926 to 43 per cent in 1937 and to 77 per cent in World War Two, then fell to 52 per cent in 1955 and 42 per cent in 1962. Most of the women who benefited were from the working class and peasantry. In 1937, 16 per cent of the elected members of the Supreme Soviet were women. By the 1940s, women held a fifth of all leading government and party posts.

Expanding education and science

The Soviet Union hugely expanded literacy and education. After a long struggle in the 1920s, the country rejected leftist claims that schools were relics of pre-modern times, that teachers and lecturers were bourgeois or even feudal, that culture was bourgeois, and that schools would wither away in socialist society. The number of teachers rose by 251 per cent between 1927 and 1939. Between 1929 and 1933, attendance at preschools rose from 838,000 to 5.9 million. By 1932, 95 per cent of 8-11 year-olds were in primary school. The number of secondary school pupils rose from 1.8 million in 1926-27 to 12.1 million in 1938-39.

The number of teachers in higher education rose from 18,000 in 1927-28 to 57,000 in early 1933. Between 1927-28 and 1932-33, the number of students grew from 159,800 to 469,800 and then to 812,000 in 1940-41. From 1928 to 1933, the number of specialists in heavy industry with degrees rose from 13,700 to 50,700 and the number of agronomists with degrees rose from 18,000 to 126,000. In 1928-29, there were 120,000 pupils in industrial and other apprenticeship schools (building, transport, forestry and farm) and 152,000 in the mainly artisan trade schools. By 1931-32, after the merging of the apprenticeship and trade schools, there were more than a million.

Spending on science tripled between 1927-28 and 1933 and doubled between 1933 and 1940. In the 1930s, the Soviet Union spent more of its national income on science than any other country. The number of research scientists grew from 18,000 in 1929 to 46,000 in 1935. Scientific thinking became increasingly widespread. The Soviet government promoted a practical materialism that enabled people to live and work effectively in a literate, industrialised society. As American historian Loren Graham pointed out, "Contemporary Soviet dialectical materialism is an impressive intellectual achievement. ... In terms of universality and degree of development, the dialectical materialist explanation of nature has no competitors among modern systems of thought."[15] Stalin defended scientific thinking and opposed Trofim Lysenko's leftist claim that "any science is class-based", asking, "What about mathematics? And what about Darwinism?"[16]

In 1917, 17 million adults were illiterate, 14 million of them women. During the 1930s, rural male literacy rose from less than 70 per cent to 85-90 per cent, female from less than 40 per cent to more than 70 per cent. In 1937, after twenty years of socialism, 90 per cent of people were literate. By contrast, in India, after 180 years of British rule, 93 per cent of the people were illiterate. As Ukraine's historian Orest Subtelny noted, "Unlike the tsarist regime, the Soviets placed a high priority on education, and their achievements in this area were truly impressive. ... Most dramatic were Soviet strides in the elimination of illiteracy."[17]

By 1933, there were 40,000 libraries, by 1938, 70,000. Between 1929 and 1933, the number of cinemas rose from 9,800 to 29,200 and newspaper circulation rose from 12.5 million to 36.5 million. In 1913, 26,200 book titles were produced in 86.7 million copies; by

1938, 40,000 titles in 692.7 million copies. The Soviet film industry flourished, with brilliant film-makers like Sergei Eisenstein (*Strike*, 1924, *Battleship Potemkin*, 1925, *October*, 1927, *Alexander Nevsky*, 1938, and *Ivan the Terrible*, 1944 and 1958) and Vsevolod Pudovkin (*The Mother*, 1926, *The End of St Petersburg*, 1927, and *Storm Over Asia*, 1928), and later Sergei Bondarchuk, whose two-part *War and Peace* (1965-67) should rank as one of the finest films ever made. The government and every organised part of Soviet life devoted time and effort to awakening interest in literature, music, theatre, dance and the visual arts. Architecture flourished.[18] In 1935, the Moscow Metro was opened, a magnificent feat of engineering and construction.

The Soviet Union promoted the values of social equality, enthusiasm for science, secularism and social responsibility. As a Moscow textile factory's paper urged, "You are yourselves responsible for your own lot. Don't leave the work to others."[19]

A new working class

The Soviet government sought to ensure that the working class really was the ruling class. In a Politburo discussion about workers, Stalin urged, "these are people, not things. And which people? From the ruling class. These are not just phrases. If some bosses or spetsy [specialists] do not relate to the workers as people of the ruling class, that is, people whom it's necessary to convince, whose needs must be fulfilled, if the worker waves his hand, twenty times asked for improvements in technology in Lisichank, and they did nothing, what kind of attitude to the worker is that, if not to a thing?"

He argued against the common view of workers as just 'labour power': "The working class is not only labour power, they're living people, they want to live ..." And again: "If a manager thinks that his working class is labour power and not the ruling class and that he needs to bang out a profit, then such a manager cannot and should not be at the factory."[20]

The Soviet government opened the gates of opportunity to the working class. The First Five-Year Plan achieved huge upskilling as peasants became industrial workers, unskilled workers became skilled workers, and skilled workers moved into management, the professions and higher education. The proportion of students from working class families rose from a quarter in 1927-28 to a half in 1932-33. On the policy of promoting workers, Sheila Fitzpatrick, the historian of Soviet education, commented, "Stalin's policy prevailed, and in retrospect it must surely be seen as a very bold and imaginative policy which did in fact serve to consolidate and legitimize the regime. At the very beginning of the industrialization drive, before there was any natural expansion of opportunity for upward social mobility, the regime demonstratively repudiated the 'bourgeois' professionals and began to promote very large numbers of workers and peasants into the administrative and specialist elite." She remarked, "The policy and its objective – the creation of a new elite, or 'proletarian intelligentsia' – were clearly stated in 1928. If one assumes that Stalin saw it as a breakthrough policy that would not be indefinitely continued, the objective was successfully reached. This was a major political achievement, and its impact on the nature of the Soviet regime and leadership was lasting." She summed up, "For the *vydvizhentsy* [those promoted], industrialization was an heroic achievement – their own, Stalin's and that of Soviet power – and their promotion, linked with the industrialization drive, was a fulfillment of the promises of the revolution."[21]

From 1929 on, the Soviet Union adopted shock movements and socialist competition, based on mass initiative, which promoted modernisation and better management. Teams of workers competed to produce more, with higher productivity, and to cut costs and improve labour discipline. Production conferences in 1928-29 adopted 83.4 per cent of suggestions made by workers.[22] As Stalin pointed out, "The decisions of single persons are always, or nearly always, one-sided. Out of every one hundred decisions made by single persons, that have not been tested and corrected collectively, ninety are one-sided."[23]

American trade union organiser Robert Dunn observed at the time, "the trade union fabkom [factory committee] is a growing force in the Soviet Union. It brings workers not only into the unions, but into the whole economic activity of the country. It is the principal organ of workers' democracy in a government and an industrial system operated by and for workers. In no other country does this type of workers' council have so much power. ... In no other country does it have such varied and important functions. Nowhere do its members have so much freedom and responsibility as in the USSR."[24]

In 1929-32, the Soviet Union created 16-17 million new jobs, doubling the number of wage and salary earners. The dependents/wage-earners ratio improved from 2.26 in 1927 to 1.59 in 1935. From 1932 to 1940, the number of wage and salary earners grew from 24 million to 34 million. In 1926, 26 million people lived in towns and cities; by 1939, 56 million. From 1926 to 1939, the number of people in non-agricultural jobs rose from 11.6 million to 38.9 million. This shift out of agriculture took from 30 to 50 years in other countries.

But even so, creating an industrial working class, a stable and reliable class that had cut its ties to the land, was a difficult and lengthy process.[25] Industrial skills were developed through learning-by-doing in a factory environment. It was one thing to build new factories, but it took time before new industries became efficient.

Ukraine

1931 had an unusually cold spring, delaying the sowing. An unusually hot summer brought drought and cut grain yields. The 1931 crop was disastrous: gross production in the principal eastern grain districts was 10.7 million metric tons below the 1927-30 average. 1932's March was even colder than 1931's, May and June were even hotter than 1931's. Again, the dreadful weather caused a disastrously low harvest.

Kulaks in Ukraine made the resulting famine even worse. Isaac Mazepa, leader of the Ukrainian Nationalist movement, admitted, "At first there were mass disturbances in the kolkhosi [collective farms] or else the Communist officials and their agents were killed, but later a system of passive resistance was favoured which aimed at the systematic frustration of the Bolsheviks' plans for the sowing and gathering of the harvest. ... The opposition of the Ukrainian population caused the failure of the grain-storing plan of 1931, and still more so, that of 1932. ... The autumn and spring sowing campaigns both failed. Whole tracts were left unsown. In addition, when the crop was being gathered last year, it happened that, in many areas, especially in the south, 20, 40 and even 50 per cent was left in the fields, and was either not collected at all or was ruined in the threshing."[26]

Stalin wrote in May 1933 to the novelist Mikhail Sholokhov, "the esteemed grain growers of your region (and not only your region) carried out a sitdown strike (sabotage!) and would not have minded leaving the workers and the Red Army without bread. The fact that the sabotage was quiet and apparently harmless (bloodless) does not alter the fact that the esteemed grain growers were basically waging a 'quiet' war against Soviet power. A war by starvation (voina na izmor), dear com. Sholokhov ..."[27] Michael Ellman recently commented, "Stalin's idea that he had faced a peasant strike was not an absurd notion indicating paranoia. It seems that there really were numerous collective refusals by collective farmers to work for the collective farms in 1932."[28]

On 17 February 1932, almost six months before the harvesting of the new crop, the Soviet government loaned the collective farms in the eastern part of Ukraine more than six million quintals of grain to set up both seed and food funds. Certain areas, such as the Ukraine and North Caucasus which had to consume all the available grain, remained with little or no seed funds, so the Soviet government loaned to Ukraine's collective farms three million quintals of seed, and to those of the North Caucasus, more than two million quintals.[29]

The government accepted Stalin's proposal to cut grain procurement from Ukraine by 40 million puds [640,000 tons].[30] This 11 per cent reduction was followed by a 17 per cent reduction in October. In February 1933, the government authorised the issue of more than 800,000 tons of grain as seed to Ukraine, North Caucasus, the Lower-Volga Region,

Urals and Kazakhstan, and a further 400,000 tons before the end of the spring sowing. Between February and July, the government authorised the issue of 320,000 tons of grain for food.[31] This included 194,000 tons of food aid to Ukraine. In total, nearly two million tons were issued for seed, food and fodder. Further, "Considerable efforts were made to supply grain to hungry children."[32] The organisation of the farms was improved and several thousand more tractors, combines and trucks were delivered.

Leading scholars of Russian history have refuted the claim that the famine was an act of genocide. Terry Martin concluded, "The famine was not an intentional act of genocide specifically targeting the Ukrainian nation."[33] David Shearer noted, "Although the famine hit Ukraine hard, it was not, as some historians argue, a purposefully genocidal policy against Ukrainians. ... no evidence has surfaced to suggest that the famine was planned, and it affected broad segments of the Russian and other non-Ukrainian populations both in Ukraine and in Russia."[34] Diane Koenker and Ronald Bachman agreed, "the documents included here or published elsewhere do not yet support the claim that the famine was deliberately produced by confiscating the harvest, or that it was directed especially against the peasants of Ukraine."[35] Barbara Green also agreed, "Unlike the Holocaust, the Great Famine was not an intentional act of genocide."[36] Steven Katz commented, "What makes the Ukrainian case non-genocidal, and what makes it different from the Holocaust, is the fact that the majority of Ukrainian children survived and, still more, that they were *permitted* to survive."[37] Adam Ulam agreed too, writing, "Stalin and his closest collaborators had not willed the famine."[38] Ellman concluded, "What recent research has found in the archives is not a conscious policy of genocide against Ukraine."[39]

Tauger explained, "The evidence that I have published and other evidence, including recent Ukrainian document collections, show that the famine developed out of a shortage and pervaded the Soviet Union, and that the regime organized a massive program of rationing and relief in towns and in villages, including in Ukraine, but simply did not have enough food. This is why the Soviet famine, an immense crisis and tragedy of the Soviet economy, was not in the same category as the Nazis' mass murders, which had no agricultural or other economic basis."[40] He summed up, "Ukraine received more in food supplies during the famine crisis than it exported to other republics. ... Soviet authorities made substantial concessions to Ukraine in response to an undeniable natural disaster and transferred resources from Russia to Ukraine for food relief and agricultural recovery."[41]

Hans Blumenfeld pointed out that famine also struck the Russian regions of North Caucasus and Lower Volga: "This disproves the 'fact' of anti-Ukrainian genocide parallel to Hitler's anti-semitic holocaust. To anyone familiar with the Soviet Union's desperate manpower shortage in those years, the notion that its rulers would deliberately reduce that scarce resource is absurd ... Up to the 1950s the most frequently quoted figure was two million [famine victims]. Only after it had been established that Hitler's holocaust had claimed six million victims, did anti-Soviet propaganda feel it necessary to top that figure by substituting the fantastic figure of seven to ten million ..."[42]

In 1933, rainfall was adequate and the 1933 harvest was good. In 1936, when the weather was again dreadful, the government averted a famine by organising food stocks and grain collections to ensure that food got to the people. By 1940, Ukraine's industrial capacity was seven times greater than it had been in 1913. Its productive capacity equaled France's.

The Second Five-Year Plan (1932-37)

The Soviet Union financed industry from the national budget – direct subsidies to restore fixed capital, and advances of working capital, to buy raw materials – the approach that favoured heavy industry. Borrowing and spending served industrialisation. The banking system gave long-term credit for industry, electrification, agricultural improvements, and for financing foreign trade. Industry's requirements, not finance, dictated policy. The national economic plan determined the state budget and the credit plan, removing financial limits on industrialisation.

Industry and its trusts and factories had to meet their production targets, couched mainly in terms of physical output, and their financial targets, particularly their targets for cutting costs. The increased investment spending did not have to be matched by a corresponding increase in revenue. The Soviet Union rejected the option of financing industry through credit from banks on the basis of tangible security and potential profits, the approach that favoured light industry. But consumers' needs were not ignored: Stalin urged in July 1935, "everything that increases the production of consumer goods for the mass market must be given more emphasis from year to year."[43] National income grew by 56.4 per cent between 1932 and 1937.[44]

In the Russian republic alone, the number of kilowatt hours of energy generated increased from 3.2 billion in 1928 to 31 billion in 1940. Between 1929 and 1937, the Soviet Union moved from 15th to 2nd in Europe in electricity production. It went from importing natural gas to exporting it, producing 560 million metric tons by 1932. Between 1928 and 1938, its oil output nearly tripled. Coal production increased from 10 to 73 million tons per year, iron ore from 1 to 5.5 million tons, steel from 2 to 9 million tons. The productive capacity of major capital goods industries doubled between October 1928 and January 1934. Blast furnace capacity rose by 111 per cent and open-hearth capacity by 63 per cent. Production of high-quality steel more than quadrupled between 1934 and 1936. Soviet machinery output increased ninefold between 1927-28 and 1937. In 1930, it had 34,000 tractors and 1,700 combine harvesters, but by 1938, it had 483,500 and 153,500 respectively. The Soviet Union became the world's largest producer of tractors and railway engines.

Soviet aircraft were among the world's best and Soviet pilots set many world aviation records in the 1930s, for flight altitude, distance and endurance. Between 1933 and 1937, labour productivity rose by 65 per cent in industry, 83 per cent in construction and 48 per cent in railway transport. Workers improved their skills: by the end of

1937, three-quarters of workers in industry and transport reached the 'technical minimum'.

Developing Central Asia

In the Central Asian republics, the Soviet government planned and built new industrial enterprises to provide work for the peoples of the republics. It also raised education and health services to the level of the more advanced areas. Investment in the Soviet Far East was eight times higher in the Second Five-Year Plan than in the First. By 1934, the region was receiving nearly half of all Soviet investment. Investments per person in the Central Asian republics grew more swiftly than in the Russian republic and so industrial production did too. So did education.

Educationists Hessen and Hans concluded in 1930, "The achievements of the Soviet Government in the field of national education are very considerable. ... These results were possible through a special system of financial subvention from central funds to the minorities. Thus whereas the Russians in the RSFSR receive from the treasury about 1-2 chernovetz rubles per head for educational needs, the autonomous republics and regions receive from the same source about 3.8 chernovetz rubles per head. Without this central help the autonomous territories, usually the most backward ... would not have been able to undertake the enormous task. This policy of the Soviet Government may be just and generous, being the only way to repay Russia's debt to these original inhabitants of territories conquered during the centuries by Russians, and left neglected by the Imperial Government. In spite of the partisan character of education imparted, the national renascence of all Russian minorities is an actual fact which brings within itself immense possibilities in the future."[45]

The Soviet Union raised tens of millions of former colonial subjects to full practical equality with the Russian people. Martin summed up, "New national elites were trained and promoted to leadership positions in the government, schools, and industrial enterprises of these newly formed territories. In each territory, the national language was declared the official language of government. In dozens of cases, this necessitated the creation of a written language where one did not yet exist. The Soviet state financed the mass production of books, journals, newspapers, movies, operas, museums, folk music ensembles, and other cultural output in the non-Russian languages. Nothing comparable to it had been attempted before ..."[46] Ellman noted, "The enormous expansion of urban employment opportunities in Soviet Central Asia during the period of Soviet power is a major achievement of Soviet power."[47]

Party workers launched a campaign against customs of female inequality and seclusion. By the early 1960s, veils were an exception, not the rule. In 1937, the government launched a campaign to attract female settlers to Central Asia. Hundreds of thousands of women volunteered. As historian Elena Shulman commented, "Such volunteers made explicit offers to put patriotic undertakings above familial duties. These were not victims appealing for aid. Rather, these women assumed that they were needed to defend the frontier and to 'bring everything to life that will win patriotism'. The presence of such strategies belies the notion that a Great Retreat pushed women into the confines of the domestic hearth. These sentiments also indicate a fervent current of support for the Soviet regime."[48] As a result of all these efforts, there was a relative calm in interethnic relations in what are today ethnic and religious trouble spots.

The Soviet government, being committed to equality, opposed all forms of racialism. Article 123 of the Soviet Constitution made discrimination of all kinds 'on account of nationality, as well as the advocacy of racial exclusiveness or hatred and contempt, punishable by law'.[49] Stalin said in 1931, "National and racial chauvinism is a survival of the misanthropic customs characteristic of the period of cannibalism. Anti-Semitism, as an extreme form of racial chauvinism, is the most dangerous survival of cannibalism."[50] In 1934, the Soviet government established a Jewish Autonomous Region, known as Birobidzhan, as the national homeland of Soviet Jewry. It still exists today.

In 1939, the Soviet Union was the only country willing to admit Jews fleeing the Nazis.[51] As Stephen Cohen pointed out, "the Soviet

Union saved more European Jews from Nazism than any other country, first by providing sanctuary for hundreds of thousands of Jews fleeing eastward after the German invasion of Poland, in 1939, and then by destroying the Nazi war machine and liberating the death camps in Eastern Europe."[52]

'An unexampled achievement'

The Soviet working class, with power in its hands, achieved much in the 1920s and 1930s. They changed the Soviet Union from the backward, semi-savage, semi-colonial land of the tsars to the second industrial, scientific and military power in the world. The Soviet Union built a viable modern industrial base in just a decade. From 1928 to 1940, industrial output grew by 17 per cent a year, agriculture by half a per cent, and overall income by 15 per cent, an unequalled rate of income growth. Eric Johnston, President of the US Chamber of Commerce, after visiting the Urals, Siberia and Kazakhstan, declared that Soviet progress since 1928 was 'an unexampled achievement in the industrial history of the whole world'.[53]

Recent scholars agreed. Davies showed how the working class transformed the Soviet Union into a major industrial power. He concluded that the Soviet industrial revolution was unique in its speed and scale.[54] Suny pointed out that Soviet and Western economists agreed that Soviet industrial growth in these years was exceptional.[55]

American historian David Hoffmann confirmed that the Soviet Union succeeded beyond all other countries in mobilising its human and natural resources, in creating an economic system driven by a common purpose, and in creating a united society without an exploiting class. He pointed out that the Soviet Union also provided for the welfare of the working class, offered workers free, universal health care and education, and guaranteed every worker a job, housing and subsidised food.[56]

Girsh Khanin noted that the Soviet Union's dynamic efficiency enabled it to mobilise centralised financial resources to develop the economy and to ensure high rates of economic development (in the 1930s the highest in the world). He explained that this was due to the high growth rates of fixed capital, the rapid growth of education and health care, planned geological exploration and the Soviet working class's effective use of Western countries' scientific and technical achievements. He observed that the third five-year plan created most of the industrial organisational and personnel that enabled the Soviet Union to win the Second World War and to recover so swiftly after the war.[57]

Michael Kort noted that the Soviet Union improved its transport significantly in the 1930s, mainly by adding to the canal and rail networks. It expanded the light industries that produced consumer goods, although these remained a poor relation to heavy industry. The industrialisation drive, because it was planned and controlled by a central authority, brought economic and strategic benefits. Much of this industrial development was in the previously backward central and eastern regions of the country, so it both contributed to their advance and made the new industrial plants and resources safer from foreign attack. Planning also brought economic benefits since the new plants were closer to their essential raw materials. By 1941 the industries built during the 1930s were producing a full range of modern weapons, including some of the world's best tanks, artillery and tactical rockets. After the Second World War, those industries provided the basis for even greater growth that made the Soviet Union an industrial power second only to the USA until Japan overtook it in the 1980s.[58]

David Kotz and Fred Weir remarked that the full employment that resulted from economic planning was another socialist feature of the Soviet system. There was virtually no unemployment in the Soviet Union after the early 1930s. In fact, there was usually an overall labour shortage. It was easy for workers to find a job quickly, and once in work they had a high degree of job security. Workers were rarely laid off or fired. This meant that they had good personal income security and enjoyed significant bargaining power on the job. Because there was a labour shortage and also because there was this tradition of almost never firing workers, managers had to take account of workers' needs and wishes. This resulted in a more relaxed pace of work than was typical of capitalist enterprises.[59] Labour experts Tim Pringle and Simon Clarke pointed out that in the 1930s Soviet workers' resistance to incompetent or unjust management was constant and widespread and that strikes were usually settled in the traditional Soviet way, with immediate concessions to meet the needs of the striking workers.[60]

British historian Kevin McDermott concluded that the Soviet Union "was fundamentally and implacably anti-capitalist. Beyond a few disgruntled Trotskyists, Stalinism represented socialism."[61]

Chapter 3
Towards world war

Threats of war

Russia has no natural borders to protect it from invaders from Asia and Europe. In 1237 the Mongols conquered Russia. Kiev and other cities were burnt to the ground; a tenth of the people were enslaved. Between 1250 and the early 1400s, Russia was invaded every year, by the Tatars in 45 wars, by the Lithuanians in 41, by German crusading orders in 30, and by the Swedes, the Bulgarians and others in 44 more. Russia regained her independence only in the 15th century. But in 1571, the Tatars burnt down most of Moscow. 112 of the next 200 years were spent in six wars with Sweden, four with the Ottoman Empire and 12 with Poland. Russia was at war for 48 of the years 1740 to 1815, fighting eight wars. Then followed the three great defeats of the Crimean war (1854-56), the war with Japan (1905) and World War One. After the revolution came the War of Intervention.

In the early 1930s, international relations were increasingly fraught with war. In September 1931, Japan invaded Manchuria, posing a threat to the Soviet Union. So the Soviet Union had to move fast to defend itself. Stalin said in 1931, "To slacken the tempo would mean falling behind. And those who fall behind get beaten. But we do not want to be beaten. No, we refuse to be beaten! One feature of the history of old Russia was the continual beatings she suffered because of her backwardness. She was beaten by the Mongol khans. She was beaten by the Turkish beys. She was beaten by the Swedish feudal lords. She was beaten by the Polish and Lithuanian gentry. She was beaten by the British and French capitalists. She was beaten by the Japanese barons. All beat her - because of her backwardness, because of her military backwardness, cultural backwardness, political backwardness, industrial backwardness, agricultural backwardness. They beat her because it was profitable and could be done with impunity.

"You remember the words of the pre-revolutionary poet: 'You are poor and abundant, mighty and impotent, Mother Russia.' Those gentlemen were quite familiar with the verses of the old poet. They beat her, saying: 'You are abundant,' so one can enrich oneself at your expense. They beat her, saying: 'You are poor and impotent,' so you can be beaten and plundered with impunity. Such is the law of the exploiters – to beat the backward and the weak. It is the jungle law of capitalism. You are backward, you are weak – therefore you are wrong; hence you can be beaten and enslaved. You are mighty – therefore you are right; hence we must be wary of you. That is why we must no longer lag behind."[1]

So the Soviet Union hastened to collectivise and industrialise. Collectivisation was a battle which cost many lives. But in the long run it saved many more lives, Soviet, British and American. In World War One, the feudal countryside had failed to feed the cities and the army, but in World War Two the collective farms fed Soviet cities and the Red Army. As *Life* magazine observed on 29 March 1943, "Whatever the cost of farm collectivization ... these large farm units ... made possible the use of machinery ... which doubled output ... [and] released millions of workers for industry. Without them ... Russia could not have built the industry that turned out the munitions that stopped the German army."

Without collectivisation the Soviet Union could not have industrialised. Without industrialisation the Soviet Union could not have had a modern army. Without a modern army it could not have beaten the Nazis. If the Nazis had defeated the Soviet Union, even more Soviet people would have been killed. Then with no two-front war to worry about and with the Soviet Union's resources at his disposal, Hitler could have turned West and killed even more Allied soldiers and civilians.

Fifth columns

After Hitler seized power in 1933, pro-Nazi fifth columns grew in almost every country and came to power in 16 countries. The German, Japanese and Polish governments all carried out Contra-style raids into the Soviet Union, to kill and destroy. The Nuremberg trials confirmed that the Nazis sent armed teams of White Russians on missions to kill Soviet leaders.[2]

The Soviet government knew that Nazi Germany and Japan were preparing to attack the Soviet Union, that they had allies inside the Soviet Union and that exposing and defeating these agents would weaken the Axis drive to war. Many modern historians agreed that, as Hoffmann judged, "What historians term 'the Great Terror' was in fact a number of related yet discrete operations instigated by Stalin and his fellow leaders to strike down potential political opponents and fifth columnists in anticipation of the coming war."[3] Oleg Khlevnyuk agreed, "This operation was conceived as a means of eliminating a potential 'fifth column' in a period when the threat of war was increasing …"[4] Acton agreed too, "A proposition currently finding renewed favour among historians is that the overarching motive behind them was preparation for war and an all-encompassing pre-emptive strike against any potential source of internal opposition liable to take advantage of military crisis."[5]

Bukharin, Grigory Zinoviev, Lev Kamenev and others had "engaged in opposition, had had contacts with Trotsky and leaked secret documents to the West, and had wanted to remove Stalin, all of which they had lied about, while proclaiming their complete loyalty."[6] Bukharin's friend Jules Humbert-Droz wrote in his memoirs, "Before leaving I went to see Bukharin for one last time not knowing whether I would see him again upon my return. We had a long and frank conversation. He brought me up to date with the contacts made by his group with the Zinoviev-Kamenev fraction in order to coordinate the struggle against the power of Stalin." And, "Bukharin also told me that they had decided to utilise individual terror in order to rid themselves of Stalin."[7]

Oppositionist Karl Radek testified that Bukharin had said that he had 'taken the path of terrorism'. Oppositionist Grigori Sokolnikov testified that the 'united centre' of Zinovievites and Trotskyists had agreed to plan terrorist attacks on Stalin and Politburo member Sergei Kirov 'as early as the autumn of 1932'.[8] Trotsky's son Sergei Sedov informed Trotsky in mid-1932 that the bloc "is organized. In it have entered the Zinovievites, the Sten-Lominadze group and the Trotskyists …"[9]

In December 1934, Kirov was murdered. The assassin, Leonid Nikolaev, was arrested at once. As Arch Getty and Oleg Naumov noted, "Nikolaev began talking freely from the start. He admitted to having planned the killing for some time because he blamed Kirov for persecution of the Zinoviev group and his resulting unemployment. He said that he had initially planned the killing alone but had then talked to [Ivan] Kotolynov [a 'former Zinoviev supporter'] and others, who at first tried to dissuade him. According to Nikolaev, they wanted to kill someone higher up, like Stalin, but they later approved his plan."[10]

Interrogations of Nikolaev's opposition contacts followed. Getty and Naumov observed, "In some cases, the accused refused to confess to belonging to any conspiracy and maintained his or her innocence … Others admitted to belonging to a 'counterrevolutionary organization' but not to knowing of Nikolaev's plans. … Another group admitted to the full accusation: belonging to a criminal conspiracy that organized the assassination."[11] Nikolaev was the gunman for this opposition conspiracy.[12] Kamenev and Zinoviev admitted that they had planned the assassination: Kamenev said, "we, that is the Zinovievist center of the counterrevolutionary organization, the membership of which I have named above, and the Trotskyist counterrevolutionary organization in the persons of Smirnov, Mrachkovskii and Ter-Vaganian, agreed in 1932 about the union of both, i.e. the Zinovievist and Trotskyist counterrevolutionary organization for cooperative organization of terrorist acts against the leaders of the CC and first of all against Stalin and Kirov."[13]

On 2 June 1937, Bukharin admitted, straight after his arrest, with no protest, that he had been "a participant in the organization of the Rights up to the present, that he was a member of the center of the organization together with Rykov and Tomsky, that this organization had set as its goal the forcible overthrow of Soviet power (uprising, coup d'état, terror), that it had entered into a bloc with the Trotskyite-Zinovievite organization." He confirmed these statements at the close of the investigation and then again at his 1938 trial.[14] Every country's legal system treated as valid admissions made by a suspect during investigation and repeated at trial. At his trial, Bukharin admitted, "If my programme conception were to be formulated practically, it would be in the economic sphere, state capitalism, the prosperous muzhik individual, the curtailment of the collective farms, foreign concessions, surrender of the monopoly of foreign trade, and, as a result - the restoration of capitalism in the country."[15]

The 1961 Commission that investigated Bukharin's case found no evidence that he was coerced. Only a small part of the investigative material for the three Moscow trials has been released. If any of the material had undermined the verdicts, it would surely have been released. As Sarah Davies and James Harris recently concluded, "It would appear that Stalin believed, and had good reason to believe, the essence of the prosecution case as it was presented at the Moscow trials."[16]

There were other opposition conspiracies, one involving Marshal Mikhail Tukhachevsky, the Red Army's commander in chief. French journalist Genevieve Tabouis related that on 29 January 1936, "Tukhachevsky ... had just returned from a trip to Germany, and was heaping glowing praise upon the Nazis. Seated at my right, he said over and over again, as he discussed an air pact between the great powers and Hitler's country: 'They are already invincible, Madame Tabouis!'"[17] Should the Soviet Union have allowed a known defeatist to stay in post?

Later in 1936, Tukhachevsky held secret talks with Czechoslovakia's President Eduard Benes and its Commander-in-Chief General Jan Sirovy. There were no secretaries at these talks and no minutes were kept. Tukhachevsky then left Prague for talks in Berlin. Later, the Czech secret service told Benes that the Nazis knew all the details of the Prague meeting. Benes had to conclude that only Tukhachevsky could have given the Nazis these details.

As Churchill affirmed, "communications were passing through the Soviet Embassy in Prague between important personages in Russia and the German Government. This was a part of the so-called military and old-guard Communist conspiracy to overthrow Stalin and introduce a new régime based on a pro-German policy. President Benes lost no time in communicating all he could find out to Stalin. Thereafter there followed the merciless, but perhaps not needless, military and political purge in Soviet Russia, and the series of trials in January 1937, in which Vyshinsky, the Public Prosecutor, played so masterful a part."[18] In 1991, Colonel Viktor Alksnis read the transcript of the trial of Tukhachevsky and the seven other generals. Before Alksnis read the transcript, he believed that the generals had been framed. After reading it, he concluded that they were indeed guilty.[19] Since then, the Russian state has not allowed anyone to read the transcript.

Josef Goebbels, Hitler's Minister of Propaganda, wrote in May 1943, "The Führer recalled the case of Tukhachevskii and expressed the opinion that we were entirely wrong then in believing that Stalin would ruin the Red Army by the way he handled it. The opposite was true: Stalin got rid of all opposition in the Red Army and thereby brought an end to defeatism."[20] The French government let its defeatist generals stay in command - its army's resistance lasted just 40 days.

In 1937, Trotsky increased his efforts to overthrow the Soviet government, urging in November, "It is high time to launch a world offensive against Stalinism."[21] He wrote, "Since the principal condition for the Trotskyites coming into power, if they fail to achieve this by means of terrorism, would be the defeat of the USSR, it is necessary, as much as possible, to hasten the clash between the USSR and Germany."[22] Radek stated that he had recommended to Trotsky that Vitovt Putna, a military commander loyal to Trotsky, negotiated with the Germans and Japanese on Trotsky's behalf.[23] Trotsky called on the Soviet people to overthrow the Soviet government when Hitler attacked the Soviet Union.[24] He called for a 'revolutionary uprising', an 'insurrection', writing, "It would be childish to think that the Stalin bureaucracy can be removed by means of a Party or Soviet Congress. Normal, constitutional means are no longer available for the removal of the ruling clique. ... They can be compelled to hand over power to the Proletarian vanguard only by FORCE."[25] And, "Inside the Party, Stalin has put himself above all criticism and the State. It is impossible to displace him except by assassination. Every oppositionist becomes ipso facto a terrorist."[26]

Trotsky forecast, "If the war should remain only a war, the defeat of the Soviet Union would be inevitable. In a technical, economic and military sense, imperialism is incomparably more strong. If it is not paralysed by revolution in the West, imperialism will sweep away the present regime."[27] Trotsky tried to organise anti-Soviet groups in every country and received support from powerful figures. For example, the American press tycoon and fascist Randolph Hearst published Trotsky's books, which were sold openly in fascist Italy and Nazi Germany.

Under Nikolai Yezhov, the NKVD became the seat of another conspiracy, carried out by "enemies of the people and spies for foreign intelligence, who made their way into the organs of the NKVD at the centre and in the localities, and who continued to carry out their subversive work, striving by all means to muddle up the investigative and information-collecting work, consciously perverting Soviet laws, carrying out mass and unfounded arrests." Yezhov used impermissible methods, imposing quotas in every part of the Soviet Union for mass arrests, which led to huge numbers of illegal arrests and punishments of innocent people. For far too long, the NKVD was out of party and government control, largely because Nikita Khrushchev protected

Yezhov and adopted his methods. When Khrushchev was First Secretary in Moscow, and then in the Ukraine, he had more people executed than in any other parts of the Soviet Union, far more than the government had authorised.[28] The Soviet government eventually exposed Yezhov and regained control of the NKVD. A resolution of 17 November 1938, *On the new processes for arrests, procurator control, and investigation*, forbade 'any sort of mass operations relating to arrests and exiles' by the NKVD and the procuracy.[29] More than 100,000 persons wrongly arrested were released from camps and prisons.

In 1990, Lazar Kaganovich, a Politburo member from 1930 to 1957, said, "Look, if you investigate everything in detail, and look at every single case, then of course it is possible to find flaws and mistakes, no doubt about it. But if we approach the issue historically, then it was necessary to cleanse the country. This is shown by the current situation. Are there no people today who are open enemies of socialism and of the October revolution? There are lots of them! Therefore, those who want to defend the October revolution have to beat the enemies of this revolution, beat the enemies of Soviet power and of the Soviet state. The present situation demonstrates that we were right."[30] Schuman commented later, "had it not smashed ruthlessly the conspiracies of the 1930's, the Soviet Union and all the United Nations would have suffered irreparable defeat in World War II at the hands of insanely savage foes …"[31]

World war

By 1938, a second world war had begun across the world from Gibraltar to Shanghai, involving at least 500 million people. Japanese forces had invaded China and were launching border attacks on the Soviet Union, which Soviet forces repelled. After the 1938 Japanese-Soviet battle at Changkufeng, the US military attaché in Moscow judged, "any adverse effects on Red Army efficiency which may have been occasioned by the purges have now been overcome. … The recent events around Lake Hassan have shown that the personnel of the Red Army is not only dependable, but that it can be called upon for extraordinary exploits of valor, that the material with which the Red Army is equipped is adequate and serviceable, if, indeed, it is not entitled to higher rating." The US military attaché in China, Colonel (later General) Joseph Stilwell, agreed, "the Russian troops appeared to advantage, and those who believe the Red Army is rotten would do well to reconsider their views."[32] In August 1939, the Red Army defeated Japanese forces at the battle of Khalkhin-Gol in Mongolia, a victory which saved the Soviet Union from facing a two-front war.

In the late 1930s, Hitler encouraged a Sudeten German fifth column in Czechoslovakia to secede. Prime Minister Neville Chamberlain, whom the French neatly called Monsieur J'aime Berlin, assisted Hitler's scheme. In October 1938, Chamberlain signed the Munich Agreement, which gave Czechoslovakia to Hitler. The Trotskyist ILP MP John McGovern praised Chamberlain for this, saying, "Well done thou good and faithful servant."[33] Anna Louise Strong pointed out at the time, "British diplomacy granted to Hitler Germany everything that it had refused for more than a decade to the German republic: the remilitarization of the Rhineland, the Nazi-terrorized plebiscite in the Saar, German rearmament and naval expansion ... British finance, which had strangled the struggling German democracy with demands for impossible war reparations, supported Hitler's regime with heavy investments and loans. It was no secret to any intelligent world citizen that the British Tories made these concessions to Hitler because they saw in him their 'strong-arm gangster' who would eventually fight the Soviets, which important sections of British finance capital have always seen as their greatest foe."[34]

Many modern historians accepted that the Chamberlain government schemed for Hitler to attack the Soviet Union. As Louise Shaw explained, Chamberlain "was so consumed by his suspicion of the Soviet leadership and his hatred of communism. His repeated attacks upon the Soviet leadership in the letters to his sisters during this period are unparalleled in any other collection of private papers."[35] Paul Hehn noted the "upper class hatred of the Soviet Union on the part of Chamberlain and his friends. This same hatred led them to place class survival over the interests of the country which in the end led to the debacle of World War II. Chamberlain and his friends in the government desired to give Hitler at Munich a 'free hand in the east' – and probably before Munich – well into the opening months of 1939 and beyond, even after it became apparent that Hitler's aggressive policy and ambitions placed Great Britain and France in mortal danger."[36] Their policies 'could be explained by the unspoken hope and expectation that he would ultimately turn east and attack the Soviet Union and destroy Communism'.[37] Warren Kimball agreed, writing of Munich's 'implied invitation to Hitler to move eastward'.[38] Andrew Alexander agreed too: "British and French policy seemed so ready to solve the problem of Hitler by turning him eastwards."[39]

Clement Leibovitz and Alvin Finkel summed up, "those in the [British] ruling group before May 10, 1940 were bloody-minded protectors of privilege whose fixation with destroying communists and communism led them to make common cause with fascists. They were not honest, idiotic patriots; they were liars and traitors who would sacrifice human lives in their defense of property and privilege ... Blame for the tragedy of World War II, including the Holocaust, must rest partly with Stanley Baldwin, Neville Chamberlain, Lord Halifax and their close associates, who, far from being naïve appeasers anxious to avoid wars in Europe, were visceral anti-communists who single-mindedly pursued an alliance with Hitler."[40]

After the Munich Agreement, Chamberlain schemed with the Nazi and French governments to use Ukraine to destroy the Soviet Union, just as they had used the Sudetenland to destroy Czechoslovakia. In talks with the French government, on 24 November 1938, Chamberlain said, "there might be in the minds of the German Government an idea that they could begin the disruption of Russia by the encouragement of agitation for an independent Ukraine."[41] He asked Georges Bonnet, the French Foreign Minister, "what the position would be if Russia were to ask France for assistance on the grounds that a separatist movement in the Ukraine was provoked by Germany. M. Bonnet explained that

French obligations towards Russia only came into force if there were a direct attack by Germany on Russian territory. Mr. Chamberlain said that he considered M. Bonnet's reply entirely satisfactory."[42] So aggression by Hitler, on the Sudeten pattern, would leave the Soviet Union isolated.

Hitler called for a Ukraine separate from the Soviet Union.[43] The British and French governments secretly backed Ukrainians based in Germany who wanted to break Ukraine away from the Soviet Union.[44] And in April, May and July 1939, Trotsky too called for an independent Ukraine.[45]

On 17 April 1939, the Soviet government proposed a mutual assistance treaty with Britain and France. As Churchill commented, "The alliance of Britain, France and Russia would have struck deep alarm into the heart of Germany in 1939 and no one can prove that war might not even then have been averted." On 8 May, Chamberlain rejected the Soviet proposal, making war inevitable. (As Schuman commented later, "The verdict of the record is unmistakable and obvious: responsibility for the breakdown of collective security rests on the Western democracies, not on the Soviet Union."[46]) The British and French governments knew that Germany would invade Poland, but refused to join the alliance with the Soviet Union that alone could have saved Poland. The British and French governments, not the Soviet Union, betrayed and sacrificed Poland.

On 22 May, Hitler signed the Pact of Steel with Mussolini. The next day, he decided to attack Poland on 1 September. This was three months before he signed the non-aggression pact with the Soviet Union.

The non-aggression pact was a consequence, not a cause, of the breakdown of the Anglo-Soviet-French alliance negotiations. The pact laid down a line within Poland beyond which German forces could not pass, so that the Polish army and the Polish government could retreat behind this line. The Soviet Union would have a buffer state, still armed and hostile to Germany, between the Reich and the Soviet frontier. The pact foiled Chamberlain's scheme to set Hitler on the Soviet Union and gave the Soviet Union two more years to prepare itself against attack.

Historians generally accept that the pact was not an alliance. As Geoffrey Roberts pointed out, "There was no specific agreement or intention on 23 August to partition Poland. ... the first clause of the secret additional protocol to the pact concerned not Poland but Soviet-German spheres of influence in the Baltic. This was a curious textual order of priorities for two states that had just decided to carve up between them another major state. It makes much more sense to posit that there was no such agreement and to assume that what was agreed on 23 August was an eastern limit of German military expansion into Poland."[47] Richard Overy agreed: "The secret protocol drawn up in August only delimited spheres of interest; it did not arrange partition or control."[48] Samantha Carl noted, "The Non-Aggression Pact was not an alliance between the two nations, but instead called for neutrality if the other was attacked. ... negotiations between the Soviet Union and the West broke down prior to the completion of the Non-Aggression Pact, not as a result of it. ... the Non-Aggression Pact, although important because it prevented a two-front war in 1939, was not integral to the German war movement."[49]

The Soviet Union used well the two years' grace brought by the pact. In 1940, the Soviet government spent 56 billion rubles on defence, more than twice as much as in 1938, more than 25 per cent of all industrial investment. As a result, the defence industry developed at three times the rate of all other industries. During the time between the signing of the pact and the Nazi invasion, the value of the Soviet Union's material resources nearly doubled, an impressive achievement.[50]

Roy Medvedev commented, "Of course he [Stalin] and his entourage always kept in mind the possibility of war with the capitalist countries, and in the late 30s this meant specifically Germany and Japan. Preparations for such a war were made by creating a modern defense industry, military aviation, an up-to-date navy, civil-defense training for the whole population, and so on. In 1939-1941 the army increased by 2.5 times, many troops and supplies were transferred to the western districts, war production increased, and the number of military schools grew. Especially after the war with Finland, a great deal of work was done toward retraining the Army. The development of new weapons was speeded up. More than a 100,000 men were put to work on the fortification of the new western borders. Airfields were modernized, ordnance depots and ammunition dumps set up, and military exercises for troops and commanders carried out."[51] Roberts summed up, "In the long run the pact paved the way for the Soviet victory over Nazi Germany."[52]

Hitler attacks Poland

On 1 September 1939, Germany broke its 1934 non-aggression pact with Poland by invading. The Polish army was routed, suffering 210,000 casualties (70,000 killed, 140,000 wounded) and 700,000 captured. The German army lost 16,000 killed and 30,000 wounded. On 7 September, the Polish leaders fled to Romania, taking the country's gold with them. Uniquely in World War Two, they appointed no successor government, leaving the Polish people unrepresented and defenceless.

Soviet forces entered eastern Poland on 17 September, dashing across Belarus and the West Ukraine for the Curzon line, beating the Nazis to it. The Polish Supreme Commander, Marshal Edward Rydz-Smigly, ordered his troops not to fight the Soviet forces, although he ordered them to continue fighting the German invaders. Hitler offered the Soviet Union all of eastern Poland up to the River Vistula and Warsaw, but Soviet troops moved only to the River Bug, that is, only into those lands that Polish forces had seized in 1920. American historian Timothy Snyder accepted that in occupying eastern Poland, "Usually the Red Army behaved well …"[53]

The Soviet occupation of western Ukraine and western Belarus saved these peoples from Nazi rule. The only alternative would have been to let Hitler send the Nazi army right up to the Soviet border. What would this have meant for Poland's people? On 9 September, Hitler's Chief of Staff General Franz Halder said, "it was the intention of the Führer and Goering to destroy and exterminate the Polish people."[54]

As Soviet Foreign Minister Vyacheslav Molotov explained to the Supreme Soviet on 31 October 1939, "Our troops entered the territory of Poland only after the Polish state had collapsed and actually ceased to exist. Naturally, we could not remain neutral towards these facts, since as a result of these events we were confronted with urgent problems concerning the security of our state. Furthermore, the Soviet government could not but reckon with the exceptional situation created for our brothers in Western Ukraine and Western Byelorussia, who had been abandoned to their fate as a result of the collapse of Poland."

American professor of international law George Ginsburgs later agreed, "*De facto*, then, one may well accept the view that the Polish Government no longer functioned as an effective state power. In such a case the Soviet claim that Eastern Galicia was *in fact* a *terra nullius* may not be unjustified and could be sustained. If one accepts the more controversial Soviet assertion that the Government of Poland had disintegrated and disappeared, implying in addition that all territorial titles vested in it lapsed *de jure* too, then Eastern Galicia may be viewed on September 17, 1939, as *terra nullius* both *de facto* and *de jure*. In such circumstances the Soviet legal title by virtue of effective occupation of abandoned territory would be clear …"[55]

Article 16 of the League of Nations Covenant required members to impose sanctions on any member who 'resorted to war'. But the League did not judge that the Soviet Union had done so. No country imposed sanctions on the Soviet Union, none broke off diplomatic relations. Romania and France did not declare war on the Soviet Union, although both had military treaties with Poland. All countries, including Poland's allies Britain and France, agreed that the Soviet Union was not a belligerent.

Ex-Prime Minister David Lloyd-George pointed out, "The German invasion was designed to annex to the Reich provinces where a decided majority of the population was Polish by race, language and tradition. Russian armies marched into territories which were not Polish and which were forcibly annexed to Poland after the Great War despite fierce protests and armed resistance by the inhabitants. Inhabitants of the Polish Ukraine are of the same race and speak the same language as their neighbours in the Ukraine republic of the Soviet Union ... White Russia was originally annexed by Poland as a result of a victorious war against Russia."[56] Ginsburgs later agreed that the Polish title to these territories "derives from a direct act of force and military conquest, not even remotely claiming parentage with the concept of national self-determination ... on this particular item the Soviet plea was, by and large, successful in carrying its point."[57]

Churchill, in a speech broadcast on 1 October, said, "that the Russian armies should stand on this [Curzon] line was clearly necessary for the safety of Russia against the Nazi menace. At any rate the line is there, and an Eastern front has been created which Nazi Germany does not dare assail."[58] He pointed out that the Soviet move into Poland was good for Britain, because it blocked Hitler's path to the Balkans. Conservative MP Robert Boothby told the House of Commons on 20 September, "I think it is legitimate to suppose that this action on the part of the Soviet government was taken ... from the point of view of self-preservation and self-defence ... The action taken by the Russian troops ... has pushed the German frontier considerably westward ... I am thankful that Russian troops are now along the Polish-Romanian frontier. I would rather have Russian troops there than German troops."[59]

In October, the Soviet Union sent forces into the Baltic states, throwing out the pro-Hitler dictatorships that had run them since the early 1930s, and signed treaties of mutual assistance with the new governments. Churchill acknowledged that these actions were 'dictated by the imminence and magnitude of the German danger now threatening Russia, in which case the Soviet Govt. may well have been justified in taking in self-defence such measures as might in other circumstances have been open to criticism'.[60] As he noted, "It was to our interests that the U.S.S.R. should increase their strength in the Baltic, thereby limiting the risk of German domination in that area."[61] Lippmann wrote, "Every day it becomes clearer that Russia is constructing a great defense area from the Baltic to the Black Sea."[62]

In 1939, the Soviet government persistently tried to reach an agreement with the Finnish government to protect the northern approaches to the Soviet Union.[63] The Soviet Union needed the room in which to defend Leningrad, its second city, which was only 25 miles from the Finnish border.[64] But the Finnish government, encouraged by the Nazi, British and French governments, refused. These governments then backed Finland's war against the Soviet Union. By contrast, Churchill was 'in favour of the Soviet demands for naval bases in Finland'. He explained that they were needed to 'prevent German aggression in the Baltic Provinces or against Petrograd'. Britain should try 'to persuade the Finns to make concessions'.

But from November 1939 to March 1940, Chamberlain sent more arms to Finland to fight the Soviet Union than he sent to France, Belgium and Holland to fight the Nazis.[65] He hoped to turn the Finnish war into a joint attack led by the British and French governments against the Soviet Union in 'a sort of glorified Crimean War brought up to date', as Conservative MP Leo Amery put it.[66] The British and French governments proposed using Polish troops against the Red Army in Finland.[67] French Prime Minister Edouard Daladier told the Finnish government that an Anglo-French expedition was ready to sail to its aid. The British government recruited 500 people for the Finnish Volunteer Force.[68] Lippmann later admitted, "The most foolish thing I can remember in my many human errors is that during World War II I was one of the people who joined the hue and cry for war against the Soviet Union to save Finland. That was the most nonsensical thing that anybody ever proposed, but I can remember doing it."[69]

Finland's Commander-in-Chief General Carl Mannerheim told Chamberlain that he would not need help until May, but Soviet forces cracked the 'impregnable' Mannerheim line in a month and the Finns sued for peace in March. The Soviet Union won enough land to save Leningrad from Nazi occupation.[70] These Soviet actions towards Poland, the Baltic states and Finland pushed its defence lines further west, increasing the distances that the Wehrmacht had to cover before it could reach Moscow and Leningrad, making it harder for Hitler to beat the Soviet Union.

Meanwhile, the British government was making preparations to destroy the Soviet oil industry. By April 1940, it had drawn up detailed plans to bomb Soviet oil wells in the Caucasus, including Baku, Batum and Grozny, a scheme known as Operation *Pike*. The attacks were to be launched from bases in Turkey and Iran.[71] Fortunately, Turkey and Iran refused, wrecking the scheme.

In June 1940, the Soviet Union strengthened its defensive ties with the Baltic states. It insisted that Lithuania form a government that would honour the treaty of mutual assistance it had signed the previous autumn. The new government ended the 14-year dictatorship of President Antanas Smetona. It freed 1,000 political prisoners, legalised trade unions and dissolved the Concordat with the Vatican. It also dissolved the old parliament which had been elected under Smetona's terror and with a small electorate restricted by property qualifications (in Vilna, only 30,000 of the city's 250,000 inhabitants had been allowed a vote). It held elections for a new parliament. By December 1940, the Soviet government had given Estonia's peasants 24,755 new farms and given more land to 27,609 farms. In Latvia, the Soviet reform created 52,000 new farms and 23,000 small farms increased their acreage. The Soviet government cancelled the debts peasants owed to the former governments.

In 1940, Nazi Germany stepped up its preparations for attacking the Soviet Union. It signed military treaties with the governments of Bulgaria, Romania, Hungary and Finland. By allying with the aggressor Hitler, these governments broke their non-aggression treaties with the Soviet Union. In March, the Finnish government decided to fight as Hitler's ally. In May, the first Nazi soldiers entered Finland and supervised the building of the Petsamo airbase later used by the Luftwaffe to attack Allied shipping.

On 13 October 1940, Germany formally proposed that the Soviet Union join the Axis, but the Soviet government refused.[72] In order to isolate the Soviet Union, the Nazis lied that there was a Nazi-Soviet alliance, that the Soviet Union wanted to divide up the British Empire with the Axis and that the Soviet Union was preparing to attack Germany.

General Halder more accurately called Soviet deployments in June 1941 'purely defensive'.[73] The Soviet government did all it could to give Hitler no excuse to accuse the Soviet Union of aggression, an excuse that the pro-Hitler groups in the British and French governments could have used to justify joining Hitler's attack. If the Soviet Union had mobilised, Hitler would have declared it the aggressor. As Stalin told Marshal Zhukov 'Mobilization means war', as it had in 1914 when Germany declared war on Russia as soon as Russia mobilised.

The Nazis boasted they would defeat the Soviet Union in two months. The British government thought that a blitzkrieg on Russia would be 'a campaign of little difficulty', over in between '3 and 6 weeks'.[74] The General Staff told the Cabinet that the Soviet Union would collapse in weeks. The Joint Intelligence Committee forecast that Moscow would fall in six weeks. Laurence Steinhardt, briefly US Ambassador to the Soviet Union, advised his government that "the Stalinist regime could not survive any invasion."[75] If Hitler had beaten the Soviet Union swiftly, he could then have turned his 240 victorious divisions against Britain.

Chapter 4

World War Two

Genocide

On 22 June 1941, the Nazis invaded the Soviet Union in 'a totally unprovoked and unconditional attack'.[1] The invasion force, the largest in history, of 3.6 million troops, included four panzer groups fielding 19 panzer and 15 motorised divisions, with 3,350 tanks and 2,770 fighter and bomber aircraft, against 2.9 million defenders. This battle-hardened army had already conquered Poland, France and most of the rest of Europe. Nazi transport capabilities were ten times those of the Soviet forces. Romanian, Hungarian, Italian, Croat, Bulgarian, Finnish and Slovakian forces also joined the invasion.

Molotov said, "Our cause is just. The enemy will be beaten. Victory will be with us." The war became a war fought by the peoples of most of the world's countries allied to defend their national independence against the Axis powers.

Operation Barbarossa "was not only the most massive military campaign in history, but it also unleashed an unprecedented campaign of genocidal violence."[2] As Hitler told two hundred Wehrmacht officers on 30 March 1941, "We are talking about a war of extermination." He wrote in *Mein Kampf*, "If our hearts are set on establishing our great German Reich, we must above all things force out and exterminate the

Slavonic nations – the Russians, Poles, Czechs, Slovaks, Bulgarians, Ukrainians, Byelorussians. ... Twenty million people must be wiped out."[3] His deputy, Hermann Goering, echoed, "Kill everyone opposed to us. Kill, kill! Not you will answer for this, but I! Hence, kill!"[4] The invading forces mercilessly assaulted Soviet civilians, they raped, pillaged and murdered wherever they went.

Hitler said, "The destruction of the major Russian cities is a prerequisite for the permanence of our power in Russia."[5] His 'Hunger Plan' was to cut Moscow and Leningrad off from the grain-producing Ukraine and seize Soviet food production to feed the German people. Erich Koch, Reichskommissar for Ukraine, aimed to 'smash Ukrainian industry and drive the proletariat back to the country'.[6] De-industrialising the Soviet Union would destroy the working class and turn the country back into the wheat supplier for Western Europe that it had been before the revolution.

The head of the Wehrmacht, Field Marshal Wilhelm Keitel, signed the final version of the infamous 'Commissar Order' on 6 June, "In the struggle against Bolshevism, we cannot count on the enemy acting according to the principles of humanity or international law. In particular the political commissars at all levels, as the real leaders of resistance, can be expected to treat prisoners of war in a hate-filled, cruel, and inhuman manner." Having projected onto the enemy the treatment the Nazis themselves intended to inflict, Keitel went on, "The troops must be made aware: 1. In this struggle to show consideration and apply principles of international law to these elements is wrong. ... 2. Political commissars are the originators of barbaric, Asiatic methods of fighting. Thus, they have to be dealt with immediately and ... with the utmost severity. As a matter of principle, therefore, they will be shot at once."[7]

The Soviet Union and Germany both recognised the 1907 Hague Convention on the treatment of POWs, but, as Overy pointed out, "When the Soviet government tried in the first weeks of the conflict to reach agreement through the International Red Cross on mutual respect for prisoners' rights, the German government refused to comply."[8] Of

5.74 million Soviet soldiers captured during the war, 3.3 million died. The Nazis carried out what Berkhoff rightly called a 'genocidal massacre' of Soviet POWs.[9] The Soviet government could not have saved them.

Active defence

The Soviet government knew that in May 1940 the French had been defeated because they had massed their forces on the border, as well as in Belgium, so instead it planned defence in depth. Marshal Zhukov pointed out, *"the Nazi command had seriously counted on our rushing the main forces of the Fronts closer to the frontier, where it planned to encircle and destroy them. That, indeed, was the main objective of Plan Barbarossa at the start of the war."*[10] And, "the Soviet Union would have been smashed if we had organized all our forces on the border."[11]

Historians now largely agreed that the Soviet Union was not unprepared for the invasion but had a strategy to oppose it. As military historians Bryan Fugate and Lev Dvoretsky concluded, "It is an enduring myth of the twentieth century that the German invasion of the Soviet Union in June 1941 caught Stalin and the Red Army totally by surprise. . . . Stalin and the Soviet High Command were not caught off guard by the invasion but in fact had developed a skilful, innovative, and highly secret plan to oppose it . . . . This strategy would ensure the nation's ability not only to survive the biggest and most violent invasion in history but indeed to prevail over it."[12] Overy agreed, "the absence of preparation is a myth. The Soviet political and military leadership began to prepare the country from the autumn of 1940 for the possibility of a war with Germany."[13] Mawdsley noted, "It is unfair, however, to charge Stalin and his government with not preparing the USSR for war."[14] Fugate summed up, "Viewed from any standpoint, the USSR was as well-prepared for war in June 1941 as it possibly could have been."[15]

British military historian Chris Bellamy noted of the first days of the invasion, "German accounts are unanimous about the unexpected strength and savagery of the Soviet resistance across most of the front."[16]

Soviet forces inflicted 750,000 casualties on the invaders in the first six months. Von Hardesty and Ilya Grinberg pointed out, "For the VVS [Soviet Air Force] in August 1941, there were signs of resiliency – even renewal. Indeed, the Nazi blitzkrieg had achieved dazzling tactical victories, but in a strategic sense, the enemy had been denied a clear and decisive victory. ... The Soviet military – and the VVS – fought desperately, even in the face of enormous losses. The VVS remained severely weakened and disorganized, but it persisted as a viable force."[17]

American military historian David Glantz stated, "In addition to slowing and temporarily halting German blitzkrieg war, the prolonged and bloody fight for Smolensk damaged Germany's vaunted war machine and ultimately contributed to its unprecedented defeat at the gates of Moscow in early December 1941. ... rather than trading space for time by accepting defence passively throughout the summer and fall, as some have argued, instead, Stalin and the Soviet Union's military leadership insisted the Red Army stand and fight whenever and wherever possible. Although this military strategy proved unquestionably costly in terms of lost lives, weaponry, and military equipment, ultimately it helped produce Red Army victories in the Leningrad and Rostov regions in November 1941 and at the gates of Moscow in December 1941. ... The military strategy Stalin, the Stavka, and Western Main Direction Command pursued was far more sophisticated than previously believed. ... This attrition strategy inflicted far greater damage on Army Group Center than previously thought and ultimately contributed significantly to the Western and Kalinin Front's victories over Army Group Center in December 1941."[18] Hardesty and Grinberg confirmed, "Moscow – unlike Paris two years before – stopped the advance of Nazi Germany. For the Soviet Union, as well as the Allied cause itself, this was indeed a momentous turning point in the war."[19] As American historian Stephen Ambrose summed up, "The Russians, alone, stemmed the Nazi tide, then began to roll it back."[20]

An unprecedented mobilization gave weight to this strategy. American historian Walter S. Dunn, Jr., remarked, "The actual reason the Soviets were able to stop the Germans in late 1941 was an unbelievable mobilization of men and weapons beginning in September 1941, which created a new Red Army. The Soviet formed and sent into combat in a few months more new divisions than the United States formed in the entire war. ... Beginning in the summer of 1941, an incredible effort was made not only to form new divisions and other units to replace those destroyed by the Germans, but also to equip them with modern weapons capable of matching German weapons. The herculean effort culminated in the defeat of the German Army at the gates of Moscow, the first defeat inflicted on Germany during World War II."[21] Overy summed up, "The reconstruction of an almost entirely new army on the ruins of the collapse in 1941, one capable of holding its own against the attacker, ranks as the most remarkable achievement of the war."[22]

Soviet arms production

Bellamy applauded the Soviet government's key decision to move 2,593 industrial enterprises, including 1,360 arms factories, to the Volga, Siberia and Central Asia, and to reassemble them between July and November 1941.[23] Other historians agreed. Glantz asserted, "this massive relocation and reorganization of heavy industry was an incredible accomplishment of endurance and organization."[24] Hardesty and Grinberg observed, "The ultimate fate of the VVS – as well as the larger Soviet military – would rest on the State Defense Committee's crucial decision, in early 1941, to evacuate Soviet war industries to the East. The herculean effort to transplant more than 1,500 industrial enterprises beyond the Ural Mountains at the height of the German invasion marks one of the Soviets' most impressive wartime achievements."[25]

During the war, the Soviet Union produced 100,000 tanks, 130,000 aircraft, 800,000 guns and mortars, one billion artillery and mortar shells and bombs, 30 million small arms (including 12 million rifles), 40 billion cartridges and more than 500,000 guns and mortars, all despite the Nazi occupation of the most industrialised part of the country. A better system produced 'some of the best weapons systems in the world'[26] – the T-34 tank, which German tank generals Paul von Kleist and Heinz Guderian called 'the deadliest tank in the world', the Katyusha multiple rocket-launcher and the Kalashnikov assault rifle.

American historian Stephen Fritz pointed out, "in 1942 the Soviet Union alone, even without the contributions of Great Britain and the United States, would once again outproduce the Reich in virtually every weapons category. In the key areas of small arms and artillery, the advantage was three to one, while, in tanks, it was a staggering four to one, accentuated by the higher quality of the Soviet T-34."[27] As David Glantz and Jonathan House wrote, "In addition, 1942 witnessed weapons production and force generation for the Red Army like never before – a miracle of industrial output and military might that created the building blocks, especially tanks and mechanized corps, of eventual Soviet victory."[28]

British and American lend-lease played a huge part by sending arms, trucks, canned rations, boots, uniforms, radios and other equipment, but did not have a significant impact until 1942. In spring 1943, the US Ambassador, Admiral William Standley, called a press conference to claim that the Soviet press was silent about US aid. The Soviet ambassador in Washington showed Undersecretary of State Sumner Welles a long list of articles from the Soviet press detailing the US aid. Standley resigned in May. Stalin praised lend-lease's 'extraordinary contribution' to Allied victory.[29] He said, "Without American production, victory would not have been possible."[30]

Allies

A grand alliance against the Axis powers was created. On 12 July 1941, the Anglo-Soviet alliance was signed, guaranteeing mutual assistance and no separate peace. On 18 July, the Soviet Union signed an agreement with the Czech government-in-exile and on 30 July with the Polish government-in-exile. On 2 August, the US-Soviet trade agreement was renewed and the US government sent an official message to the Soviet government stating that "the strengthening of the armed resistance of the Soviet Union ... is in the interest of the national defense of the United States." On 4 December, Poland and the Soviet Union made a Declaration of Friendship and Mutual Assistance.

The Anglo-Soviet and Soviet-American communiqués of June 1942 both declared that in the negotiations 'complete understanding was reached with regard to the urgent tasks of creating a second front in Europe in 1942'. The US and British governments promised a Second Front before the end of that year. In talks with Molotov, President Franklin D. Roosevelt 'authorized Mr. Molotov to inform Mr Stalin that we expect the formation of a Second Front this year'.[31] Churchill then changed '1942' to '1943'. On 10 June 1942, he told the Soviet government, "Finally, and this is most important of all, we are concentrating our maximum efforts on organization and preparation of the large scale invasion of the continent of Europe by the British and American forces in 1943. We do not set any limits for the scale and aims of this campaign, which at the beginning, will be carried out by the British and American forces numbering more than one million men, with the appropriate support of aviation."[32] Mawdsley has commented that the Soviet government was 'right, too, to accuse Roosevelt and Churchill of bad faith'.[33] US General Albert Wedemeyer explained the delay: "The second front, he told [Ambassador Joseph] Davies, should be postponed to maximize the number of Germans and Russians killing each other."[34]

On 21 June 1942, Panzer Army Africa, commanded by Colonel-General Erwin Rommel, took Tobruk: 33,000 British troops surrendered to a smaller German force. Rommel pursued British forces into Egypt and engaged the British Eighth Army at El Alamein. On 5 July, Roosevelt cabled Stalin, "The crisis in Egypt with its threat to the supply route to Russia has led Prime Minister Churchill to send me an urgent message asking whether forty A twenty bombers destined for Russia and now in Iraq can be transferred to the battle in Egypt. It is impossible for me to express a judgement on this matter because of limited information here. I am therefore asking that you make the decision in the interest of total war effort." Stalin replied, "In view of the situation in which the Allied forces find themselves in Egypt I have no objection to forty of the A 20 bombers now in Iraq en route to the USSR being transferred to the Egyptian front."[35] As Churchill said later, "I know of no Government which stands to its obligations, even in its own despite, more solidly than the Russian Soviet Government."[36] The Soviet Union was a better ally to Britain than vice versa.

Collaborators

Back on the eastern front, the Nazis carried out mass murders in all the countries of Eastern Europe that they occupied. They killed an estimated 13.7 million Soviet civilians.[37] This total included a quarter of Belarus's people and 4.1 million Ukrainians, a fifth of the population. American historian Wendy Lower summed up, "In Ukraine's history of man-made disasters, mostly imposed from the outside, the Nazi occupation stands out as the worst episode."[38] She concluded, "what the Nazis attempted to achieve in the region and how they implemented their imperialistic, criminal policies represented a dramatically different episode in Ukraine's history, unlike the Stalinist campaigns of the 1930s and the subsequent, relatively relaxed Soviet policies of the postwar period."[39] Berkhoff affirmed, "the Nazi regime in the 'East' was driven by the Nazi conviction that Ukraine was, or should become, a clean national minorities' slate for the German people. ... This extreme German nationalism combined with anti-Bolshevism, anti-Semitism, and a racist view of the 'Russians', and the results were terror, murder, massacre, and genocide. ... never before in the history of Ukraine did so many social and ethnic groups suffer so much during one period."[40]

Yet some Ukrainians collaborated with the Nazi occupier. Since the early 1920s, the *Abwehr*, the German intelligence service, had funded the Organisation of Ukrainian Nationalists [OUN] and its predecessor, the Ukrainian Military Organization. The OUN proclaimed, "Our system will be horrible for its opponents: terror against the enemy – foreigners and their accomplices."[41] A Nationalist leaflet of 1941 said, "Moscow, Poland, the Hungarians, Jewry are your enemies. Destroy them."[42]

OUN leaders admitted that the Ukrainian Insurgent Army [UPA] aimed to 'exterminate Ukraine's national minorities'.[43] Iaroslav Stets'ko, the OUN's second in command, said, "We are raising a militia that will assist the extermination of the Jews." Orthodox Church leaders in the Ukraine condemned 'Jewish-Bolshevism'. UPA Commander Roman Shukhevych ordered the killing of East Ukrainians 'on shaky grounds or without any grounds, and contemplated their total extermination, including even OUN or UPA members'.[44] Special German units supported by far more numerous units of local collaborationists reduced Ukraine's Jewish population from 870,000 to 17,000.[45]

In east Poland, in June 1941, local militias killed 19,655 Jews. *Antyk*, the Polish Home Army's propaganda arm, declared in the summer of 1942, when the Nazis were shipping 5-6,000 Warsaw Jews a day to Treblinka, "The extermination of the Jews in Europe by the Germans, which will be the final result of the German-Jewish war, represents from our point of view an undoubtedly favorable development …"[46] Polish historian Andrzej Paczkowski noted, "thousands of Jews were handed over to the Germans, and similar numbers were murdered by Poles themselves."[47] Hubert van Tuyll agreed: "The holocaust in eastern Poland could not have been accomplished without the active participation of hundreds of thousands of locals recruited by the Nazis to control and then slaughter Jews in the field."[48]

In the Baltic states too, some collaborated with the Nazi invaders. The Lithuanian Activists' Front and Estonian guerrillas rose against Soviet forces on the first day of the invasion.[49] The Estonian Legion in 1944 became part of the new 20th SS Waffen Grenadier Division (First Estonian).[50] All too many Latvians joined the 19th SS Waffen Grenadier Division (2nd Latvian).[51]

These bodies were not just anti-Soviet. They were anti-Semitic, and they killed Jews in what historian Prit Buttar rightly called the Baltic Holocaust.[52] Other historians agreed. Andrejs Plakans judged that the Nazi occupiers and their local allies 'succeeded in turning the first six months of the German occupation (June to December) into the most murderous period in the modern history of the Baltic littoral …

the Baltic littoral's Holocaust'.[53] Statiev pointed out, "In the Baltic region, too, the police actively helped the Nazis to exterminate nearly all the Jews. At least 20 Lithuanian, 4 Estonian, and 4 Latvian police battalions participated directly in the Holocaust. ... In 1941-1942, German collaborators, scores of whom later joined the anti-Communist resistance, killed many more people in every borderland region except Estonia than did the Soviets throughout the entire period of their struggle against nationalists from 1939 to the 1950s."[54] Statiev summed up, "Each major nationalist group slaughtered or helped the Nazis slaughter far more members of ethnic minorities and local peasants than they killed Soviet soldiers."[55]

The post-Soviet Baltic governments tried to deny that their SS Legions committed war crimes, which meant denying the verdicts of the Nuremberg Tribunal. For example, the Estonian government claimed that the Estonian SS legion only engaged in combat operations at the front to defend Estonia's independence and that it played no part in Nazi war crimes.[56] On 18 June 2002, the Riigikogu, the Estonian Parliament, adopted a 'Declaration on Crimes of the Occupation Regimes' which tried to equate Estonia's incorporation into the Soviet Union with the invasion by Nazi Germany and falsely accused the Soviet Union of aggression and genocide. It did not mention that Estonia's Self-Defence Commando killed all 963 Estonian Jews.[57]

Early in the war, the Soviet government deported numbers of Lithuanians, Latvians and Estonians. Lithuanian historians later noted that the anti-Soviet underground 'was somewhat impaired by the mass deportations of 14 June 1941'. Franz Stahlecker, commander of *Einsatzgruppe A*, complained that "it was much harder to stage pogroms in Latvia, mainly because the Soviets had deported the nationalist leaders."

The Soviet government also had to send away from the front the Tatars, the Chechens and the Ingush, with far more reason than the US government had for interning its Japanese citizens. In 1939, there were 218,000 Crimean Tartars, including about 22,000 men of military age. By 1941, 20,000 Crimean Tartar soldiers had deserted the Red Army.

20,000 of them joined the Nazi forces. There were about 450,000 Chechens and Ingush, including about 40,000-50,000 men of military age. When the Soviet government called up 14,576 men for military service, 13,560 of them deserted.

And by deporting 58,852 Jewish refugees from Poland, the Soviet government saved them from being killed by the Nazis and their allies. As Snyder observed, Soviet deportations 'preserved Polish Jews from German bullets'.[58] Again, in autumn 1944, the Soviet government ordered the deportation of all Poles from western Ukraine and of all Ukrainians from south-eastern Poland. This policy 'had by autumn 1945 ended the worst era of ethnic cleansing in the Ukrainian-Polish civil war for Galicia'.[59]

At the Potsdam Conference of August 1945, "the three governments, having considered the question in all its aspects, recognise that the transfer to Germany of German populations, or elements thereof, remaining in Poland, Czechoslovakia and Hungary, will have to be undertaken."[60] The Allies saw these transfers as practical measures to prevent future conflicts between nationalities.[61] The Hungarian, Polish and Czech governments all carried out the Allies' decision to expel their German minorities. The Polish authorities told their camp commanders that beating or abusing prisoners was illegal and that anyone doing so would be punished.[62]

In the extraordinary circumstances of 1945, acts of revenge were understandable, although not justifiable. In particular, revenge rapes by soldiers of the Red Army and of the Polish, US, British and French armies were inexcusable.

Chapter 5
Stalingrad and victory

Stalingrad, the battle that saved the world

Stalin's order 227, issued on 28 July 1942, said, "Every commander, soldier and political worker must understand that our resources are not unlimited ... To retreat further would mean the ruin of our country and ourselves. Every new scrap of territory we lose will significantly strengthen the enemy and severely weaken our defence of our Motherland. ... Not a Step Back! This must now be our chief slogan. We must defend to the last drop every position, every metre of Soviet territory, to cling to every shred of Soviet earth and defend it to the utmost."[1]

Lieutenant Anatoly Mereshko said, "Order 227 played a vital part in the battle. It opened the eyes of the army and the people, and showed them the truth of the situation facing the country. It led to the famous slogan at Stalingrad: 'There is no land for us beyond the Volga.' We were no longer just fighting for a city. It inspired us to fight for every metre of ground, every bush and river, each little piece of land. Order 227 brought an incredible ferocity to our defence of Stalingrad."[2] Machine gunner Mikhail Kalinykov said, "To be honest with you, there was considerable uncertainty about the fate of the city – whether we could hold it or not. And yet, after Order 227, we felt that we had to hold out at Stalingrad regardless of that uncertainty – somehow, we had to make our stand there. You see, the soil was now precious to us, and we had to defend every metre of it. It was our promise to the Motherland."[3]

The Nazi lie was that the Soviet Union won the battle only because of its great numbers of men and munitions. At Stalingrad the opposite was the case. The Red Army was hugely outnumbered and outgunned and the Nazis also had total command of the air. Yet the Nazis lost because of the Red Army's better strategy, better tactics (especially in street-fighting) and better morale. As military historian H. P. Willmott concluded, "The point that emerges from any detailed examination of the conduct of operations on the Eastern Front in 1942 is that the *Wehrmacht* was outfought at *every* level …"[4] It was not the Soviet Union's greater numbers that made the victory possible. It had had greater numbers in World War One, which had not saved it from defeat. Nor did 'General Winter' win the war; it was winter for the Red Army too.

Bellamy rated the Soviet counter-offensive at Stalingrad, Operation Uranus, as 'the greatest encirclement of all time'.[5] By the end of the battle, in February 1943, the Nazis and their allies had lost 50 divisions, 1.5 million men, 3,500 tanks, 12,000 guns and 3,000 aircraft. Never before had the Wehrmacht suffered such a defeat. US Secretary of State Edward Stettinius said at the time, "The American people should remember that they were on the brink of disaster in 1942. If the Soviet Union had failed to hold on its front, Germany would have been in a position to conquer Great Britain." Recent historians agreed that, as Acton noted, "Stalingrad marked the turning point."[6]

Goebbels tells a lie

After the Soviet victory at Stalingrad, it was clear that Germany could not win the war if the Allies stayed united, so the Nazis tried to split the Allies. In April, Goebbels alleged that Jewish commissars had killed 10,000 Polish officers at Katyn, near Smolensk in Western Russia, in 1940. But documents with dates from 12 November 1940 to 20 June 1941 were found in the graves, proving that the prisoners were alive until the Nazis invaded. *Pravda* commented on 19 April 1943, "Feeling the indignation of the whole of progressive humanity over their massacre of peaceful citizens and particularly of Jews, the Germans are now trying to arouse the anger of gullible people against the Jews. For this reason they have invented a whole collection of 'Jewish commissars' who, they say, took part in the murder of the 10,000 Polish officers. For such experienced fakers it was not difficult to invent a few names of people who never existed - Lev Rybak, Avraam Brodninsky, Chaim Fineberg. No such persons ever existed either in the 'Smolensk section of the OGPU' or in any other department of the NKVD …"

Goebbels wrote on 17 April, "the Polish Government-in-exile now demands that the International Red Cross should take part in the investigation. That suits us perfectly."[7] (Later, in 1944, the Red Cross gave the Nazi concentration camp Theresienstadt a good report.[8]) The 'Free Polish government' in London endorsed the Nazi claims, breaking its relations with the Soviet government. Goebbels boasted in his diary, "This break represents a one-hundred-per-cent victory for German propaganda and especially for me personally … we have been able to convert the Katyn incident into a highly political question." *The Times* commented on 28 April, "Surprise as well as regret will be felt that those who have had so much cause to understand the perfidy and ingenuity of the Goebbels propaganda machine should themselves have fallen into the trap laid by it. Poles will hardly have forgotten a volume widely circulated in the first winter of the war which described with every detail of circumstantial evidence, including that of photography, alleged Polish atrocities against the peaceful German inhabitants of Poland."

On 8 May, Goebbels admitted, but only in his diary, "Unfortunately, German ammunition has been found in the graves at Katyn … It is essential that this incident remains a top secret. If it were to come to the knowledge of the enemy the whole Katyn affair would have to be dropped." The bullets found in the graves were mainly 7.65mm bullets made in Germany. The others were 9mm bullets - the Soviet Union did not have a 9mm pistol until after the war. The Anti-Soviet Polish

General Wladyslaw Anders accepted that all the men were shot with German 'Geco' brand bullets and that no Soviet ammunition was used.

The official German report contained photos of the German shell casings found in the graves. The photos were of the casings' sides, not of their ends where their dates of production were stamped. If they had been stamped 1940 or earlier, the Nazis would surely have photographed them, to prove Soviet guilt.

In 2011-12, a Polish-Ukrainian archaeological team partially excavated an SS Einsatzgruppe mass murder site at the town of Volodymyr-Volyns'kiy in Ukraine.[9] More than 96 per cent of the shells found in these graves were made in Germany in 1941, mostly the same 'Geco' bullets found at Katyn. The team dated the site as 1941 at the earliest. They also found the badges of two Polish policemen previously thought to have been murdered hundreds of miles away in Katyn. In sum, the evidence was that the Nazis, not the Soviets, shot the Polish officers at Katyn.

The battle of Kursk and Operation Bagration

At the battle of Kursk, July-August 1943, Germany lost 30 divisions (including 7 Panzer divisions), 500,000 troops, 1,500 tanks, 3,000 guns and 3,500 warplanes. Glantz and House summed up, "The battle of Kursk meant an end to blitzkrieg in a strategic and operational sense. For the first time in the war, a German offensive was contained in the tactical or shallow operational depths. ... the Soviets had learned ... that the only effective defense was one that exploited all arms and possessed both depth and flexibility. ... As a result, the Soviets proved that a determined and properly constructed infantry-based defense could defeat the tactics of blitzkrieg. Hence, Kursk marked a turning point in the war strategically, operationally and tactically. Building on the lessons of Kursk, the Soviets also applied their new combined-arms techniques to offensive situations, at first tentatively and later with greater effect."[10]

Fritz observed, "As far back as the autumn of 1943, Hitler had planned to stabilize the eastern front in order to transfer troops west to defeat the Allied invasion of France. ...The Soviets, however, had refused to cooperate and play their assigned role. Instead of sitting passively through the winter, the Red Army had launched a series of continuous offensives that had drained German resources and brought the Ostheer to the breaking point."[11]

At the Teheran conference in December 1943, the Allies agreed that the Curzon Line would be the Polish border. Churchill said on 22 February 1944, "I cannot feel that the Russian demand for a reassurance about her Western frontiers goes beyond the limits of what is reasonable or just."[12] But, on 21 March, he told Stalin that 'all questions of territorial change must await the armistice'. Stalin saw this as 'a betrayal of the agreement reached at Teheran, which in fact it was …'[13]

Also at the Tehran conference, Stalin stated that Soviet forces would launch an offensive at the same time as D-Day, to stop Hitler transferring forces from the Eastern to the Western front. On 22 June, 1.6 million Soviet soldiers launched Operation Bagration over a 500-mile-long front. This offensive was larger than Overlord, both in the forces engaged and in the cost to the Wehrmacht. In three months, the Red Army destroyed 28 German divisions, while there were just 15 German divisions on the Western front in France on D-Day and the weeks thereafter. Without this Soviet operation, D-Day might have failed. As the late Forrest Pogue, an official US Army historian, summed up, the Soviet forces 'broke Germany and made the [D-Day] landing possible'.[14]

The American military historians Williamson Murray and Allan Millett observed that Operation Bagration was 'the single most impressive ground operation of the war'.[15] Mark Mazower called it 'not only the most effective Soviet offensive of the war but perhaps the most overwhelming and devastating single military assault in history'.[16] Murray and Millett concluded, "the Soviets displayed the greatest abilities at the operational level of war. From Bagration, which took out virtually all of Army Group Center in summer 1944, to the operations that destroyed German forces in East Prussia and Poland in winter 1945, Soviet commanders exhibited outstanding capabilities in deception, planning, and the conduct of operations. Their victories were far superior to anything the Germans had achieved early in the war."[17]

The struggle for Warsaw

Russian historian Irina Mukhina observed, "Already in early 1944, the London Poles shifted the strategy of AK [Armia Kraiova] from anti-Nazi to anti-Soviet. ... the AK did not abandon their anti-Soviet actions in newly liberated cities (like Wilno). Their continuing resistance involved armed struggle and was not always limited to wearing white and yellow bows, a sign of Polish patriotism. This clandestine, often forgotten anti-Soviet struggle of forces connected to the London Poles continued well into 1945, intensifying after the dramatic failure of the Warsaw Uprising and spreading over the 'traditional' Polish territories of Warsaw, Lublin, Krakow, Bialystok and other regions, thus creating pockets of anti-Soviet resistance behind the frontlines of the Red Army and slowing the Allied advance to Berlin. But already in the first two weeks after the liberation of Wilno, and before the onset of the Warsaw Uprising, the extent of the Polish actions became evident to Soviet authorities. Members of AK killed Red Army soldiers and representatives of the newly established civilian occupation administrations created by the Soviets."[18]

Mukhina noted of the Warsaw rising, "the Poles had repeatedly attempted to stage similar uprisings in other towns and cities when the Red Army was approaching. Polish rebels also actively resisted Soviet domination after the Red Army had liberated these cities. Hence, the Warsaw Uprising was not a unique event but just one among many such pre-emptive uprisings, even if it was unique in the scale of the resulting devastation. Moreover, Moscow knew well that Western Allied forces secretly participated in this ultimately anti-Soviet action. ... British and American involvement in anti-Soviet uprisings in Poland and the Baltic states behind the front lines of World War II reinforced Stalin's suspicions of his wartime Allies. Stalin's knowledge that the two Allied governments trained the leaders of anti-Nazi/anti-Soviet uprisings was one more factor leading to the systematic breakdown of the Grand Alliance."[19]

Mukhina pointed out, "[O]n 17 and 18 July 1944 British forces parachuted the leaders of the Warsaw Uprising into Warsaw so that these men could prepare a successful anti-Soviet revolt that would put the Polish capital in Polish hands before the Red Army could take Warsaw. The British not only parachuted the leaders of the rebellion into Warsaw, but they, in collaboration with the United States, had also previously trained these men to lead this and other anti-Soviet revolts in Eastern Europe."[20]

In July, the Red Army, including four Polish divisions, entered Poland after liberating Vilna and Lvov. By the end of the month, they freed an area the size of Britain, on a 600-mile front. But the Nazis had built up a powerful defensive system around Warsaw. They transferred four panzer divisions from France and counter-attacked on 1 August. The same day, the AK launched its rising in Warsaw, on orders from the 'Free Polish Government' in London, which had not consulted any of the Allies.[21]

General Tadeusz Bor-Komorowski, the commander of the AK, also refused to liaise with any of the Allies.[22] Zhukov wrote, "On instructions by the Supreme Commander, two paratroop officers were sent to Bor-Komorowski for liaison and coordination of actions. However, Bor-Komorowski refused to receive the officers … our troops did everything they possibly could to help the insurgents, although the uprising had not been in any way coordinated with the Soviet command."[23] (Historian Anthony Tucker-Jones recently commented, "In light of Rokossovsky's efforts to the north-east and south-east of Warsaw in the face of the tough Waffen SS, this is largely true."[24]) Bor-Komorowski stated publicly, "The Bolshevik enemy will face the same merciless struggle that shook the German invader. Actions in favor of Russia are treason to the motherland. … The Germans are running. Time is coming to fight the Soviets."[25]

As Sir Max Hastings noted, "the Polish commander wanted it both ways: the success of his revolt hinged upon recognising Russian military support, while its explicit objective was to deny the Soviet Union political authority over his country. ... the British Joint Intelligence Committee had concluded that, if the Poles carried out their long-planned uprising, it was doomed to failure in the absence of close co-operation with the Russians, which was unlikely to be forthcoming. It seems lamentable that, after making such an appreciation, the British failed to exert all possible pressure upon the Poles to abandon their fantasies."[26]

Red Army General Konstantin Rokossovsky's forces were in no position to free Warsaw, as many historians agreed. Tucker-Jones affirmed, "In five weeks of fighting Rokossovsky had covered 450 miles (725km) and was within reach of Warsaw. The Polish capital now looked a tempting prize as a culmination of Bagration's remarkable success, but Stalin's summer offensive was beginning to lose momentum. Rokossovsky's 1st Byelorussian Front was at the very limit of its supply lines; ammunition and rations were exhausted, as were his men. In many ways the defence of Warsaw echoed that of Minsk – the eastern approaches of the Polish capital were protected by a 50 mile (80km) ring of strongpoints. The only difference was that this time Model had sufficient mobile reserves with which to parry Rokossovsky's forces. ... Rokossovsky simply could not fulfil his orders to break through the German defences and enter Praga by 8 August. ... Rokossovsky was facing twenty-two enemy divisions, including four security divisions in the Warsaw suburbs, three Hungarian divisions on the Vistula south of Warsaw, and the remains of six or seven divisions which had escaped from the chaos of Bialystok and Brest-Litovsk, that could be deployed between the Narev and the Western Bug. At least eight divisions were identified fighting to the north of Siedlice, among them two panzer and three SS panzer or panzergrenadier divisions."[27]

Overy asked, "Could the Red Army have captured Warsaw in August 1944 and saved its population from further German barbarities? The answer now seems unambiguously negative. Soviet forces did not sit and play while Warsaw burned. The city was beyond their grasp. ... German war memoirs ... confirm that the Red Army was prevented from helping Warsaw by the sudden stiffening of the German defence. ... On 10 September the attack was renewed ... The Polish 1st Army then launched its own attack across the Vistula into Warsaw itself, but after heavy losses was forced on September 23 to retreat back across the river. Even at this late stage the Polish Home Army distrusted their pro-Communist compatriots so profoundly that they refused to co-ordinate their operations with the new attacking force."[28]

Willmott agreed, "in military terms, the capture of Warsaw was probably beyond Soviet resources in August and September: the 1st Belorussian Front alone sustained 123,000 battle casualties in July and August."[29] Alan Bullock also agreed, "It occurred at a time when the Russian advance in the centre had run out of steam and preparations for the next phase of the campaign had not yet begun."[30] Acton too, "In retrospect, too, it appears that the Red Army was not in fact in a position to break through to Warsaw in time to save the uprising."[31] As Mazower pointed out, "the Soviet troops were exhausted, out of fuel and supplies and needed to regroup and they had been brought to a halt by a determined German defensive line."[32] Fritz noted, "after weeks of unbroken fighting, the Soviets had outrun their supply capabilities and passed the culmination point of the offensive."[33] Robin Edmonds confirmed, "Subsequent research suggests that the Red Army's need for a pause of months - not just weeks - on the Vistula, after an advance of four hundred miles, was genuine, as indeed Stalin assured Churchill in Moscow (an assurance accepted absolutely by Churchill at the time)."[34] Snyder concluded, "there is no reason to believe that Stalin deliberately halted military operations at Warsaw."[35]

The Polish Prime Minister said in a broadcast from London to Warsaw, on 19 September, "Today the Soviet air force is giving you air cover and A.A. artillery. The Russians are shelling enemy forces and are already dropping some arms and food, thus making it possible to continue the fight. On behalf of the Polish Government I acknowledge this help with gratitude, and at the same time I appeal for further help."[36] Bor-Komorowski acknowledged, on 18 September, "Since the night of

September 13th-14th we have received daily arms and food dropped by the Russian air force on the centre of the city. Supplies were also dropped on the suburbs."[37] As Churchill said on 26 September, "The Soviet armies were at that time engaged in heavy fighting with strong German forces to the east and north-east of Warsaw, but when their operational plans permitted and direct contact had been established with the Polish Commander-in-Chief in Warsaw, they sent supplies to the Polish forces and provided them with air cover and anti-aircraft support. This assistance has been gratefully acknowledged by the Polish Prime Minister and by the Polish Commander-in-Chief in Warsaw."[38]

The Nazi counterattack drove the Red Army back nearly 60 miles. In revenge for the rising, the Nazis destroyed Warsaw and killed 200,000 of its people. No wonder that General Anders called the rising a 'disaster', 'madness', a 'flagrant crime'.[39] The Red Army planned to liberate Warsaw by outflanking and surrounding the Nazi forces. This it did on 17 January 1945, three months after the rising, when the river and the marshes north and south of the city had frozen solid, giving firm track for tanks and heavy weapons. In all, 600,000 Soviet troops died freeing Poland from Nazism. Of this Vistula-Oder offensive, Fritz wrote, "in three weeks, the Red Army had won perhaps its most spectacular victory of the war."[40] And American historian Robert Messer noted "the crucial timing of the spectacular Soviet winter offensive, launched ahead of schedule on the eve of the Yalta conference; in part as an effort to relieve the beleaguered Western front after the disappointing setbacks of the Battle of the Bulge."[41]

The Yalta Conference and after

At the February 1945 Yalta Conference, the Allies agreed that the peoples of Eastern Europe had the right to build their own societies in peace. The US and British governments knew that they could not defeat Hitler without Soviet forces entering eastern Europe. As Willmott pointed out, "eastern Europe was neither Britain's nor America's to abandon and betray: it did not lie within an Anglo-American power of gift."[42] He noted of Yalta, "the Americans had much the better of the bargains struck at this conference. The United States yielded nothing that the Soviet Union did not already have or could take for herself without seeking American agreement …"[43] American historian Michael Schaller commented, "Often blamed for the 'loss' of Eastern Europe and China to Communism, Yalta did nothing of the kind. The Soviet Red Army already occupied most of Eastern Europe in February 1945 …"[44] Robert Nisbet agreed, "It is not true that Yalta gave Stalin authority to subjugate the Baltics, Balkans, and large parts of Poland and Eastern Europe. Yalta couldn't have given this permission to the Soviets, for they already had these countries in their possession when the Yalta summit began."[45]

On Poland, the Allies agreed to back the provisional government of national unity, based in Lublin and led by Boleslaw Bierut, the president of Poland. As Churchill wrote to Stalin just after Yalta, "We and the Americans agreed, therefore, that there was to be no sweeping away of the Bierut government."[46] US Secretary of State James Byrnes said, "there was no question as to what the spirit of the agreement was. There was no intent that a new government was to be created independent of the Lublin government. The basis was to be the Lublin government."[47] Byrnes acknowledged, "there was no justification under the spirit or letter of the agreement" for insisting on a new government in Poland.[48] Roosevelt explained, "we want a Poland that will be thoroughly friendly to the Soviet for years to come."[49] As Churchill had said earlier, "The Russian armies … offer freedom, sovereignty and independence to the Poles. They ask that there should be a Poland friendly to Russia. This seems to me very reasonable considering the injuries which Russia has suffered through the Germans marching across Poland to attack her."[50]

On 21 April 1945, the Soviet Union and Poland signed a Treaty of Friendship, Mutual Assistance and Post-war Collaboration. As Stalin said, "The importance of this Treaty consists in the first place in that it signifies the radical turn of relations between the Soviet Union and Poland towards alliance and friendship, a turn which took shape in the course of the present liberation struggle against Germany and which is now being formally consummated in this Treaty. ... In the course of the last two World Wars the Germans succeeded in making use of the territory of Poland as a corridor for invasion of the East and as a springboard for attack on the Soviet Union. This became possible because at that time there were no friendly allied relations between our countries. The former rulers of Poland did not want to have relations of alliance with the Soviet Union. They preferred a policy of playing about between Germany and the Soviet Union. And of course they played themselves into trouble. . . . Poland was occupied, her independence abolished, and as a result of this whole ruinous policy German troops were enabled to appear at the gates of Moscow." The Treaty pledged the signatories to carry the war against fascism to victory, to preserve and strengthen friendly relations after the war, and to work together on the basis of the principles of mutual respect for independence, sovereignty and non-interference in the internal affairs of states.

The Soviet Union also agreed to declare war on Japan. The US Chiefs of Staff said that this would save 200,000 American lives. The Soviet government advanced the date of its attack on Japan's Kwantung Army in China, outmanoeuvring the US government, which had hoped to force Japan's surrender before the Soviet Union entered the war. In August, the Red Army shattered the Kwantung Army in seven days and achieved total victory over Japan in less than three weeks. They killed or wounded 674,000 Japanese troops, losing 12,031 killed and 24,425 wounded.[51] As Glantz concluded, "The massive scale of the Soviet attack was matched by the audaciousness, skill, and relentlessness with which it was conducted."[52]

'The greatest military achievement in all history'

World War Two involved 61 countries with a total population of 1.7 billion. 110 million people were mobilised into armed forces. In Europe, the war killed more than twice as many people as had been killed in the wars of the previous 350 years. The Soviet Union suffered 65 per cent of all Allied military casualties, China 23 per cent, Yugoslavia 3 per cent, Britain and the USA 2 per cent each, and Poland and France 1 per cent each.

The Soviet Union's role in defeating the Nazi forces was decisive. From June 1941 to May 1944, it fought virtually alone against the vast majority of Germany's armed forces; it never faced fewer than 180 German divisions, three quarters of the German army. British Empire forces faced from two to eight German divisions. Even at the height of the US and British forces' efforts, they engaged just a third of the total Axis forces. In the whole war, the Red Army destroyed 607 Axis divisions, the US and British forces destroyed 176.

As Churchill said, "Russia tore the guts out of the German Army." Roosevelt noted, "the Russian armies are killing more Axis personnel and destroying more Axis material than all the other twenty-five United Nations put together."[53] Field Marshal Bernard Montgomery pointed out, "Russia had to bear, almost unaided, the full onslaught of Germany on land; we British would never forget what Russia went through."[54] US Chief of Staff General George C. Marshall stated in his final report on the war, "It is certain that the refusal of the British and Russian peoples to accept what appeared to be inevitable defeat was the great factor in the salvage of our civilization."[55]

US General Douglas MacArthur said, "The hopes of civilization rest on the worthy banners of the courageous Russian army. During my lifetime I have participated in a number of wars and have witnessed others, as well as studying in great detail the campaigns of outstanding leaders of the past. In none have I observed such effective resistance to the heaviest blows of a hitherto undefeated enemy, followed by a smashing counter-attack which is driving the enemy back to his own land. The scale and grandeur of the effort mark it as the greatest military achievement in all history."[56]

Sumner Welles asserted, "The achievements represented by the victorious struggle of the Soviet Union have never been excelled by any other nation. They would not have been possible save through the efforts of a united and selflessly patriotic people."[57] Roosevelt cabled Stalin on 22 February 1943, "On behalf of the people of the United States, I want to express to the Red Army, on its twenty-fifth anniversary, our profound admiration for its magnificent achievements unsurpassed in all history."[58]

Many present-day historians agreed. Dunn summed up, "Few nations could have survived such an onslaught. In World War I, Russia had succumbed under much less pressure. Somehow Stalin had convinced the many Soviet nationalities to fight for their country, which the czar had failed to do in 1917."[59] Andrew Roberts wrote, "it was the Eastern Front that annihilated the Nazi dream of *Lebensraum* ('living space') for the 'master race'. Four in every five German soldiers killed in the Second World War died on the Eastern Front, an inconvenient fact for any historian who wishes to make too much of the Western Allies' contribution to the victory."[60] Hastings concluded, "It was impossible to dispute, however, that Stalin's people were overwhelmingly responsible for destroying Hitler's armies."[61] Fritz agreed, "the Red Army, at the cost of perhaps 12 million dead (or approximately thirty times the number of the Anglo-Americans) broke the back of the Wehrmacht."[62] Willmott judged, "In terms of scale the Nazi-Soviet conflict was unprecedented, and it was infinitely more important in deciding the outcome of the Second World War than any other theatre, perhaps even more important than all others combined."[63] As Geoffrey Roberts noted, the Soviet view was that "the Anglo-Soviet-American coalition had won the war together, but the greatest contribution had come from the Red Army, which had turned the tide of war in the Allies' favour a full year before the D-Day landings in France. It was the Soviet Union that had largely liberated Europe from German occupation and thereby saved European civilization."[64] Schuman confirmed, "Defeat would've meant not only the enslavement of the Soviet peoples but the ultimate conquest of Britain and China and the reduction of America to helplessness before the unchallenged masters of Eurasia and Africa."[65]

Every sector of Soviet society contributed to the victory. The Soviet economy produced what was needed to win the war. As Mawdsley wrote, "the victory was in the end a victory for the Stalinist economic campaigns of the 1930s."[66] Mark Harrison observed, "Stalin proposed that World War II had proved 'an all-round test' of the Soviet Union's 'material and spiritual forces'. In so far as this idea had a scientific kernel, the Soviet economy passed the test; in fact, judged by historical and comparative criteria, the Soviet success in World War II was very striking."[67] Overy judged, "the Soviet war effort still remains an incomparable achievement, world-historical in a very real sense."[68] It was above all the victory of the Soviet people. The peoples of the world owe them a huge debt.

The victory of socialism in the Soviet Union was the decisive factor in the Allies' victory. The American people's contribution was enormously significant. The heroic struggle of the British people, civilians and armed forces alike, should be singled out, for making an impact out of all proportion to their numbers. The whole nation mobilised for war, and planned all their work to defeat Nazism. Soviet planning provided many models for Britain's war effort. Churchill admitted that Britain's central planning of production in both world wars 'constitute the greatest argument for State Socialism that has ever been produced'.[69]

As Bellamy observed, "the socialist victory in the 1945 general election owed something to the upsurge of pro-Russian, and therefore, at that time, pro-communist – certainly socialist – feeling among the British people during the war. After all, the British people had faced the Germans alone for a year in 1940-41, and the Russians had held them and knocked them back, pretty well alone, apart from the limited support the western Allies could send, in 1941-2."[70] All this was achieved without the City of London, which virtually closed in the world wars.

Schemes for a new world war

Even before the war had finished, some wanted a new world war, against the Soviet Union. The Polish 'prime-minister-in exile' said in 1943, "the only thing that will settle Polish relations with the Soviet Union will be a war between the Soviet Union and the United States and Great Britain, with the latter countries on Poland's side."[71] Some in the British state wanted war too. Orme Sargent of the Foreign Office called for a 'showdown' with the Russians. His friend Robert Bruce Lockhart told him that "the Anglo-American armies in the west could go through the Russian armies quite easily because of their enormous preponderance in armour and air power." The British government's Joint Intelligence Committee urged 'getting tough with the Russians'.

Churchill telegraphed Field Marshal Montgomery ordering him 'to be careful in collecting German arms, to stack them so that they could easily be issued again to the German soldiers whom we should have to work with if the Soviet advance continued'. Churchill asked the Joint Planning Staff to draw up a plan, known as Operation UNTHINKABLE, for an attack on the Soviet Union.[72] Britain's Secret Intelligence Service [SIS] had carried out operations in the Soviet Union during the war, gathering information for use in such an attack.[73]

So the Chiefs of Staff drew up a plan for a surprise Anglo-American attack, a two-pronged attack to seize eastern Germany and Poland through Stettin and Poznan, to start on 1 July using 45 British and American divisions plus, among others, 12 Wehrmacht divisions.[74] The Chiefs warned, "if we are to embark on war with Russia, we must be prepared to be committed to a total war, which would be both long and costly."

After the war's end, the British government allowed Admiral Karl Doenitz's Nazi government to continue to issue orders to the Wehrmacht. He offered to join the attack on the Soviet Union. Britain kept 700,000 German troops in military formations in its zone until December. On 20 May 1945, Stalin said, "While we have disarmed all the officers and men of the German Army and placed them in prisoner-of-war camps, the British are keeping the German troops in a state of combat readiness and establishing cooperation with them. To this day the headquarters of the German forces headed by their commanding officers are enjoying complete freedom and on Montgomery's instructions the arms and material of the German troops are being collected and put in order." Stalin continued, "the British want to retain the German troops so that they can be used later. But this is an outright violation of the agreement between the heads of government of the immediate disbandment of all German forces."[75]

As late as 1 January 1947, according to the British Command's report, there were still 81,358 German soldiers in military units, commanded by German officers. The British and US governments were also maintaining tens of thousands of troops under the command of Polish fascist General Anders in Italy and Colonel Rogozhin's Russian Whiteguard infantry corps, who had fought in Hitler's service in Austria.

Churchill knew that the USA now had atomic bombs and told Field Marshal Viscount Alanbrooke, Chief of the Imperial General Staff, "if Stalin failed to listen to the West's wishes, the US could target Moscow, Stalingrad and Kiev." Alanbrooke was appalled and privately described the Prime Minister as a warmonger. But on 29 June, Stalin ordered the Red Army to redeploy and fortify its new positions, thwarting the planned attack. And by 5 July, Churchill was out of a job.

Before dropping the atomic bombs on Japan, the new US President Harry Truman conferred with Britain's new Prime Minister, Labour's Clement Attlee, who did not demur. Stalin was not consulted: he denounced the bombing, saying, "It is a wanton act" and "the atomic bomb is to atomic energy what the electric chair is to electricity." Some claimed that the atomic bombs ended the war, but, as the official British history of the war stated, "The Russian declaration of war was the decisive factor in bringing Japan to accept the Potsdam declaration, for it brought home to all members of the Supreme Council the realisation that the last hope of a negotiated peace had gone and that there was no alternative but to accept the Allied terms sooner or later."[76]

Japanese historian Tsuyoshi Hasegawa agreed that the Soviet declaration of war, not the atomic bombs, induced Japan to surrender. He showed that the Soviet entry into the war shocked the Japanese government even more than the atomic bombs because it ended all hope of a settlement short of surrender.[77] Geoffrey Jukes affirmed that Hasegawa proved that the Soviet declaration of war forced Japan to surrender.[78]

In sum, capitalism started both world wars, and communists ended both. The Soviet Union ended World War One, because its example weakened both the imperialist alliances waging that war. It ended World War Two by defeating the Nazi and Japanese aggressors. It also prevented World War Three.

Chapter 6
The Soviet Union from 1945 to 1986

Still under threat

After the war, the Soviet Union made an extraordinary recovery from unparalleled devastation. In August 1945, General Dwight Eisenhower had flown from Berlin to Moscow and 'did not see a single house standing intact from the Russian-Polish border to Moscow. Not one'.[1] Journalist Edward Crankshaw observed, "To travel, painfully slowly, by train from Moscow to the new frontier at Brest-Litovsk in the days after the war was a nightmare experience. For hundreds of miles, there was not a standing or a living object to be seen. Every town was flat, every city. There were no barns. There was no machinery. There were no stations, no water towers. There was not a solitary telegraph pole left standing in all that vast landscape."[2]

The Nazis destroyed 1,700 Soviet cities and towns, 32,000 factories, 40,000 hospitals, 84,000 schools, 43,000 public libraries, 61 major electric power plants, 70,000 villages, 100,000 collective farms, 40,000 miles of railway track and six million homes. 25 million people were homeless. More than a third of the Soviet Union's wealth had been destroyed. The Extraordinary State Commission estimated Soviet losses at $128 billion. Much of this loss was permanent, because of the lost growth opportunities of the war years.

At the Yalta conference, the US government agreed the figure of $10 billion reparations from Germany as 'a basis for discussion'. President Roosevelt had promised to aid the Soviet Union's reconstruction. But the US and British governments broke both the agreement and the promise. In 1945, the US government abruptly ended Lend-Lease. In 1946, under US pressure, UN agencies ended their aid to the Soviet Union, even though the country was suffering its worst drought since 1880, which affected half of its farmland: the grain harvest was less than half 1940's.

Germany had twice used Poland as a highway to invade Russia, costing Russia about 40 million people. (Yet the US diplomat George Kennan claimed in 1946 that the Soviet belief that Western states would launch 'wars of intervention' was 'baseless and disproven', 'simply not true'.[3] Didn't the war of intervention and the Nazi invasion count as evidence?) So it was no surprise that the Soviet Union wanted to close that highway. This was in Poland's interests too, given how much the Polish people had also suffered in those wars, and it was also in the general interest. The Soviet Union's alliances with the countries of Eastern Europe enabled them for the first time to develop in peace. On 11 May 1953, Churchill said, "Russia has a right to feel assured as far as human arrangements can reach that the terrible events of the Hitler invasion will never be repeated and that Poland will remain a friendly power and a buffer."

Eisenhower said in November 1945, "Nothing guides Russian foreign policy so much as a desire for peace with the United States."[4] Many historians agreed that the Soviet Union wanted peace. Sir Michael Howard judged, "No serious historian any longer argues that Stalin ever had any intention of moving his forces outside the area he occupied in Eastern Europe."[5] Andrew Alexander agreed, "The opening up of the Soviet archives underlines the fantasy of the old view of the Russian 'threat'."[6] Geoffrey Roberts confirmed, "the western cold war caricature of the Soviet Union as an aggressive and expansionist power aiming at world domination can be definitely discarded. The archives reveal no such plans, intentions or ambitions."[7] He noted, "The Soviet perspective was that great-power collaboration would continue in the long term to contain Germany and to maintain a stable setting for postwar reconstruction."[8]

Vladislav Zubok and Constantine Pleshakov concluded that Stalin "was not prepared to take a course of unbridled unilateral expansionism after World War II. He wanted to avoid confrontation with the West. He was even ready to see cooperation with the Western powers as a preferable way of building his influence and solving contentious international issues. Thus, the Cold War was not his choice or his brainchild. ... Stalin's postwar foreign policy was more defensive, reactive and prudent than it was the fulfillment of a master plan."[9] Garthoff summed up, "The burden of all the available evidence from Soviet archives and memoirs confirms the view that some of us had at the time, that no Soviet leadership at any time during the Cold War ever contemplated a military attack on the West."[10]

Warren Cohen noted of the US government, "Even as they contemplated projecting American power more than five thousand miles from their shores, substituting it for declining British power in the proximity of Soviet borders, they perceived Soviet behaviour in the area as threatening, American actions as defensive."[11] In fact, as Garthoff pointed out, "On the whole the United States used its own military forces coercively more frequently . . ."[12]

The US and British governments responded to what they called the Soviet 'peace offensive' with Churchill's Fulton speech (a virtual declaration of war), the Truman Doctrine, which threatened worldwide US intervention, the formation of the North Atlantic Treaty Organization (NATO) (six years before the Warsaw Pact was created) and the Marshall Plan. The Plan was to open the Soviet Union and Eastern Europe's countries to control by Western capital. Russian historian Dimitri Volkogonov later noted that Stalin rejected the Plan because accepting it would have meant 'accepting virtual US control over the Soviet economy'. Volkogonov commented, "Stalin's understanding of the Marshall Plan had not been mistaken."[13]

In March 1945, US Assistant Secretary Struve Hensel had recorded of Roosevelt, "The President indicated considerable difficulty with British relations. In a semi-jocular manner of speaking, he stated that the British were perfectly willing for the United States to have a war with Russia at any time and that, in his opinion, to follow the British program would be to proceed to that end."[14] Later, President Truman said he agreed with Vice-President Henry Wallace when he said, "the purpose of Britain was to promote an unbreachable break between us and Russia."[15]

At the Yalta and Potsdam conferences, the Allies agreed that they would jointly occupy Germany to disarm and democratise it, to ensure that it fulfilled its obligations to the Allies and to erase its war-industrial potential. But in December 1946, the US and British governments agreed to fuse their zones, thereby splitting Germany in breach of their earlier commitments. Many historians agreed that, as Oliver Stone and Peter Kuznick wrote, "the United States and Great Britain charged towards confrontation with the Soviet Union."[16] Zubok pointed out, "Stalin left to the West the role of breaking the agreements of Yalta and Potsdam and starting a confrontation." He observed, "every Soviet step towards creating units of military and secret police inside the zone was taken after the Western powers took their own decisive steps toward the separation of West Germany: Bizonia, the Marshall Plan, and the formation of West Germany."[17]

From the late 1940s, the USA carried out secret, illegal spy flights over the Soviet Union, at the cost of losing 140 US pilots and crewmen shot down. From February 1945, "British Special Operations were already smuggling anti-Soviet agents in and out of Poland disguised as Allied ex-POWs."[18] On 18 June 1948, Truman authorised 'preventive direct action, including sabotage, anti-sabotage, demolition and ... subversion against hostile states, including assistance to underground resistance movements, guerrillas and refugee liberation groups'. As Kennan wrote of the anti-Soviet 'Operation Rollback', "this project would follow a principle which has been basic in British and Soviet political warfare: remote and deeply concealed official control of clandestine operations so that governmental responsibility cannot be shown ..."[19] (When ex-President Truman in May 1952 made some overly revealing comments about Operation Rollback, the Foreign Office told the BBC not to mention them.[20]) Between 1944 and 1953, Latvian 'national partisans' trained by Nazi counter-intelligence and backed by the CIA and MI6 killed 3,242 Red Army soldiers. As late as 1953, MI6 was still sending agents, arms, explosives and timers for sabotage operations into Ukraine and Poland.[21]

Jeffrey Burds summed up, "U.S. and British intelligence were supporting Ukrainian and Polish underground rebel actions against Soviet forces long before victory over Germany, ... the Soviet leadership was by autumn 1946 deeply cognizant of this support - information which had a powerful impact on U.S.-Soviet relations during the crucial years of postwar transition from 1944 to 1948." He concluded, "in 1946 the Soviets discovered solid evidence of Western support for paramilitary groups who were actively conducting not just espionage (sanctioned by their Western controllers) but also terror, assassinations, diversion, and sabotage against Soviet citizens and state and party officials on a wide scale. ... the Soviets did indeed have something to be concerned about vis-à-vis U.S. threats to their own national security following World War II. And Pavel Sudoplatov's claims, that "the origins of the Cold War are closely interwoven with Western support for nationalist unrest in the Baltic areas and Western Ukraine," do not seem so far-fetched. This interpretation would be wholly consistent with a new view emerging among some post-Soviet scholars, a view that interprets Soviet policy and Soviet perceptions in the early Cold War as having been driven by legitimate concerns about their own national security, and not merely by Stalin's personal foibles, Communist ideology, or traditionally presumed notions of a drive for world domination."[22]

After the USA dropped the two atomic bombs on Japan, Stalin said, "Hiroshima has shaken the whole world. The balance has been broken. Build the bomb – it will remove the great danger from us." On 29 August 1949, the Soviet Union exploded its first plutonium bomb. As Cohen later affirmed, "The Soviets had no choice but to acquire nuclear weapons." He stressed, "there was nothing unreasonable about their fear of Germany or of NATO, or about their decision to arm against the threat they perceived."[23]

The Soviet bomb ended the huge danger of the US government's believing that it could defeat the Soviet Union by nuclear attack. The leading American strategist Bernard Brodie acknowledged, "If the atomic bomb can be used without fear of substantial retaliation in kind, it will clearly encourage aggression."[24] As David Holloway, the historian of the Soviet nuclear bomb, summed up, "The great success of Stalin's military policy was that it helped to persuade the United States that the atomic air offensive would not be decisive, and that war with the Soviet Union would be prolonged and difficult."[25]

The USA exploded its first H-bomb in November 1952. In August 1953, the Soviet Union produced the world's first deliverable H-bomb, again restoring the balance. As British strategist Colin Gray conceded, US 'nuclear deterrence may have been redundant', since the Soviet Union was not bent on aggression. But the nuclear deterrent was not redundant for the Soviet Union. Soviet diplomacy, backed by the Soviet bomb, prevented any US nuclear attack. Of course, any such attack would have been suicidal: as military historians Allan Millett and Peter Maslowski noted, "A full-scale NATO wargame in 1955 discovered that West Germany could not be saved without being destroyed."[26]

In March 1952, the Soviet Union proposed creating a neutral, united Germany and withdrawing all Allied forces from Germany. In April, Stalin told the German Democratic Republic's leaders, "Whatever proposals we make on the German question the Western powers won't agree with them and they won't withdraw from West Germany. To think that the Americans will compromise or accept the draft peace treaty would be a mistake. The Americans need an army in West Germany in order to keep control of Western Europe. .. The Americans are drawing West Germany into the [NATO] pact. They will form West German forces ... In West Germany an independent state is being formed. And you must organize your own state."[27] NATO indeed turned down the Soviet proposal.

By contrast, Molotov was prepared to make a deal with NATO that would have given up the GDR in exchange for a peace treaty on Germany. Giving up the GDR would have undermined the whole Soviet bloc. In 1953, after Stalin died, Molotov and Premier Georgy Malenkov continued to push for a German peace treaty. In June, Malenkov said, "Profoundly mistaken are those who think that Germany can exist for a long time under conditions of dismemberment in the form of two independent states. To stick to the position of the existence of a dismembered Germany means to keep to the course for a new war."[28] But events proved that Malenkov and Molotov were mistaken, not Stalin.

Rebuilding, again

Yet despite the threats, sabotage and terrorism, the Soviet people rebuilt their industry and agriculture. The state kept the ownership of the means of production, which it allocated, not sold, to factories: they were not commodities. The Soviet Union recovered remarkably quickly from the effects of the war. National income increased by 64 per cent between 1940 and 1950, industrial production by 73 per cent and agricultural production by 14.2 per cent. Real wages tripled between 1945 and 1950.[29] 1940's GNP was reached again by 1948 and 1950's level was nearly 50 per cent above 1940's.[30] Soviet output grew by 7.3 per cent a year from 1947 to 1958 (a higher rate than all but Japan and West Germany). Between 1947 and 1952, output of consumer goods increased substantially every year and retail prices were cut by more than 40 per cent, thanks to productivity increases, which cut costs.[31]

In a planned system, the incentive for innovation came from its promotion by the planners, with the active participation of workers at the point of production. The Soviet Union used a comprehensive set of standardisation procedures to improve product quality.[32] From 1951 to 1965, industry's productivity grew by 6.4 per cent a year, which put the Soviet Union 'among the world leaders in this period'.[33]

Between 1946 and 1950, 652,000 students graduated, more than in any previous five-year-plan period. By 1950, there were a record 1,247,400 students in Soviet universities and professional institutes, by 1960, 2,396,100, almost three times the number in 1940. By 1950, 59 per cent more specialists with degrees were working than in 1941.[34] Enrolment of engineering specialists was 57 per cent up on 1940's figure and by 1955 had almost doubled again.

As a result of this huge investment in higher education, the decade of the 1950s was the Soviet Union's best for growth. The Soviet Union also launched the world's first satellite, the Sputnik, and sent the first man into space, Yuri Gagarin. It conducted the world's first flight of a supersonic passenger aircraft. It became a world leader in specialised metals, machines for seamless welding of railroad tracks and eye surgery equipment. Its performing artists and athletes were among the world's best.

Khanin summed up the 1950s, "at the beginning of the decade the level of consumption of basic foods was characteristic rather of a developing country, as a result of the rise in per capita consumption of high-quality goods like meat, milk, sugar, vegetables and pulses by 1.5-2 and more times, it reached the level of a number of developed countries. ... Completion of housing rose two and a half times, reaching the level of highly developed countries per head of population. ... the enormous increase in life expectancy, to 69 – the level of the most developed countries in the world at the time. ... These immense economic and social achievements, in my opinion, permit us to call the 1950s the decade of the 'Soviet economic miracle'. ... this result should be considered a unique social and economic achievement. ... The command economy in this period demonstrated its viability and macroeconomic efficiency. The Soviet economy, being in essence the largest corporation in the world, made skilful use of the strengths of any large corporation: preparing and implementing long-range plans, using colossal financial resources for development in priority directions, carrying out major capital investments in a short period of time, spending large sums on scientific research and so on. The achievements of the 1950s were based on the powerful heavy industrial and transport potential created in the 1930s-1940s ... The USSR skilfully used its limited resources for the development of sectors which determine long-term economic progress: education – including higher education – healthcare and science."[35]

US Secretary of State John Foster Dulles told the US National Security Council in 1956, "the United States had very largely failed to appreciate the impact on the underdeveloped areas of the world of the phenomenon of Russia's rapid industrialization. Its transformation from an agrarian to a modern industrialized state was an historical event of absolutely first class importance." He observed that underdeveloped countries saw "the results of Russia's industrialization and all they want is for the Russians to show them how they too can achieve it."[36] Economist Joseph Berliner told the US Congress's Joint Economic Committee in 1959, "Two generations ago people debated the question of whether a socialist economy could possibly work. History removed that question from the agenda. The last generation changed the question to whether the Soviet economy could work at all efficiently. That question has also been answered. These hearings would not otherwise be taking place. My discussion takes for granted that the Soviet economy is reasonably efficient, and that the question at issue is how efficient."[37]

Russia expert Alexander Werth affirmed in 1969, "the ordinary Russian of today ... is extremely conscious of the fact that the system works, and has on the whole been an enormous success. What's more, thanks to State control, it works without slumps, economic crises and unemployment. ... The country is, moreover, the greatest welfare state in the world, with 34 million old-age pensioners, a free health service, and a vast free education system."[38]

More recent students agreed that Soviet workers did well. Ellman pointed out, "Workers in state socialist countries are often better off from the standpoint of social security (in old age or illness) than workers in capitalist countries at comparable stages of development, or than workers in the socially backward countries (e.g. the USA)."[39] David Stuckler and Sanjay Basu observed in 2013, "In general Soviet economies tended to have much higher life expectancies than capitalist economies at similar levels of GDP [Gross Domestic Product] per capita (such as Chile, Turkey, Botswana, South Africa, etc.). On average, Soviet men had 4.8 years greater health and Soviet women had 7.7 years greater health for their country's level of income compared with capitalist economy averages."[40]

All this the Soviet Union achieved despite the permanent sanctions against all socialist countries which restricted their trade and borrowing. The US government ensured that Western Europe's countries and Japan imposed these sanctions too. The blockade made it harder for the Soviet Union to buy the technological innovations available to the rest of the developed world. And the Soviet Union still had huge problems, especially the poor quality and shortages of housing and consumer goods.

Stalin, the architect of socialism, died in 1953. Churchill said of him, "He was a man of outstanding personality who left an impression on our harsh times, the period in which his life ran its course. Stalin was a man of extraordinary energy, erudition and inflexible will, blunt, tough, and merciless in both action and conversation, whom even I, reared in the British Parliament, was at a loss to counter. His words resounded with gigantic strength. This strength was so great in Stalin that he seemed unique among leaders of all times and peoples. ... This was a man who used his enemies' hands to destroy his enemy, who made us - whom he openly called imperialists - do battle against imperialists. He found Russia with a wooden plow, but he left it equipped with atomic weapons."[41]

Carr concluded, "Stalin, in driving forward the industrial revolution at breakneck speed, in constantly urging the need to catch up with the west, proved a more pertinacious, more ruthless and more successful revolutionary than any of the other party leaders: this certainly accounted for the support he received over a long period."[42] And, "He carried out, in face of every obstacle and opposition, the industrialization of his country through intensive planning, and thus not only paid tribute to the validity of Marxist theory, but ranged the Soviet Union as an equal partner among the Great Powers of the western world. In virtue of this achievement he takes his undisputed place both as one of the executors of the Marxist testament and one of the great westernizers in Russian history."[43] Egor Gaidar, Russia's Acting Prime Minister from June to December 1992, called 1929-53 'the only period when communism triumphed'.[44] American journalist Howard K. Smith observed, "Stalin did more to change the world in the first half of the twentieth century than any other man who lived in it."[45] He had found the Soviet Union a ruin and left it a great power.

Khrushchev

After Stalin died, the government led by the new General Secretary Nikita Khrushchev weakened state control of the economy, instead favouring the Yugoslav model of 'market socialism'. It extended commodity production and commodity circulation under the slogan of 'expanding Soviet trade'. In 1957, it created organisations to sell industry's products. It replaced central directive planning by 'coordinative' planning. It cut the numbers of directive norms for the use of materials and labour. This allowed ministries to cut the production of goods which were not profitable in the short term, without regard for the needs of the wider economy. This slowed scientific and technical progress and reduced efficiency.

Khrushchev ended management of branches of industries as wholes and imposed a territorial system which led to localism and blocked the spread of innovations. Khanin pointed out, "This redirection was entirely in the interests of the economic nomenklatura, a considerable part of which wanted a lack of supervision so they could both paint a favourable picture of the situation and enrich themselves."[46] Khrushchev also divided the party into industrial and agricultural wings.

Khrushchev's scheme to farm previously uncultivated 'virgin lands' in central Asia and western Siberia failed, because rainfalls there were unreliable and inadequate and because the methods imposed by government decree turned vast areas into dustbowls. Millions of tons of topsoil were blown away. Climate scientists Nikolai Dronin and Edward Bellinger summed up, "In the mid-1950s, Nikita Khrushchev launched a grandiose plan for the ploughing up of 42 million hectares of the 'virgin lands' in Kazakhstan and Western Siberia. The plan turned out to be a fiasco. None of the planned targets were achieved. The 'virgin lands' suffered from wind erosion and supported low, unstable, and economically unprofitable (for new grain sovkhoses [state farms]) cereal production." They observed, "The virgin lands campaign had brought neither the expected increases in grain harvests nor an abundance of fodder for the country." They noted "a serious deterioration in the living standards of the Soviet people, caused by Khrushchev's reforms."[47]

Khrushchev abolished the Machine Tractor Stations [MTSs], forcing farms to buy machines they could neither use nor maintain, with money they had not got, so they were saddled with debts they could not pay. Selling off the MTSs plunged the rural population into poverty and caused long-term damage to the economy. Stalin had warned that selling the MTSs to the collective farms would ruin the farms.[48]

Economists have noted that, as Hanson wrote, "the origins of Soviet relative economic decline can be found in the liberalisation of the Soviet social order that followed the death of Stalin in 1953."[49] Joseph Ball argued, "after 1953, the means of production in the Soviet Union were sold at their prices of production, like capitalist commodities. This was in opposition to Stalin's line. Stalin was clear that the means of production should not be regarded as capitalist commodities. Stalin stated that the means of production should be distributed according to decisions made in the course of economic planning and they should be sold at subsidised prices to facilitate this. Consumer goods, unlike means of production, were sold as commodities in the Soviet Union, prior to 1953, but Stalin understood the importance of this practice being brought to an end as socialism developed. Soviet leaders after Stalin, however, changed this system as they favoured the distribution of the means of production among the various branches of the economy by means of semi-spontaneous market forces. In effect, capitalist profit criteria rather than central planning decisions were to determine the way in which the Soviet economy developed. Rather than struggling to restrict commodity production, the new leaders of the Soviet Union deliberately expanded it to the entire economy. These leaders wanted to create a market socialist system where state owned enterprises would behave just like capitalist enterprises. However, what emerged was a dysfunctional hybrid system, neither effectively planned from the center nor regulated by economic competition. Subsidies for purchasing new means of production had been used to facilitate the planned introduction of innovation up to 1953. Once this system of planning and subsidies was swept away, the incentive to innovate was largely eliminated, as economic competition did not exist to provide an alternative system of incentives. Progressive economic stagnation set in and there was the rapid growth of rent-seeking behaviour (seeking rewards unrelated to effort or quality of work) by enterprise managers and industrial ministries."[50]

Khrushchev also criticised Stalin for waging class struggle: "Stalin, on the other hand, used extreme methods and mass repression at a time when the revolution was already victorious, when the Soviet state was strengthened, when the exploiting classes were already liquidated and socialist relations were rooted solidly in all phases of national economy." But Khrushchev, as First Secretary in Moscow, then later in the Ukraine, had used extreme methods, executing more people than any other First Secretary in the Soviet Union.[51] Nor was it true that "socialist relations were rooted solidly in all phases of national economy." The billionaire oligarchs of the 1990s did not come from nowhere. Khrushchev was wrong to say that there was no danger of capitalism's return.

Khrushchev's attack on Stalin led to attacks on Lenin and on Marx. As American historian Mike Davidow pointed out, "the overestimation of the level of socialist development in the USSR led to the underestimation of the role of the working class. If the 'complete victory of socialism' had been secured, if the USSR was in the stage of 'developed socialism', if antagonistic classes had disappeared, if there already existed an all-people's state, then it would follow that the need for the working class as the leading class in society is considerably diminished, if not eliminated. ... The unacknowledged antagonistic class, existing particularly in the form of the black market forces, played an increasingly active role in the Soviet economy. ... They began to exert increasing pressure for 'legitimate' expression, in keeping with the powerful world position of capitalism. They were sustained and encouraged by the moral and material support they received from this source. The channels of democratization, glasnost and political pluralism provided these black market forces with their first real political opening and they rushed to make the most of it."[52]

American historian Grover Furr concluded, "Khrushchev was **not** trying to 'right the ship of communism'. A total trashing of the truth like the 'Secret Speech' is incompatible with Marxism, or with idealistic motives of any kind. Nothing positive, democratic, or liberating can be built on a foundation of falsehood. Instead of reviving a communist movement, and Bolshevik Party, that had strayed from its true course through grievous errors, Khrushchev was killing it off. Khrushchev himself is 'revealed' not as an honest communist but instead as a political leader seeking personal advantage while hiding behind an official persona of idealism and probity, a type familiar in capitalist countries. Taking into account his murder of Beria and the men executed as 'Beria's gang' in 1953, he seems worse still – a political thug. Khrushchev was guilty in reality of the kinds of crimes he *deliberately and falsely* accused Stalin of in the 'Secret Speech'."[53] American historian John Lewis Gaddis agreed, "Khrushchev's strategy of reforming Marxism-Leninism instead diminished its legitimacy and shattered its unity."[54] Khrushchev's reforms fuelled counter-revolution.

His policies failed to reinvigorate Soviet industry and agriculture. Similarly, in foreign policy, his impulsive and erratic policies towards Eastern Europe, China, Cuba and the USA weakened the Soviet Union. In 1960, just before talks with the US government on nuclear disarmament, a US spy plane crashed in the Soviet Union. Khrushchev used the incident to wreck the talks, overriding the need for nuclear disarmament. As a result, the USA and the Soviet Union conducted a damaging and costly arms race, building huge numbers of nuclear weapons. In 1960, each had just 10 nuclear warheads; by 1986, they had 9,000.[55] All these failures led to Khrushchev's ouster in 1964.

After Khrushchev

In 1917, Russia's industrial production had been just 12 per cent of the USA's, by 1967, it was 80 per cent. From 1928 to 1975, Soviet GNP grew 4.5 per cent a year, the USA's by 3.1 per cent. Between 1950 and 1975, Soviet farm output more than doubled - the world's fastest growth rate both in volume and per head. Soviet farm output was 61 per cent of the USA's in 1950, 86 per cent by 1973. After Khrushchev was ousted, "There were also some improvements in agricultural practice in the steppe zone of the USSR. The exploitative nature of Khrushchev's style of farming (Stalin, by contrast, was an advocate of grasslands, as it proved to be a substitute for chemical fertilizer), with its emphasis on grain and corn growing at the expense of soil conservation practices, was rejected. The bitter lessons of the virgin lands proved to the Soviet authorities that grain crops depleted the soil and actually promoted soil erosion, while grassland farming was soil conserving. ... the practice of fallow-land crop rotation was re-established. The [Khrushchev] dogma 'Fallow land is lost land; erosion is a fiction' proved to be completely false."[56]

In 1950-75, real consumption per head grew 3.8 per cent a year; in the USA, 2 per cent. In the 1970s, Soviet living standards and incomes rose dramatically. No society had ever increased the living standards of all its people so quickly. Only about 0.5 per cent of the people were unemployed, and then only for a short time. Between 1975 and 1985, the economy was still growing, if at a slower rate. Production and consumption also grew every year between 1985 and 1989, and faster than between 1980 and 1985.[57] In 1987, food production was up 130 per cent since 1980, meat by 135 per cent, dairy products by 131 per cent, fish production 132 per cent and flour 123 per cent. In the same period, the population grew by 6.7 per cent, while the average wage rose by 19 per cent. The food industry was working at full capacity, with guaranteed supplies of the agricultural products and other raw materials needed.

In 1980, the Soviet Union had 37.4 doctors and 125 hospital beds per 10,000 people; the USA had 18.2 and 58.5. The Soviet Union had free education for all, from kindergarten to university; post-secondary students also received their living costs. In the mid-1970s, workers averaged 21.2 days of holiday a year. The Soviet Union ended huge inequalities in wealth, incomes, education and opportunity. In 1983, the highest incomes were just ten times the average worker's wages; in the USA, they were 115 times. Trade unions could veto firings and recall managers.

But when Leonid Brezhnev was the Soviet Union's leader (1964-82), the Soviet working class allowed the illegal private sector to grow and this became the base for capitalism's return. There were hardly any prosecutions of illegal economic activities. Later, Mikhail Gorbachev's market reforms further strengthened the private sector. His 1987 Law on Individual Labour Activity legalised co-operatives that were really private enterprises. Another law allowed co-operatives to lease industrial property – a way of privatising state assets while keeping the fiction of public ownership. In 1988, these crime-infested fake co-operatives employed a million workers, a year later, five million. By 1991, former or active criminals ran 60 per cent of the co-operatives.[58] Even before the counter-revolution, crime levels soared, encouraged by Gorbachev's reforms.[59] As FBI director Jim Moody noted, "the transition to capitalism provided new opportunities quickly exploited by criminal organizations."[60]

Chapter 7

Eastern Europe from 1945 to 1989

Rebuilding

The working classes of Eastern Europe's countries faced huge difficulties in 1945. They had to rebuild their countries after having been exploited for centuries by the empires to their east and west, then wrecked by the battles of the First World War, then oppressed by home-grown fascist regimes in the 1920s and 1930s, and finally ruined again by Hitler's genocidal war.

Before World War Two, they had been semi-colonies, serving the needs of foreign capital. In Hungary, foreign capital owned 30 per cent of the banks. In Romania, it owned 90 per cent of the oil industry. In Bulgaria, it owned 50 per cent of the chemical industry, 30 per cent of the textile industry, almost all the sugar and flour-milling industry, and 75 per cent of the power industry. Products, largely raw materials, left the countries, as did profits, and the ruling classes put no money back in to develop their economies. During the Second World War, the British government had supported Eastern Europe's émigré governments in London, whose failures had led to fascism.

After the war, the US government and Western Europe's powers wanted to keep Eastern Europe backward, as a source of cheap food and cheap labour, so they tried to restore the prewar governments.

They wanted Eastern Europe's countries to adopt an 'open door' policy, allowing the free movement of capital, goods and labour. But, as Molotov warned, "It is surely not so difficult to understand that if American capital were given a free hand in the small states ruined and enfeebled by the war, as the advocates of the principle of 'equal opportunity' desire, American capital would buy up the local industries, appropriate the more attractive Romanian, Yugoslav and all other enterprises and would become the masters in these small states. Given such a situation, we would probably live to see the day when in your own country, on switching on the radio, you would be hearing not so much your own language as one American gramophone record after another or some piece or other of British propaganda."[1]

Instead, the Soviet victory in the war shifted the balance of power, allowing Eastern Europe's countries to progress. But when these countries sought to develop in their own interests, the capitalist states tried to stop them. In 1946, the US government cut off all aid and loans.[2] In 1948, it forbade all countries signed up to the Marshall Plan to buy Eastern European goods. In 1950, it hardened this blockade by setting up the Co-ordinating Committee for Multilateral Trade Controls (COCOM).

Eastern Europe's old pro-capitalist parties were all compromised by their collaboration with the Nazi occupiers and they had no programmes for rebuilding these shattered countries. So there was great popular support for socialism.

In Czechoslovakia's May 1946 elections, the Communist Party won 38 percent of the votes, the most of any party, and their leader, Klement Gottwald, became prime minister of a coalition government with the Socialists. But, as Suny explained, "in February 1948 the National Socialists, suspicious that the Communists were preparing a coup d'état, tried to bring down the government and force new elections by resigning. Mass meetings were held in the Old Town Square, where crowds cheered Gottwald, who accused the departing ministers of having formed a 'reactionary bloc' to obstruct further reforms. Given the popularity of the Communists and the growing dependence of

Czechoslovakia on Soviet aid and good will, [President] Beneš had little choice but to agree to appoint a new coalition government that was more firmly in Communist hands. These events, which were soon characterized as 'the Czech coup', in fact were legal and constitutional."[3] British historians Geoffrey Swain and Nigel Swain agreed that "the constitution had not been violated."[4]

In Hungary's 1947 elections, the Communist Party won most seats. With its allies, it won 45 per cent of the vote; the Smallholders party won 15 per cent. In response, the USA's Central Intelligence Agency (CIA) recruited Smallholder MPs.[5] The US and British governments criticised these elections, ignoring the fact that their fascist allies Spain and Portugal held no elections at all.

In eastern Germany, the Soviet Military Administration (SVAG) achieved 'remarkable' 'successes in reconstructing the zone', especially in setting up a food rationing system that was far better than the British occupiers' system.[6] In the most recent study, Filip Slaveski commented, "SVAG's Herculean efforts to feed the German population so soon after German occupation forces starved millions of Soviet citizens to death remains an enduring testimony to the intelligence and humanity of its officers."[7]

But, as American historian Anne Applebaum pointed out, "the proximity of West Germany and the relative openness of Berlin in the 1940s and 1950s meant that the new East German state really was surrounded, and infiltrated, by large numbers of Westerners."[8] The Woodrow Wilson International Center for Scholars, of Washington, DC, agreed, "The open border in Berlin exposed the GDR to massive espionage and subversion and … its closure gave the Communist state greater security."[9]

Indeed, the US and British governments did all they could to disrupt Eastern Europe's countries. Britain's MI6 conducted sabotage and subversion, including an attempt to overthrow Albania's socialist government in 1948-49.[10] The US government organised 'Project X', of which *US News and World Report* wrote, "strong-arm squads would be formed under American guidance. Assassination of key Communists would be encouraged. American agents, parachuted into Eastern Europe … would be used to co-ordinate anti-Communist action."[11] A US committee advised by the Joint Chiefs of Staff recommended, "we must counter-attack by political warfare activities directed against the USSR itself and against the Soviet satellites of Eastern Europe with the objective of increasing the discontent, tension and divisions known to exist in the Soviet orbit … In addition, such activities are designed to form the political bases and operational nuclei for resistance groups which, we hope, would weaken the Soviet regime in case of armed conflict."[12]

As *Newsweek* pointed out, "Observers on both sides of the Iron Curtain are fully aware that Russia is not suffering from 'spy hysteria' in declaring that the United States has undercover agents working inside the Curtain. The United States, like most other powers, of course, has such intelligence and psychological warfare groups at work. The 'spy hysteria' charge had to be made for the record and for the benefit of the neutral nations."[13]

In Poland, the anti-Soviet opposition constantly alleged that a 'Jewish-communist clique' ran the country. (Jan Gross noted "the nearly universal presence and the intensity of anti-Jewish prejudice in Polish society."[14]) Consequently, several hundred Jews were murdered.[15] This opposition linked up with the CIA, which provided $1 million and subversion training. The terrorist 'National Armed Forces' sought 'the liquidation of the workers of the Department of Public Security' using either 'quiet disappearances (drowning, kidnapping, torture) or open shooting'.[16] Remnants of the 'Home Army' carried on a war of sabotage and assassination against both the Soviets and their Polish allies. They had killed 15,000 Polish communists by 1946.

In Ukraine, Belarus and the Baltic states too, the governments had to defeat US- and British-backed counter-revolutionary terrorist organisations. They did this by combining social reforms, primarily land reform, with repression. Statiev noted that the Soviet Union 'put more effort into social reforms than have most other states conducting counterinsurgency'.[17] The OUN continued to operate in Ukraine. The

Latvian Central Council, founded in 1943, operated until 1948.[18] The Nazi-created 'Lithuanian Defense Force' was active until 1949.[19] The Armed Resistance League, formed in Estonia in 1947, was active until 1951.[20] As Mart Laar, Prime Minister of Estonia 1992-94 and 1999-2002, wrote of these anti-Soviet 'Forest Brothers', "The first to gather in the forest were those who had fought in the German army ..."[21]

In 1944-46, these anti-Soviet terrorists killed thousands of civilians and Soviet personnel – in Ukraine, 5,890 civilians and 7,182 Soviet personnel; in Belarus, 507 civilians and 699 Soviet personnel; in Lithuania, 3,929 civilians and 2,994 Soviet personnel; in Latvia, 439 civilians and 740 Soviet personnel; and in Estonia, 323 civilians and 314 Soviet personnel.[22]

Counter-revolutionaries agitated for World War Three. Paczkowski pointed out, "Many émigré groups (not just Polish) once again began hoping – especially after the outbreak of the Korean War – for an outbreak of worldwide conflict."[23] Laar noted, "Estonians hoped that with the end of the war in Europe, a new world war would start, which would bring liberty to Estonia."[24] Ukrainian Nationalist policy in 1945 was 'to hope for a new war between the Allies and the Soviets'.[25]

Despite all this, the peoples of Eastern Europe defended their countries' independence, broke up the huge landed estates that had been the economic basis of fascism and ran their industries in the national interest. The US Chamber of Commerce complained, "We have lost virtually all oil-wells and refineries in the Balkans, as well as giant industrial plants in Germany and Hungary."

Poland's national income grew by 76 per cent between 1947 and 1950; farm and industrial output more than doubled. Its Six Year Plan of 1950-55 brought vast increases in investment, especially in industry, and in industrial output, and big rises in national income and farm output.[26] In addition to its popular land reform, the government started a house-building programme that won much respect. Most Poles preferred rebuilding to terrorism and civil war and therefore supported a government that worked for national unity, reconstruction and social reform.

Land reforms across Central and Eastern Europe were widely popular. *The Times* noted that the GDR's land reform was 'an outstanding political success'.[27] Large cooperative farms were successful, raising rural incomes to urban levels. To assist, the Soviet Union exported more than 100,000 tractors to East Central Europe and the Balkans between 1946 and 1962. The Control Council set up by the Allies to carry out the Potsdam conference decisions reported in 1947, "land reform has been practically completed only in the Soviet zone."

Before the war, the Roman Catholic Church had owned 720,000 hectares of Hungary's best farmland, while 40 per cent of peasants had no land. The new government distributed two million hectares, including the Church's holdings, to 600,000 peasants. Cardinal József Mindszenty said this was 'robbery'. In Poland, one million families received land and 145,000 peasants worked land formerly owned by the Church. The Baltic states built on the successes of the earlier land reforms. In Lithuania, between 1944 and 1948, 96,330 farmer families gained land.

Albania used Stalin's *Economic Problems of Socialism in the USSR* as the programme for building its economy and society. The country's gross domestic material product, taking 1938 as 1, rose to 1.7 in 1950, 4 in 1960, 8.3 in 1970 and 10.7 in 1973. Its farm production rose to 1.2, to 1.7, 3.1 and then 3.5, its industrial production to 4, 25, 64 and 86.[28] Industrial output grew between 1950 and 1975 by more than 10 per cent a year. Consumption per head in 1951-55 grew by 45 per cent, in 1956-60 by 27 per cent, in 1961-65 by 9 per cent, in 1966-70 by 33 per cent and in 1971-75 by 20 per cent.[29] These growth rates were greater than anywhere else in Europe.[30] Average life spans rose from 38 in 1938 to 71 in 1985. On this evidence, historian Adi Schnytzer argued that Stalin's book 'provides a reasonably clear and unambiguous development strategy'.[31]

By the 1950s, import-substituting industrialisation had transformed the incomes, jobs and production potentials of the Balkan and Eastern European countries. In the early 1950s, national income grew by 11 per cent a year in Poland, 14 per cent a year in Romania, 9.5 per cent a year in Czechoslovakia, 10 per cent a year in the GDR and 8.5 per cent a year in Hungary.[32] Industrial output grew from 1940 to 1975 (counting 1940 as 1) to 37 in Latvia, 46 in Lithuania and 39 in Estonia, compared to a growth to 17 in the Soviet Union, which proved that the Soviet Union did not exploit its Baltic allies.[33] In all Eastern Europe's countries, incomes were more equitably distributed than before the war and there was far more equality of opportunity. The production of consumer goods was satisfactory in Czechoslovakia and the GDR, and rather good in Hungary.[34]

British historian Hugh Seton-Watson wrote of Eastern Europe's countries, "These far-reaching plans strike the imagination. Even a foreign observer cannot fail to be affected by the enthusiasm and optimism of the planners. Moreover it is certain that large-scale industrialisation, public works and mechanisation of agriculture are the right remedies for the rural overpopulation and poverty, and the lack of manufactured goods, which were so striking in the old Eastern Europe. It is also understandable that the new regimes should wish, from a general feeling of patriotism, to diminish their countries' economic dependence on foreign countries."[35]

Yugoslavia: a different path

On 11 April 1945, the Soviet Union and the Yugoslav government signed a Treaty of Friendship, Mutual Assistance and Post-war Collaboration. The UN reported, "Of special importance for the implementation of the Five-Year Plan is the conclusion of a trade agreement with the Soviet Union, officially reported on July 30, 1947. According to the terms of this agreement, Yugoslavia will receive metallurgical plants and equipment, both ferrous and non-ferrous, and plants for oil and chemical industries and for coalmining. Yugoslavia's deliveries of goods will not take place until 1950 …"[36] President Josip Tito acknowledged in 1946, "the principal and most substantial aid came from our great ally, the Soviet Union."[37] In 1947, the Soviet Union met Yugoslavia's wishes and dropped a plan to set up joint stock companies. Instead it supplied equipment and technical aid to build industrial enterprises in Yugoslavia.[38]

But after this good start, Yugoslavia took a different path. In 1948, the Tito government broke away from the socialist camp, causing 'a second civil war' in which 51,000 people were arrested or disappeared.[39] As early as January 1945, Tito had tried to get the Soviet Union to back his territorial claims against Austria, Hungary, Italy and Romania, but Stalin told him to moderate his claims. Tito also sought to 'swallow' Albania, ordering his troops to occupy it.[40] The Soviet Union stopped this aggression.

Tito said in June 1951, "in the event of a Soviet attack anywhere in Europe, even if the thrust should be miles away from Yugoslavia's own borders", he would "instantly do battle on the side of the West ... Yugoslavia considers itself part of the collective security wall being built against Soviet imperialism."[41] In 1952, Tito called the Soviet Union 'state capitalist' and imperialist, saying it had 'colonies' in Eastern Europe.

Kennan wrote, "Tito in being is perhaps our most precious asset in the struggle to contain and weaken Russian expansion."[42] As *Business Week* noted in 1950, "For the United States in particular and the West in general this encouragement of Tito has proved to be one of the cheapest ways yet of containing Russian Communism. To date the West's aid to Tito has come to $51.7 million. This is far less than the billion dollars or so that the United States has spent in Greece for the same purpose. ... Yugoslavia has had to settle for a Western credit policy based on these two principles: (1) Priority assistance for industries having the best potential for volume exports readily marketable in the West: minimum of aid for basic industries ... just enough to meet security needs and to facilitate exports. (2) Extension of credit in instalments. This would act as incentive to put their best efforts into foreign-aided projects. The better their efforts, the better their chances of getting favourable consideration on further dollar requests."[43]

Tito's counter-revolution opened the country to IMF loans and credits. The leading historian of Yugoslavia, Susan Woodward, wrote,

"The regime survived thanks to U.S. military aid; U.S.-orchestrated economic assistance from the International Monetary Fund, World Bank, U.S. Export-Import Bank, and foreign banks; and the restoration of trade relations with the West after August 1949. In exchange, socialist Yugoslavia played a critical role for U.S. global leadership during the cold war: as a propaganda tool in its anticommunist and anti-Soviet campaign and as an integral element of NATO's policy in the eastern Mediterranean. Yugoslavia became an important element in the West's policy of containment of the Soviet Union."[44]

In 1951, the Tito government abolished Yugoslavia's planning body. It adopted 'market socialism', with profit-making enterprises, decentralised investments and material incentives. It gave workers' councils control of enterprise funds and investment.[45] This favoured the more profitable enterprises, causing uneven growth and unequal incomes. The goal of profit maximisation encouraged enterprise members to use the profits to pay themselves short-term wage rises rather than invest in the future. Where they did invest in their enterprises, they financed these investments by borrowing rather than by setting aside savings from their earnings. This caused a low rate of savings, high inflation, ever-higher levels of debt, and inadequate investment.

The *Economist* enthused, "the federal government ... proposes to relinquish detailed economic planning to the separate republics, and they in turn will delegate to the local authorities and the individual 'economic enterprises'. ... the enterprises themselves are to be allowed to retain their net profits."[46] The *Daily Mail* too praised Tito's policies: "price of goods ... determined by the market – that is, by supply and demand ... wages and salaries ... fixed on the basis of the income or profits of the enterprise" which "decide independently what to produce and in what quantities" and rightly concluded, "there isn't much classical Marxism in all of that."[47] The *Economist* also praised the collective farms, run by kulaks.[48] Yugoslavia, unlike the Soviet Union, encouraged bourgeois nationalism in its republics. Labour Minister Hector McNeil said in 1949, "It is of the utmost importance 'to encourage the line of thought developed by Marshal Tito in opposing Russia's attempt to eliminate nationalism among the peoples of Eastern Europe'."[49]

Threats of counter-revolution

After Stalin's death, Khrushchev and Malenkov invited the Hungarian leadership to Moscow. Contrary to Stalin's practice, they chose which Hungarians came and excluded József Revai and Mihály Farkas, Prime Minister Matyas Rakosi's two closest colleagues. They then ousted Rakosi and appointed Imre Nagy Prime Minister.

In 1956, the US government raised its spending on de-stabilising Eastern Europe to $125 million, focusing on Hungary, where it produced 'a revolt plotted for a year', as the *Daily Mail* admitted.[50] MI6's historian Michael Smith noted, "MI6 had been active behind the scenes for some time providing covert assistance to potential Hungarian rebels."[51] One rebel slogan was 'Down with the Jews'. Khrushchev let the counter-revolution grow to the point where the Soviet Union had to send forces into Hungary to defeat it.

In 1950-70, the first two decades of central planning, the socialist countries in Eastern Europe grew by 7 per cent a year, better than the best inter-war year.[52] Their average annual GDP per head grew by 3.81 per cent between 1950 and 1973, as against the Soviet Union's 3.35 per cent and Western Europe's countries' 4.05 per cent. The percentage of the net material product originating in industry rose from 23 in 1948 to 55 in 1970. This was partly because the Soviet Union supplied energy 'on the most generous of terms until the second half of the 1980s'.[53] Wilfried Loth concluded, "Altogether, the modernization of the Eastern Bloc proceeded even more rapidly than that of Western Europe."[54]

But later, under worse policies, Eastern Europe's countries contracted large external debts. Their governments borrowed not to invest but to prop up consumption. In the 1970s, cheap loans encouraged import-led growth, luring them to depend on outside demand and on sucker loans. For example, Poland's debt to the West rose from $8.4 billion in 1975 to $33.5 billion in 1986. So the 1980s' high interest rates hit hard.

In 1986, Gorbachev ruled that market forces would govern relations between the Soviet Union and Eastern Europe's countries: he then charged them world prices for Soviet oil and gas, adding hugely to their production costs.

Internal weakness brought yet more pressure from outside. The NATO powers never ceased their attacks. In Poland, the US government secretly aided Solidarity, an anti-socialist political party masquerading as a trade union.[55] American historian Charles Gati admitted that the Soviet government's claim that there was a 'plot' to end socialism in Poland was true.[56]

Chapter 8
China

Feudal China

In ancient and feudal China, famine was ever-present. From 100 BC to 1911, the Chinese people suffered 1,828 major famines. From 1850 to 1932, 4.5 per cent of each generation died of hunger. The 1876 famine in northern China left 15 million dead.

After its defeats in the Opium Wars, China endured a 'century of humiliation', foreign occupation, defeat and disunity. In 1850, China's GDP per head was $600; by 1950, it was just $439. Lucien Bianco wrote, "[F]rom one end of rural China to the other ... poverty, abuse and early death were the only prospects for nearly half a billion people."[1]

A French correspondent, Robert Guillain, wrote of China before the revolution, "Before, it was appalling – that truth predominated over every other. Poverty, corruption, inefficiency, misery, contempt for the people and for the commonweal, these were the elements which made up the most wretched nation on earth. And I knew China then."[2] Life expectancy in 1930 was 24. In the 1930s, millions died every year in famines, epidemics and floods. China was the most oppressed of the world's semi-colonies, the most under attack and the most backward. Foreign powers ran China through their vast economic interests, the treaty ports, the leased territories, foreign residents' and diplomats' privileges, armed forces, missionaries, the foreign-run Maritime Customs Service, the Post Office and the Salt Administration.[3]

In September 1926, Royal Navy warships shelled Wanhsien, killing 2-3,000 civilians. The Foreign Office admitted, "our naval people … were spoiling for a fight."[4] In January 1927, the British government sent 15,000 troops, the biggest British deployment between the world wars, to secure British finance's interests in Shanghai. In April, Chiang Kai-Shek carried out his coup. On 6 April, the forces of Chinese warlord Chang So-lin (whose adviser was a British officer, Captain Sutton), aided by White Russians, raided the Soviet Embassy in Peking. The British government had agreed to the raid, which resulted in 'executions' of embassy staff. The same day, Chiang's forces, again aided by White Russians, raided the Soviet Consulate in Shanghai. On 13 December, Chang's forces raided the Soviet Consulate in Canton, destroyed the building and killed six of its staff in the street. On 27 May 1929, Chinese police stormed the Soviet Consulate in Harbin.

In July, Chiang said, "We want first to take the Chinese Eastern Railway [CER] into our hands …"[5] This railway was the Soviet Union's single dependable link with Vladivostok and the Maritime Provinces. Sino-Soviet treaties of 1924 had acknowledged Soviet ownership of the CER. On 10-11 July, Chiang's forces seized the railway and arrested its Soviet employees. Then Chinese forces and White Russian bandits launched raids into the Soviet Union.[6] In October-November, Soviet forces responded in self-defence with a limited invasion of Manchuria, to restore the status quo ante on the basis of the treaties.[7] They defeated and disarmed the bandits, making further attacks impossible, then promptly withdrew to Soviet territory.

On 18 September 1931, Japanese forces invaded and occupied Manchuria. Western newspapers forecast that they would go on to attack the Soviet Union. Japan's Imperial Way Faction, a fascist military group, openly urged such a war. In December, the Soviet Union proposed a non-aggression pact, as it had in 1926, 1927 and 1928, which the Japanese government yet again refused.

Chiang's government failed to defend China against Japanese aggression.[8] The Japanese empire's war on China killed 18 million Chinese civilians and three million soldiers and displaced 100 million people from their homes. It wrecked 55 per cent of China's industry and mines, 72 per cent of its shipping and 96 per cent of its railway lines.

From 1937 to 1940, China fought alone against a Japanese aggressor that was armed and aided by its Axis allies and also by the USA and the British Empire. Then throughout the Second World War, the Chinese people held down half of Japan's fighting strength. As British historian Andrew Roberts observed, "Western accounts of the war often minimize, to the point of ignoring it altogether, the experience of China, despite the fact that 15 million of those who died in the conflict – a full 30 per cent – were Chinese."[9] The Chinese people, led by their Communist Party, were our ally, fighting the same enemy, the Japanese empire.

After the war, Chiang's Kuomintang [KMT] still ran most of China. But the Chinese people increasingly opposed Chiang's gangster rule. In 1946-47, there was an upsurge of working class action in the cities, particularly by women workers, for more pay, better conditions and shorter hours, and against inflation, unemployment and civil war.[10] There were 1,700 strikes in Shanghai alone. Across the country, the peasants sought land reform. There were also significant student struggles.

In response, the US 7th Fleet ferried KMT troops to north China. The United States Air Force, in the largest airlift in history, transported KMT troops to Shanghai, Nanking and Peiping. US General Wedemeyer declared his 'determination to keep the fifty-three thousand marines operating on behalf of the Nationalists in north China'.[11] But the Chinese people chose to reject the KMT and to support the revolutionary forces. Schaller summed up, "The collapse of the American-supported regime in China resulted not from Soviet-American collusion but from essentially internal causes, only compounded by incredible American bungling."[12] Despite the US state's huge intervention, the Chinese people freed their country from imperial and feudal oppression, in an epic struggle for freedom.[13]

The 1949 revolution

In April 1949, People's Liberation Army forces crossed the Yangtze River, to free Shanghai. American journalist Jack Belden wrote, "The crossing of the Yangtze – like the crossing of so many other river barriers in history, from the Rubicon to the Rappahannock or the Rhine – may stand as a decisive date in world history. … the day which sounded the death knell of imperialism in Asia. The crossing of the Yangtze rang down the curtain on an era of history. … Gone was the era of gunboat diplomacy, gone the treaty port concessions, gone the specially conceded naval bases, the military missions, the ill-disguised interference in Chinese affairs."[14]

The Chinese people's revolution restored unity and independence to China. British economic historian Angus Maddison summed up, "The establishment of the People's Republic in 1949 marked a sharp break with the past. It provided a new mode of governance, a new kind of elite and a marked improvement on past economic performance."[15] Once 'the sick man of Asia', China now awakened as a modern nation-state with full national independence.

Stalin generously acknowledged, "True, we, too, can make a mistake! Here, when the war with Japan ended, we invited the Chinese comrades to reach an agreement as to how a modus vivendi with Chiang Kai-Shek might be found. They agreed with us in word, but in deed they did it their own way when they got home: they mustered their forces and struck. It has been shown that they were right, and not we."[16] In June, the Soviet Union offered China a $300 million loan. It also offered technical and educational aid, help to build and supply ships, and training for sailors and pilots. By contrast, the US government at once imposed sanctions on China, trying to strangle the new state at birth. In 1949, just 8 per cent of China's trade was with the socialist countries; by 1952, 87 per cent. President Truman said on 5 January

1950, "The United States Government will not pursue a course which will lead to involvement in the civil conflict in China. Similarly, the United States will not provide military aid and advice to the Chinese forces on Formosa."[17] He broke both pledges within six months.

Faced with the huge task of rebuilding China in 1949, no government could have left the job to market forces. Every country which has industrialised, including Britain and the USA, has used the state to protect industry, because infant industries are unprofitable in the short and perhaps even medium term.[18] So the new Chinese government chose to develop a wide range of industries and rejected the World Bank's advice to put textiles first.

Land reform ended the abuses of the feudal system. It destroyed the landlord-gentry class that had ruled China for 2,000 years. The landlord could not get an income directly from the land, but the peasant could cultivate the land without the landlord. But the landlords did not yield power peacefully. Their Kuomintang agents committed acts of terrorism and sabotage, killing communist officials, 'perhaps as many as 40,000' in 1950.[19] To assist them, the CIA in 1950 dropped 212 agents into Manchuria. Within days, 101 had been killed and the other 111 captured. Chiang's planes bombed Shanghai, killing more than 500 people. Yet "the vast majority of China's 2 million landlords, while they may have lost their estates, survived the land reform."[20]

In June 1949, just after the communist victory, speculators manipulated silver dollar quotations on Shanghai's currency exchange, pushing food and energy prices up threefold. On 10 June, the new government closed down the currency exchange and arrested a large number of speculators, widely popular moves.

In China, as in Russia, the small scale of private farming, based on individual household work, prevented both the use of farm machinery and investment in irrigation, conservation and infrastructure. The people had to end this ownership structure in order to modernise farming. They created mutual aid teams, working collectively, and set up producers' cooperatives, where land, implements and cattle were pooled, then they created socialised cooperatives, with collective land ownership.

As Chun Lin observed, "[T]he lack of thoroughgoing land reform is a major developmental obstacle in large parts of the postcolonial world. The fact that China has done a great deal better – in meeting basic needs, alleviating poverty, raising the general standard of living, and giving political recognition to the social standing of labor and the common people (as in the Maoist legacy) – is an awesome testimony. It carries a universal implication: By transforming 'feudal' structures and relations, land reform, broadly defined to also include cooperative farming, eradicates backward and reactionary social power while empowering hitherto subjugated and marginalized classes. In so doing it can be a decisive promoter of economic growth and social development. ... historical evidence has amply vindicated the superiority of revolutionary paths in transforming large, poor, agrarian, illiterate, and patriarchal societies."[21] This programme was highly effective: by 1958, agricultural production was 185 million tons, up from 108 million tons in 1949. It also won huge popular support.

With the land reform, the government gave peasants full rights at meetings freely to criticise and impeach all cadres of the government and peasant organisations, and full rights to remove and elect all cadres.[22] Peasants had a more accountable and more honest local leadership than before the revolution and they made more decisions about their daily lives than ever before.[23]

From the start, the new government worked to end discrimination against women. It gave women the rights to divorce and to own land. It banned the practice of abandoning wives and children and gave all children, male and female, the right to be cared for and to inherit property from their parents. It banned foot-binding, child-bride marriages, forced widowhood chastity, mercenary and arranged marriages, the trafficking of women, and wife-beating.[24] The government also worked to end discrimination against China's minority peoples. China's minorities made real gains in education, poverty reduction, population growth and public welfare.[25]

China experienced very rapid mortality decline during the 1950s. The death rate fell from 20 per 1,000 in 1949 to 10.8 in 1957. Xihze Peng summed up, "This monumental achievement to a large extent was attributable to the cessation of warfare, a reduction in the degree of extreme poverty, and great improvements in health care."[26]

Tibet

Nearly every government in the world, including the US government, recognised Tibet as part of China: "The Government of the United States has borne in mind the fact that the Chinese Government has long claimed suzerainty over Tibet and that the Chinese constitution lists Tibet among areas constituting the territory of the Republic of China. This Government has at no time raised a question regarding either of these claims."[27] In 1949 and 1950, the United Nations rejected claims that it should recognise Tibet as independent and that it should condemn 'Chinese aggression'.

Mao said that 'Chinese' meant 'all those who live in the territory of China'.[28] Xinhua News Agency stated that "the Tibetan people are an integral part of the Chinese."[29]

In May 1951, the Dalai Lama's court signed an Agreement with China accepting that Tibet was part of China. On 24 October, the Dalai Lama telegraphed the Chinese government, "The local government of Tibet and the Tibetans, lamas, and the entire Tibetan people unanimously support this agreement."[30] Subsequently, China tried to turn Tibet's feudal land-owning class into agents of gradual modernisation, but the landlords fought all attempts at reform. In 1958, Khampa tribesmen, 'trained in Colorado by the CIA', and directed and armed by the CIA and MI6, rose in revolt.[31]

The Dalai Lama's court then reneged on the 1951 Agreement. Ever since, the Dalai Lama has refused to recognise China's sovereignty over Tibet. From 1959 to 1971, the CIA covertly paid the Dalai Lama $180,000 a year and gave his cause another $1.5 million every year. After the 1951 Agreement, Tibetan life expectancy increased from 36 years to 67 by 2003 and rates of infant mortality and poverty steadily fell.[32] Far from suffering 'genocide', Tibetans have doubled in number in the last 50 years.[33] The USA still officially recognises Tibet as part of China, but the US Congress and the Presidency unofficially backed the campaign for Tibet's secession. US strategists also backed Uighur separatists, who called for 'Xinjiang independence' and called on the Uighur people to carry out 'violent struggle' 'as in the fight against Japanese aggression'.

Development

China was always keen to use foreign technology. In 1950-51, the Soviet Union and China worked together to set up metal manufacturing plants, civil aviation and shipbuilding in China. On 31 December 1952, the Soviet Union transferred to China all her rights in the Chinese Eastern Railway and its subsidiary enterprises. Mao thanked Stalin for this 'tremendous contribution to railway construction in China'.[34] Soviet credits amounted to 3 per cent of China's state investment between 1953 and 1957.

In its first five-year plan (1953-57), China aimed to build 694 large industrial enterprises. 156 of these were Soviet aid projects, 'one of the largest transfers of technology in history'.[35] They included 52 energy enterprises, 20 metallurgical companies, seven chemical plants, 24 mechanical processing plants, three light industry factories and 44 military enterprises. The Cambridge History of China states, "The importance of Soviet technical assistance and capital goods would be difficult to overestimate. Its effort to transfer design capability has been characterized as unprecedented in the history of the transfer of technology. Moreover, China appears to have received the most advanced technology available within the Soviet Union, and in some cases this was the best in the world. In the iron and steel industry, the most important sector of Soviet assistance, the Soviets during the 1950s built and operated the world's best blast furnaces."[36] China, like Eastern

Europe's countries, paid Soviet specialists the same salaries as their own specialists.

The government tried to balance the need to develop heavy industry with due attention to light industry and farming. Consumer goods output rose by 29 per cent a year during 1950-2 and by 13 per cent a year during 1953-57. Foodgrain output grew by 7 per cent and by between 2.9 and 3.7 per cent over the two periods. Both grew faster than the population. In 1953-57, national income grew by 8.9 per cent a year, farm output by 3.8 per cent a year and industrial output by 18.7 per cent a year. Wages rose 30 per cent in real terms, peasant income by 20 per cent. Life expectancy rose from 36 in 1950 to 57 in 1957, as against poor countries' average of 42.

State-led defence industrialisation was a priority to safeguard China. The US threat of first use of nuclear weapons during the Korean War drove China's nuclear programme in the 1950s. The US government posed a constant threat. For example, on 27 July 1953, a US F-86F Sabre pilot shot down a Soviet civilian Aeroflot Il-12 over China, killing all 21 people on board.[37] Chiang's defeated troops, many of whom had fled to Burma after 1949, also posed a threat. The CIA used them to launch attacks on China from 1950 to 1959. Chiang's forces on Taiwan conducted naval raids against the mainland and sent in agents. In 1958, the USA sold Taiwan modern missiles, increasing the threat of a US-backed attack on China and forcing China to switch resources to defence.

The British government built an intelligence-gathering site in Hong Kong in the 1950s which operated until the 1980s. Western aircraft regularly intruded into China's airspace to generate electronic intelligence responses from China's defences.

The British Empire left no agreed boundaries in the Indian subcontinent, leaving these problems to the newly independent successor states to solve. In 1960, China reached border agreements with Nepal and Burma, in 1963 with Pakistan, and also with Afghanistan, Tajikistan, Kazakhstan, Kyrgyzstan, Mongolia, Korea, Vietnam and Laos. As Premier Zhou Enlai had pointed out in 1953, "We are the ones who advocate resolving all international disputes through peaceful consultation and negotiation, and the other side is the one who insists on the use of force or hostility in resolving conflicts."[38] Of Asia's countries, only India refused to negotiate, claiming that its borders with China were already defined and were therefore non-negotiable.[39] But its claim line, the McMahon Line, based on a British diplomat's forgery, was never a legal border.[40]

In August 1959, India started a border war with China.[41] Indian patrols crossed the border at Longju and attacked Chinese border guards. Yet Khrushchev claimed that China 'started the war'.[42] In September, Khrushchev visited the USA for talks. The talks covered China, among other issues.[43] Afterwards, he lied that the talks 'had not touched on issues involving third countries'.[44] Khrushchev tried to turn the Warsaw Pact against China, an act that the Sino-Soviet alliance prohibited.[45]

In October, after a more serious clash on the Kashmir-Xiangkiang border, the Chinese government ordered a 20-kilometre withdrawal of Chinese guards all along the border and asked India to do likewise. The Indian government refused. China sought negotiations; India demanded unilateral Chinese withdrawal from all territory claimed by India.[46] In April 1960, Zhou Enlai met President Jawaharlal Nehru in an attempt to negotiate but was rebuffed. On 3 October 1962, China again sought negotiations. India instantly rejected this proposal. At this time, US forces were attacking Vietnam, Chiang Kai-Shek was threatening to invade China, and the Soviet Union was turning hostile, so the Indian government reckoned that China would not risk a war. On 4 October, Nehru's daughter, Indira Gandhi, secretly approached Dean Rusk, the US Secretary of State, who approved India's attack.[47] On 9 October, Indian forces attacked Chinese border guards.[48] China repulsed the attack, then withdrew its forces.

In early 1959, the Soviet government broke its 1957 agreement to provide China with modern military technology. In June 1960, Khrushchev publicly criticised all China's domestic and foreign policies. On 25 July, he ended all Soviet aid and ordered the 1,400 Soviet scientists and engineers who had been working in China to leave by

1 September, tearing up their contracts. (The Soviet Ambassador in Beijing had warned Khrushchev that unilateral termination of these agreements 'would be a violation of international law'.) They took with them the blueprints of the industrial plants they had been planning to build. Two-thirds of the projects were left unfinished.

Natural disasters and recovery

1959, 1960 and 1961 were years of record natural disasters in China. In July 1959, the Yellow River flooded in East China, killing about two million people. In 1959, the harvest was 175 million tons, down from 1958's 250 million tons. In 1960, drought and other bad weather affected 55 per cent of the country's farmland. Some 60 per cent of the farmland in the north received no rain at all. 1960's harvest was 142 million tons.[49] But even during this period, China was growing more than 50 per cent more grain per head than India and the nutritional level was higher than India's.[50]

Between 1961 and 1965, China bought a total of 30 million tons of grain from Australia, France, Sudan, Burma and Canada at a cost of $2 billion.[51] As Henry Liu pointed out, "More would have been imported except that US pressure on Canada and Australia to limit sales to China and US interference with shipping prevented China from importing more."[52] For example, in March 1962 the US government stopped the International Trading Corporation of Seattle from selling 10.5 million tons of wheat and barley to China.[53]

The poor quality of the 1953 census, which was based largely on random samples, made it impossible to number the population accurately and opened the door to wild claims about famine deaths. The 1953 census claimed that China's population had risen from 450 million in 1947 to 600 million in 1953, figures both suspiciously round. The 1960s censuses found that tens of millions of Chinese had 'gone missing', compared with the 1953 figure. But this claim was worthless, since it was most unlikely that the 1953 figure was accurate.

As Utsa Patnaik observed, "[T]he 'missing millions' totalling 27 millions in the population pyramid during 1958 to 1961 have been identified with 'famine deaths'. The problem with this is that not only the people who were actually living and who died in excess of normal numbers are included in the missing millions, but so are all those hypothetical persons included, who were never born at all and who 'should' have been born if the birth rate had not fallen. This is not a common-sense definition nor is it a logical definition of famine deaths: for, to 'die' in a famine, a minimum necessary condition is to be born in the first place."[54] Wim Wertheim agreed, "Often it is argued that at the censuses of the 1960s 'between 17 and 29 millions of Chinese' appeared to be missing, in comparison with the official census figures from the 1950s. But these calculations are lacking any semblance of reliability."[55] Population deficits based on projected birth and death rates may be many times the real death rate.

To cope with the famine, the government maintained a strict rationing system.[56] Robert North judged, "Undoubtedly the Communist regime was unique among Chinese governments of the 19th and 20th centuries with respect to the efforts it made toward alleviating the inevitable mass suffering that accompanied these catastrophes."[57]

But even so, the death rate in these years was tragically far higher than normal. The worst year's death rate was 25.4/1,000 in 1960, as against 1957's 12/1,000. This 1960 figure was close to India's 'normal' death rate, 24.6/1,000, Indonesia's 23/1,000 and Pakistan's 23/1,000. It was much lower than China's 1949 figure (38/1,000) and much lower than in any year before the revolution. It was also lower than India's in any year of British rule, which was always 30/1,000 or more. China, by cutting death rates from 38/1,000 in 1949 to 12/1,000 in 1957, had saved tens of millions of lives, the largest mortality reduction in history. In the same period, India reduced mortality only from 28 to 23/1,000 and Indonesia only from 26 to 23/1,000.

The Chinese people worked hard to improve agriculture. They irrigated 20 per cent of the land in 1952, 50 per cent in 1978.[58] This expansion, combined with the increased productivity achieved by large collective farms, allowed for big increases in double cropping.[59] The communes also spread the use of improved technology, made greater use of fertilisers, and planted high-yield semi-dwarf rice on 80 per cent of China's rice land. Michael Dillon commented, "The People's Communes did have positive aspects, notably economies of scale when compared with small family farms and the ability to engage in the long-term planning of agricultural production."[60]

Between 1949 and 1978, food production rose by 169.6 per cent, while the population grew by 77.7 per cent. So food production per person grew from 204 kilograms to 328 kilograms. Grain output increased by 2.4 per cent a year from 1952 to 1978. By 1977, China was growing 40 per cent more food per person than India, on 14 per cent less arable land, and distributing it more equitably to a population which was 50 per cent larger.[61] China had become self-sufficient in food.[62] As Y. Y. Kueh pointed out, "by the close of Mao's period China's historic food problem was basically solved."[63]

In 1986, India's death rate was 12 per 1,000; China's was 7 per 1,000. India's population was 781 million in 1986, so its excess mortality was 3.9 million in that year.[64] As economists Jean Drèze and Amartya Sen observed of India and China, "the similarities were quite striking" in 1949, but by 1989 "there is little doubt that as far as morbidity, mortality and longevity are concerned, China has a large and decisive lead over India."[65]

More threats of war

On 5 August 1963, US Secretary of State Dean Rusk, Soviet Foreign Minister Andrei Gromyko and British Foreign Secretary Lord Home signed a partial test ban treaty, which was aimed at isolating China. As Gordon Chang later observed, the treaty "could have been the avenue for a surprise attack on China. ... [President John F.] Kennedy and his associates sought to aggravate tensions between the Soviet Union and China to the point that the Soviets would join with the US, possibly even in a military action against the PRC."[66] In 1964, President Lyndon

Johnson proposed 'joint action' with the Soviet Union, including 'possible agreement to cooperation in preventive military action' against China. US officials debated a joint US-Soviet nuclear attack on China's nuclear weapons facilities.[67] So China had to prepare itself against this threat.[68] In August 1964, the US government fabricated the Tonkin incident, to justify its illegal assault on Vietnam. In September, it threatened to pursue North Vietnamese planes into China's territory.[69]

The Brezhnev government, like the Indian government, refused to negotiate its borders with China, claiming that they were already defined and therefore non-negotiable. In 1968, Brezhnev stationed 16 divisions armed with heavy weaponry and missiles on the Sino-Soviet border. In the 1969 border conflict, the first casualties were Chinese. In March, Brezhnev threatened a nuclear attack on China.[70] In August, a Soviet official asked the US State Department "what the US would do if the Soviet Union attacked and destroyed China's nuclear installations."[71] Again, China had to prepare itself against this threat.[72]

Rapid growth

The World Bank's first report on China concluded that Chinese development had been impressive. Workers' real wages were 35 per cent higher in 1970 than in 1952. China's state-owned enterprises provided secure jobs, cheap and decent housing, health care that was usually free of charge, social care, pensions for retired workers, and education for workers' children.[73] Workers had better food, housing, medical care, education and training opportunities than ever before. GNP per head had grown at between 2 and 2.5 per cent a year between 1957 and 1977, in spite of a 2 per cent yearly population growth. Other low-income countries had grown on average by only 1.6 per cent.

Industry's net output grew by 10.2 per cent a year between 1957 and 1979, well above other low-income countries' average of 5.4 per cent.[74] In the mid-1950s, China produced only 20,000 barrels of petroleum a day; by 1965, it produced 200,000 and was basically self-sufficient. Between 1952 and 1976, steel output increased from 1.4 to 31.8 million tons, coal from 66 to 617 million tons, cement from 3 to 65 million tons, timber from 11 to 51 million tons, electric power from 7 to 256 billion kilowatt hours, crude oil from virtually nothing to 104 million tons and chemical fertiliser from 39,000 to 8,693,000 tons. By the mid-1970s, China was producing large numbers of jet airplanes, heavy tractors, trains and oceangoing vessels. It became a nuclear power, with intercontinental ballistic missiles. It produced its first atomic bomb in 1964 and its first hydrogen bomb in 1967. It launched a satellite into orbit in 1970.

By 1976, China was one of the world's six largest industrial producers. Between 1952 and 1978, energy production grew by 10.3 per cent a year. The industrial working class grew from 3 million to 50 million. The number of scientists and technicians grew from 50,000 in 1949 to 5 million in 1979. From 1965 to 1985, China's GDP grew by 7.49 per cent a year, more than India's 1.7 per cent, the USA's 1.34 per cent, Britain's 1.6 per cent, Japan's 4.7 per cent, South Korea's 6.6 per cent and West Germany's 2.7 per cent.

From 1952 to 1972, China grew 64 per cent (34 per cent per head) per decade, compared to the Soviet Union's 54 per cent (44 per cent per head) from 1928 to 1958, Germany's 33 per cent (17 per cent per head) between 1880 and 1914 and Japan's 43 per cent (28 per cent per head) between 1874 and 1929.[75] The Chinese people achieved all this by their own efforts, using their country's resources. Apart from the Soviet aid of the 1950s, which was repaid in full (and with interest) by the mid-1960s, China industrialised without foreign loans or investments.[76]

The government consistently invested heavily in the health of China's people. By the late 1970s, the health service covered, according to the World Bank, 'nearly the entire urban and 85% of the rural population, an unrivalled achievement among low-income countries'.[77] Its health care system prioritised mass sanitation, universal immunisation and preventive medicine. Opium smoking was banned. Chris Bramall, the British historian of China's economic development, pointed out, "Large-scale vaccination programmes and improvements in sanitation (such as the anti-schistosomiasis campaigns) had a major effect in reducing death from infectious disease, especially in rural areas. In this regard China's strategy was far more effective than India's; in fact barely a country in the world has matched the pace of mortality reduction achieved by the People's Republic in the postwar era. It is a classic demonstration of how a poor country can reduce mortality even in the absence of large increases in GDP per head."[78]

Between 1949 and 1957, 800 hospitals were built, the number of beds rising from 90,000 to 390,000. From 1949 to 1965, the number of doctors rose from 40,000 to 150,000. Smallpox, cholera, typhus, typhoid fever, plague and leprosy were ended. The government increased the number of midwives from 15,700 in 1950 to 35,290 in 1960. Infant mortality fell from 250/1,000 before the revolution to 20/1,000 in 1980. Between 1949 and 1980, life expectancy at birth nearly doubled, from 36 to 67, the biggest improvement in the world.

The World Bank's 1981 development report said, "China's most remarkable achievement during the past three decades has been to make the low-income groups far better off in terms of basic needs than their counterparts in most other poor countries. They all have work; their food supply is guaranteed through a mixture of state rationing and collective self-insurance; most of their children are not only at school but are also comparatively well taught; and the great majority have access to basic health care and family planning services. Life expectancy – whose dependence on many other economic and social variables makes it probably the best single indicator of the extent of real poverty in a country – is outstandingly high for a country at China's per capita income level." The Bank pointed out in 1983, "the poorest people in China are far better off than their counterparts in most other developing countries."[79]

The government also consistently invested heavily in the education of China's people. In 1949, most children did not attend school at all, fewer than 7 per cent completed primary school, about 2 per cent completed junior middle school, fewer than 1 per cent completed senior middle school and even fewer attended college. In the late 1950s and early 1960s, hundreds of thousands of primary schools and tens of thousands of secondary schools were built in rural areas to ensure that China had the skilled workers it needed for industrial growth across the country.[80]

By 1976, almost all children finished primary school, more than two-thirds completed junior middle school and more than a third completed senior middle school. By 1979, primary school enrolment was 93 per cent, 30 per cent higher than developing countries' average. Secondary school enrolment was 46 per cent, 20 per cent higher than developing countries' average. But tertiary enrolment was below average – only 10 per 10,000, as against India's 60.

Bramall concluded, "China was very unusual amongst developing countries in bringing about a rapid and sustained reduction in the illiteracy rate. ... late Maoist educational policy ... in so far as it allowed students to gain work experience in industry ... may well have accelerated the rate of growth. Late Maoist China did even better in terms of reducing educational inequality. The gap between average levels of attainment in urban and rural areas narrowed. The educational opportunities enjoyed by girls vastly increased. And the traditional link between the level of parental education and the educational opportunities enjoyed by their children was broken. ... late Maoist policy expanded urban middle-school opportunities as well as opportunities in the countryside. It is therefore hard to escape the conclusion that the mass of the Chinese population gained far more than the populations of other developing countries from their government's educational programme during the late Maoist era."[81]

As historian Jack Gray concluded, "integrated village development on the basis of the employment of surplus rural labour is probably the best way forward for most poor countries ..."[82] Bramall observed, "it was the diffusion of skills from urban core to rural periphery, and the learning-by-doing in the primitive rural industries of the Maoist era, which ensured that China entered the 1980s with the workforce needed for rapid industrial expansion. By 1978, an extensive manufacturing capability had been created in rural areas. ... One of the attractions of this learning-by-doing hypothesis is that it explains the gradual acceleration in the growth of rural industrial output during the late 1970s. If policy change had been critical to the process, a much more abrupt discontinuity in the pace of the growth in the early 1970s (following fiscal decentralization) or in the early 1980s (as a result of liberalization of controls on ownership) would be observed. In fact, however, the change was much more gradual. ... this process of urban to rural diffusion was without parallel in the developing world. It is hard to believe that the rural industrial explosion of the 1980s would have occurred in its absence."[83] Bramall summed up, "Mao in his twilight years presided over a remarkable expansion of rural industrial capability – especially skills – which laid the foundation for the extraordinary growth of the 1980s and 1990s and hence provided the basis for rural China's ascent out of poverty."[84]

Female literacy and employment were vital to development and freedom and had the only proven effect on lowering fertility. So China's fertility fell from 6.4 children per woman to 2.7 in the 1970s, before the one-child policy was introduced in 1979.

Students of China agreed that Chinese women made great gains at this time. Sen praised 'China's excellent achievements' in raising the quality of life for women in education, health care, employment and other aspects of gender equality.[85] Delia Davin agreed, "Life expectancy, health, education, work roles, and opportunities for women all improved. Ideas about the transformation of gender roles reached far beyond the urban educated classes to which they had once been largely confined. Maoism was by no means successful in establishing gender equality, but it did preside over an impressive transformation of existing gender divisions. Perhaps most important, by successfully challenging and moving traditional gender boundaries, Maoism showed that these boundaries are not static and can be contested."[86] As Chun Lin noted, "new China's record of pursuing gender equality was outstanding, despite many problems such as in political representation."[87] Nicholas Kristof judged, "The emancipation of women ... moved China from one of the worst places in the world to be a girl to one where women have more equality than in, say, Japan or Korea."[88]

Modern scholars pointed to the Chinese people's great achievements during the Mao era. Sen asserted, "the Maoist policies of land reform, expansion of literacy, enlargement of public health care and so on had a very favourable effect on economic growth in post-reform China. The extent to which *post-reform* China draws on the results achieved in *pre-reform* China needs greater recognition."[89] Kueh judged, "what Mao did as an economic strategist was absolutely necessary ... the economic heritage of Mao has to be assessed in its entirety to include the massive material foundation in both agriculture and industry, that he helped to create with the particular economic strategy practised."[90] Maurice Meisner concluded that China's progress resulting from the revolution 'must be seen as one of the greatest achievements of the twentieth century'. He summed up, "few events in world history have done more to better the lives of more people."[91]

Counter-revolution

China's capitalist class launched its coup d'état in October 1976, after Mao died in September. Mao had warned of the danger of capitalist restoration. Deng Xiao-Ping like Gorbachev promised that his reforms would democratise and revitalise the revolution. But instead they too led to counter-revolution. In 1979, a new Criminal Law listed 14 new 'counter-revolutionary offences' punishable by death.

In 1975, the Fourth National People's Congress, on Mao's recommendation, had added to China's constitution the rights of the people to 'speak out freely, air views freely, hold great debates and write big character posters'. In 1980, the Fifth National People's Congress removed from the constitution these freedoms and the right to strike. In 1982, 5,000,000 people were purged from the party and the state; in Beijing alone, 200,000 government employees were sacked. In 1983, 5,000 people were executed.[92]

When Deng introduced the Household Responsibility System in 1978, rural China returned to the class system of landowners and peasants that had existed before the revolution.[93] Under this system, households owned most of the means of production – capital and farm machinery. Commercial cash crops were developed, agricultural markets liberalised and US agro-business entered the Chinese economy.[94] In northern China, after the collectives were dissolved, herds were distributed to individual households, which bred bigger herds leading to overgrazing.

Some credited decollectivisation with producing faster growth, but actually the faster growth came first. Farm output increased by 8.9 per cent in 1978 and 8.6 per cent in 1979, when by early 1980 only about 1 per cent of farm households had adopted the household responsibility system.[95] Similarly, very fine weather, not decollectivisation, was responsible for the very good grain harvests of 1982 and 1983.[96]

With the ending of the commune system and the commercialisation of agriculture, nearly 200 million rural workers, about half the total, were made redundant. Inequality grew hugely. All forms of social insurance worsened – pensions, social security and health cover.[97] After 1980, 120 million peasants moved into cities, the world's largest migration. Peasant smallholders became wage labourers in 'probably the most massive class transfer in world history'.[98] The working class grew from 118 million in 1978 to 369 million in 2002. It comprised 25 per cent of the world's workers.

China reduced poverty most in the early 1980s when the volumes of trade and foreign direct investment were still tiny.[99] Domestic investment drove this economic growth, not foreign trade and capital flows. Investment accounted for more than 40 per cent of GDP.

When the government opened the door to foreign capital, this brought major financial and industrial joint ventures, special economic zones, coastal free ports and cheap labour export-processing industries.[100] The government designed the tax system, subsidies, trade rules and access to finance, all to favour foreign over domestic firms. It even failed to negotiate technology transfers. So foreign multinationals soon controlled China's high-tech exports and China came to depend on foreign technologies. The opening-up meant a loss of the power to protect infant industries, so with these policies China could never become more than a middle-income country.[101]

Speculation grew bubbles in shares, real estate and unregulated shadow banking. Capitalism brought privatisation, which brought corruption, as officials, cadres and managers stole and sold public goods. Private entrepreneurs got their start-up capital by seizing control of collective fixed assets. Village governments sold their enterprises at extremely low prices.

Mao's successors discriminated against people from poor rural backgrounds, even though devoting resources to rural education was the best way to promote development.[102] The government ended free health care and education, imposing fees for both. In 1994, it shifted responsibility for health care, education and welfare to cash-strapped local government.[103] There were fewer rural primary schools and medical facilities. So, under the new regime, health, productivity, rural incomes and education all worsened. Regional, gender and ethnic inequalities in health and education grew. Between 1980 and 2000, life expectancy rose by only 3.5 years, one of the smallest improvements in the world. Even so, by 2003, it was 71.8 years for men and 73 for women, compared to 64 years in India in 2002.

In the 1990s, China spent only 3 per cent of GDP on education, in 2000, only 2.5 per cent; low-income countries averaged 3.4 per cent. Many schools charged for textbooks and other services.[104] More than twice as many girls as boys did not go to school. Between 2000 and 2005, the number of illiterate adults grew by 30 million, to 113.9 million.

In the 1970s, community medical schemes had covered 90 per cent of the rural population, but by 2003, only 20 per cent. Only 15 per cent of health spending went to rural China, where 70 per cent of people lived. In 1998, 37 per cent of sick rural residents were not treated, because they could not afford the costs of health care. Some local governments charged for immunisation. By 2000, the World Health Organisation ranked China's health care system 144th in the world and ranked it as 188th in 'fairness in financial contributions'.

The UN World Development Report said that China was one of the world's most unequal societies. In particular, women's status worsened dramatically.[105] Many employers openly discriminated against women in hiring. In the large-scale lay-offs in the state-owned industries, women were usually the first to be sacked. The notion that men were more able than women was widely expressed, despite the many years of Maoist education to the contrary. The media and adverts treated women as sex objects or showed them only in domestic roles. Local governments sponsored beauty competitions. Prostitution returned. Young women from poor rural regions were trafficked into sex work.[106]

Capitalism brought layoffs, land thefts, non-payment of wages and pensions, and longer hours. At the end of the 1990s, the state-owned enterprises laid off 30-40 million workers: employment in the public sector was cut from 24 per cent of the labour force in 1996 to 7 per cent in 2003. There were 27 million unemployed in 2002, up from 7 million in 1993. In 2006, fewer than 30 per cent of unemployed men and 25 per cent of unemployed women got unemployment benefits. In 2000, 14 million workers in China's state and collective enterprises were owed wages, up from 2.6 million in 1993. In 1996-2001, in Shenyang, 26.4 per cent of retired workers were owed pensions. 100 million (internal) migrant workers made up 57.5 per cent of China's industrial working class: 75 per cent of them had been owed wages. In Guangdong in 2001, 80 per cent of migrant workers worked more than 10 hours a day, most for between 12 and 14 hours. The change in welfare from a work-unit-based entitlement to a universal human right worsened workers' conditions.[107]

Between 1978 and 2005, labour's share of GDP was cut from 57 per cent to 37 per cent. There were growing divides between rich and poor, between city and countryside and between the east and the west of the country. Household consumption's share of GDP was cut from 45 per cent in 2001 to 34 per cent in 2010, the smallest share in any large economy.[108] The rural tax burden grew. Peasants lost land. Land grabs increased. For example, in 2000, the state seized the land of 40 million villagers, leaving them without land, jobs or social security. Industrial accidents killed an estimated 20,000 workers a year in the early 1990s and injured many more.[109] In 2003, there were 130,000 work-related deaths, in 2010, 79,552.

Poverty grew: in 2002, 45 per cent of people got less than $2 a day. The government declared managing to be legitimate work (which was never in dispute), but did not distinguish between return on capital invested and payment for work done. So the concepts of exploitation and class vanished. China's public ethic in Mao's time was 'serve the people', under Deng it was 'to get rich is glorious'. In 2012, seven billionaires attended the 18th Party Congress.

Exploitation was rife. Wages and working conditions were appalling. In 2004, in a Puma shoe factory run by a Taiwan businessman employing 30,000 workers in Guangdong, the average hourly wage rate was 31 US cents, while the company made $12.24 per worker per hour. Working hours were 7.30 am to 9 pm, sometimes till 12 pm, at the same hourly rate at best. Workers slept in the factory compound, 12 to a room, one bathroom for 100 people. They were not allowed to talk at work and could not leave the compound without permission. There were no health and safety regulations.

Workers making Microsoft mice worked 80-plus hour weeks for 52 cents an hour. Workers making Microsoft keyboards worked 74-hour weeks for 41 cents an hour. Foxconn, which produced iPhones and iPads for Apple, paid its workers 83 cents an hour. Apple had a 64 per cent gross profit margin on its iPhones.[110] But in 2010, there were strikes across China's high-tech export sector, in which workers won 30 per cent wage rises at Foxconn's iPod production centre in Shenzhen and at Honda's factory in Foshan, and 25 per cent wage rises at the Hyundai supplier in Beijing.

China's exploitation of its natural resources caused huge losses of farmland, soil and forest. It cut down half its forests between 1970 and 2010. Air pollution soared. Every year 650,000 to 700,000 people died early because of air pollution. In the most polluted cities, people breathed the equivalent of two packs of cigarettes a day. The World Health Organisation said that 25 micrograms or less of particles of dangerous air pollutants per cubic metre was safe and that 250 micrograms was the danger level. Beijing in January 2014 had 671 micrograms. China had 20 of the world's 30 worst-polluted cities.

Water pollution also increased. Three quarters of China's river water were unfit for drinking or fishing. 700 million people drank water contaminated with human and animal waste. Capitalism had been restored in China, but it was failing China's people.

Chapter 9

Korea

The war against Korea

Korea, like Vietnam, was a single country until 1945. The USA, Britain and the Soviet Union recognised Korea's unity and independence at the Cairo and Moscow conferences.

In 1945, Soviet forces entered the north of Korea to create a defensive barrier against any renewed Japanese aggression. They could have occupied the whole country, but Stalin wanted not territorial gain but an end to Japanese power over the region. So when the US government proposed a temporary division of Korea at the 38th parallel, Stalin accepted, because the USA could help to neutralise Japan.[1] US forces occupied the south.

The three allies agreed that the country would be divided for only a short time and pledged that no foreign troops would stay in Korea. In the north, the Democratic People's Republic of Korea (DPRK) was founded in 1948. American historian Melvyn Leffler wrote, "With the help of Soviet occupation forces and with considerable indigenous support, Kim assumed power in North Korea …"[2] Many of its leading figures had been guerrilla fighters against the Japanese Empire. The DPRK asked all occupying forces to leave. The Soviet Union withdrew its forces in late 1948. The DPRK gave equal rights to women and land to the peasants, nationalised basic industries and set about rebuilding the country. GNP doubled between 1946 and 1949.

The south had most of the country's good farmland (only 18-20 per cent of the north was arable land) and most of its industry. To run the south, the US occupiers appointed wealthy landlords and businessmen who had collaborated with the Japanese occupiers. Some had even been officers in the Japanese Imperial Army. Leffler noted, "In 1948 they formed a government in South Korea under Syngman Rhee, a conservative authoritarian nationalist who aspired to unite all of Korea under his own auspices."[3] In the late 1940s, US aid to the Republic of Korea [ROK] was $220 million a year - more than its aid to Greece and Turkey combined. An American journalist wrote, "only American money, weapons, and technical assistance enable [the ROK] to exist more than a few hours."[4] The ROK was a disaster: even the British Foreign Office admitted its 'black reaction, brutality and extreme incompetence'.[5]

The US and British governments claimed that the Korean War started in June 1950, but war started well before then. In April 1947, Ryu, the US-appointed governor of the South Korean island of Cheju-do, 'initiated a yearlong reign of terror' against the island's civilian population.[6] American historian Sheila Miyoshi Jager pointed out, "[W]hole villages became targets, innocent suspects were beaten and hanged, and women and children massacred. A reign of terror largely perpetrated by government forces, the police, and the Republic of Korea Army ... gripped the island. ... By the end of June 1949, an estimated thirty thousand had been killed in Cheju-do, many of them innocent civilians massacred by government forces. ... Some of the worst atrocities were committed by South Koreans against South Koreans. ... Caught in the roundup of suspected leftists and communists were innocent civilians, including women and children who were summarily executed in the thousands in the name of fighting the communists. It is estimated that at least a hundred thousand South Koreans were killed in the summer of 1950."[7] The US Military Mission to Korea organised and armed these forces, gave them their best intelligence materials, planned their actions and sometimes commanded them.[8]

Fighting at the 38th parallel started in January 1949 and flared up in the summer. US Army staff stated that ROK forces started most of the skirmishes.[9] The ROK army tried to occupy Haeju, attacking across the 38th parallel from Ongjin.[10] In October 1949, General William Roberts, Head of the US Military Mission, said, "Certainly there have been many attacks on the territory north of the 38th parallel on my orders . . . From now on, the invasion by the land forces of the territory north of the 38th parallel is to be carried out only on the basis of orders of the American military mission." In March 1950, the US government voted an extra $11 million military aid to the ROK. In early May, fighting along the 38th parallel grew into battles between thousands of soldiers with hundreds of casualties.[11]

In the ROK's May 1950 elections, President Rhee's party got just 18 seats in an Assembly of 218, which voted overwhelmingly for peaceful reunification. UN Resolutions obliged the US government to end its military support for Rhee by June 1950. Rhee publicly proposed invading the North and incited raids across the 38th parallel.[12] In early June, ROK forces crossed the parallel.

Bruce Cumings, the leading American historian of Korea, noted, "Then there was John Burton, mild-mannered professor of Political Science at George Mason University, who had been the very young head of the Australian Foreign Office in 1950. He told us of telegrams coming from South Korea to the Foreign Office just before the war broke out, reporting South Korea patrols crossing the border, trying to provoke the North Koreans. Dr Burton took these straight to the Foreign Minister and the Prime Minister, 'and we sent a very strongly worded telegram to the State Department', asking them to curb South Korea adventurism. Before a reply came back from Washington, the war began. ... Thereafter the telegrams, according to Dr Burton, disappeared from Australian Foreign Office files."[13]

The Korean War was far from being a simple matter of the 'North' invading the 'South'. Even on this account, it would be a war of Koreans against Koreans, a civil war, in which no other country had any right to interfere. The notion that a country called Korea was 'invading' another country, also called Korea, surely raised questions in people's minds. As Richard Stokes, Britain's Minister of Works, commented in 1950, "In the American Civil War the Americans would never have tolerated for a single moment the setting up of an imaginary line between the forces of North and South, and there can be no doubt as to what would have been their reaction if the British had intervened in force on behalf of the South. This parallel is a close one because in America the conflict was not merely between two groups of Americans, but was between two conflicting economic systems as is the case in Korea."[14]

Or imagine that in 1861 Korea had sent troops to the USA to attack Union forces fighting against the Confederate states and that after three years of war, and killing two million US citizens, they held the Mason-Dixon Line and kept the country divided, allowing the South to keep its slaves. That would be the equivalent of what US forces did in 1950-53.

In the UN Security Council, the US government, to secure the enabling Resolution, claimed that the Soviet Union was involved in starting the war. But when a US State Department team combed the archives of the occupied DPRK, later in 1950, for evidence of Soviet complicity, it found none.[15] Further, the Resolution which supposedly authorised the UN intervention was invalid, since Article 27(3) of the UN Charter stated that substantive Resolutions must receive the 'concurring votes' of all the Security Council's permanent members, yet the Soviet representative was absent.

President Truman ordered US armed forces into war in Korea. He ordered the Seventh Fleet into the Taiwan Strait between the mainland of the People's Republic of China (PRC) and Taiwan - an undeclared act of war, which saved Chiang Kai-Shek's regime in Taiwan. Truman sent a Military Mission and more aid to the French forces fighting against Vietnam and started secretly to supply Tibetan rebels (even though the USA recognised Tibet as part of China). Britain's Labour government at once sent British forces into Korea.

The British armed forces yearbook for 1951 reported, "the war was fought without regard for the South Koreans, and their unfortunate country was regarded as an arena rather than a country to be liberated. As a consequence, fighting was quite ruthless, and it is no exaggeration to state that South Korea no longer exists as a country. Its towns have been destroyed, much of its means of livelihood eradicated, and its people reduced to a sullen mass dependent upon charity. The South Korean, unfortunately, was regarded as a 'gook', like his cousins north of the 38th parallel."[16]

The US Army banned all fraternisation with Koreans. It 'treated the South Koreans like untouchables', as First Lieutenant Robert Shackleton, an American advisor to the Korean Constabulary, complained.[17] Private Mario Scarselleta of the 35th Infantry admitted, "I couldn't get over how cruel we were to the prisoners we captured."[18] Millett observed, "[T]he Commonwealth Brigade, especially the Australians, shot first and asked questions later."[19] In the 1950 No Gun Ri massacre, in South Korea, as Robin Andersen noted, "Roughly three hundred civilians, many of them women and children, were bombed and strafed from the air by U.S. gunner pilots under direct military command to do so."[20]

On 7 October 1950, the UN General Assembly passed a resolution proposed by Britain's Labour government, "1.a) All appropriate steps be taken to ensure conditions of stability throughout Korea; b) all constituent acts be taken, including the holding of elections, under the auspices of the U.N., for the establishing of a united, independent and democratic government in the sovereign state of Korea." That same day, US troops first invaded the DPRK, crossing the 38th Parallel. This threatened China's north-east. The next day, Chinese forces entered the war. As Warren Cohen later judged, "prudence required China to intervene in Korea."[21]

In October 1950, the USAF bombed targets in China. On 9 October, two USAF jets raided 'by mistake' a Soviet airfield 60 miles inside the Soviet border, near Vladivostok. In July 1952 and May 1953, the USAF again bombed towns in China.

In the war against Korea, the USAF dropped more bombs on Korea than it had on Europe in World War Two. It dropped more than a million gallons of napalm. The US Army joined in the destruction. US Colonel Harry Summers wrote of "the horrors of the 'scorched earth' policy during our retreat from North Korea in the winter of 1950. On the explicit orders of the Eighth U.S. Army commander [General Walton Walker], all houses were burnt, all livestock killed, and all food supplies destroyed."[22] MacArthur ordered his forces to "destroy every means of communication, every installation, factory, city and village from the front line to the Yalu River."[23] He later admitted that his scorched earth policy had created 'a wasteland' in the DPRK.[24] Dean Rusk, then Assistant Secretary of State for Far Eastern Affairs, said that the USAF bombed 'everything that moved, every brick standing on top of another brick'.[25] An official communiqué said, "It's hard to find good targets, for we have burned out almost everything."[26] General Curtis LeMay, who ran the bombing war, said, "over a period of three years or so ... we burned down *every* town in North Korea and South Korea, too."[27] President Eisenhower ordered the bombing of all the dams in the DPRK - a war crime.

It was, as Cumings summed up, "three years of genocidal bombing by the US Air Force which killed perhaps two million civilians (one-quarter of the population), dropped oceans of napalm, left barely a modern building standing, opened large dams to flood nearby rice valleys and kill thousands of peasants by denying them food, and went far beyond anything done in Vietnam in a conscious program of using air power to destroy a society ..."[28] He rightly called it 'one of the most appalling, unrestrained, genocidal bombing campaigns in our genocidal twentieth century ...'[29] The war caused three million military casualties. A tenth of Korea's people were killed, wounded or missing.

Still no peace

But at last the Armistice was signed in July 1953. Eisenhower accepted the deal that Truman had rejected: the US government, not the DPRK, changed its position. General Mark Clark became the first US general to agree to end a war with no official victor. The Chinese and Korean forces had 'fought the world's greatest power to a standstill' and defeated its plans to occupy all Korea and invade China.[30] The American people rejected the war and its author: Secretary of State Dean Acheson admitted that the war 'demolished' Truman's administration.

In the five years after the 1953 Armistice Agreement, the US government broke all the terms stopping it turning the ROK into a military and nuclear base. The Agreement banned the introduction of qualitatively new weapons, but the US government introduced nuclear weapons.[31] The US government backed the military dictatorships which ran the ROK from 1960 to 1987, even when General Chun Doo-hwan's regime killed 2,000 pro-democracy demonstrators in Kwangju in 1980. It also broke Article 15 of the Agreement by starting a blockade of the DPRK which it has maintained ever since.

In the 1950s and the early 1960s, the DPRK grew by more than 20 per cent a year. As Cumings observed, "Industrialisation on the Soviet model made North Korea perhaps the fastest growing postcolonial country in the world in the 1950s and 1960s."[32] Machine-building and metal-working industries' share of the economy rose from 1.6 per cent in 1944 to 31.4 per cent in 1967. Industrial output grew from 16.8 per cent of GNP in 1946 to 57.3 per cent in 1970. Between 1946 and 1987, the proportion of industrial workers in the population grew from 12.5 per cent to 57 per cent. A CIA study "acknowledged various achievements of this regime: compassionate care for children in general and war orphans in particular, 'radical change' in the position of women; genuinely free housing, free health care and preventive medicine; and infant mortality and life expectancy rates comparable to the most advanced countries until the recent famine."[33]

After the collapse of the Soviet Union, the DPRK faced huge problems. The US government maintained its punitive sanctions. The Russian government cut its oil supplies to the DPRK by 90 per cent. Nicholas Eberstadt, of the American Enterprise Institute, forecast 'The coming collapse of North Korea' in the *Wall Street Journal* as early as 25

June 1990.[34] In 1992, Aidan Foster-Carter, Honorary Senior Research Fellow in Sociology and Modern Korea at Leeds University, forecast that the DPRK would collapse by 1995.[35] Deputy Secretary of Defense Paul Wolfowitz said in June 2003, "North Korea is teetering on the brink of collapse."[36]

In 1993, the DPRK withdrew from the Non-Proliferation Treaty, so it was no longer bound by its provisions. In 1994, the USA and the DPRK signed the Agreed Framework, the only agreement ever signed between the two countries.

In 1995-96, the DPRK suffered catastrophic floods, hurricanes and drought. The 1995 floods wrecked 330,000 hectares of arable land just before harvest time, destroying nearly two million tonnes of grain (half the year's harvest) and three million tonnes of emergency grain stores. The floods made five million people homeless. The damage cost the country $15 billion. In 1997, drought destroyed 70 per cent of the country's corn. In 2000-01, the country suffered the worst drought in its history.

Despite all these hardships, the DPRK honoured the 1994 Agreement. It carried out its one specific commitment, to suspend its plutonium production facilities (Provision I.3). It warned that if the US government did not supply the promised energy sources, it would have to restart its nuclear power programme.

The US government, on the other hand, failed to install the promised 2,000 megawatts of nuclear-powered generating capacity to replace the DPRK's plutonium-producing reactors. It did not normalise political and economic relations, as it had promised, and it did not give 'formal assurances against the threat or use of nuclear weapons by the United States' (Provision III).[37]

In January 2002, President George W. Bush named the DPRK as part of the 'Axis of Evil' and named it as a target in the Nuclear Posture Review and again in September in the National Security Strategy. The DPRK declared that it had the right to develop nuclear weapons in response to these US threats. In October, the DPRK offered to shut down its nuclear programme if the US government committed itself again to normalise relations and not to attack the DPRK. The US government refused, and rejected any more negotiations. In December, the US government cancelled its promised oil shipments. The US government had torn up the treaty.

In 2005, Bush wanted the UN to impose sanctions on the DPRK; China, Russia and the ROK refused. In 2007, the US government still had 37,000 troops illegally occupying the ROK and planned to spend an extra $11 billion tightening its grip there. The Defence Minister of Japan, the US government's main ally in the region, sought a law allowing Japan to launch a pre-emptive strike on the DPRK.

The DPRK had every right to defend itself against threats to its existence. Even ROK President Roh Moo-hyun pointed out, "North Korea professes that nuclear capabilities are a deterrent for defending itself from external aggression. In this particular case it is true and undeniable that there is a considerable element of rationality in North Korea's claim."

NATO's illegal attack on Libya showed that if a country gave up its nuclear programme, it would be more vulnerable to attack. Within days of the NATO attack, a senior North Korean official said that NATO's 2003 deal, that Gaddafi gave up his nuclear programme in exchange for better relations with the West, had been 'an invasion tactic to disarm the country'.[38] The NATO powers would not bomb nuclear-armed North Korea the way they bombed Gaddafi's denuclearised Libya.

Chapter 10
Vietnam and South-East Asia

Colonial wars

At the end of World War Two, across South-East Asia, the major colonial powers, Britain, France and the Netherlands, sought to restore their rule. But the peoples of all South-East Asia's countries had no wish to be ruled in the old way. The French government sent armed forces into Vietnam and Laos, and the Dutch government sent troops into Indonesia. The British and US forces in the region did all they could to assist the French and Dutch governments.

In late 1945, the Labour government sent troops to Indonesia. They rearmed Japanese troops, who had killed 3.7 million Indonesians during their occupation and who now killed another 7,000 Indonesians. The Royal Navy ferried in Dutch troops. The British forces killed more than 15,000 Indonesians.[1]

The Labour government also sent forces to Malaya to restore Britain's colonial rule. Malaya was the Empire's biggest asset. Between 1949 and 1953, it sent £204 million in profits, interest and dividends to shareholders in Britain. The war lasted from 1948 to 1960. Field Marshal Sir Gerald Templer, who was both High Commissioner and Director of Operations, admitted that the people of Malaya opposed British rule when he said, "If only I had the support of the Malayan people I could bring this war to a speedy ending." The government called the war 'the emergency' because, as the Colonial Secretary admitted, "if we called this war we should presumably have to deal with our prisoners under international Conventions, which would not allow us to be as ruthless as we are now."[2]

The army forcibly resettled 1.2 million people, a seventh of the population, into barbed wire-enclosed 'strategic hamlets' that were no better than concentration camps.[3] British forces used chemicals to destroy food crops. In 1955 alone, the RAF dropped 5,089 1000-pound bombs, 5,712 500-pound bombs, 2,660 20-pound fragmentation bombs and 3,096 rocket projectiles.[4]

Templer said he used "special squads of jungle fighters . . . they will really be 'killer squads' (though I promise you I won't call them that, with a view to the questions in the House.)"[5] British forces sometimes massacred innocent civilians. A subaltern serving with 6th Malay Regiment wrote in 1953, "No Chinese rubber tapper is safe when we search an estate, my men are trigger-happy with Chinese, and several platoon commanders have had to plant grenades on tappers and call them bandits when their men have made 'a small error in judgement'."[6] British forces effectively operated a shoot-to kill policy in Malaya.[7] An estimated 4,000 civilians were killed.

Historians have detailed the repression. Bruno Reis pointed out, "In the Malayan campaign manual there was a detailed section devoted to Emergency Regulations. However, the dominant tone was enabling not restrictive: it was oriented towards showing how this special legislation could be put to the best possible operational use. These regulations included: the right to shoot without warning in war areas; or in all areas after due warning; or in order to prevent captured insurgents from escaping, which amounted to a potential blank cheque for summary executions; as well as virtually unlimited powers of detention, deportation, resettlement and collective punishment."[8] The manual laid down a mandatory death penalty for carrying arms, and life imprisonment for providing food or other support to the rebels.

As Calder Walton wrote, "during the Emergency, Malaya effectively became a police state."[9]

All this left a dreadful legacy: as Caroline Elkins stated, "repressive laws and undemocratic institutions, not peace and progress, were the primary bequest of the British to Malaya."[10] Christopher Hale summed up, "The Emergency War in Malaya was a nasty and brutal business that had unintended consequences which punish and divide the people of Southeast Asia to this day."[11]

But this war was all too typical of Britain's wars to keep the empire. Between 1945 and 1968, the British state deployed its military forces overseas more often than either the USA or the Soviet Union, in more than 20 countries in nearly every region of the world. These were dirty wars. As military historian David French asserted, "British counter-insurgency doctrine, as it was practised in Palestine, Malaya, Kenya, and Cyprus, deliberately targeted the civilian population. Coercion took various forms, ranging from cordon and search operations, collective punishments, detention without trial on a sometimes massive scale, right up to the creation of free fire zones. But in every case civilians were always in the front line."[12] As Hale noted, "Violence was integral to 'the British way in counter insurgency'."[13]

Douglas Porch wrote of these wars, "most proved to be protracted, unlimited, murderous, expensive, total-war assaults on indigenous societies. ... the true key to success was pitilessly to target anyone and anything that sustained the insurgency. In this way, colonial warfare simply boiled down to national displacement and ruining the countryside by making it unlivable. ... imperial Britain's small wars retained their dirty, violent, racist character ..."[14] As he summed up, all these wars resulted in "the institutionalization of collective punishment, torture, resettlement, internment, special night squads/ferret forces/counter gangs, and RAF terror bombing for imperial policing. The key to success was to rebrand these kinetic methods as hearts and minds and prosecute it out of public view. ... villages might be bombed from the air, shelled, burned, or simply knocked down, wells poisoned, crops fumigated or destroyed, livestock slaughtered, the wounded executed, and the population displaced."[15]

Vietnam's victory

Vietnam, like Korea, was until 1945 a single united country. In 1945, the people of Vietnam made their revolution and evicted the French, in the first overthrow of a colonial state, and President Ho Chi Minh declared the Democratic Republic of Vietnam (DRV), establishing state power in the north of the country.

But in October, the Labour government authorised British troops 'throughout Southern French IndoChina, to maintain order in support of the French government'. British forces assisted the French coup against the Viet Minh administration in Saigon and imposed martial law throughout South Vietnam. Their commander, General Douglas Gracey, boasted, "I was welcomed on arrival by the VietMinh . . . I promptly kicked them out." The British and US governments divided Vietnam, supposedly temporarily.

From 1946, French governments fought to reimpose their colonial rule over Vietnam. But the Vietnamese people gradually wore down the French forces. Finally, the French risked a set-piece battle at Dien Bien Phu in April 1954. Towards the end of the battle, the French government, desperate to avoid defeat, begged the Eisenhower government to launch a huge bombing raid on the Vietminh forces. Eisenhower said that he would only intervene if the Churchill government did too. To their credit, Churchill and Foreign Secretary Anthony Eden refused. Eisenhower then tried to get the Australian government to intervene. It too refused. Its allies forced the US government not to intervene.

This Vietnamese victory crowned their successful struggle. As American historian Fredrik Logevall summed up, "The Battle of Dien Bien Phu was over. The Viet Minh had won. Vo Nguyen Giap had overturned history, had accomplished the unprecedented, had beaten the West at its own game. For the first time in the annals of colonial warfare, Asian troops had defeated a European army in fixed battle."[16]

But in their eight-year war, French forces killed 175,000 Vietminh fighters and at least 300,000 civilians. The French wrecked much of the country. When they left, they dismantled hospitals and stripped factories of tools, machinery, even lightbulbs.[17]

Vietnam's 1953 Law on Farm Land Reforms confiscated the farms of colonial and feudal owners, landlords and capitalists, and gave the land to more than half of all families, under the slogan of 'farms to the cultivators'. Ho Chi Minh tried to curb any excesses. When a people's tribunal had a woman landlord executed, he said, "The French say that one should never hit a woman, even with a flower, and you, you allowed her to be shot!" On 8 February 1955, at a conference on land reform, he said, "Some cadres are using the same methods to crush the masses as the imperialists, capitalists, and feudalists did. These methods are barbaric. ... *It is absolutely forbidden to use physical punishment.*"[18]

At the 1954 Geneva Peace Conference, the British, French, Chinese and Soviet governments agreed, "In their relations with Cambodia, Laos and Vietnam, each member of the Geneva Conference undertakes to respect the sovereignty, the independence, the unity and the territorial integrity of the above-mentioned states and to refrain from any interference in their internal affairs."[19] President Eisenhower pledged the USA not to violate the Accords. The four governments, and the USA, all promised to back 'general elections which will bring about the unification of VietNam'.[20] These 'free general elections by secret ballot' were to be held under UN supervision in July 1956. The Final Act of the Accords defined Vietnam as one state and nation. Part 6 stated, "the military demarcation line is provisional and should not in any way be interpreted as constituting a political or territorial boundary."

On 21 July 1954, a US government spokesman pledged that it 'will refrain from the threat or use of force to disturb [the Accords] ... [and] shall continue to seek to achieve unity through free elections'. But, as they all knew, Ho Chi Minh would have won about 80 per cent of the votes in an election. So the US and British governments backed the regime in the South, the Republic of Vietnam led by President Diem, when it attacked those calling for an election. As American historian George Herring commented later, "Violating the letter and spirit of the Geneva Accords, the United States backed Diem's refusal to participate in the national elections."[21] The regime killed 76,000 people between 1954 and 1961. American historian Joseph Buttinger noted, "thousands of Communists as well as non-Communist sympathizers of the Vietminh were killed and many more thrown into prison and concentration camps . . . all of this happened more than two years before the Communists began to commit acts of terror against local government officials."[22] Douglas Valentine, the historian of the USA's Phoenix programme, concluded, "Diem's security forces terrorized the Vietnamese people more than the VCI [Vietcong infrastructure]."[23]

The US government attacks Vietnam

Successive US governments had no intention of honouring their pledges. Walt Rostow, President Kennedy's deputy special assistant for national security affairs, said on 28 June 1961, "The sending of men across international boundaries ... is aggression."[24] But the Geneva Accords had explicitly stated that the demarcation line between the North and South of Vietnam was not an international boundary. So when the DRV sent men into the South, it was not aggression. But when the USA sent men into Vietnam, it was aggression.

Walter Lippmann affirmed, "the easy way to avoid the truth is to persuade ourselves that this is not really a civil war but is in fact essentially an invasion of South VietNam by North VietNam. This has produced the argument that the way to stabilize South VietNam is wage war against North VietNam."[25] The claim that a country called Vietnam was 'invading' another country, also called Vietnam, surely raised questions in people's minds.

The US government violated the Accords' neutrality provisions by giving huge support to Diem. It carried out covert military operations and psychological warfare against the North.[26] Kennedy started the war when he sent 16,000 military 'advisers' to Vietnam, far more than allowed by the Accords.[27] Some of these 'advisers' fought alongside

Diem's army units and a hundred of them were killed. US pilots flew combat and bombing missions.[28]

Kennedy never wanted negotiations.[29] As Logevall commented, "In 1963, the Kennedy administration opposed any move to bring about an early diplomatic settlement, as it had since it came into office and as its predecessor had done before that. From January 1961 to November 1963, the administration adhered firmly to the position that the insurgency in the South had to be defeated and that no diplomacy should be undertaken until that result was ensured. Negotiations should be entered into only when there was nothing to negotiate."[30]

Kennedy's successor, President Johnson, also opposed negotiations. In the US election of November 1964, the American people voted for peace and got war. Logevall noted, "Goldwater's general Vietnam policy before election day would become Johnson's Vietnam policy thereafter. A Herblock cartoon some months later got it right – it showed LBJ looking into a mirror and seeing Goldwater's face staring back at him."[31] Johnson promised 'no wider war' and then sent more than 500,000 US troops. The supposed rationale was the 'domino' theory. As Wyoming Democrat Senator Gale McGee told his colleagues, "If Vietnam goes, Cambodia goes, Thailand goes, Malaysia goes, Indonesia goes, the Philippines go …"[32] Except that they didn't go. Even the dominos did not believe in the domino theory.

The US government's supposed justification for attacking Vietnam was the Tonkin Gulf Incident of 4 August 1964, when US naval vessels attacked Vietnam.[33] As the CIA's Director testified, "The North Vietnamese are reacting defensively to our attacks on their offshore islands."[34] The USA attacked Vietnam, not vice versa. The British government backed the US aggression by all means short of direct military intervention, including 'in country' operations by SIS and special forces.[35]

The British and US governments support the coup in Indonesia

The US and British governments both wanted to oust Indonesia's President Dewi Sukarno, who had led Indonesia's independence struggle against the Dutch government. From 1958 to 1965, the US government trained, funded, advised and supplied Indonesia's army so that it could launch a coup.[36] The army's scheme was to blame the Indonesian Communist Party [PKI] for an attempted coup, launch a full-scale war on the party, keep Sukarno as a figurehead president and take over the government. The army kept the US embassy informed, and knew that it could count on US diplomatic, military and economic support.[37] In 1962, President Kennedy and Prime Minister Harold Macmillan 'agreed to liquidate President Sukarno'.[38]

Edward Peck, assistant secretary of state in the Foreign Office, said on 27 November 1964, "there might therefore be much to be said for encouraging a premature PKI coup during Sukarno's lifetime."[39] The US Ambassador to Indonesia, Howard P. Jones, said on 10 March 1965, "From our viewpoint, of course, an unsuccessful coup attempt by the PKI might be the most effective development to start a reversal of political trends in Indonesia."[40] In May, the Indonesian government released a copy of a telegram from the British Ambassador to the Foreign Office which noted that 'our local army friends' were working on a secret 'enterprise'.[41]

On 5 October, the US Ambassador urged Washington to 'Spread the story of PKI's guilt, treachery and brutality', adding that this was 'perhaps the most needed immediate assistance we can give army if we can find way to do it without identifying it as solely or largely US effort'.[42] Also on 5 October, the British Ambassador in Jakarta, Sir Andrew Gilchrist, told the Foreign Office, "a little shooting in Indonesia would be an essential preliminary to change.... The crucial question still remains whether the generals will pluck up enough courage to take decisive action."

The Foreign Office replied that the generals are 'going to need all the help they can get' and pledged British backing.[43] The Foreign Office hoped to 'encourage anti-Communist Indonesians to more vigorous action in the hope of crushing Communism in Indonesia altogether'.[44] On 9 October, it reported that it was mounting 'short term unattributable ploys designed to keep the Indonesian pot boiling'.[45] In February 1965, the Foreign Office's Information Research Department, which produced black propaganda, set up the South East Asia Monitoring Unit in Singapore to focus the propaganda war. In July, the Foreign Office appointed a Political Warfare Coordinator in Singapore.[46] The governments of Britain, the USA, Australia and Malaysia all used the media to blame the PKI.[47]

In November, the leading Indonesian general, Major-General Suharto, ordered the destruction of the PKI, claiming he was preventing a revolution. The generals and their apologists accused the PKI of being innately genocidal, a projection to excuse their own genocide.[48] Neither the PKI, nor President Sukarno, had prepared a coup.[49] As the Australian Joint Intelligence Committee acknowledged, "evidence of actual PKI involvement – that is of prior planning by the Central Committee – is largely circumstantial."[50]

The US Ambassador wrote that he 'made it clear that Embassy and USG generally sympathetic with and admiring of what army doing'.[51] When the generals approached the US and British governments for more arms for the killing, they duly provided. The CIA gave the army lists of names – list A, those to be killed, list B, those to be imprisoned - just as it had given lists of names to the Guatemalan army for its 1954 coup.[52] This was standard CIA procedure, also used in Chile in 1971.[53]

Harold Wilson's Labour government also supplied the generals with intelligence. Britain became the largest seller of arms to Indonesia and gave Suharto £2 billions' worth of export credits. British companies supplied bombs, Hawk ground-attack aircraft, Tactica riot-control vehicles and machine-guns. British warships escorted a ship taking Indonesian troops through the Malacca Straits so that they could join in the killing. The government downgraded its commitment to Borneo in order to avoid 'biting the Generals in the rear', as the British Ambassador said.[54]

The army and other forces killed perhaps a million trade unionists, members of peasant organisations and others. President Richard Nixon boasted that the US aggression in Vietnam 'provided a shield behind which the anti-communist forces found the courage and capacity to stage their counter-coup'.[55]

US war crimes in Vietnam

Meanwhile, in Vietnam, every US army division in Vietnam between 1965 and 1973 committed war crimes, as a 1970s Pentagon study found. A 1968 memorandum by a US Deputy Chief of Staff admitted, "The incidents authoritatively alleged show a cruel, sophisticated, calculated torture for information and make pious hypocritical arguments of statements about our treatment of POWs by the President …"[56] Chief of Staff Harold K. Johnson stated that American prisoners in the hands of the Vietnamese seemed to have been better treated than vice versa.[57] Lieutenant Francis Reitemeyer recalled that he was taught to use 'the most extreme forms of torture' at the Army Intelligence School at Fort Holabird.[58]

The USA's Phoenix programme was an assault on the Vietnamese people. After the 1971 Congressional hearings, Congress members Pete McCloskey, John Conyers, Ben Rosenthal and Bella Abzug concluded, "the Phoenix program is an instrument of terror; that torture is a regularly accepted part of interrogation … U.S. civilians and military personnel have participated for over three years in the deliberate denial of due process of law to thousands of people held in secret interrogation centers built with U.S. dollars."[59]

Corporal Bart Osborn testified of the operations he knew about, "I never knew in the course of all those operations any detainee to live through his interrogation. They all died. There was never any reasonable establishment of the fact that any one of those individuals was, in fact, cooperating with the VC, but they all died and the majority were either tortured to death or things like thrown out of helicopters."[60] The CIA's chief of operations in I Corps in 1970 admitted, "Sure we got involved in assassinations. That's what PRU [Provincial Reconnaissance Units] were set up for – assassination. I'm sure the word never appeared in any outlines or policy directives, but what else do you call a targeted kill?"[61]

Journalist Don Luce called the South a 'Prison Regime' and wrote, "Phoenix was created, organized and funded by the CIA. The district and provincial interrogation centers were constructed with American funds, and provided with American advisers. Quotas were set by Americans. The national system of identifying suspects was devised by Americans and underwritten by the U.S. Informers are paid with US funds. American tax dollars have covered the expansion of the police and paramilitary units who arrest suspects."[62] By 1972, there were an estimated 200,000 political prisoners in the South.

Vietnam's victory

It was always a national liberation struggle, waged by the whole Vietnamese people. Even CIA consultant Thomas L. Ahern Jr. acknowledged, "It is now clear that Hanoi directed an insurgency based on indigenous cadre organization drawn largely from the Southern peasantry."[63] Ho Chi Minh asked President Johnson in 1966, "Who has sabotaged the Geneva Agreements which guaranteed the sovereignty, independence, unity and territorial integrity of Vietnam? Have Vietnamese troops invaded the United States and massacred Americans? Or isn't it the US government which, on the contrary, has sent US troops to invade Vietnam and massacre the Vietnamese people?"[64]

Tran Thi Tung, a Viet Minh member, said, "I never felt guilty about the killing I did. It was war. Wouldn't you shoot me if you saw me holding a weapon and pointing it at you? I think it was justified. But if I went to America and killed people there, I would feel very sorry and guilty. Since the Americans came to my country, I don't feel guilty."[65]

The best estimate, by researchers from Harvard Medical School and the Institute for Health Metrics and Evaluation at the University of Washington, is that the US war caused 3.8 million deaths, including two million civilians killed.[66] In addition, 5.3 million civilians were injured, a quarter of them children under 13 years old. Years later, years too late, US Defense Secretary Robert McNamara admitted that the war was 'wrong, terribly wrong'.[67]

The USAF dropped more bombs on Vietnam than on all targets in all history. The US assault caused 'the utter destruction of much of the country of Vietnam and large portions of Laos and Cambodia'.[68] Author Arthur Westing reported, "Despite a year of frontline combat experience in Korea, and despite three previous trips to Indochina to study the war zones of Cambodia and South Vietnam, I was unprepared for the utter devastation that confronted us wherever we turned. Our tour took us through much of the lowland region and some of the central hilly region. Never were we out of sight of an endless panorama of crater fields. As far as we could determine not a single permanent building, urban or rural, remained intact: no private dwellings, no schools, no libraries, no churches or pagodas and no hospitals. Moreover, every last bridge and even culvert had been bombed to bits."[69]

US forces dropped 19 million gallons of defoliants on the South, destroying 12 million acres of forest. US forces evicted five million peasants from their homes. Valentine observed, "The massive bombing campaign turned much of Laos and Cambodia into a wasteland. The same was true in South Vietnam, where the strategy was to demoralize the Communists by blowing their villages to smithereens. Because of the devastation the bombing wrought, half a million Vietnamese refugees had fled their villages and were living in temporary shelters by the end of 1965, while another half million were wandering around in shock, homeless."[70] As McNamara told Johnson, "the picture of the world's greatest superpower killing or seriously injuring 1,000 non-combatants a week, while trying to pound a tiny, backward nation into submission on an issue whose merits are hotly disputed, is not a pretty one."[71]

The US tried to impose such costs on the Vietnamese people that they would give up their struggle for independence. Yet in 1975, all US forces left Vietnam. The Vietnamese people instead imposed such costs on the invader that it had to leave. They decisively defeated the USA.

After the war, the British and US governments, and the EEC, punished Vietnam, Cambodia and Laos by cutting off all food shipments, aid and trade. The $4.75 billion reconstruction aid that Nixon had promised was never given.

Vietnam did its best to rebuild its economy. It put more resources into education and health care, so literacy levels soared and disease rates fell. It also aided Cambodia. It sent 100,000 tons of rice, 20,000 tons of seed rice, three million metres of cloth and 500,000 ploughs to help feed and clothe the Cambodian people and to revive their farms. It sent medical aid, nurses and doctors. It also sent workers to purify the water, build schools and hospitals, generate electricity and repair Kampong Sam, the country's only deep-water port. Laos and Vietnam signed a treaty of friendship and cooperation in 1977. Cambodia and Vietnam did likewise in 1979 and so did Cambodia and Laos.

But in Cambodia, Pol Pot's Khmer Rouge government killed a fifth of the population and destroyed industry and services. Then, backed by the US government, it attacked Vietnam in 1977-79, killing 30,000 Vietnamese and displacing hundreds of thousands of people.

The Vietnamese defeated these attacks and in January 1979 the National United Front for the Salvation of Kampuchea, supported by Vietnam's armed forces, overthrew Pol Pot. Vietnam acted in accordance with UN Resolutions on the rights and duties of nations to support national liberation movements. And, as British journalist William Shawcross judged, "For the overwhelming majority of the Cambodian people the invasion meant freedom."[72] The new Cambodian government ended the killing, started to rebuild the country and quickly got food and aid to the people.

But the NATO powers and the EEC, now joined by the Chinese government, did all they could to make it hard for Vietnam, Cambodia and Laos to rebuild their shattered societies. The EEC withheld UNICEF food aid from Vietnam and Cambodia.[73] In 1979, Chinese forces, backed by the US government, invaded Vietnam, laying waste its six northern provinces before Vietnamese forces threw them out.

The UN Legal Bureau ruled that aiding Pol Pot was unjustifiable. But for a decade US and British governments recognised, funded and armed his forces. Prime Minister Margaret Thatcher sent 250 'special forces' personnel to train Pol Pot's forces in sabotage and laying anti-personnel mines.[74] Yet she told Parliament that there was 'no British Government involvement of any kind in training, equipping or cooperating with the Khmer Rouge forces or those allied to them'.[75]

The US government imposed sanctions on Vietnam, Laos and Cambodia until 1995. US ally Thailand waged border wars against Laos in 1984 and 1987-88, and China backed anti-government rebels in Laos, Cambodia and Vietnam until 1990.

Sugar-coated bullets

But Vietnam, having defeated first Japanese, then French and then US military aggression, succumbed to the sugar-coated bullets of the NATO powers' economic aggression. Vietnam had been continuously under attack for some 35 years. Its people faced the huge task of rebuilding their war-torn country. Yet its economy was still largely based on subsistence farming and small-scale local trade. Just five per cent of the relatively advanced part of Vietnam's economy was under state control.

Were they to rely on their own resources, or on foreign investment? Investing in increasing output per worker was the best way to raise living standards.[76] But instead, and unlike Cuba, the Vietnamese government chose to try to compete with other poor countries in a race to the bottom by offering low-wage workers to foreign companies. The government chose to obey IMF/World Bank orders to encourage foreign investment. Vietnam embraced capitalism. The Vietnamese government accepted the usual IMF 'austerity' programme, which shifted public funds from serving the public to paying off the South Vietnamese regime's debts to Western banks. Debt payments rose tenfold between 1986 and 1993. Of the 12,000 state enterprises, 5,000 were driven into bankruptcy. More than a million workers and some 200,000 public employees, including tens of thousands of teachers and health workers, were laid off.[77]

Public spending cuts forced people to pay for health care and education. Health clinics and hospitals were closed down. More people got infectious diseases. Recorded malaria deaths tripled during the first four years of the reforms. 750,000 children dropped out of the school system. When capitalism returned, so did high levels of petty trading, begging and prostitution.

Food aid, more imports and the dumping of subsidised US grains all helped to destroy local farms. The Asian Development Bank acknowledged, "While trade liberalization in rice has had a substantial positive impact on the economy as a whole, the benefits have largely accrued to wealthier and land-rich households, while the poor have not reaped significant benefits."[78] Food subsidies ended, causing local famines that affected a quarter of the country's population. By 1995, Vietnam had levels of malnutrition second only to Bangladesh.

The country's natural resources were sold off for short-term profit. Rare wildlife was sold to be eaten in posh restaurants. Fish stocks were destroyed. Illegal logging destroyed 2.5 million hectares of forest between 1976 and 1990.[79] Cities had poor or no sanitation. Untreated industrial waste was dumped. So much ground water was extracted that houses collapsed. The rivers around Ho Chi Minh City were biologically dead and air pollution was dangerously high.[80]

In 2000, Vietnam's government opened a stock market in Ho Chi Minh City. This boomed in 2006-07 and crashed in 2008. 'State' enterprises operated without state support as virtual private enterprises and moved into finance, blowing up a huge property bubble. Criminal networks bound the communist party to the new private sector.[81] The US government, the IMF and the World Bank approved it all. In 2007, Vietnam was admitted to the World Trade Organization. By 2013, GDP per head was $1,911.

In Cambodia too, capital ruled. It remained one of Asia's poorest countries. About four million Cambodians lived on less than $1.25 a day and 37 per cent of children suffered from chronic malnutrition. By

2013, GDP per head was $1,007. A government spokesman, Siphan Phay, said, "We are not communists any more, we are not socialists any more. We believe in freedom of choice."[82] This meant high inequality and rampant crony capitalism, where a few robber barons seized vast tracts of forest and land to strip timber and set up sugar and rubber plantations.

Laos remained a centrally planned economy. Its economy grew by 6 per cent a year between 1988 and 2008 and by 7 per cent a year between 2008 and 2013, by 8.3 per cent in 2013. It cut its poverty rate from 46 per cent in 1992 to 22 per cent in 2013. Just 1.9 per cent were unemployed. By 2013, GDP per head was $1,661.

In all three countries, low GDP per head meant low wages, so their governments could compete for foreign investment even with China.

Chapter 11
Cuba, to 1990

Batista's dictatorship

Before the Revolution, Cuba was a dictatorship. In 1952, Batista cancelled elections that the progressive forces were about to win. The US government backed his coup. US embassy officials wrote, "every one is aware of the support which the Cuban armed forces have received from our own armed forces before and since the *coup d'état*."[1]

US Treasury Secretary George Humphrey said in 1954 that US officials should "stop talking so much about democracy, and make it clear that we are quite willing to support dictatorships of the right if their policies are pro-American."[2] Throughout the 1950s, US governments backed Batista's dictatorship.[3] They knew quite well what Batista was like. US Ambassador George Messersmith had said in 1940 that Batista's 'principal interest is to be in power for the material advantage which it gives him'. The next US Ambassador, Spruille Braden, agreed: "Batista and his gang would like to free themselves from such few shackles as the Cuban creole democracy imposes and which prevent their unbridled acquisition of even more complete power and personal wealth."[4]

President Kennedy stated, "Fulgencio Batista murdered 20,000 Cubans in seven years – a greater proportion of the Cuban population than the proportion of Americans who died in both World Wars."[5] CIA director Allen Dulles later acknowledged that "in some cases, especially in South America, a dictator has later taken over an internal security service previously trained to combat Communism and has diverted it into a kind of Gestapo to hunt down his local political opponents. This happened in Cuba under Batista."[6] Kennedy also said, "there is no country in the world, including all the African regions, including any and all the countries under colonial domination, where economic colonization, humiliation and exploitation were worse than in Cuba, in part owing to my country's policies during the Batista regime ..."[7]

In the 1950s, Cuba had just one rural hospital. The Batista government's 1952 census called 75 per cent of rural dwellings 'ruinoso'. Only 3 per cent of rural homes had inside toilets, more than half had no toilet at all. Two-thirds had only dirt floors, only 9 per cent had electricity, only 2 per cent had running water. Between 80 and 90 per cent of rural children were infested with intestinal parasites.[8] In 1951, a World Bank team estimated that 30 per cent of urban dwellers and 60 per cent of rural dwellers suffered from malnutrition.

Less than a quarter of rural children attended school, and less than a half of urban children. The World Bank commented, "The general trend in the school system as a whole has been one of retrogression. A smaller proportion of the school-age children are enrolled today than a quarter of a century ago; the number of hours of instruction has been cut; the quality and morale of the teaching and supervisory force have gone down."[9]

Income per head in constant prices averaged $200 a year in 1956-58, the same as in 1903-06. But, as the World Bank noted, "Any figure for average *per capita* income is rather fictitious, especially where – as in Cuba – there is a very wide gap between the incomes of a relatively few high-income receivers at the top and the mass of income receivers."[10]

A 1957 report by the Catholic University Association said, "rural areas, especially wage workers, are living in unbelievable stagnant, miserable, and desperate conditions ... It is time our country cease being the private fiefdom of a few powerful interests. We firmly hope that, in a few years, Cuba will not be the property of a few, but the true homeland of all Cubans."[11] The US Embassy's commercial attaché summed up, "Cuban farmers and their families with few exceptions are undernourished, inadequately clothed, illiterate or semi-literate, readily susceptible to a variety of diseases, and at the mercy of country merchants and middlemen whose prices are what the traffic will yield and whose interest rates are generally exorbitant."[12]

Before the revolution, 80 per cent of Cuba's foreign exchange came from selling sugar, mostly to the USA. To get access to the US market, Cuba had to give 'most favoured nation' status to imports from the USA. By 1959, Cuba relied on the USA for 65 per cent of its exports and 73 per cent of its imports. US companies were often exempted from paying taxes and could repatriate all their profits: they took from, not gave to, the Cuban economy. Between 1950 and 1960, the balance of payments favoured the USA, by one billion dollars.[13] When Batista and his cronies fled Cuba on 1 January 1959, they took $500 million stolen from Cuba's treasury.[14]

Revolution in 1959

The Cuban working class led the revolution from the start. They created mass organisations, like the Workers' Central Union of Cuba, the 800,000-strong Committees for the Defence of the Revolution, the Revolutionary National Militias, the Federation of Cuban Women and the Literacy Campaign.

From the start, the US state fiercely opposed the Cuban revolution, because it threatened US economic interests. Philip W. Bonsal, the US Ambassador to Cuba, later wrote, "In appraisal of the prospects for Cuban-American relations under Castro the extensive private American interests in Cuba were of major significance."[15] Assistant Secretary of State Roy Rubottom said, "'Real U.S. goals in Cuba' included 'receptivity to U.S. and free world capital and increasing trade' and 'access by the United States to essential Cuban resources'."[16]

As early as 24 June 1959, the US state began to consider imposing sanctions on Cuba. The State Department knew what this would do: "The sugar industry will suffer a rapid and abrupt decline that will entail general unemployment. Many persons will be without work and go hungry."[17] On 6 April 1960, Lester Mallory, Deputy Assistant Secretary of State for Inter-American Affairs, wrote in an internal memorandum: "The majority of Cubans support Castro ... The only foreseeable means of alienating internal support is through disenchantment and disaffection based on economic dissatisfaction and hardship. ... every possible means should be undertaken promptly to weaken the economic life of Cuba." Mallory proposed 'a line of action which, while as adroit and inconspicuous as possible, makes the greatest inroads in denying money and supplies to Cuba, to decrease monetary and real wages, to bring about hunger, desperation and overthrow of government'.[18]

Yet the CIA claimed in 1961 that Fidel Castro 'became convinced that the US would never understand and accept his revolution, that he could expect only implacable hostility from Washington. This was the conclusion of his own disordered mind, unrelated to any fact of US policy or action'.[19]

The US government knew quite well that "there is no effective political opposition."[20] It early played the theme, "Castro betrayed Cuba."[21] In 1961, the Eisenhower administration started the blockade. On 3 February 1962, President Kennedy made the blockade total by banning the sale of drugs and food products, which was a breach of international humanitarian law.

On 1 November 1960, the US Ambassador to the UN called Cuba's allegation of a planned US attack 'monstrous distortions and downright falsehoods'.[22] On 12 April 1961, Kennedy pledged at a press conference, "there will not be, under any conditions, any intervention in Cuba by United States armed forces. This government will do everything it possibly can, and I think it can meet its responsibilities, to make sure that there are no Americans involved in any actions inside Cuba."[23] Five days later, on 17 April, he ordered the Bay of Pigs attack, launched from

US bases, with US mercenaries alongside Cuban exiles. The Cubans defeated the attack in four days.

In March 1962, the Defense Department presented to the Joint Chiefs of Staff what it called 'Pretexts to justify military intervention in Cuba', including:

"2. A series of well coordinated incidents will be planned to take place in and around Guantanamo to give genuine appearance of being done by hostile Cuban forces."

"3. a. We could blow up a US ship in Guantanamo Bay and blame Cuba."

"4. We could develop a Communist Cuban terror campaign in the Miami area, in other Florida cities and even in Washington."

"5. A 'Cuban-based, Castro-supported' filibuster could be simulated against a neighboring Caribbean nation."

"8. It is possible to create an incident which will demonstrate convincingly that a Cuban aircraft has attacked and shot down a chartered civil airliner en route from the United States to Jamaica, Guatemala, Panama or Venezuela." "The passengers could be a group of college students."

And, "9. It is possible to create an incident which will make it appear that Communist Cuban MIGs have destroyed a USAF aircraft over international waters in an unprovoked attack."

By 1962, the CIA's anti-Cuba Task Force W had grown to 400 US operatives running the sabotage and guerrilla operations of more than 50 front organisations, with its own fleet of fast boats, a rudimentary air force and 2,000 Cuban agents. By 1962, Miami housed the largest CIA station in the world, whose sole task was to overthrow the Cuban government.[24] The CIA colluded with gangsters to try to kill Castro.[25] Henry Kissinger admitted, "Robert Kennedy personally managed the operation on the assassination of Castro."[26]

In October 1962, the US government came close to starting a nuclear war over Cuba. Kennedy's reckless policy of aggression forced Cuba to install missiles on the island to safeguard itself from US assault. As Kennedy's defense secretary Robert McNamara admitted years later,

"I want to state quite frankly that with hindsight, if I had been a Cuban leader, I think I might have expected a U.S. invasion …"[27] The US government responded by imposing a naval blockade, an act of war, and claimed that it was acting in self-defence.

But many professors of international law agreed that Cuba, not the US government, acted in self-defence. As D. W. Greig commented, "it is difficult to accept the American contention that it was their naval quarantine which was necessitated on the grounds of self-defence … the plea of self-defence would justify Cuba's acceptance of Russian missiles, rather than United States' prevention of their being installed in Cuba."[28] The late Quincy Wright concluded, "It is difficult, therefore, to support the allegation that the Soviet Union violated international obligations in sending and installing missiles in Cuba."[29]

The US government continued to attack Cuba. In 1976, CIA paid asset Luis Posada Carriles bombed a Cuban civilian airliner, killing 73 people. He said, "The CIA taught us everything. They taught us explosives, how to kill, bomb, trained us in acts of sabotage." The US government also waged biological warfare against Cuba. As the US magazine *Newsday* reported on 8 January 1977, "with at least the tacit backing of US Central Intelligence Agency officials, operatives linked to anti-Castro terrorists introduced African swine fever virus into Cuba in 1971" forcing the slaughter of 500,000 pigs. In 1981, the CIA created an epidemic of hemorrhagic dengue fever, which infected 340,000 people in a country which had never before experienced a single case of the disease. 116,000 were hospitalised; 158 people, including 101 children, died.

Cuba grew slowly from 1959 to 1970, faster from 1970 to 1985. Between 1961 and 1965, gross social product rose 1.9 per cent a year, between 1966 and 1970 by 3.9 per cent a year and between 1971 and 1975 by 10 per cent a year. Real income growth per person from 1960 to 1985 was 3.1 per cent a year; Latin America's average was 1.8 per cent. Between 1961 and 1965, industrial output rose by 2.3 per cent a year and between 1965 and 1984 by 6.3 per cent a year.[30]

Between 1971 and 1975, industry received 21 per cent of all investment, agriculture 29 per cent. In 1976, Cuba introduced its System of Economic Management and Planning. Between 1976 and 1980, industry received 35 per cent of all investment, agriculture 19 per cent. Between 1970 and 1980, industrial production grew by 80 per cent, agriculture by 27 per cent. Cuba's whole economy grew by 7.8 per cent a year between 1972 and 1981. In 1981, Cuba introduced production brigades (self-managing subunits of state farms) to promote worker participation in decision-making and to enhance work incentives through linking effort and reward more closely. Between 1981 and 1985, labour productivity grew 5.2 per cent a year.

Between 1980 and 1985, Cuba's gross social product grew by 7 per cent a year, as against Latin America's average of a 1.7 per cent fall. Between 1975 and 1985, Cuba increased fourfold its production of non-electrical machinery (including transport equipment and agricultural machinery) and of electrical machinery threefold. It more than doubled its output of metal products. Cuba pursued both export promotion and import substitution in its development strategy.

Social progress

A 1972 report for the Joint Economic Committee of the US Congress said, "The genuine socio-economic and political accomplishments of the Cuban revolution have attracted international attention. These accomplishments include: A highly egalitarian redistribution of income that has eliminated almost all malnutrition, particularly among children; Establishment of a national health care program that is superior in the Third World and rivals that of numerous developed countries; Near total elimination of illiteracy and a highly developed multi-level educational system; and Development of a relatively well-disciplined and motivated population with a strong sense of national identification."[31]

Cuba's constitution guaranteed the right to work, equal pay for equal work, health and safety protection at work, an eight-hour day, paid annual leave and social security. The law guaranteed local collective bargaining with unions. Cuba continually worked to raise the wages of lower-paid workers. The salary scale limited the highest basic salaries, 650 Cuban pesos (CUP) a month, to 2.89 times the national minimum salary of 225 CUP.

Cuba did more than most developing countries to achieve equality.[32] Most Latin American countries instead embraced the IMF's 'austerity' - poverty - policies, which only deepened their slumps, cutting jobs and wages, worsening class and gender inequities.[33] As Steve Ludlam concluded, "the Revolution has maintained a level of social equality that puts to shame the achievements of most social democrats and socialists elsewhere."[34] American economist James K. Galbraith commented, "the efforts made by the Cuban authorities to slow down the rising trend in wage inequality in the nineties are remarkable …"[35]

The constitution guaranteed access to health care as a human right for all citizens, regardless of wealth, status, race or geographical origin. Cuba provided low-cost, sustainable primary health care, using prevention, health education, dietary advice, vaccination and low-tech options, involving the community. Women had free access to high-quality prenatal and postnatal services. Tuberculosis, typhoid fever, diphtheria and polio were eradicated.[36]

Cuba invested hugely in health care. It had 59 hospitals in 1959, 257 in 1969. In the 1950s, it had just one rural hospital, by 1983 it had 55, plus 218 medical posts built in rural areas. By 2007, it had one doctor for every 170 people, more per head than any other country; the USA had one to 188 and the UK one to 250. The World Bank reported that the USA had 2.4 doctors per 1,000 people in 2009. Cuba had 6.7 doctors per 1,000 in 2010. The proportion of women doctors rose from 6 per cent in 1953 to 48 per cent in 1990 and of dentists from 18 per cent to 69 per cent. Between 1953 and 1992, the number of nurses increased fifteen-fold to 70,000.

In the 1980s, Cuba was the first of 113 countries in Asia, Africa and Latin America for life expectancy, health and education. It had the most equal income distribution in Latin America, the lowest unemployment, the lowest infant mortality and the highest literacy rate. In Latin

America in the 1980s, only Cuba and Nicaragua improved their infant mortality rates. Between 1975 and 1984, Cuba's was reduced from 27/1,000 to 15. By 2003, Cuba had the lowest infant mortality rate in Latin America and the Caribbean, 6/1,000: the average was 27/1,000.

Cuba also invested heavily in education. There were four times more teachers in 1970 than in 1959. By 2007, there were eleven primary school students per teacher – the best ratio in the continent.[37] The UN reported in 2007 that only Cuba in Latin America and the Caribbean met the UN's Millennium Goal for universal education. A 2008 UNESCO survey of 196,000 primary school students in sixteen Latin American countries put Cuba first in mathematics, language and sciences. Erwin Epstein, president of the Comparative and International Education Society, praised Cubans' "heroic efforts to raise their standard of education and make learning a natural part of their everyday lives. … Few, if any other nations can claim the use of schools to achieve such a pervasive transformation of social, political and economic life."[38]

Medea Benjamin, Joseph Collins and Michael Scott of the California-based Institute for Food and Development Policy wrote in 1986, "the Cuban revolution declared, from the outset, that no one should go malnourished. No disappointment in food production, no failed economic take-off, no shock wave from world economic crisis has deterred Cuba from freeing itself from the suffering and shame of a single wasted child or an elderly person ignominiously subsisting on pet food.

"No other country in this hemisphere, including the United States, can make this claim. Ending hunger is not the revolution's only accomplishment. The streets of old Havana are no longer lined with prostitutes. A former slave society with many blacks and a history of discrimination, Cuba is now the most racially harmonious society we have ever experienced ... Illiteracy has been virtually eradicated and the current campaign is to ensure everyone, even the oldest small farmer, at least a ninth-grade education. Health care is free, and Cuba's health indicators are perhaps the best in Latin America. Every effort is made to guarantee full employment. All this makes for a society with a pervasive sense of dignity and confidence in the future."[39]

Internationalism

Cuba backed the peoples of Guinea-Bissau, Mozambique and Angola in their struggles for independence from Portuguese colonial rule. In 1966 Cuba sent military instructors and doctors to Guinea-Bissau, where they stayed until the people won independence in 1974. This liberation war brought down the Portuguese empire and Portuguese fascism and won independence for Guinea-Bissau and Mozambique.

But South Africa, with US backing, intervened to prevent Angola's people also winning their independence. As Piero Gleijeses wrote, "Washington urged Pretoria to intervene. On October 14 [1975], South African troops invaded Angola, transforming the civil war into an international conflict. As the South Africans raced toward Luanda, MPLA [Movimento Popular de Libertacao de Angola, the national liberation movement] resistance crumbled; they would have seized the capital had not Castro decided on November 4 to respond to the MPLA's appeals for troops. The evidence is clear – even though many scholars continue to distort it – the South Africans invaded first, and the Cubans responded. The Cuban forces, despite their initial inferiority in numbers and weapons, halted the South African onslaught. The official South African historian of the war writes, 'The Cubans rarely surrendered and, quite simply, fought cheerfully until death.'"[40]

On 1 July 1977, US Secretary of State Cyrus Vance said that the US government would supply Somalia with arms. This gave the Somali government the green light to attack Ethiopia. As Paul Henze, the US National Security Council specialist on the Horn of Africa, later wrote, "The crucial decision [to intervene] seems to have been taken only ... when the Somalis concluded they had a good chance of securing American military aid."[41] On 17 July, Somalia invaded Ethiopia. The Ethiopian government asked the Soviet Union and Cuba to help it to defend itself. The US government then tried to get the UN to condemn, not the aggressor, but those defending Ethiopia.[42] But, as Henze pointed out, "The Soviets and Cubans have legality and African sentiment on their side in Ethiopia – they are helping an African country defend its territorial integrity and countering aggression."[43]

In 1987-88, Cuba again sent forces to assist Angola to defend itself against South African aggression. Contrary to US government claims, Cuba was entitled under international law to do so. Professor of international law Henry J. Richardson III judged, "the presence of Cuban troops in Angola is quite lawful - a legality underscored by repeated South African military aggression on Angolan territory, and that contrasts sharply with the patent illegality of the South African presence in Namibia."[44] Gleijeses wrote, "The Reagan administration helped Pretoria flaunt [flout] UN Resolution 435 by introducing the principle of linkage: South Africa's withdrawal from Namibia, the White House declared, would have to occur concurrently with the withdrawal of the Cuban troops from Angola. This blurred the distinction between a legal act (Cuba's troops were in Angola at the express invitation of the government) and an illegal one (South Africa was occupying Namibia despite the express disapproval of the United Nations). As the Canadian ambassador told the Security Council with unusual candour, this linkage "had no warrant in international law, … is incompatible with resolution 435 and … has been rejected by this Council. Perhaps worst of all, … [it] is totally unnecessary, is a deliberate obstacle and is the cause of grievous delay …. To hold Namibia hostage to what this Council has previously described as 'irrelevant and extraneous issues' is palpably outrageous"."[45]

Gleijeses commented, "It was the Cubans who pushed the Soviets to help Angola. It was they who stood guard in Angola for many long years, thousands of miles from home, to prevent the South Africans from overthrowing the MPLA government. It was they who in 1988, with the reinforcements Castro sent against Gorbachev's wishes, forced the South African army out of Angola. It was they who forced Pretoria to abandon Savimbi and hold free elections in Namibia – which SWAPO [South West Africa People's Organisation] won. In the words of Nelson

Mandela, the Cuban victory over the South African army in southern Angola in 1988 'destroyed the myth of the invincibility of the white oppressor ... [and] inspired the fighting masses of South Africa.' This was Cuba's contribution to what Castro has called 'the most beautiful cause' – the struggle against racial oppression in southern Africa."[46]

Gleijeses concluded, "On 22 December 1988, the New York agreements stipulated that Namibia would become independent, that the South African army would leave Namibia within three months. ... the New York agreements would not have been possible without the Cubans' prowess on the battlefield and skill at the negotiating table. Despite Washington's best efforts to stop it, Cuba changed the course of southern African history. Throughout the 1980s the Cuban military shield prevented the SADF [South African Defence Force] from wreaking even more destruction on Angola and bringing down its government. The Cubans were steadfast in their support for SWAPO, and they were instrumental in forcing Pretoria to accept the independence of Namibia."[47]

Speaking in Havana at the traditional 26 July celebration in 1991, Nelson Mandela said that Cuba's efforts, culminating in the unprecedented defeat of South African regular troops at Cuito Cuanavale in Angola in 1988, was a victory for all of Africa. He said, "That impressive defeat of the racist army ... gave Angola the possibility of enjoying peace and consolidating its sovereignty." He added that it gave the people of Namibia their independence, demoralised the white racist regime of Pretoria and inspired the anti-apartheid forces inside South Africa. "Without the defeat inflicted at Cuito Cuanavale our organisations never would have been legalised", he asserted. "The Cuban people hold a special place in the hearts of the peoples of Africa. The Cuban internationalists have made a contribution to African independence, freedom and justice, unparalleled for its principled and selfless character."

As Mandela said, "Cuito Cuanavale was the turning point for the liberation of our continent - and of my people – from the scourge of apartheid."[48] He summed up, "We come here with a sense of the great debt that is owed the people of Cuba. What other country can point to a record of greater selflessness than Cuba has displayed in its relations to Africa?"[49] At Mandela's inauguration as President in 1993, after the defeat of the apartheid system, he embraced Fidel Castro: "You made this possible," he whispered audibly.[50] Cuba's revolution also inspired other countries to become more independent and self-reliant.[51]

Chapter 12

The Soviet Union - counter-revolution and catastroika

Afghanistan

In April 1978, the Afghan people overthrew the country's feudal regime. The new government promoted social justice for ethnic minorities, freed 13,000 political prisoners, introduced free medical care for the poorest, abolished peonage and launched a mass literacy programme. It aimed to provide 'a modern educational system in which girls as well as boys would go to school, at which young women did not have to wear the veil, in which science and literature would be taught alongside Islam'.[1]

It gave full rights to women. A 1986 US Army manual praised the new government's policies towards women: "provisions of complete freedom of choice of marriage partner, and fixation of the minimum age at marriage at 16 for women and 18 for men ... abolished forced marriages ... extensive literacy programs, especially for women ... putting girls and boys in the same classroom ... changing gender roles and giving women a more active role in politics."[2] By the late 1980s, half the university students, nearly half the doctors and most teachers were women.

In response, the US government began a war of intervention against Afghanistan, running armed raids from Pakistan. As President Jimmy Carter's national security adviser Zbigniew Brzezinski admitted, "According to the official version of history, CIA aid to the mujehadin began during 1980, that is to say, after the Soviet army invaded Afghanistan, 24 December 1979. But the reality, secretly guarded until now, is completely otherwise: indeed, it was July 3, 1979 that President Carter signed the first directive for secret aid to the opponents of the pro-Soviet regime in Kabul. And that very day, I wrote a note to the president in which I explained to him that in my opinion this aid was going to induce a Soviet military intervention."[3]

This US act breached UN Resolution 2625 of 1970, which stated that every state had to refrain from organising or encouraging armed bands to violate another state's territory. The UN Definition of Aggression adopted on 19 December 1974 explained, "Aggression is the use of armed force by a State against the sovereignty, territorial integrity or political independence of another State" and that included "the sending by or on behalf of a State of armed bands, groups, irregulars or mercenaries, which carry out acts of armed force against another State."

The US government, the IMF, the World Bank and the Pakistan Aid Consortium (led by the US and British governments) gave Pakistan's government more than $5 billion to build and supply bases for attacking Afghanistan. The CIA spent $1.5 billion arming and training the mujehadin, Contra-style opponents of the new government, in its biggest operation since Angola. It raised the money by selling drugs to the USA. MI6 supplied the mujehadin with Blowpipe surface-to-air missiles and trained them at secret bases in Saudi Arabia and Oman. Foreign Secretary Lord Carrington said that the mujehadin 'have got to receive weapons and that's that', to 'keep the pot boiling'.

The mujehadin raided civilian targets, destroying over 1,800 schools, 40 hospitals and 110 first aid centres. RAND expert Cheryl Benard explained, "We made a deliberate choice. At first, everyone thought, there's no way to beat the Soviets. So what we have to do is to throw the worst crazies against them that we can find, and there was a lot of collateral damage. We knew exactly who these people were, and what their organizations were like, and we didn't care. Then, we allowed them to get rid of, just kill all the moderate leaders. The reason we don't have moderate leaders in Afghanistan today is because we let the nuts kill them all. They killed the leftists, the moderates, the middle-of-the-roaders. They were just eliminated, during the 1980s and afterwards."[4]

The Afghan government, in accordance with Article 51 of the UN Charter, called on the Soviet Union to help it defend itself. The Soviet Union did so. In August 1980, a House of Commons Committee described the Soviet action as defensive. George Kennan agreed that it was 'defensive rather than offensive'.[5] D. W. Greig observed, "there is no conventional rule prohibiting a state from answering the call of another state to provide it with troops to operate solely within the territory of the latter."[6] Garthoff wrote that the Soviet leaders saw it as 'the only solution to a specific situation on their borders that was threatening Soviet security'. He concluded, "the Soviet decision was a reluctant recourse to defend vital interests."[7]

Counter-revolution

Gorbachev and his allies proposed 'new thinking', 'universal human values' and 'market socialism'. In the name of democracy and glasnost, they gave anti-Soviet forces free, full access to the TV, radio and press.[8] In the name of restoring the rule of law, they rehabilitated everyone arrested for counter-revolutionary acts including collaboration with the Nazis. Perestroika, under the label of correcting socialism, rejected socialism. From the start, it was a counter-revolution in the name of revolution.

In particular they attacked the Communist Party of the Soviet Union (CPSU). This strengthened the growing capitalist forces led by Boris Yeltsin - the separatists, corrupt elements in the economy and the party, the mafia.⁹ Gorbachev's Third Way led straight to robber baron capitalism, which meant cutting down democracy.¹⁰

Unsurprisingly, Trotskyism backed Gorbachev and Yeltsin. When *Temps Nouveaux* asked Ernest Mandel, the leader of Trotsky's 'Fourth International', "Mikhail Gorbachev, does he proclaim that perestroika is truly a new revolution?" Mandel replied, "Yes, he actually proclaims this, and it is again very positive. Our movement has defended the same idea for 55 years, for which reason we have been taxed with being counter-revolutionary."¹¹ Mandel also praised Yeltsin, writing, "The reformer Yeltsin represents the tendency which wants to reduce the gigantic state apparatus. Consequently he follows in Trotsky's footsteps."¹²

In December 1987, Gorbachev cut the state purchase of industrial output by half, so half of industry could buy and sell in a new wholesale market. This caused chaos: production fell, shortages grew, wages were not paid and prices inflated for the first time since 1945. His reforms cut wages, job security and social services. Despite better harvests, shortages of the most necessary food items became chronic. His reforms caused economic decline, not vice versa.

The Soviet working class responded with strikes, go-slows and other protests. In the first half of 1989, two million working days were lost in strikes. In the coal industry alone, there were twelve strikes, which won concessions from the employer. On average, 15,000 workers were on strike every day.

At the Houston summit in July 1990, Gorbachev endorsed the World Bank programme of shock therapy (all shock, no therapy). He passed a Law on Enterprises which allowed managers to turn factories into private concerns without consulting the workers. In response, the Union of Works Collective Councils and Workers' Committees, representing two million workers, demanded that workers decided who owned their factories. Workers in the building materials plant of Pollioustrovo held a 21-day strike demanding workers' ownership of plants.

The Independent Union of Coal Industry Employees, the miners' union affiliated to the Federation of Independent Trade Unions of Russia (FNPR), tried to save their industry. Union chairperson Vitaly

Budko announced, "In essence we are demanding one thing - the funds needed to preserve the Russian coal industry. Above all, funds for the development of new mines and the reconstruction of existing enterprises, for the materials and equipment needed to create safe working conditions and to build housing for miners." The FNPR achieved wage rises in 1991.

When workers struggled to increase their wages, save social protections, take control of their workplaces, rebuild their industries and keep workers' ownership of plants, they were fighting for socialism. Opinion polls showed that by large majorities the Soviet people opposed capitalism and supported key features of the Soviet system - public ownership of large-scale economic assets, a state-regulated market, guaranteed employment, controls on prices, standard-of-living subsidies, and free education and health care.[13]

In April 1991, nine republic leaders agreed to form a new 'Union of Soviet Sovereign Republics' which preserved an all-Union state, economy and military. As late as November, Yeltsin said, "The Union will live!"[14] On 25 November, leaders of seven republics agreed another treaty which also retained a Union state, economy and military. But Yeltsin aborted all these agreements by his coup of 8 December 1991. In a declaration that was 'neither legitimate nor democratic', he ended the Soviet Union:[15] "The USSR as a subject of international law and as a geopolitical entity has ceased to exist." Even Western admirers called it his 'autumn putsch'.[16]

The Soviet Union's collapse was not due to inherent flaws, economic crisis, popular discontent, lack of democracy, or US pressure. The US war build-up strained the Soviet Union but did not crush it. Its economy grew continually: the CIA judged that Soviet output increased every year from 1946 to 1989 except for 1963 and 1979, years of particularly bad harvests. The Soviet Union had huge popular support: in the March 1991 referendum, 112 million people, 76 per cent of those who voted, voted to keep the Soviet Union. The Central Asian Republics voted 90 per cent for the Union.

Historians largely agreed with Fidel Castro: "Socialism did not die of natural causes." David Kotz and Fred Weir summed up, "We came to the view that the Soviet system had been dispatched, not by economic collapse combined with a popular uprising, but by its own ruling elite in pursuit of its own perceived interests." They concluded, "The desertion of the state socialist system by the party-state elite did not happen *because* of the demise of the old system. The reverse is true - the demise of the system occurred because the party-state elite deserted it."[17] Roger Keeran and Thomas Kenny agreed, writing of "the key events of 1989-91 – the overthrow of socialist governments in Eastern Europe, the Party's destruction, the rise of the 'democrat' opposition, the deepening economic crisis, and the USSR's dismemberment. They were interacting processes. In the final analysis one process drove them all: the leadership's determination to end the dominant role of the CPSU which, even at this late date, remained a latent obstacle to Gorbachev's policies."[18] Peter Nolan also agreed: "The fundamental cause of the Soviet collapse lies in the destruction of the state administrative apparatus and the nation-state under Gorbachev."[19] The Soviet Union's rulers killed it off. The working class resisted, but not strongly enough to save it.

When the parliament in 1991 opposed the shock therapy, Yeltsin illegally dissolved the parliament and imposed the shock by decree. The 6th Congress of the Russian Federation voted against the shock. Daily mass pickets in Red Square demanded Yeltsin's resignation. 100,000 people marched in Moscow on May Day in 1992. Medical workers and teachers went on strike. In September, collective farmers and members of the Moscow Federation of Trade Unions demonstrated across the country. In November, 100,000 marched to celebrate the October Revolution. Parliament too opposed Yeltsin's dictatorial powers. So on 4 October 1993, he launched a tank assault on parliament to crush the opposition, killing 146 people and injuring more than a thousand. He dissolved and outlawed the CPSU, seizing its assets and purging its members.

In the 1990s, Russia's new capitalist class seized through privatisation the great wealth that the country's workers had produced during the

Soviet era. The nation's wealth ceased to benefit the working class; instead it benefited the tiny capitalist minority, who put the money into thousands of offshore bank accounts, real estate holdings and offshore companies.

The Yeltsin government, backed by the Russian Union of Industrialists and Entrepreneurs, let directors and workers buy 51 per cent of the voting shares in their workplaces at nominal prices, using the enterprises' own funds. All too often, workers agreed not to interfere with the directors in exchange for promises of job security, soon broken. Directors bought workers' shares before they had any market value or in collaboration with banks outbid the workers.

Yeltsin issued special decrees to exclude other buyers, to aid his cronies. He set up an incentive system that drove money into Swiss bank accounts and made domestic investment virtually impossible. Directors used joint ventures, shell companies and offshore havens to leach cash and raw materials out of public enterprises. They created banks and trading companies that seized the factories' output and stripped their assets.

But the biggest money-spinner for the new capitalist class was the theft of Russia's vast natural resources through the Loans for Shares scam: the capitalists lent money to the state. In exchange, they bought at auction, for a fraction of their market value, the shares that the government put up as collateral for the loans. When the government could not repay the loans, the capitalists sold the shares to themselves very cheaply as repayment for the loans. In these corrupt insider deals, the government let capitalists seize the companies.

As the basis for these auctions, the government used companies' book values as fixed in January 1992. That month, Yeltsin's deputy prime minister, Egor Gaidar, had freed prices, causing 2,500 per cent inflation. So capitalists could buy Russia's energy resources for tiny fractions of what they were worth. (It also wiped out workers' life savings — seventy million accounts in the state-owned Sberbank alone.)

In November and December 1995, the government sold off twelve of Russia's biggest companies. A handful of private banks, owned by the new capitalists, ran the auctions, disqualified their rivals, bid in the auctions and - surprise, surprise - won the auctions. For example, in a closed auction run by his own bank, Uneksimbank, Vladimir Potanin (the deputy prime minister in charge of finance) bought Norilsk Nickel, the world's biggest producer of nickel and platinum, for just $170.1 million. Its profits that year were $1.2 billion. His bank had disqualified a rival bid of $350 million, on a technicality.

Yeltsin's friend Boris Berezovsky loaned the government $100 million for 51 per cent of Sibneft, Russia's sixth biggest oil company, worth $2.8 billion, then sold it to himself in another sham auction 18 months later for $110 million. Russia's Audit Chamber later reported that the sale was conducted with 'multiple legal violations' and 'should be considered invalid'. In 2000, Sibneft bought 27 per cent of its shares for $542 million from shareholders. Less than a year later, it secretly sold back those shares, for far less, to the same shareholders. It then gave a $612 million dividend to the shareholders — one of whom, Roman Abramovich, was lucky enough to own 87 per cent of the shares. The Blair government gave Berezovsky political asylum, while Roman Abramovich bought Chelsea Football Club.

The Yeltsin government sold off other national assets cheaply, including tax concessions, TV channels, radio frequency licences, export licences and government bank accounts. Yeltsin privatised the TV company Channel One, which reached 200 million Russians, without the legally required auction, selling it to Berezovsky for a knock-down price of $2.2 million.

Successive Russian governments privatised 80 per cent of Russia's 22,500 industrial enterprises, which produced 90 per cent of Russia's industrial output. Eight oligarch groups controlled 85 per cent of the revenues of Russia's 64 largest private companies. By 2002, five people controlled 95 per cent of Russia's aluminium, 18 per cent of her oil, 40 per cent of her copper, 20 per cent of her steel and 20 per cent of car production. Criminal gangs, which had been growing since the 1960s, ran nearly half the private sector and owned half Russia's largest banks. In 2004, the World Bank reported that 30 people controlled 40 per cent of the $225 billion output of Russia's key sectors. The 100 richest Russians owned 25 per cent of Russia's entire GDP. By contrast, in the USA, the 227 richest owned 6 per cent.

The capitalists also looted state funds and the Soviet gold reserves. The new banks took billions of rubles of party, government and trade union funds, transferring these too to foreign bank accounts and offshore tax havens. In 2006, the government deregulated all capital accounts. By 2014, an estimated $500 billion of capital had fled the country since 1991.

In sum, the privatisations of the 1990s sold off a trillion dollars' worth of state assets for just $5 billion.[20] Anatoly Chubais, head of the State Privatization Committee, said of Russia's capitalists, "They steal and steal and steal. They are stealing absolutely everything and it is impossible to stop them." The American economist Milton Friedman admitted, "In the immediate aftermath of the fall of the Soviet Union, I kept being asked what the Russians should do. I said, 'Privatize, privatize, privatize.' I was wrong."[21] As civil society disintegrated, private firms, cartels, crony networks and mafia gangs burgeoned. Local bosses, protected by racketeers, ran any remaining production. State-planned internal exchange was not replaced by a national free market, but by the petty trade of intra-regional deals between local bodies defined by ethnicity and religion, and by local networks of barter, a parody of socialist exchange.

Kort concluded that the 1990s saw 'a spasmodic descent into a morass of political dysfunction, economic hardship, social disorder, unchecked criminality, and corruption on a massive scale'.[22] Jerry Hough summed up, "Without question, Russia in the 1990s featured a great deal of illegality and corruption. ... The utter scandal is that so much of the 'corruption' in Russia has been legal and has been the logical consequence of the policy that has been advocated by the West."[23]

Catastroika

Yeltsin's shock therapy caused 'the worst economic and social devastation ever suffered by a modern country in peacetime' and 'the unprecedented demodernisation of a twentieth century country'.[24] Russia's vice president Alexander Rutskoy denounced Yeltsin's programme as 'economic genocide'.[25] The Russian people called its effects 'catastroika'.[26] The UN's investigative team warned, "a human crisis of monumental proportions is emerging in the former Soviet Union, as the transition years have literally been lethal for a great many people."[27] In the 1990s, Russia's rate of population loss was more than double the rate in the first half of the 1930s. Stuckler and Basu estimated that there were 10 million excess deaths in Russia in the early 1990s.[28]

Between 1991 and 1998, national income was cut by more than 50 per cent, as against 27 per cent in the USA in the Great Depression. Oil production fell by half. Investment in 1999 was a fifth of 1990's total. Direct foreign investment in Russia during the 1990s was only a little more than in Hungary, which had a fifteenth of Russia's population. Most of that investment went into extractive industries. The privatisation of housing provision led to a huge fall in house building.

In Russia, in 1994-98, 40-60 per cent of workers were owed wages. In 1995, pay was just half 1990's level and average real pensions were less than half 1990's level. Unemployment rose from 3.6 million in 1992 to 8.9 million – a tenth of the working class – in 1998. By 1998, more than 80 per cent of Russia's firms had gone bankrupt and 70,000 factories had closed. Industrial jobs were cut from 32 million in 1990 to fewer than 20 million by 1999. Science lost half its workers.

Livestock and dairy herds fell by 75 per cent. By 2008, Russia was importing 40 per cent of its food, including 75 per cent of its meat. Meat and milk production were half what they had been in 1990. Russia had reverted to its 19th-century role as a source of raw materials: it depended on its oil and gas exports.

The 2000 labour code reform allowed wider use of temporary contracts, expanded employers' rights to dismiss workers, and reduced the powers of trade unions in dismissals. Responsibilities for housing, health care and pensions were transferred to individuals, markets and insurance mechanisms. Access to public transport, housing, utilities and other goods and services was further reduced.

The extensive social services of Soviet times, from free kindergartens to free health care and paid holidays, all went. As a former supporter of Yeltsin lamented in 1992, "Our children used to rest at well-provided camps; we were able to buy things at prices we could afford; we received free medical care from doctors who respected their Hippocratic Oath; we ate at lunchrooms at prices within our reach; we walked the streets till early in the morning without fear. Now all is falling apart."[29]

Vitamin deficiency was widespread. Tuberculosis cases rose by 75 per cent, HIV cases from 400 in 1994 to 250,000 in 2000. A tenth of newborns suffered from serious birth defects and about half all schoolchildren suffered from chronic diseases. By late 1998, two million Russian children were living without families, two-thirds of them on the streets. Ten million children were not in school. In 1999, about 35 per cent of the people were living below the poverty line and many more hovered just above it. The suicide rate was up 60 per cent since 1989. Russia's birthrate had dropped by a third since 1990 and its mortality rate had risen by a quarter. The population fell to 146 million in late 1999, down more than two million since 1991. In 1989, lifespans had been 66 for men and 75 for women; by 2008, they were 62 and 74. By 2007, Russia ranked 164th of 226 countries for life expectancy.

The UN Human Settlements Programme concluded in 2003, "The region where the increase in extreme poverty was the most pronounced comprised the former socialist countries of Eastern Europe and Central Asia. Poverty rates moved to over 50 per cent in half of the transitional countries in the transition period of 1988 to 1995; and persons in poverty increased from 14 million to 168 million in the region, as a whole. The number of people in poverty in Russia rose from 2 million to 74 million, in the Ukraine from 2 million to 33 million and in

Romania from 1.3 million to 13.5 million. These massive changes were due to lower incomes, to increased income inequality and especially to inflation, which lowered purchasing power substantially."[30]

Yet the working class fought back. The government proposed to abolish the United Tariff Scale (UTS) that governed the wages of all public employees. It also proposed to devolve responsibility to regional and local authorities for public-sector finances, for providing public services and for wage-setting, which would cause large differentials in pay between more and less wealthy regions. The health service workers' union demanded that the UTS be kept, to guarantee equal pay for equal work. In October 2004, a million health workers struck. As a result, the lowest grade workers won a pay increase from 110 to 600 rubles and public sector wages rose by 20 per cent from 1 January 2005 and then by 50 per cent in stages over the next three years. Early in 2005, trade unions organised demonstrations and transport blockades across more than 70 cities in protest at the 'austerity' measures.

The chairman of the building workers' regional committee in Samara said, "The trade union is a fighting organisation, not a charitable one. ... Only competently organised pressure upon employers brings a positive result."[31] This union waged about five disputes a year, winning most of them. In 2001, it prevented the bankruptcy of a large building materials combine and in 2006 it stopped the closure of a large project. Metal workers at Siberian Ore won a 20 per cent wage increase in 2007. Ford workers won a big pay rise in 2009 and a 12 per cent rise the next year.

The world crisis hit Russia hard. In 2009, its output fell by 7.9 per cent; in 57 out of 83 regions, disposable income per person was cut by 30 per cent or more. 75 per cent of the people lived at or below subsistence level. In 2013, the health of Russian men was still worse than it was before 1991.[32]

Reactionaries rejoiced at Russia's plight. Charles Krauthammer, the *Washington Post*'s political commentator, wrote, "it is in our interest that their economy *not* recover"[33], an opinion shared by Britain's International Institute for Strategic Studies. The 'young-reformer', privatiser and businessman Alfred Kokh said, "the Russians deserved their miserable fate."[34]

Yet Russia still had huge resources: the World Bank said in 2013 that it was the world's fifth largest economy. It needed to direct investment into industrial and agricultural enterprises, to borrow to invest and to pay workers' unpaid wages and pensions, to support education, science and welfare, to put tariffs on imported goods to protect domestic enterprises, to tighten controls to stop bank malpractices and capital flight, to regulate key prices (especially of food and energy) and to renationalise key privatised enterprises like oil, gas, timber and strategic metals. Even US economist Joseph Stiglitz agreed that some renationalisation was needed.[35] Russia should default on its debts. Restructuring the debt, the usual IMF 'remedy', would only add interest due, perpetuating the debt bondage.

Central Asia

The counter-revolution threw the peoples of the five countries of Central Asia, Tajikistan, Uzbekistan, Kyrgyzstan, Kazakhstan and Turkmenistan, into poverty. American historian Sally Cummings summed up, "Debt remained a serious problem. To date, trade has benefited the richest, not the poorest. Social problems have increased as access to basics, for example education and health care, have declined. Basic state infrastructures have declined. ... In all five, state capacity in the sectors of welfare and infrastructure has been enormously neglected."[36]

These countries became avenues for the heroin trade to Russia and Europe, which increased heroin use in these countries too, spreading addiction, disease, misery, corruption and crime. A UN agency concluded, "in the past ten years, Central Asia has experienced the highest increase in prevalence of drug abuse worldwide."[37] Their states became repressive kleptocracies, dictatorships where capitalist criminals seized both state power and the countries' resources. Their economies were reduced to sales of raw materials, money-lending, dodgy corporate takeovers aided by Western banks and the sale of contracts to supply fuel to the US military bases set up to wage NATO's war against Afghanistan.

The US government and the EU used Islamist terrorists to fragment and destabilise countries across Asia.[38] In Tajikistan, a civil war in 1992-97 killed 50,000 people. Uzbekistan and Russia aided Tajikistan's government; the US government funded the opposition. In Uzbekistan, the Islamic Movement of Uzbekistan [IMU], linked to Al-Qaeda, funded its weapons purchases by selling Afghan opium. It ran 70 per cent of Central Asia's drug trade. It opposed the Moscow peace accord which ended the war in Tajikistan. It de-stabilised Kyrgyzstan by launching raids in 1997 and 2000. NGOs also destabilised Kyrgyzstan. As journalist Boris-Mathieu Pétric wrote, "international organisations and NGOs in Kyrgyzstan are ... co-producing a policy that has exacerbated and strengthened ethnic differences instead of producing a common social contract ..."[39] This led to the killings in inter-communal violence of hundreds of Uzbek and Kyrgyz inhabitants of the Kyrgyzstani city of Osh in 2010.

But the Uzbekistan government bucked the trend. In May 2005, it cracked down on the IMU and on the Chechen terrorists in the country (who also funded their weapons purchases by selling Afghan opium and were also linked to Al-Qaeda). This brought a halt to the wave of 'colour' counter-revolutions in countries of the former Soviet Union. The government also evicted the USA from the Karshi-Khanabad Air Base and expelled the NGOs. The Uzbek economy grew by 7 per cent in 2013 and only 4.9 per cent were jobless.

In Mongolia, the counter-revolution made life worse. 9 per cent were unemployed in 2011 and 29.8 per cent lived below the poverty line. Craig Janes and Oyuntsetseg Chuluundorj noted, "as most Mongolians now recognize, it is clear that the social protections afforded by the old socialist regime provided households and individuals far more health, economic, and social security than are now afforded under the new capitalist system."[40]

US and EU governments stir up trouble

On 2 February 1990, the US and German governments agreed "there was no interest to extend NATO to the East."[41] But this was untrue. NATO's top priority was to extend across Eastern Europe. When Gorbachev met Germany's Chancellor Helmut Kohl on 10 February, he conceded what Kohl wanted - German unification - without getting Kohl to agree to what Russia wanted - no eastward expansion of NATO.[42] The Czech Republic, Hungary and Poland joined NATO in 1999. After 9/11, the Russian government was the first to back the US war against jihadism. The US response was to withdraw from the Anti-Ballistic Missile Treaty and to expand NATO yet more. Bulgaria, Romania, Slovakia, Slovenia, Estonia, Latvia and Lithuania joined in 2004, and Albania and Croatia in 2009. Before 1989, Leningrad was 1,200 miles from NATO's nearest border. By 2004, with Estonia's entry into NATO, it was just 100 miles away.

When NATO installed a new anti-ballistic missile system, it told Russia that it was not usable against Russia, but, as Karl Lieber and Daryl Press wrote in *Foreign Affairs*, "If the United States' nuclear modernization were really aimed at rogue states or terrorists, the country's nuclear force would not need the additional thousand ground-burst warheads it will gain from the W-76 modernization program. The current and future US nuclear force, in other words, seems designed to carry out a preemptive disarming strike against Russia or China."[43] The US government continued to build a force able to win a nuclear war.

Former Secretary of Defense and CIA Director Robert Gates noted, "When the Soviet Union was collapsing in late 1991, [Defense Secretary Dick Cheney] wanted to see the dismemberment not only of the Soviet Union and the Russian empire but of Russia itself, so it could never again be a threat to the rest of the world."[44] Brzezinski urged, "both EU and NATO expansion should continue, thereby eliminating any geopolitical ambiguities or temptations in the areas immediately west of Russia."[45] The *Wall Street Journal* explained NATO's aggressive expansion as 'a strategy that will permanently guarantee Western overall interests in the

South Caucasus and Central Asia. Such interests include: direct access to energy resources ... and forward bases for allied operations."[46] The *Washington Post* opined, "The West wants to finish the job begun with the fall of the Berlin Wall and continue its march to the east."[47]

The US government continued to stir up trouble on Russia's borders. When the second Chechen-Russian war broke out in August 1999 with the Chechen invasion of Dagestan, the US government backed the invasion, ignoring its jihadi nature. Brzezinski and retired general Alexander Haig, a former secretary of state under President Ronald Reagan, set up an advocacy group for the Chechens.

In 2003, Russia and Moldova agreed the Kozak Memorandum, which settled the conflict in Moldova's republic of Transnistria, but the US government and the EU sabotaged the agreement: US Secretary of State Colin Powell and EU foreign policy chief Javier Solana pressured Moldova's President Vladimir Voronin into rejecting the Memorandum. Later, in the referendum held in Transnistria in September 2006, the vast majority voted for association with Russia.

In 2004 NATO and the EU backed the pro-NATO, pro-EU 'colour revolutions' in Georgia and Ukraine. When the vast majority in South Ossetia voted in November 2006 for independence from Georgia, the US and EU governments encouraged Georgia to attack South Ossetia. Georgian forces bombed South Ossetia's capital Tskhinvali, killing 100 civilians and 19 Russia peacekeepers. Only then did Russian forces intervene. This led to a short war, in which Russia defeated Georgia's forces. An EU study concluded that Georgia 'started an unjustified war' against Russia not the other way round.

The US and EU governments caused trouble in other ways too. Their proposed Transatlantic Trade and Investment Partnership (TTIP) was an attack on all other states, especially those that had started to cooperate independently of the USA, like Brazil, Russia, India, China and South Africa in the BRICS group, the Latin American countries in ALBA, Russia, China, Uzbekistan, Tajikistan, Kyrgyzstan and Kazakhstan, linked to Iran, in the Shanghai Cooperation Organization, and Southeast Asia's nations in the Association of Southeast Asian

Nations Economic Community. TTIP would override all previous trade rules and cause worldwide damage. As the European Commission admitted, "China, India and the ASEAN region will face decreases in their relative terms of trade on the world market, as the result of an ambitious EU-US FTA [Free Trade Agreement]."

In response, the BRICS group agreed in July 2014 to create the Asian Infrastructure Investment Bank as an alternative to the IMF. Russia strengthened its ties with the countries of Latin America, China, Iran and its longtime ally Syria. It decided to conduct its trade with Iran in rubles and its trade with China in both rubles and the Chinese yuan, instead of in US dollars. Russia also agreed two huge deals with China to build pipelines and sell oil and gas, cleaner-burning fuels which would reduce China's huge pollution problems.

In November, the G20 summit strengthened the US-led drive to war. NATO, the EU, Canada, Australia, New Zealand, Japan, Saudi Arabia and the Gulf despots united against Russia. The Saudi autocracy, acting as usual on the US government's behalf, used its dominance of the world's oil market to drive down oil prices, to hurt Russia and therefore Syria (and also Venezuela and Iran). Financial markets in New York and London 'shorted' the ruble, selling it short to undermine its value. The US, Australian and Japanese governments agreed on 'increasing military cooperation and strengthening maritime security' in the Pacific against China.

Chapter 13
Eastern Europe – counter-revolution and war

Yugoslavia under attack

In 1970, Yugoslavia changed its constitution to recognise its six republics - Serbia, Croatia, Slovenia, Bosnia-Herzegovina, Macedonia and Montenegro - as 'sovereign'. It upheld 'the right of every nation to dispose of its own realised surplus value'.[1] This made each republic, not the Yugoslav working class, the driving force of self-management.[2] It led to the resurrection of Croatian separatism, backed by the fascist ustashe organisation based in West Berlin. The state also promoted Islamism in Bosnia: between 1950 and 1970, it built 800 new mosques in Bosnia. By 1970, there were more mosques than there had been in 1930.

Yugoslavia adopted another new constitution in 1974 which granted even more powers to the republics and to the two autonomous provinces. This fragmented the national market into eight sub-markets, each with its own taxes, foreign exchange system, investment policy, and regulations. The result was wasted investment, as each republic tried to develop a full range of industries.[3]

Pavel Kolář summed up the moves towards splitting the country: "In Yugoslavia the 1963 reformist constitution, amended in 1968, brought in elements that reinforced national differences between the federal republics. The legislative independence of each republic was increased by enhancing the power of the Chamber of Nationalities and by granting Kosovo and Vojvodina the status of provinces within Serbia. The whole of political and economic life, including worker self-management, was increasingly organized along ethnic lines. The Constitution of 1974 promoted decentralization still further, practically transforming Yugoslavia into a confederation. During the 1980s, internationalism and class consciousness, embodied by the Yugoslav slogan 'Brotherhood and Unity', gave way to ethnic identification in the working class itself."[4]

Yugoslavia borrowed hugely in the 1970s, making it vulnerable to high interest rates. Between 1975 and 1981, its debt quadrupled to $19.3 billion. The government agreed with the IMF to refinance the debt, exposing the people to the usual IMF poverty programme of spending cuts, wage cuts, higher prices, privatisation, marketisation and the ending of food subsidies. So, in the 1990s, more than a tenth of the peoples of Kosovo, Bosnia, Montenegro and Serbia emigrated.

After the Soviet Union's demise and the counter-revolutions in Eastern Europe, the Yugoslav government, unlike the other Eastern European governments, refused to let NATO base its forces in the country and refused to apply to join the EEC. So the NATO and EEC powers decided to destroy it. As Warren Zimmerman, the US ambassador to Yugoslavia, said, "We are aiming for a dissolution of Yugoslavia into independent states."[5] The EEC declared the internal borders between Yugoslavia's republics to be international and inviolable and that the majority people in each republic, not the Yugoslav people as a whole, had the right to self-determination.[6]

The UN tried to keep Yugoslavia united. UN Security Council Resolution 1244, adopted on 10 June 1999, reaffirmed the sovereignty and territorial integrity of the Federal Republic of Yugoslavia.[7] Rosalyn Higgins, a former President of the International Court of Justice, stated,

"Contrary to popular belief, international law does *not* permit self-determination, by way of national secession, to national minorities."[8] There was no right to secede.[9]

UN Secretary-General Boutros Boutros-Ghali warned that recognising Slovenia and Croatia would 'fuel an explosive situation especially in Bosnia'. Lord Carrington also warned that recognition 'might well be the spark that sets Bosnia-Herzegovina alight'.[10] President Izetbegovic of Bosnia-Herzegovina asked Germany not to recognise Croatia because it would mean war in Bosnia-Herzegovina.

But Thatcher called for recognising and arming the individual republics. On 16 December 1991, the EEC said it intended 'to recognise the independence of all the Yugoslav republics' and on 23 December, Germany recognised Croatia. The Vatican recognised Slovenia and Croatia on 13 January 1992. The EEC and Thatcher followed suit on 15 January.

As Higgins stated, "By recognizing Croatia and Slovenia prematurely, the United Kingdom actively assisted in transforming the matter from an internal war to an international war. These countries were recognized as independent states at a time when they manifestly did not fulfil the criteria of statehood that the United Kingdom has always insisted upon for recognition – they were not in effective control of their own territory. This premature recognition, in subservience to German pressure, has been an unfortunate exemplar for a common EC foreign policy."[11]

Susan Woodward summed up, "For those who were the object of sanctions, European actions had been duplicitous. Europeans told Yugoslavs to honor the sanctity of international borders while they were themselves violating the norm of sanctity by applying it to the republican borders instead of Yugoslav and after some European nations had counselled secession and helped secretly to supply alternative national armies in the republics."[12]

In the Croatian war (1991-95) that followed, 20,000 people were killed and 550,000 people became refugees or were displaced.

Three bodies – NATO, the EU and the Warsaw Pact – had all claimed to keep the peace in Europe. When the Warsaw Pact went, the

EU, composed of NATO members, sparked this war, proving that it was the Pact that had kept the peace.[13] With the Pact gone, war also broke out in the Middle East with the first Gulf War. The end of the Soviet Union brought a new round of wars: from 1990 to 2000, four million people were killed in 49 countries.

On 25 January 1992, the Bosnian government held a referendum on secession, approved by the EEC. On 6 April (the anniversary of Hitler's attack on Yugoslavia), the EEC recognised the Republic of Bosnia and Herzegovina, sparking the war. Al-Qaeda, with Saudi support, used the Bosnian war to build itself, just as it had used the Afghan war in the 1980s. The US and British governments backed the Bosnian jihadists, just as they had backed the Afghan jihadists. One outcome of this disastrous policy was 9/11: Khalid Sheikh Muhammad, the so-called 'mastermind' of 9/11, had been a jihadist in Bosnia. So had two of the hijacker pilots.

In September 1993, Izetbegovic told Srebrenica's representatives, "President Clinton told me that if the Chetniks enter Srebrenica and massacre five thousand Muslims, then there will be military intervention."[14] Izetbegovic then weakened Srebrenica's defences, enabling local Serb forces to take the city in July 1995. NATO at once accused President Slobodan Milosevic of ordering the killing that followed. But, as the leading expert on the events at Srebrenica, the Dutch scholar Cees Wiebes, testified at The Hague, "we never found evidence that Milosevic was involved or ordered the mass murder at Srebrenica."[15]

The International Criminal Tribunal for the Former Yugoslavia estimated in November 2004 that the 1992-95 war in Bosnia killed 102,622 people. Two million people became refugees or were displaced, of a population of 4.3 million. Production fell by 80 per cent. The war cost tens of billions of dollars in devastated factories and real estate.

There was peace in Kosovo until February 1998, when the Kosovo Liberation Army [KLA] launched its terrorist campaign. KLA leaders traced their roots back to a fascist unit set up by the Italian occupiers during World War Two.[16] The UN condemned 'acts of terrorism by the

Kosovo Liberation Army'.[17] *The Scotsman* wrote, "the KLA was being armed, trained and assisted in Italy, Turkey, Kosovo and Germany by the Americans, the German external intelligence service and former and serving members of Britain's 22 SAS Regiment."[18] *Jane's Defense Weekly* confirmed that SAS units and US Special Forces aided the KLA.

President Clinton admitted on 23 March 1999, "And if we're going to have a strong economic relationship that includes our ability to sell around the world, Europe has got to be a key ... Now, that's what this Kosovo thing is all about."[19] The *New York Times* denounced Milosevic's determination to 'keep state controls and his refusal to allow privatization'.[20] The *Washington Post* complained, "Milosevic failed to understand the message of the fall of the Berlin Wall ... while other communist politicians accepted the Western model ... Milosevic went the other way."[21] The US government and the EU imposed the 1999 Rambouillet Accords which stated, "The economy of Kosovo will function in accordance with free market principles. ... There shall be no impediments to the free movement of persons, goods, services, and capital to and from Kosovo."

Clinton and Blair accused Serbia of committing genocide against ethnic Albanians in Kosovo. David Scheffer, US State Department ambassador-at-large for war crime issues, claimed that '225,000 ethnic Albanian men aged between 14 and 59' might have been murdered. But after the war, a UN tribunal concluded that the final count of the dead in Kosovo was 2,788, including combatants on both sides and Serbs and Roma killed by the KLA.

NATO's 1999 attack on Yugoslavia even violated the NATO treaty, whose Article 5 defined NATO's function as only defensive. The UN General Assembly condemned NATO's attack as illegal in Resolution 54/172. NATO Commander General Wesley Clark wrote that the Kosovo war "was coercive diplomacy, the use of armed forces to impose the political will of the NATO nations on the Federal Republic of Yugoslavia, or more specifically, on Serbia. The NATO nations voluntarily undertook this war."[22]

International lawyers agreed that, as Jonathan Charney asserted, "Indisputably, the NATO intervention through its bombing campaign violated the United Nations Charter and international law."[23] John Murphy stated, "NATO's use of force in Kosovo could not be justified under existing international law. ... the Charter requires that Security Council resolutions afford more than 'some measure of legitimacy' for the use of force by states to be legally justified. They must authorize the use of force, and none of the Council's resolutions adopted before the bombing began provides such authorization."[24]

NATO's attack killed 10,000 people and wrecked industry and infrastructure, costing Serbia more than $17 billion. General Herteleer, Chief of Staff of the Belgian Army, said, "Maybe we do have to make the bombings felt by hurting the Serb population itself. Let's inflict losses on them. Let's hit them where they're comfortable."[25]

The British press backed NATO's war. For example, when the Serbian government deported Kosovans to safety in Macedonia, the *Daily Mirror* commented, "The forced evacuation was reminiscent of SS troops sending Jews to the gas chambers."[26] The *Guardian* made the same comparison.[27] Both newspapers thus equated sending civilians away from war-zones with killing them. The *Mirror* called NATO's destruction of the RadioTV Serbia building, killing 16 civilians and wounding 19, 'a vital blow against Slobodan Milosevic's evil propaganda machine'.[28] The *Mirror*'s warmongering surely qualified it as an 'evil propaganda machine'.

The Greek people opposed the NATO/EU attack on Yugoslavia. NATO then destroyed the Greek consulate in the southern city of Nis.

After the wars ended, the only multi-ethnic country in the region was Serbia – one inhabitant in five was not Serbian. It had the largest number of refugees in Europe, one million people who had fled from Kosovo, Bosnia and Croatia (territories run by NATO), including 70,000 Muslim refugees.

After the war, the US government and the EU said they would only end their sanctions against Yugoslavia if the people ousted Milosevic in the presidential election of 2000. The US government spent $100 million backing the pro-US candidate Vojislav Kostunica. The EU gave $6 million to media which backed him. But Milosevic supporters won a majority in parliament, so the US government backed the 5 October coup which overthrew the elected government. Then the US government said it would not allow Yugoslavia an IMF loan unless Milosevic was arrested by 31 March 2001 and then that Yugoslavia would not get the loan unless it handed Milosevic over to the International Criminal Tribunal for the Former Yugoslavia by 29 June.

NATO forces have occupied Kosovo since 1999. In the following years, Kosovans drove out hundreds of thousands of Serbs and Roma in acts of 'reverse ethnic cleansing'. Kosovo was run by a UN Special Representative, backed by Kosovo Force (KFOR), which was complicit in trafficking women for the sex slave trade.[29] The *Washington Post* reported, "The sex-slave traffic in East European women, one of the major criminal scourges of post-communist Europe, is becoming a major problem in Kosovo, where porous borders, the presence of international troops and aid workers, and the lack of a working criminal-justice system have created almost perfect conditions for the trade. ... The first case of sex-slave trafficking came to light in October [1999] – four months after NATO-led peacekeepers entered the province ... In the last 10 years, according to women's advocacy groups, hundreds of thousands of women from the former Soviet republics and satellites have been trafficked to Western Europe, Asia and the United States."[30]

Kosovo's citizens were the poorest in Europe, with GDP per head just $7,600 in 2013. 30 per cent of the people lived below the poverty line. By November 2014, 40 per cent were unemployed. It housed a US military base which was a Guantanamo-style torture camp. NATO also had other new bases in Croatia, Bosnia and Macedonia.

From 2000 onwards, the US government and the EU pushed for Montenegro to secede from Yugoslavia. The US government spent $62 million, the EU $36 million, 'to advance Montenegro toward a free market economy'. NATO destabilised Macedonia, using the KLA, reborn as the National Liberation Army. The BBC reported, "Western forces were training guerrillas."[31] Albanian terrorists also founded the

'Liberation Army of Chameria' to 'free' Thrace ('Chameria') from Greece.

In 1989, the World Bank had demanded the closing down of 2,435 Yugoslav companies, putting two-thirds of Serbia's workers out of work. In 2002, the Bank said, "At least 800,000 Serbian workers in public services and state-run enterprises must be laid off."[32] Two decades after the wars, millions were still in poverty in all parts of former Yugoslavia.[33] The UN said that two-thirds of Yugoslavia's people lived on less than $2 a day. In 2008, Montenegro's GDP was 91 per cent of its 1989 GDP, Croatia's 83 per cent and Serbia's 72 per cent. In 2012, 19 per cent of Montenegro's workers were unemployed. From 2008 to 2013, Serbia's unemployment was about 20 per cent and half the 18-29-year-olds were out of work.

In Croatia, President Franjo Tudjman's privatisation policy damaged industry and trade: he wanted to create 200 wealthy families to start up a 'successful' economy. Economist Zarko Modric observed, "But only his aides could get funds for such privatisation. Once-successful production and export companies were sold for small amounts to people who had no knowledge of how to run them."[34] Croatia's accumulated foreign debt soon equalled its GDP, $55 billion. By 2013, unemployment was 21.6 per cent and 21 per cent were below the poverty line. Slovenia's economy shrank by 2.5 per cent in 2012, 1.1 per cent in 2013 and 1 per cent in 2014. Unemployment was 13.1 per cent and 13.5 per cent were below the poverty line.

In Bosnia, a Saudi-US-British alliance fostered Islamism, corruption and crime. Between 1995 and 2000, the US government and the EU gave Bosnia $5 billion, $1 billion of which Bosnia's leaders simply stole. The Saudis paid for 150 new Wahhabi mosques. In October 2002, the EU Special Representative for Bosnia and Herzegovina, Lord Ashdown, fired Munir Alibabic, head of Bosnian state security, who opposed Islamist extremism. Ashdown backed Islamists against reformers and secularists. In August 2005, the EU Force commander, Major General David Leakey, denied there were any mujehadin in Bosnia, yet in 2006 there were still 1,200. The EU, the US Treasury, the IMF and the World

Bank imposed the standard destructive 'austerity' package.[35] Through privatisation, companies were sold for a few euros and the new owners mostly did nothing with them. By 2013, the unemployment rate was 44.3 per cent and growth was 0.8 per cent.

The 2009 study by the United Nations Development Program (UNDP), 'Privatisation of State Capital in Bosnia-Herzegovina', named corruption and ethnic divisions between Bosniak Muslims, Croats and Serbs, 'entrenched in their entities', as the main reasons for Bosnia's economic disaster. It had even higher youth unemployment than Greece. Like Montenegro, Kosovo and Croatia, Bosnia became 'a hostage state', whose rulers let mafia gangs make profits 'through corruptive transactions with public officials and politicians in power'. The US firm Dynocorp hired US police officers to serve in the UN's International Police Task Force. For years, this UN body connived at the sex slave trade there.[36]

In February 2014, workers at Tuzla demanded an end to privatisation. So did workers in Zenica, Bihac, Mostar and Sarajevo. The EU Representative, Valentin Inzko, threatened EU military intervention if the protests continued.

Counter-revolutions

Before the events of 1989-91, not all Eastern Europe's countries were suffering crises, budget deficits, shortages, debts, inflation and collapses in production. Czechoslovakia, in particular, was stable. Yet its Czech and Slovak leaders, with no popular mandate, still split the country in two.

The events of 1989-91 are often called 'revolutions', but were really counter-revolutions, attacks on the working class. The capitalist classes of Eastern Europe gained; the working classes lost out. The US government and the EU turned Eastern Europe's countries back into colonies of the West. The 'newly-independent' countries became new protectorates, with German employers and US occupiers. Foreign investors cherry-picked the most profitable firms and stripped their assets.

Wages in Central and Eastern Europe were cut more than in any country during the 1930s Great Depression. In 1990-92, they were cut by 22 per cent in the Czech Republic and by 27 per cent in Slovakia in 1989-93. Hungary's wages were cut by 20 per cent in 1990-94 and again by 18 per cent in 1995-96. So across the region, poverty increased from around 4 per cent in the late 1980s to 45 per cent in 1993-95.[37] Education and R&D budgets were cut; school enrolment rates and literacy rates fell.[38] The stress of rising unemployment and poverty caused rising death rates and falling marriage and birth rates.[39]

Under Eastern Europe's countries' huge privatisation programmes, firms were sold for next to nothing to asset-strippers, speculators and criminal groups who got rich by looting publicly-owned assets.[40] Profits were privatised and losses nationalised. It was all too easy to strip national assets and transfer wealth abroad.

The new governments did not even back their own new domestic capitalist firms, giving most help to foreign companies.[41] Banks, foreign and domestic, provided little finance for investment, instead promoting parasitic activities that enriched the few at the expense of the many. The EU's expansion into Eastern Europe gave West European banks and well-connected insiders windfall profits as they loaded big mortgages onto previously debt-free East European properties. But it was a de facto tax on the mass of the people who had to take on huge mortgages to get housing.[42]

As even the European Commission admitted, "corruption, fraud and economic crime are widespread in most candidate countries, leading to a lack of confidence by the citizens and discrediting the reforms."[43] Poland suffered 'a veritable explosion of economic crime'.[44]

After the counter-revolutions, all Eastern Europe's countries suffered crises, budget deficits, shortages, debts, inflation and collapses in production. In 23 of the 25 countries in Central and Eastern Europe and the former Soviet Union, real GDP in 1999 was still lower than in 1989. The new governments' policies worsened the slump.[45] In Hungary, for example, the 'structural adjustment' of 1988-95 destroyed more economic assets than did World War Two - 20 per cent of GDP and 1.5 million jobs. By 2013, 10.5 per cent of Hungarians were unemployed, 14 per cent were below the poverty line and growth was just 0.2 per cent.

In Poland, Solidarity's 1987 programme demanded wage cuts, job cuts and welfare cuts. Its 1990 'shock therapy' cut real wages by 30 per cent in just one month. US economist Jeffrey Sachs, the shock therapist-in-chief, urged in 1990, "Western observers should not over dramatise lay-offs and bankruptcies. Poland, like the rest of Eastern Europe, now has too little unemployment, not too much."[46] Poland's unemployment rose from zero to 16 per cent in 1993-94, 18 per cent in 2002 and 10.3 per cent in 2013. GDP was slashed by 8 per cent. Poland's poorest people had a life expectancy 15 years lower than the richest. Abortion was made illegal in 1993. A third of health care jobs disappeared between 1995 and 2003. There were 1,553 child care centres in 1989, by 2006 just 371. As American historian David Ost observed, "[W]hen Solidarity won, Polish workers lost."[47] Solidarity's membership fell from 10 million in the early 1980s to 400,000 in 2013. By 2013, just 2.1 million workers, 8 per cent of the population, were members of a trade union.

In 1990-92, the Czech Republic's real GDP fell by 13 per cent and Slovakia's by 23 per cent.[48] Unemployment in Slovakia rose from 39,603 in 1990 to nearly 500,000 in 1999. From 1999 to 2005, there were 9 per cent unemployed in the Czech Republic. In 2012, the Czech economy contracted by 1 per cent and by 0.7 per cent in 2013; 7.1 per cent were unemployed. In Slovakia, growth was just 0.8 per cent in 2013 and 14.4 per cent were unemployed.

Bulgaria's GDP fell by a quarter between 1989 and 1994. By 1997, pensions were $2 a month and 90 per cent of people were below the poverty line of $4 a day. In 2013, 11.6 per cent were unemployed.

Albania's economy grew by just 0.7 per cent in 2013, but only through 'buoyant earnings from drug smuggling, arms dealing, money laundering and people trafficking'.[49] 16.9 per cent were unemployed and 14.3 per cent were below the poverty line. Criminal gangs trafficked

Albanian men, women and children for sex. The government cut back its trafficking investigations and punished trafficking's victims, not its agents. Gangs also increasingly trafficked money, arms, contraband and Afghan opium.

The GDPs of Georgia, Tajikistan and Moldova in 2008 were just 60 per cent of 1989's. In 2013, Georgia had 15 per cent unemployed, Tajikistan 2.5 per cent (officially, but, as the CIA noted, the real rate was far higher) and Moldova 5.8 per cent.

Eastern Europe's countries depended on vast imports of capital from the West, but when the 2008-09 crash hit, the capital inflows dried up. Between 2007 and 2012, their GDP rose by only 11 per cent in total.

By the mid-1990s, 40-60 per cent of the peoples of the Baltic states were in poverty. Pensions and savings were slashed. Suicides and murders increased. These states too depended on imports of foreign capital, so in the 2008-09 crash Estonia lost 17 per cent of its GDP, Lithuania 15 per cent and Latvia 20 per cent.

In June 2009, Latvia's government cut spending and raised taxes. It cut public sector wages by almost 40 per cent and pensions by 10 per cent, and increased health care fees.[50] Unemployment rose to 21.7 per cent in 2010, the highest in the EU. By 2013, it was 12 per cent, even after its population fell by 7.6 per cent between 2007 and 2012.

In 2013, unemployment was 10.9 per cent in Estonia and 17.5 per cent of the people lived below the poverty line. Growth was just 1.5 per cent.

Lithuania played an increasingly large part in global money laundering and tax evasion. It became hugely unequal. In 2010, wages were cut by 11.3 per cent and by another 6.7 per cent by late 2011. Unemployment fell from 17.8 per cent in 2010 to 12.4 per cent in 2013, but again, only because of increased emigration. Its population fell by 10.1 per cent between 2007 and 2012.

In 2013, Latvia's GDP was still 9 per cent below its pre-crisis peak. Lithuania and Estonia were back to where they were, after suffering huge slumps. Latvia's cumulated loss between 2008 and 2013 was 89 per cent of the country's pre-crisis annual output, Lithuania's was 43 per cent and Estonia's 39 per cent.

By 2007, unemployment among Eastern Europe's young people was 40 per cent. So millions of these new EU citizens voted with their feet and left their countries to find work abroad.[51] Two million Poles (one in 20 of the population) emigrated, 700,000-1,000,000 of them to Britain. More than a million Albanians (one in six), 1.9 million Romanians (a tenth) and 750,000 Bulgarians (a tenth) emigrated.

This huge migration helped to cut the wages of the worst-paid workers wherever they went. For example, immigration led to wage reductions for the worst-paid fifth of British workers.[52] A 10 per cent rise in the proportion of immigrants working in semi-skilled and unskilled sectors like care homes, bars and shops, led to a 5.2 per cent pay cut in the sector.[53]

But across the region, there were signs of resistance to the EU 'austerity' measures: workers went on strike in Slovakia in 1991, Slovenia in 1992 (defeating a wage freeze), Hungary in 1990, when drivers struck successfully against a 65 per cent rise in the price of petrol, and in Latvia and Romania in 1999. In Slovenia, trade unions were still well organised and relatively strong. In 2005, they organised the largest trade union public protest in Slovenia's history against the government's proposed flat tax rate. In 2010, Hungary's government refused to enforce the cuts in wages, pensions and public spending demanded by the IMF.

In Poland in 1990, transport workers and miners went on strike; in 1991, workers in industry, education and agriculture struck. On 13 January 1992, Solidarity declared its first strike against the government: a one-hour strike against a proposal to raise energy prices. Another, two-hour, strike took place on 14 December. In 1992-93, the number of strikes rose to some thousands a year, many in education, as teachers demanded higher pay and more funding for education. In 2013, steelworkers and rail, mine and health workers in Silesia struck for better job security, higher pensions and better health care.

Across Eastern Europe's countries, most people rejected the capitalist counter-revolution. The American magazine *USA Today* wrote in 1999,

"When the Berlin Wall crumbled, East Germans imagined a life of freedom where consumer goods were abundant and hardships would fade. Ten years later, a remarkable 51% say they were happier with communism." In 2010, 72 per cent of Hungarians said they were worse off than before the counter-revolution. A 2013 CBOS poll found that just 33.4 per cent of Poles thought that the free market was better than a planned economy; 85 per cent thought that the government should provide jobs and 85 per cent expected free health care.

The Belarus exception

After the collapse of the Soviet Union, Belarus suffered greatly. In 1989-93, GDP was down by 14 per cent and real wages by 85 per cent. Between 1991 and 1994, $15 billion fled the country.

But then Belarus chose a different route. In July 1994, 80 per cent of the people voted for Alexander Lukashenko to become President. The new government at once rejected IMF policies. President Lukashenko said, "First of all, we need to support our domestic manufacturers." 80 per cent of industry stayed state-owned. Collective farms produced food for the people.

Belarus largely avoided the crisis that hit the other former Soviet states. Entry and exit were relatively simple, but there was no mass exodus to its free market neighbours. In 2001, more people moved into it than left, unlike every other East European state.

In 2004, the World Bank reported, "overall health expenditures are progressive, in the sense that the poor benefit relatively more than the better off. ... Pensions are found to be the most adequate benefit, in part as a result of the policy of indexing pensions to real wages. Child allowances are also found to provide adequate protection. ... Belarus can be justly proud of the elaborate system of social services it provides to its population. The ability of households to access quality education, health and social protection services makes a large difference to their living standards in the present, and their prospects for the future." It summed up, "The poverty reduction and inequality performance of Belarus is impressive."[54]

GDP in 2008 was 160 per cent of 1989's. In 2013, the economy grew by 2.1 per cent, poverty was below 2 per cent and just 1 per cent were unemployed. State pensions from the Soviet era were still paid on time. It was the most equal country in the world: the highest income was only five times the lowest. It had free education and health care. Male life expectancy in 2011 had risen to 65.6 years, female to 77.4. Its adult literacy rate was 99.7 per cent, according to the UN.

These policies proved popular. Lukashenko held and won referendums in 1995 and 1996. He won presidential elections in 2001 with 78 per cent of the votes, 2006 with 82 per cent and 2010 with 79.65 per cent. The country also held parliamentary elections in 1995, 2000, 2004, 2008 and 2012 and local elections in 1995, 1999, 2003, 2007 and 2010.

In the 2001 election, Gerard Stoudmann, the head of the Office for Democratic Institutions and Human Rights, of the Organization for Security and Co-operation in Europe [OSCE], said there was 'no evidence of manipulation or fraud of the result'. The Association of Central and Eastern European Election Officials confirmed that the election had been 'free and open in compliance with universal democratic institutions'.[55]

In response to Belarus' achievements, the NATO powers treated Belarus as an enemy. In 1995, the IMF suspended loans, on the grounds that Belarus subsidised its agriculture – as did the USA. President Lukashenko expelled the IMF commission, calling them 'swindlers'. The US government accused Belarus of sex trade trafficking, but, as the International Office for Migration pointed out, "Belarus has been globally recognised as one of the world's most resolute fighters against the slave trade."[56] US Senator John McCain said absurdly, "September 11th opened our eyes to the status of Belarus as a national security threat."

The USA passed the Belarus Democracy Act in 2004 demanding that Belarus introduce democracy - when Belarus had 18 registered political parties. The Act claimed that Belarus harassed its Jewish community, though Belarus' chief rabbi said that he had 'no qualms with any aspect of Lukashenko's rule' and the USA-based National Conference of Soviet Jewry noted that 'long suppressed Jewish life has rebounded and is flourishing'.[57] When Belarus' government closed down two newspapers that regularly printed anti-Semitic articles, the US government accused it of stifling independent media - Belarus had 555 independent newspapers. In 2004, Belarus banned the White Legion, a fascist, terrorist group - the US government accused the government of infringing their human rights.

At the 2004 meeting of the UN Commission on Human Rights Belarus and Russia tabled a resolution warning of the 'resurgence and spread of neo-Nazism, neo-fascism and aggressive nationalism'. The majority backed it, but the US government and the EU member states voted against. In 2004, the US government called Belarus an 'outpost of tyranny'. In 2006, President Bush ordered sanctions against the country and tried to isolate it. The Polish government called on the USA to bomb it.

A 2006 poll paid for by the US Republican party found that the ratings of Alexander Milinkevich and other opposition leaders were in single figures.[58] In 2006, the US government wasted $14.2 million on backing the opposition, in 2007, $27 million and in 2008, another $27 million.

Ukraine: counter-revolution and war

After the Soviet Union dissolved, Ukraine suffered a sharp decline. Its governments cut wages and services. By 1999, wages were less than half 1989's level. GDP in 1999 was 60 per cent below the 1989 level. In 2008, it was still 30 per cent below. Its governments built monuments to Stepan Bandera, the OUN leader, who joined the Nazi invasion of the Soviet Union. President Viktor Yushchenko declared Bandera and fellow Nazi Roman Shukhevych 'heroes of the Ukraine'.

The 2004 'Orange Revolution' in Ukraine divided much of its economy from Russia, causing yet more decline. In 2009, GDP fell another 15 per cent, wages were cut by 10.9 per cent and unemployment rose to 9.6 per cent. The birth rate was very low and the death rate high. Government-backed persecution of Russians and Jews cut the number of ethnic Russians living in Ukraine from 11.4 million in 1991 to 8.3 million in 2001 and the number of Jews from 486,326 to 103,600.[59] The population fell from 52.2 million in 1994 to 45.5 million in 2009.

In 2009, it was estimated that 35 per cent of the people lived below the poverty line, while the fifty richest owned almost half the wealth. In 2010, the IMF demanded public spending cuts and a 50 per cent rise in gas prices. Most of the IMF $15 billion package of 2014 went straight out to Western banks to pay off loans.

NATO wanted to seize control of Ukraine, to complete the hostile line of armed nations to Russia's west, even though neutrality was part of Ukraine's constitution.[60] In April 2008, NATO stated that both Ukraine and Georgia 'will become members of NATO'. The US government spent more than five billion dollars funding at least 65 pro-NATO, pro-EU NGOs in Ukraine, as Victoria Nuland, the US Assistant Secretary of State for European Affairs, admitted. In May 2008, the EU unveiled its Eastern Partnership initiative, to integrate countries like Ukraine and Georgia into the EU.

In November 2013, the EU triggered a crisis when it told President Viktor Yanukovych (elected in February 2010) to sign a free trade deal with the EU. The deal would have imposed the usual EU 'austerity', ending food and energy subsidies and ending all prospects for development. When Yanukovych refused to sign the deal, the EU and the US government started moves to oust him. They fomented civil war in Ukraine, arming and funding the fascists of Svoboda and Pravy Sektor (Right Sector, a paramilitary group). The European Parliament had called Svoboda 'racist, anti-Semitic and xenophobic' in 2012, but when Svoboda backed the EU deal, the EU rebranded its members 'pro-democracy activists'.

The Russian, French and German governments and Ukraine's government and opposition reached an agreement for a peaceful transfer of power after new elections. But the Ukrainian opposition illegally overthrew the elected president on 22 February 2014. The NATO powers celebrated this as a 'democratic revolution'. Many in Ukraine, especially in eastern Ukraine, resisted the coup. The post-coup regime at once signed the free trade deal with the EU.

The EU and the US government wanted Arseniy Yatsenuk as Prime Minister and so it happened. One of his first acts was to tell Russia to leave its naval base of Sebastopol in the Crimea, breaking Ukraine's 1997 agreement with Russia on the Status and Conditions of the Black Sea Fleet Stationing on the Territory of Ukraine. Khrushchev had in 1954 illegally split Crimea from Russia. On 16 March 2014, Crimea held a referendum on whether to rejoin Russia. Voter turnout was 83 per cent; 97 per cent voted to rejoin. The NATO powers denounced the referendum, saying that all Ukraine should have been polled and that a referendum in Crimea alone was invalid. But when Khrushchev split Crimea from Russia, he held no referendum in Russia or Crimea. And when NATO split Kosovo from Serbia in 1999, it held no referendum in Serbia or Kosovo.

In April, NATO Secretary General Anders Fogh Rasmussen announced the reinforcement of NATO forces across Eastern Europe: "air policing aircraft will fly more sorties over the Baltic region. Allied ships will deploy to the Baltic Sea, the eastern Mediterranean, and elsewhere as required." The US government deployed troops to Poland and the Baltic states 'for military exercises'. Finland and Sweden signed Memoranda of Understanding with NATO stating their readiness to host NATO forces.

On 27 May, his second day in office, the new president of Ukraine, billionaire Petro Poroshenko, launched an 'anti-terrorist operation' against eastern Ukraine, with airstrikes and ground assaults. NATO pledged military support for Poroshenko. His air and artillery attacks on residential areas forced more than 250,000 Ukrainians to flee to Russia. By 3 February 2015, 5,350 people had been killed.

On 17 July, commercial airliner MH17 was shot down over eastern Ukraine. US intelligence officials said that there was no evidence of Russian involvement. President Vladimir Putin called for an independent investigation by 'a fully representative group of experts to be working at the site under the guidance of the International Civil Aviation Organization (ICAO)'. The preliminary report into the tragedy, conducted by representatives of all the countries involved, did not assign blame to any side.

But NATO and the EU pushed NATO armed forces right up to Russia's western borders, imposed more sanctions and ratcheted up the 'hate Russia' propaganda war. They were pursuing Brzezinski's strategy of trying to draw Russia into a 'prolonged and costly' war in Ukraine. Brzezinski had used a similar strategy in the 1980s when he armed Islamic fundamentalists in Afghanistan as part of a proxy war against the Soviet Union. On 4 December, the US Congress passed resolution H. Res. 758, by 411 votes to 10. The resolution did everything except openly declare war on Russia. It stated that 'military intervention' by the Russian Federation in Ukraine 'poses a threat to international peace'. It proffered no proof, no pictures of any Russian military units. It demanded the withdrawal of Russian forces from Ukraine. It urged the regime to resume military operations against eastern Ukraine, calling for the 'disarming of separatist and paramilitary forces in eastern Ukraine'. This would mean the deaths of many more civilians.

The resolution urged the US president to 'provide the government of Ukraine with necessary defense articles, services, and intelligence in order to defend its territory and sovereignty'. The German daily newspaper *Süddeutsche Zeitung* warned that Russia would take a US decision to arm the Kiev regime with offensive weapons as equivalent to a declaration of war.

The resolution also demanded that Russia 'cease its support for the Assad regime in Syria'. It called on NATO to increase its war-readiness. It called for the return of Crimea to Ukraine, of Abhazia and South Ossetia to Georgia and of Transnistria to Moldova.

The US Congress also passed a 'Ukraine Freedom Support Act' which President Barack Obama signed into law on 19 December. This provided for increased sanctions against Russia. It authorised spending $350 million on military aid to Ukraine, including anti-tank and anti-armour weapons; crew weapons and ammunition; counter-artillery radars; fire control and guidance equipment; surveillance drones; and secure command and communications equipment. The Act also designated Ukraine, Moldova and Georgia as major non-NATO allies, to speed up the transfer of military equipment. Finally, the Act authorised $30 million to 'counter Russian propaganda' in the countries of the former Soviet Union. The Pentagon's 2016 budget proposal asked for an extra $168 million to 'counter Russian aggressive acts', $117 million for Ukraine and $51 million for Moldova and Georgia, plus $789 million to bolster NATO in the European Union.

As part of the war preparations, Britain aimed to send 1,000 troops and four RAF Typhoon jets to add to NATO 'Force Integration Units' to be set up in new NATO command posts in Estonia, Latvia, Lithuania, Poland, Romania and Bulgaria. There were also plans to deploy such a unit in Hungary. 30,000 NATO troops were to be deployed in the region in what the new NATO Secretary General Jens Stoltenberg called 'the biggest reinforcement of our collective defense since the end of the cold war'.

NATO's aggression was based on the big lie that there had been a Russian invasion. But the Chief of Ukraine's General Staff, Colonel-General Viktor Muzhenko, revealed on 29 January 2015, "Now we have only the facts of participation of individual citizens of the Russian Federation and the Russian Army, who are members of illegal armed groups. I will also say that currently the Ukrainian army is not fighting with the regular units of the Russian army."

But NATO continued to escalate the conflict. NATO deputy general secretary Alexander Vershbow said on 2 February, "NATO is doing its part. To help Ukraine to modernize and reform its armed forces, we have launched five trust funds to assist in areas like command and control, logistics, cyber defense and military medicine." Vershbow continued, "We are sending more advisors to Kiev and will be carrying out exercises with Ukraine's armed forces. And we are helping Moldova and Georgia to strengthen their defense capacity in similar ways, and, in Georgia's case, to help it prepare for future membership in the Alliance." NATO defence ministers also discussed 'the nuclear threat scenario from Russia in the past few months' and 'the consequences for the nuclear strategy of the alliance'.

At a press conference at the Munich Security Conference on 7 February US Air Force General Philip Breedlove, the head of both the US European Command and NATO in Europe, insisted that NATO could not 'preclude out of hand the possibility of the military option' in Ukraine. By contrast, President Putin said, "We repeatedly called upon all conflicting sides to stop the bloodshed immediately and sit down at the negotiating table."

On 12 February, the governments of Ukraine, Russia, Germany and France concluded the Minsk peace agreement, later approved by the UN Security Council:

1. Immediate and full bilateral ceasefire
2. Withdrawal of all heavy weapons by both sides
3. Effective monitoring and verification regime for the ceasefire and withdrawal of heavy weapons
4. From day one of the withdrawal begin a dialogue on the holding of local elections
5. Pardon and amnesty by banning any prosecution of figures involved in the Donetsk and Luhansk conflict
6. Release of all hostages and other illegally detained people
7. Unimpeded delivery of humanitarian aid to the needy, internationally supervised
8. Restoration of full social and economic links with affected areas
9. Full Ukrainian government control will be restored over the state border, throughout the conflict zone
10. Withdrawal of all foreign armed groups, weapons and mercenaries from Ukrainian territory

11. 11. Constitutional reform in Ukraine, with adoption of a new constitution by the end of 2015.

The peace agreement was achieved because resistance forces in eastern Ukraine had pushed the regime's forces, fascist militias and mercenaries out of the Donbass/Donetsk region. And because EU Commissioners and US, British, Polish and other Eastern European governments were kept out of the peace talks.

In direct violation of point 10 of the agreement, the US government announced in late February that it would send 300 troops to Ukraine to help train the regime's forces and Prime Minister David Cameron announced on 24 February that 75 British troops would do likewise.

Chapter 14

Cuba, the Special Period – workers in control

The Special Period, 1990-2010

When the Soviet Union and Eastern Europe collapsed, Cuba lost 80 per cent of its trade and more than 40 per cent of its GDP. It suffered power cuts and hunger, with shortages of everything. The US government tightened its blockade to try to make Cuba collapse too. The Torricelli-Graham Act of 1992 and the Helms-Burton Act of 1996 banned US companies from trading with Cuba and also made it illegal for foreign companies to do so. The sanctions blocked Cuba's access to US markets and to loans and aid, restricting investment and growth.[1]

The sanctions cut Cubans' access to medicines and medical goods. In 1990, Cuba imported $55 millions' worth, in 1996, just $18 million. WHO officials noted, "In the health sector, the consequences of the embargo have a negative multiplier effect on the cost of basic everyday health products, on the difficulties in acquiring health products, on the availability of basic services and, therefore, on the overall living conditions of the population … The embargo affects the individual health care of all people, regardless of age or gender, through its impact on Cuba's unified health system institutions, research facilities, epidemiological surveillance institutions and disease control agencies."[2] The US government admitted, "The embargo on Cuba is the most comprehensive set of American sanctions ever imposed upon a country."[3]

The EU backed the US blockade. It refused to sign any cooperation agreement with Cuba, the only Latin American country with which it had no such agreement. EU Commissioner Chris Patten pressed for Cuba to be indefinitely banned from membership of the Cotonou Agreement for African, Caribbean and Pacific countries.

President Yeltsin too banned all trade with Cuba. He went on to give away the assets of the Soviet working class to the new breed of gangsters running the country. Cubans saw what would happen to their country if they did not take charge.

The US government also continued to sponsor terrorism against Cuba. Some 3,500 Cubans were killed during mercenary attacks, all launched from the USA. Five brave Cubans volunteered to infiltrate the mercenary organisations to stop these attacks. When they told US authorities about possible terrorist attacks against Cuba, they were jailed in 1998 for long sentences. The last three of the five were finally freed in December 2014.

In response to the US/EU blockade, Salud International asked London Ambulance Unison if it could add an ambulance to a shipment of buses, fire engines and other aid from British trade unions. In the end, with the help of generous union and individual donations, London Ambulance Unison sent more than 50 ambulances. It was a historic day when the *Luric* docked in Havana and delivered its cargo.

With the Soviet Union gone and the US government intensifying its assault, Cuba faced unprecedented difficulties. So the Cuban government declared a 'Special Period not in time of war'. This put Cuba on a footing like Britain's Special Period during World War Two. Despite severe hardship, there was a strong sense of working class unity. Cuba's other assets included the welfare state, price controls, the monopoly of international exchange, national ownership of the means of production, a capacity for a state-led, collective response, and a tradition of winning voluntary support through mass mobilisations after public participation and debate. The Special Period, for all its pain, was the first time since colonisation that Cuba was a fully free and independent country, no longer dependent on a major power.[4]

Specially convened 'workers' parliaments' attended by 85 per cent of Cuba's workers discussed the way forward. Special Congresses of the Cuban Communist Party and of the mass organisations like the trade unions, the Union of Communist Youth, the Committees for the Defence of the Revolution and the Cuban Federation of Cuban Women were held.

The Committees for the Defence of the Revolution took care of their local communities and made sure that no one fell through the safety net. Trade union farms were opened to grow food. The health workers' union looked after the health of the people and the health system's infrastructure. The transport union looked after the transport system. The government distributed half a million bicycles to workers and students. The education and science union maintained educational standards despite lack of equipment and supported pioneering developments in biotechnology and genetics. The Institute of Innovators and Rationalisers was set up to help workers to solve the problems caused by the blockade.

Cuba maintained basic food security even in these conditions of acute scarcity. The state distribution body used the food-rationing system and networks like the *vías sociales*, which provided free or subsidised meals at workplaces, schools and health centres. Thanks to the ration-system's fixed prices, the cost of meeting basic food needs, around 40 pesos a month per person, was kept below the minimum social-security allowance of 85 pesos a month. The monthly ration basket, for which the average Cuban family paid about $4.70 in 2009, actually cost $61. Similarly, the average family quarterly electricity bill was 32.22 CUP, while the actual cost of the energy supplied was 708.84 CUP.[5] The government introduced a Food Programme which encouraged local self-provisioning and small-scale experimentation, including using animal traction, organic fertilisers, biological pest control, sustainable farming and renewable energy sources.[6]

Foreign investment was sought to develop tourism as the only short-term way to get hard currency to buy the goods needed to survive. Tourism brought with it the new problem of a dual currency, which meant that those with access to hard currency were better off than others, and this had to be managed.

Cuba also addressed its security concerns. Previously, it had relied on its relationship with the Soviet Union to defend it from the constant threat of US invasion. Now Cuba relied on its own ability to defend itself. It learned from the Vietnamese the lessons of developing a strategy of a 'war of all the people'. The whole population had a role in the defence of the country. Trade unions had their own armouries. Previously, the watchword had been that the enemy would never step foot on the island. Now it was to defeat an invading army by guerrilla struggle.

In 2000, Cuba launched its Battle of Ideas, a nationwide campaign to reassert and develop honest, humanitarian, working class morals. They took this campaign into schools, youth organisations, trade unions and all the other mass organisations. It gave birth to a new worker called a 'social worker'. The government opened new schools for these social workers, mainly young women from poor families. 28,000 had graduated by 2005. These workers visited every family and individual, learned the specific problems facing different groups – families, single mothers, unemployed, children, pensioners – and tried to find solutions for them. This nationwide door-to-door survey discovered that 37,000 elderly people were living alone and in need of personal attention, so the government launched programmes to help them.

These young people went into communities and sought out disaffected youth. They tried to befriend them, win their trust and convince them with ideas and arguments to find a rewarding life-project that chimed with the larger collective project of the Cuban revolution.

They also dealt with the corruption that developed during the Special Period. First they tackled the country's 2,000 petrol stations, where half the revenue from fuel sales had gone missing. 10,000 of them took over the pumps and accompanied delivery drivers, monitoring the deliveries from the refineries. In two months, the state's income from petrol stations doubled. This aided the country's economic revival and redistributed wealth from the 'new rich' to the working class.

Their next mission was to replace every domestic incandescent light globe in the country with an energy-efficient compact fluorescent bulb and to replace ancient Soviet fans and refrigerators with new, more efficient appliances. This was part of Cuba's 'energy revolution', which started in 2006 and aimed to save the country $1 billion a year.

As another part of its survival strategy, Cuba developed more links with countries around the world, especially with its neighbours in Latin America. In December 2004, Cuba and Venezuela founded ALBA, the Bolivarian Alliance for the Peoples of Our America.[7] By 2014, it had eleven members. In December 2011, all 33 countries south of the USA founded CELAC – the Community of Latin-American and Caribbean States. In 2013, Cuba was elected to its second Presidency.[8]

The Special Period officially ended as the economy recovered. Between 1996 and 2000, it grew by 3.9 per cent per head a year. By 2005, Cuba had recovered its pre-crisis GDP. In 2006, it introduced its own hard currency. Tourism, biotechnology and the scientific and medical services sectors had all contributed. By 2013, real national income per head was 40 per cent above 1990's level. The Cuban working class could only do all this because it held state power.

Internationalism

In 1999, Hurricane George devastated Haiti, followed by Hurricane Mitch, which destroyed much of Honduras and Nicaragua. More than 60,000 people lost their lives. Cuba, along with many other countries, sent doctors to help the survivors in all three countries.

After a month, most other aid agencies left, but the Ernesto Che Guevara Cuban Medical Brigade stayed in Haiti, as agreed with the government. It comprised 575 doctors and health professionals and operated the same Integral Health Programme, based on the Cuban domestic model, as the Cuban brigades in 62 other countries. It covered 70 per cent of the Haitian population.

The work of each unit started with a comprehensive analysis of people's health, the risks to health and the resources available. Then each unit took measures to provide clean drinking water, to improve diet, sanitation and sewage disposal, and to visit every house in the area. This would usually be the first time that most Haitians had ever seen a doctor. On their visits, the doctors saw every member of the household and made basic health checks. They then organised various 'circles' for the elderly, pregnant women, adolescents and children, to discuss and identify risks and find solutions. Some medical problems required surgery, but other problems were solved by measures as basic as exercise, the use of condoms, prenatal examinations and better family hygiene.

The brigades mostly comprised young people, many of whom studied together in the same medical school, along with some experienced professionals, specialists in internal medicine, orthopaedics, surgery, paediatrics, gynaecology and obstetrics. They provided health care to the people of Haiti despite the personal risk of malaria and dengue and the two-year absences from home. They were also committed to their country, to the Cuban revolution and to their union. In the corner of every brigade house there was a 'patriotic corner', with their flag and items reminding them of Cuba. But they maintained strict political neutrality in Haiti.

Part of the agreement with the Haitian government was that young people from the poor areas where the Cubans were working would be educated as doctors and health professionals, to return to these areas to work for at least three years. As they were all being educated in the Cuban model, it was hoped that they would develop the same revolutionary professionalism as the Cubans.

Between 1999 and 2007, the Cuban Medical Brigade sent 1,000 doctors, nurses and other personnel to Haiti. They conducted almost 15 million patient visits. Life expectancy rose from 54 to 61 and the rates of maternal death, infant mortality and child mortality were all reduced by more than half, resulting in a verified saving of 81,856 lives.

Haiti's President Jean-Bertrand Aristides, a former Catholic priest, said that there were stars in the sky and on earth – those on the earth were the Cuban doctors.

After Haiti's 2010 earthquake, the US Navy treated 871 patients and performed 843 surgical operations in seven weeks. In the same period, the Cubans treated 227,443 patients and performed 6,499 operations.[9] In 2010, the organisation 'Project Censored' called 'Cuba Provided the Greatest Medical Aid to Haiti after the Earthquake' one of the year's 'outstanding stories ignored by the US corporate media'.

Cuba gave medical aid to many other countries too. 14,000 Cuban aid workers, mostly medical, worked overseas in the late 1970s, mostly in Latin America and Africa. Otto Reich, Bush's representative for Latin America and a former organiser of anti-Cuban terrorism, threatened US intervention in Venezuela because of the growing number of 'military-style' Cubans in the country. Castro responded that the doctors were there at the invitation of the Venezuelan government and that if the US government would replace Cuba's 10,169 doctors in Venezuela with American doctors, Cuba would gladly withdraw them.

In the areas of Ghana where Cuban medical professionals worked, infant mortality was cut from 59/1,000 to 7.8/1,000. After the Pakistan earthquake of 2005, Cuba sent 2,465 medical workers, including 1,430 doctors. Almost all the other aid teams left after five weeks; Cuba's stayed for eight months, treating more than a million people and leaving behind 32 fully-equipped field hospitals. In 2014, Cuba mobilised 461 doctors and nurses to West Africa, the largest medical contingent of any country, to help in the fight against Ebola.

By 2009, 38,000 Cuban health workers, including 17,000 doctors, were working overseas. By 2010, Cuban health workers had performed more than 2.2 million operations, assisted 768,858 births and vaccinated more than 9.2 million people.[10] By 2012, surgeons working on Cuba's Operation Milagro had performed free eye surgery on more than three million people in 34 countries.[11] They restored the eyesight of more than a million people, including that of one of the Bolivian soldiers who had killed Che Guevara. Cuban medical staff had provided 745 million free medical consultations. They had cared for more people (more than 70 million) and had saved more lives in the developing countries (1.5 million) than all the G-8 countries, the World Health Organisation and Médecins Sans Frontières put together.

Since 1959, Cuba has provided free medical education for 52,000 people from 130 other countries. It has helped to set up ten medical schools in other countries. In 1999, Cuba set up the world's largest medical school, the Latin American Medical School, with more than 8,000 students from countries in Asia, Africa and Latin America. Most were from working class and peasant families and half were women.[12] It educated more health workers from other countries than did all the G8 member countries combined.

Cuba was the only country in the world's history to create a WHO-validated, six-year course of medical education, with no fees and with full food and board, for adequately-schooled people from anywhere in the world who could not afford medical school in their own country. The graduates' only commitment was to return to their home countries and provide medical care to those who could least afford it. By contrast, in Zambia, only 50 of the 600 doctors educated there since independence were still working there in 2008.

Giving medical aid had been a basic principle of the Cuban Revolution from the first, flowing from its belief that medicine is not a business but the right of every citizen and the duty of every doctor. Cuba has done more to aid underdeveloped and developing nations than any other country in the world.

Working class democracy

Two decades after the crisis that followed the collapse of the Soviet Union, the Cuban working class was still in control. The dictatorship of the proletariat still meant democracy for the workers, the direct application of power and control by Cuban workers. Cuba is, constitutionally, a 'socialist state of workers'. There were no capitalists apart from foreign entrepreneurs in mixed companies and a few clandestine workshop owners.[13] As the 19th Congress of the Cuban trade union congress, the Central de Trabajadores de Cuba (CTC), stated, "the principal conquests of the Revolution have been preserved, first of all, the political power of the workers."[14]

This meant that workers as the ruling class were not to be treated as just labour power. So Cuba decided not to compete with other countries in a race to the bottom by offering low-wage workers to foreign companies. Instead it would invest in its people's skills, especially in health care, education, biotechnology, medications and other high-value goods. The saving of material resources and a more productive workforce had to be the key sources of this investment. So Cuba needed better organisation and better education and technical skills. As workers improved their skills, they increased productivity, so fewer were needed to carry out particular jobs. Workers could then be redeployed to other areas of work to develop new lines of production and to upgrade their skills. This would again raise productivity and workers' skill and educational levels, in a virtuous circle.

So Cuba re-engineered its economy, developed a new Labour Code and debated the nature of the future workforce. The new task was to move from crisis management to restoring normal working practices, including full use of the working day. It meant modernising management under Cuban standards, professionalising administration and re-drafting workers' legal rights and responsibilities. It also meant addressing the distribution of incomes.

So the people consulted, as they had in the earlier workers' parliaments in which workers and unions had a complete veto. 1.5 million proposals on job descriptions and redeployment, health and safety, productivity, incentives and salaries were discussed and voted on at more than 20,000 workplace meetings.

Those moving out of the direct state sector were from over-manned sections and those services that should not be maintained by the state, such as hairdressing. All were offered full pay in higher education, skills training or new areas of work like small-scale manufacturing and repair workshops. New areas of work also arose from the economic integration with other countries through ALBA. This required novel relations with private capital in those countries as joint companies were developed on the island. But Cuban workers decided the regulations governing these ventures, insisting that the people would decide, not market forces.

Yamil Eduardo Martinez, a young trade unionist, said, "Sections of the western, hostile, media are claiming that these changes are a retreat from socialism. In fact, they are about making our economy more efficient so that we can develop further in health and education – with the public sector not having to directly manage everything. One thing we really want to do is to raise agricultural production, so in a world of uncertain food security we can be as close to being self-sufficient as possible."[15]

So at all stages, workers were in control. Unions initiated laws; trade unionists sat in the National Assembly and participated in ministerial decision-making. Legislative proposals affecting workers were always referred to the unions for their agreement or criticism.

In 1995, the unions rejected a draft law to allow foreign companies to directly employ Cuban workers on their own terms. The unions insisted that those workers must be employed through a state agency and under Cuban labour laws. In the 1990s, the unions defeated a proposal to raise the retirement age. In 2002, the radical restructuring of Cuba's biggest industry, the sugar industry, followed negotiations with unions and meetings with all its 900,000 workers. 207,000 went to new jobs, or to 'study as a form of work', or to early retirement with enhanced pensions; none was discarded.

Resolución No. 8/2005 provided that no worker could be dismissed through redundancy, redeployment or temporary lay-off. Any such had to be negotiated with the unions and management had to pay the worker 100 per cent of his or her salary for a month, then 60 per cent until an alternative was agreed. This would be either another job, with training if necessary, or 'study as a form of work', with workers keeping their salaries and employment rights. In 2008, in conditions of full employment, this proposal was revived with improved pension rates and another CTC mass consultation exercise was launched. 3,085,798 workers met in 85,301 workplace assemblies to discuss the proposals: 99 per cent voted for the changes.

The drafting of new employment laws involved detailed and extensive consultation with the CTC. And, for implementation across workplaces, the laws explicitly required the agreement of unions and of the monthly workers' assemblies. Resolución No. 9/2007 specified managerial responsibilities for health and safety, required written health and safety policies and workplace health and safety manuals, listed hundreds of hazards to be addressed and restated the role of unions in all aspects of health and safety policy. As a result, recorded workplace accidents fell from 8,280 in 2002 to 6,015 in 2007 and fatal accidents fell more rapidly, from 111 to 47.[16]

Cuba also had the world's best programme of community-based disaster preparedness.[17] During the three devastating hurricanes Fay, Gustav and Ike that hit Cuba in 2008, causing $8 billion worth of damage, the working class worked selflessly and collectively to repair the damage and to care for those who lost homes and property, under the slogan 'every human life is sacred'. The Cuban Civil Defence Authority took responsibility for the population in such events and guaranteed to save all lives if people and organisations did as instructed. In Cuba seven people died. When visiting British health workers expressed their condolences during their visit, they were respectfully told that the seven had died because they ignored instructions from the Civil Defence Authority. When the same three hurricanes hit neighbouring Haiti, more than 1,000 people were killed.

In 2010, unions accepted some dilution of the 2005 rights. The right of redeployed workers to take up 'study as a form of work' with their salary and continuity of employment retained or to enhanced early retirement (as in the sugar industry restructuring in 2002) was no longer available as of right, though they remained options in practice. Temporarily redeployed workers would no longer have the right to continue to draw their original salary if it was higher than the salary in the job to which they were redeployed. Earnings-related salary protection would be paid at 100 per cent of salary for a month, then at 60 per cent for the next one to five months for those with 10 to 30 years' service. Thereafter welfare benefits in cash and kind were available, subject to regular household income and availability-to-work assessments.[18]

As the economy recovered, modest salary increases across the board followed, with the minimum wage more than doubled and minimum pensions tripled. In April 2008, the minimum monthly pension was raised again, by more than 20 per cent to 200 CUP, and social security payments were raised by 20 per cent. In 2012, the economy grew by 3.1 per cent.

People's Power

People's Power was piloted in the province of Matanzas in 1974 and set up nationally in 1976. Cuba held competitive elections for delegates to its municipal assemblies, in which the people, not the Communist Party, proposed the candidates.[19] There were usually four to seven candidates, never fewer than two. There was no campaigning for or against any candidate; negative campaigning was not allowed. There were no electoral promises or bribes or funding. There were no lobbyists to promote private interests over the general good. [20]

Delegates were unpaid and their work was on top of their regular work, so Cuba had no caste of professional politicians. The delegates did not represent themselves or parties; they had to act in the interests of the whole people. Delegates had to live in their electoral districts and had to account to their constituents at all times. The constituents formally instructed the delegates and had the right to recall them at once at any time. The delegates held weekly and six-monthly meetings to report back to their constituents, who held them to account.

This system was not perfect, but it worked. For example, in June 1978 in a passionate debate in the National Assembly, delegates raised the matter of housing repair, a matter of great concern when 80 per cent of Cubans owned their own homes. In response, the government's 1979 plan put 70 per cent of the monies for building into housing repair and maintenance and Cuba doubled the number of houses built every year.[21]

Cuba's 169 municipal and 14 provincial assemblies met at least twice a year. Since 1993, there have been direct elections to the provincial assemblies and the National Assembly. The National Assembly met twice a year, for two days each time. It had ten permanent commissions. The people were sovereign, so their elected delegates worked to ensure that the people participated as much as possible in making the laws. This was a key part of democratising the country.[22]

In 2007, 5.1 million Cubans participated in meetings to discuss what reforms they wanted and they made 1.3 million proposals. In 2011, in preparing for the 2011 Party Congress, 8.9 million people attended 163,000 meetings and generated more than three million suggestions. This was democratic centralism in action, where the Cuban people consulted together, then decided policy.

Cuba persistently sought to keep high standards of behaviour. All those in leading positions and their families were expected to live in a manner no different from other people. Those found guilty of corruption were punished severely. Cuba did well on the World Bank and Transparency International scores of corruption. A thorough US-sourced study which set out to show the extent of corruption in Cuba ended by confirming the extent of the efforts to contain it.[23]

Cuba's 1992 Constitution banned discrimination based on race, skin colour or sex. Its Article 44 said, "men and women have equal rights in the economic, political, cultural and social realms and in the family." In 1994, the Federación de Mujeres Cubanas [FMC] had 3.6 million members, 82 per cent of the adult female population. It was the largest organisation in Cuba and the largest women's organisation in Latin America. It helped to improve women's health, education, legal rights and rights at work. National control of the economy and the government's policy of encouraging women's work brought women more independence, professional opportunities and social mobility.24[24]

The FMC's 1985 Congress successfully called for more childcare centres, more provision of contraception, better sex education and more emphasis on the need to share housework, in line with the 1975 Family Code which required men and women to share household duties and child care. By 1996, Cuba had 1,156 childcare centres. The FMC also organised voluntary health workers into programmes of screening for cervical cancer. It helped to find absconding fathers to assist them to support and legally recognise their children. It arranged care and subsidies for children in need. The country also had a network of shelters for victims of domestic violence and child abuse.

In 2006, 36 per cent of the members of the National Assembly were women, the seventh highest proportion in the world. In 2008, 43 per cent of members were women and 36 per cent of members were between 18 and 30. After February 2013's general election, 37.9 per cent of the Assembly's members were people of colour. The average age of members was 48.

By 2014, 48.9 per cent of members were women, the fourth highest proportion in the world. Britain came 60th, with 22.6 per cent. The USA was 75th equal with Panama at 19.3 per cent. In Cuba, women held 66 per cent of professional and technical jobs. 49 per cent of judges were women.

In April 2011 Cubans elected a new Central Committee of the Communist Party. 48 of the 115 members were women, 41.7 per cent, triple the proportion elected at the previous Congress.

There were 36 blacks and mestizo members, 31.3 per cent, the highest ever, 10 per cent more than on the previous Central Committee. Cuba was the only country in the world in where blacks and mestizos had the state and the government as their ally. But they still needed to make more use of the state and the government as their allies to achieve full equality. The government and the party were not racist. But there was still some discrimination by some individuals.

The black and mestizo population in Cuba was the healthiest and best-educated mass of Afro-descendants in the hemisphere. No other country has done as much as Cuba to end racial discrimination and injustice.

Defending the revolution

US governments, Cuban exiles and 'dissidents' always told the Cuban people to abstain or to spoil their ballot papers in elections, without great success. In the 1993 National Assembly elections, 7.67 per cent abstained or spoilt their ballot papers, in 1995, 11.3 per cent, in 1998, 6.65 per cent, in 2003, 6.25 per cent, in 2007, 7.01 per cent, in 2010, 8.89 per cent and in 2012, 9.42 per cent.

Successive US governments have attacked, blockaded and bombed Cuba for 50 years. The US government funded the Cuban American National Foundation, a former board member of which publicly admitted that its leaders had created a paramilitary group to destabilise Cuba and to kill Fidel Castro.[25] James Cason, head of the United States Interests Section (USIS), was told in 2002 to create so much 'chaos' that Cuba would expel him, causing a complete break in diplomatic relations. Cuba did not fall into the trap. Instead it arrested 75 Cubans for taking aid from a foreign power in order to engage in activities harmful to the country. Such acts were also deemed crimes in the USA and most other countries. But USIS had to admit that Cuba's dissidents could show no proof of house searches, interrogations, detentions or arrests.[26]

Also, it was sheer hypocrisy for the US government to accuse Cuba of censorship: in 1971, the US Treasury Department closed down the First New York Festival of Cuban Cinema, seized all the prints and drove the co-sponsor of the festival, American Documentary Films, out of business. In January 2013, Cuba lifted restrictions on Cubans wishing to travel abroad. The USA still stopped its citizens from travelling to Cuba as tourists, threatening any such tourists with ten years' jail.

USIS and some EU embassies in Havana openly backed subversion. The Polish diplomat Jacek Padee, in charge of political affairs, often attended opposition activities. The Dutch embassy provided the opposition with office supplies and Internet access. The Czech Republic gave the opposition appointments at the embassy to document their claimed violations of their human rights. Peter Brandel, an embassy official, played a leading role in these activities. Sweden's delegation was also involved. The German embassy's counsellor, Volker Pellet, came out on the street to support the *damas en blanco*, the Ladies in White, relatives of imprisoned opposition members.

President Bush wasted $166 million between 2001 and 2008 trying to restore capitalism in Cuba. In 2005, the USA's National Endowment for Democracy (NED) paid the governments of Poland, Romania and the Czech Republic $2.4 million to fund their anti-Cuba groups, for example Poland's Lech Walesa Institute. In 2006, the US government set up a 'Cuba Fund for a Democratic Future' with an $80 million budget for building an opposition in Cuba.

President Obama wasted $60 million between 2009 and 2011 trying to destabilise Cuba, much of it given to NGOs like Spain's Solidarity with Cuba, which also got $615,000 from the International Republican Institute between September 2008 and December 2009. Payment of counter-revolutionary bloggers has also been privatised. Opposition blogger Yoanni Sanchez received $500,000 in international prizes awarded by corporate agencies. In 2010, the US Agency for International Development sent 50 people a month into Cuba to deliver technical and financial aid to opposition members. The Spanish government and the NED funded the opposition website Cuba Encuentro.[27]

Carlos Manuel Serpa, a Cuban security agent who infiltrated many of Cuba's tiny, US-funded counter-revolutionary groups between 2001 and 2011, said that it was easy to organise an anti-Cuba media campaign. All he had to do was invent a piece of news and call Radio Martí. Without any confirmation or verification, they would put it out on air.[28]

Social progress

In 1990, Cuba spent 20 per cent of its GDP on social services (education, social security and health care all provided free of charge to all), as against other Latin American countries' 10 per cent. By 1998, Cuba had raised this spending by 60 per cent (against a Latin American average rise of 30 per cent) to 32 per cent, again the highest proportion in Latin America.

Cuba maintained its comprehensive early childhood support programmes.[29] Save the Children, an internationally-acclaimed children's advocate organisation, annually ranked the best and worst places to be a mother. In 2010, it ranked Cuba number one of the 81 less developed countries. (It ranked the USA 28th of the 43 more developed countries.[30])

In 2008, Cuba's infant mortality rate, 5/1,000, was lower than the USA's 7/1,000, and the same as Britain's 2006 figure. In 1958 it had been 60/1,000. By 2012, on the CIA's estimate, it was 4.83/1,000. Cuba's child mortality rate in 2008 was 6/1,000, the USA's 8/1,000. In the 1950s, the maternal mortality rate was 120 per 100,000 live births, by 1992, it was 32.

During the Special Period, the proportion of physically active adults doubled. Between 1997 and 2002, deaths from diabetes were reduced by 51 per cent, from coronary heart disease by 35 per cent and from stroke by 20 per cent. In 1958, Cuban life expectancy was 55 years. By 2011, it was 78, higher than in the USA.

Cuba's success in achieving good health for its people was shown in its sporting prowess. In the 2012 London Olympics, Cuba came 16th in the medals table, the highest-ranked Latin American country.

But the US government persisted in attacking Cuba: in January 2011, it even seized $4.2 million in funds allocated to Cuba by the United Nations Global Fund to Fight AIDS, Tuberculosis and Malaria.

Much has changed in Cuba. Several years ago, hardly anyone contemplated openly coming out on the island. Until the 1990s, gays were socially excluded: they got disapproving looks around the neighbourhood and even lost their jobs. But in 2010, Fidel Castro expressed regret for the government's earlier attitude towards gays. Now the Cuban government rejects all discrimination against gays. Mariela Castro Espin, the daughter of Cuban President Raul Castro, heads the National Centre for Sex Education. She has campaigned for years for gay rights and called for same-sex marriage to be allowed. The

Communist Party stated that it favoured allowing same-sex marriage, but the legislation had yet to be drafted.[31] On 17 May 2013, Cuba held lectures and workshops to mark the International Day Against Homophobia and Transphobia.

Cuba made great strides in education. By 2012, its illiteracy rate was 2 per cent (the USA's was 12 per cent.) Its literacy programme 'Yo, sí puedo' became a model for developing countries.[32] Cubans assisted other countries' literacy campaigns. In 2006, UNESCO awarded Cuba its Literacy Award for its contribution to literacy campaigns in 15 countries.

Cuba devoted 13 per cent of its GDP to education – more than twice as much as any other country in the world. Primary schooling and pre-primary schooling had become almost universal in Cuba by 1969. There were 300,000 enrolled in secondary technical schools in 1983-84. Every secondary school child could prepare for university entrance. Class sizes were constantly reduced. In the 1980s, women made up nearly half of all students attending high schools, 44 per cent of those at technical schools and more than half of all university students. Emulation, not competition, was the ethic. Racial and gender inequalities vanished as educational opportunities grew.

By 1990, there were eight universities and 35 research institutes. There were 280,000 students, eight times the number in the late 1950s. By 2010, there were one million university students. There were universities in every province and education up to postgraduate school was free. Cuba focused on providing higher education courses in technology, medical sciences, pure sciences, agricultural sciences, economics and teaching, to meet the economy's needs. Cuba achieved one of the highest educational levels in the world and one of the highest numbers of scientists per head of any country in Asia, Africa and Latin America.

The battle of ideas and the future

In 2014, the UN, for the 23rd year in a row, called for an end to the blockade. 188 countries voted to end the blockade; the USA and Israel voted against. Three small island states, the Marshall Islands, the Federated States of Micronesia, and Palau, abstained. The blockade had cost Cuba an estimated $1.1 trillion up to October 2014.

Yet Cuba continued to win support from countries around the world and to develop trade links with countries around the world, especially with Latin America.

Cuba developed its economy in such a way that it also cared for the environment. Cubans achieved the world's largest conversion from conventional farming to organic, environmentally sustainable farming. The people stopped using costly, harmful petroleum-based pesticides. They adopted a soil management programme that helped to preserve the natural environment. They reintroduced traditional peasant practices where appropriate. They reduced tillage and rehabilitated the soil. They used green manures, biofertilisers and organic fertilisers rather than chemical ones. They used integrated pest-management methods, biological control and biopesticides. They used crop diversity, crop rotations and intercropping. They recycled waste and experimented in biotechnology. Cuba's farming became the most organic in the world.

Cuba's urban farming movement employed 326,000 people. They reared small animals in kitchen gardens. From home gardens in the cities they sold fruit, vegetables, meat, herbs, plants and flowers in farmers' markets. Havana grew 90 per cent of its fruit and vegetables on more than 7,000 organiponicos, covering more than 80,000 acres. So there was no need for costly refrigerated transport, which saved energy, time and spoilage.

Gardener Monty Don judged that no other country in the world had organised its food production so effectively through gardens. He wrote that he was hugely inspired by this and full of admiration for the intelligence and dignity of the Cuban people.[33]

Cuba protected her environment through environmental education at all stages of schooling to enable people to take part in making decisions on the environment.[34] Cubans understood the need for environmental ethics and aesthetics. They had a duty to protect Cuba's unusually rich biological diversity. They worked hard to reforest Cuba – forest covered 15 per cent of the island in 1970, 23.6 per cent in 2004. Cuba was the only country in the Caribbean and Central America region to reforest.

Cuba's socialist efforts reflected the people's long-term care of nature for the good of future generations. As part of these efforts, Cuba developed eco-tourism. Sites included Sierra del Rosario, a UNESCO-declared biosphere reserve, the Viñalas Valley, the fish-and-game preserve in the Zapata Swamp, the Topes de Collantes Hills, the Turquino National Park and Saetia Cay.

The blockade forced the Cuban people to husband their energy sources. They had to achieve self-reliance, sustainability in one country. They had to develop and use a variety of energy sources.

A 2012 conference on renewable sources of energy praised Cuba's use of alternative sources of energy. Enrico Turrino, founding member of Eurosolar and honorary member of CubaSolar, said that the island was a model other countries should adopt in order to make good use of clean sources of energy for the benefit both of people and of the environment. He highlighted the solarisation projects carried out in the municipalities of Bartolome Maso and Guama in the eastern provinces of Granma and Santiago de Cuba, where thermal, photoelectric, wind, water and biomass sources were used for the sustainable development of these communities.

So Cuba met its people's needs using small amounts of natural resources. Cuba was the only country in the world that lived within its environmental footprint while achieving high levels of human development. This was due to its unique combination of good environmental management with excellent provision of health care and education.[35] The World Wildlife Fund said that Cuba was the only country on Earth to meet the minimum requirements for sustainable development. It had both a quality of life above the Fund's threshold of 0.8 on the Human Development Index and an ecological footprint that was sustainable.[36]

The Cuban people continued to work to improve their health, welfare, education and culture. The Battle of Ideas grew to encompass more than 170 educational, cultural and social programmes. These included cutting class sizes to 20 students at the primary-school level and 15 at the junior-high level; higher education campuses and youth computer clubs in the municipalities; and 15 new arts colleges which have graduated thousands of young instructors who teach music, dance and fine arts in schools and in the community. Two new TV channels were dedicated solely to educational programmes, including tertiary-level courses. An annual travelling book fair drew huge crowds in 35 cities and towns. Schools in remote areas, even those schools with just one or a few students, were fitted with solar panels to power TVs, VCRs and computers.

On 17 December 2014, the USA and Cuba agreed to restore diplomatic ties that the USA severed 54 years before. President Obama called for an end to the embargo. He ordered the restoration of full diplomatic relations with Cuba. The US government acknowledged, almost uniquely, that its previous policy had failed and had been wrong.

Obama instructed Secretary of State John Kerry to begin the process of removing Cuba from the list of states that sponsored terrorism. Obama promised to ease restrictions on remittances, travel and banking, while Cuba said that it would allow more Internet access and would release 53 Cubans identified as political prisoners by the US government.

Cuba's revolution was for liberty, equality and fraternity; for winning through their own efforts; for education, social awareness, organisation and public service; for clear thinking, intelligence and realism; for modesty, altruism, courage; for never lying or violating ethical principles; it is a profound conviction that no power can crush the power of truth and ideas. The revolution meant unity, independence, patriotism, socialism and internationalism.

In its struggle for national unity and sovereignty and in its efforts to develop its communist morals and ideas, the Cuban working class was taking responsibility for its future.

Notes

Introduction

1. Congress '82, CPBML pamphlet, 1982, pp. 1-2 and 3.

Chapter 1 Russia, to 1927

1. See Nikolai Dronin and Edward Bellinger, Climate dependence and food problems in Russia, 1900-1990: the interaction of climate and agricultural policy and their effect on food problems, Central European University Press, 2006, p. 2.
2. Emile J. Dillon, The eclipse of Russia, New York: George H. Doran, 1918, p. 67.
3. Edward Acton and Tom Stableford, editors, The Soviet Union: a documentary history, Volume 1 1917-1940, University of Exeter Press, 2005, p. 84.
4. Cited p. 71, Adam Hochschild, To end all wars: how the First World War divided Britain, Macmillan, 2011.
5. 19 August 1914, cited p. 12, Paul N. Hehn, A low dishonest decade: the great powers, Eastern Europe, and the economic origins of World War Two, 1930-1941, New York: Continuum, 2002.
6. See Christopher Clark, The sleepwalkers: how Europe went to war in 1914, Allen Lane, 2012, pp. 537, 538 and 557.
7. V. I. Lenin, The 'United States of Europe' Slogan, Collected Works, Volume 18, Moscow: FLP, p. 232.

8. The war programme of the proletarian revolution, p. 60, in Lenin on war and peace: three articles, FLP, Peking, 1966, pp. 58-72.
9. V. I. Lenin, Speech delivered at a joint meeting of the All-Russian Central Executive Committee and the Moscow Soviet, 14th May 1918, Collected Works, Volume 23, Moscow: FLP, p. 9.
10. Cited p. 32, Peter Kenez, Civil war in South Russia, 1918, University of California Press, 1971.
11. Both quotations cited p. 106, Michael Hughes, Inside the enigma: British officials in Russia, 1900-1939, Hambledon Press, 1997.
12. Sir George Buchanan, My mission to Russia and other diplomatic memoirs, Volume II, Cassel & Co., 1923, p. 185.
13. Judiciary Committee (Senate) Hearings, 65th Congress, Third Session 1919, Bolshevik Propaganda, p. 780.
14. Report (Political and Economic) of the Committee to Collect Information on Russia, HMSO, 1921, p. 17.
15. Donald Raleigh, Revolution on the Volga: 1917 in Saratov, Cornell University Press, 1986, p. 323.
16. Evan Mawdsley, The Russian civil war, Allen & Unwin, 1987, p. 273.
17. Alexander Statiev, The Soviet counterinsurgency in the Western borderlands, Cambridge University Press, 2010, p. 15.
18. Ronald Suny, p. 175, 'Revision and retreat in the historiography of 1917: social history and its critics', *Russian Review*, 1994, Vol. 53, pp. 165-82. See Terence Emmons, 'Unsacred history', *The New Republic*, 5 November 1990, p. 36.
19. Ronald Suny, editor, The structure of Soviet history: essays and documents, 2nd edition, Oxford University Press, 2013, p. 21.
20. Hugh Phillips, p. 2, 'The heartland turns red: the Bolshevik seizure of power in Tver', *Revolutionary Russia*, 2001, Vol. 14, No. 1, pp. 1-21.
21. Hugh Phillips, p. 18, 'The heartland turns red: the Bolshevik seizure of power in Tver', *Revolutionary Russia*, 2001, Vol. 14, No. 1, pp. 1-21.
22. John Wheeler-Bennett, Brest-Litovsk: the forgotten peace, March 1918, Macmillan, 1963 (1938), p. 28.
23. Robert Service, Lenin: a biography, Macmillan, 2000, p. 267.
24. Donald Raleigh, Revolution on the Volga: 1917 in Saratov, Cornell University Press, 1986, p. 331.
25. Rex A. Wade, The Bolshevik revolution and the Russian civil war,

Greenwood Press, 2001, p. 29.
26. Karel C. Berkhoff, Harvest of despair: life and death in Ukraine under Nazi rule, Harvard University Press, 2004, p. 309.
27. Frederick Schuman, Soviet politics at home and abroad, Robert Hale Limited, 1948, p. 129.
28. Cited p. 17, Louis Fischer, The Soviets in world affairs: a history of the relations between the Soviet Union and the rest of the world, 1917-1929, 2nd edition, Princeton University Press, 1951 (1930).
29. Isaac Deutscher, The prophet armed: Trotsky 1879-1921, Oxford University Press, 1970, p. 382.
30. Cited p. 186, John W. Wheeler-Bennett, Brest-Litovsk: the forgotten peace, March 1918, Macmillan, 1963 (1938).
31. Isaac Deutscher, The prophet armed: Trotsky 1879-1921, Oxford University Press, 1970, p. 393.
32. Cited p. 381, Isaac Deutscher, The prophet armed: Trotsky 1879-1921, Oxford University Press, 1970.
33. Cited p. 384, Isaac Deutscher, The prophet armed: Trotsky 1879-1921, Oxford University Press, 1970.
34. Louis Fischer, The Soviets in world affairs: a history of the relations between the Soviet Union and the rest of the world, 1917-1929, 2nd edition, Princeton University Press, 1951 (1930), p. 68.
35. For evidence of his treachery, see Grover Furr, Evidence of Leon Trotsky's collaboration with Germany and Japan, *Cultural Logic*, 2009.
36. See Oleh S. Fedyshyn, Germany's drive to the East and the Ukrainian revolution, 1917-1918, Rutgers University Press, 1971.
37. Cited p. 352, John W. Wheeler-Bennett, Brest-Litovsk: the forgotten peace, March 1918, Macmillan, 1963 (1938).
38. Louis Fischer, The Soviets in world affairs: a history of the relations between the Soviet Union and the rest of the world, 1917-1929, 2nd edition, Princeton University Press, 1951 (1930), p. 76.
39. See Giles Milton, Russian roulette: a deadly game: how British spies thwarted Lenin's global plot, Sceptre, 2013, pp. 156-63.
40. Cited p. 217, Louis Fischer, The Soviets in world affairs: a history of the relations between the Soviet Union and the rest of the world, 1917-1929, 2nd edition, Princeton University Press, 1951 (1930).
41. Winston S. Churchill, The world crisis: Volume 4, The aftermath,

Thornton-Butterworth, 1929, p. 235.
42. See Louis Fischer, The Soviets in world affairs: a history of the relations between the Soviet Union and the rest of the world, 1917-1929, 2nd edition, Princeton University Press, 1951 (1930), p. 199.
43. Cited pp. 143-4, Evan Mawdsley, The Russian civil war, Allen & Unwin, 1987.
44. Cited p. 137, Louis Fischer, The Soviets in world affairs: a history of the relations between the Soviet Union and the rest of the world, 1917-1929, 2nd edition, Princeton University Press, 1951 (1930).
45. See Giles Milton, Russian roulette: a deadly game: how British spies thwarted Lenin's global plot, Sceptre, 2013, pp. 251-5.
46. Cited p. 315, Clifford Kinvig, Churchill's crusade: the British invasion of Russia, 1918-1920, Hambledon Continuum, 2006.
47. Walter Lippmann and Charles Merz, 'A test of the news' in Walter Lippmann, Liberty and the news, New York: Dover Books, 2010 reprint of the 1920 edition, p. 126.
48. Cited p. 127, Walter Lippmann and Charles Merz, 'A test of the news' in Walter Lippmann, Liberty and the news, New York: Dover Books, 2010 reprint of the 1920 edition.
49. Evans Clark, Facts and fabrications about Soviet Russia, Rand School of Social Science, 1920, pp. 18-22.
50. Cited p. 19, Evans Clark, Facts and fabrications about Soviet Russia, Rand School of Social Science, 1920.
51. Walter Lippmann and Charles Merz, 'A test of the news' in Walter Lippmann, Liberty and the news, New York: Dover Books, 2010 reprint of the 1920 edition, p. 63.
52. See Walter Lippmann and Charles Merz, 'A test of the news' in Walter Lippmann, Liberty and the news, New York: Dover Books, 2010 reprint of the 1920 edition, p. 139.
53. Walter Lippmann and Charles Merz, 'A test of the news' in Walter Lippmann, Liberty and the news, New York: Dover Books, 2010 reprint of the 1920 edition, p. 43.
54. Cited p. 245, Louis Fischer, The Soviets in world affairs: a history of the relations between the Soviet Union and the rest of the world, 1917-1929, 2nd edition, Princeton University Press, 1951 (1930).
55. Report (Political and Economic) of the Committee to Collect

Information on Russia, HMSO, 1921, p. 30.
56. Sir Paul Dukes, Red dusk and the morrow: adventures and investigations in Red Russia, Williams & Norgate, 1922, pp. 224-5.
57. Cited p. 136, Christopher Hill, Lenin and the Russian revolution, Penguin, 1971 (1947).
58. Cited p. 165, Frederick L. Schuman, Soviet politics at home and abroad, Robert Hale Limited, 1948.
59. Cited p. 164, Frederick L. Schuman, Soviet politics at home and abroad, Robert Hale Limited, 1948.
60. General Sir Brian Horrocks, A full life, Collins, 1962, p. 48.
61. Alexander Statiev, The Soviet counterinsurgency in the Western borderlands, Cambridge University Press, 2010, p. 33.
62. Michael Hughes, Inside the enigma: British officials in Russia, 1900-1939, Hambledon Press, 1997, p. 181.
63. Clifford Kinvig, Churchill's crusade: the British invasion of Russia, 1918-1920, Hambledon Continuum, 2006, p. 318.
64. Edward Acton and Tom Stableford, editors, The Soviet Union: a documentary history, Volume 1 1917-1940, University of Exeter Press, 2005, p. 114.
65. Cited p. 178, Peter Kenez, Civil war in South Russia, 1918, University of California Press, 1971.
66. See Peter Kenez, Civil war in South Russia, 1918, University of California Press, 1971, p. 79.
67. Cited p. 387, Jonathan Smele, Civil war in Siberia: the anti-Bolshevik government of Admiral Kolchak, 1918-1920, Cambridge University Press, 1996.
68. Cited p. 93, Walter Lippmann and Charles Merz, 'A test of the news' in Walter Lippmann, Liberty and the news, New York: Dover Books, 2010 reprint of the 1920 edition.
69. Cited p. 129, Edward Acton and Tom Stableford, editors, The Soviet Union: a documentary history, Volume 1 1917-1940, University of Exeter Press, 2005.
70. Cited p. 130, Edward Acton and Tom Stableford, editors, The Soviet Union: a documentary history, Volume 1 1917-1940, University of Exeter Press, 2005.
71. Cited pp. 164-5, Frederick L. Schuman, Soviet politics at home and

72. Cited p. 163, Michael Hughes, Inside the enigma: British officials in Russia, 1900-1939, Hambledon Press, 1997.
73. Frederick L. Schuman, Soviet politics at home and abroad, Robert Hale Limited, 1948, p. 149.
74. V. I. Lenin, Speech at a Plenary Session of the Moscow Soviet, 1922, Collected works, Volume 27, Moscow: FLP, p. 366.
75. V. I. Lenin, On cooperation, 1923, Collected works, Volume 33, Moscow: FLP, p. 467.
76. E. H. Carr, Socialism in one country, 1924-1926, Volume 2, Macmillan, 1959, p. 48.
77. See Stephen Dorril, MI6: fifty years of Special Operations, Fourth Estate, 2000, p. 268.
78. Stephen Dorril, MI6: fifty years of special operations, Fourth Estate, 2000, p. 8.
79. Gabriel Gorodetsky, Grand delusion: Stalin and the German invasion of Russia, Yale University Press, 1999, p. 2.
80. Stephen Dorril, MI6: fifty years of special operations, Fourth Estate, 2000, p. 402.
81. Raymond L. Garthoff, A journey through the cold war: a memoir of containment and coexistence, Brookings Institution Press, 2001, p. 383.
82. Cited p. 218, Keith Jeffery, MI6: the history of the Secret Intelligence Service, 1909-1949, Bloomsbury, 2010. For an account of the whole affair, see his pp. 214-22.
83. See Michael Kort, The Soviet colossus: history and aftermath, 7th edition, M. E. Sharpe, 2010, p. 197.
84. E. H. Carr, Socialism in one country, 1924-1926, Volume 1, Macmillan, 1969, pp. 329-30.
85. See Sarah Davies and James Harris, Stalin's world: dictating the Soviet order, Yale University Press, 2015, pp. 65, 77 and 87.
86. On the Arcos raid, see Louis Fischer, The Soviets in world affairs: a history of the relations between the Soviet Union and the rest of the world, 1917-1929, 2nd edition, Princeton University Press, 1951 (1930), pp. 686-92.
87. See Christopher Andrew, The defence of the realm: the authorized

history of MI5, Allen Lane, 2010, p. 154.
88. *The Observer*, 29 May 1927.
89. See James Harris, Intelligence and threat perception: defending the revolution, 1917-1937, Chapter 2, pp. 29-43, in James Harris, editor, The anatomy of terror: political violence under Stalin, Oxford University Press, 2013.

Chapter 2 The Soviet Union from 1927 to 1939

1. Cited footnote 1, p. 189, Sidney and Beatrice Webb, Soviet communism: a new civilization, 3rd edition, Longmans, Green and Co., 1947.
2. See E. A. Rees, Iron Lazar: a political biography of Lazar Kaganovich, Anthem Press, 2012, p. 97.
3. Cited p. 73, E. H. Carr and R. W. Davies, Foundations of a planned economy, 1926-1929, Volume 1 Part 1, Macmillan, 1969.
4. Moshe Lewin, Russian peasants and Soviet power: a study of collectivization, George Allen & Unwin, 1968, p. 488.
5. See Anna Louise Strong, I change worlds, Routledge, 1935, p. 290.
6. Thomas D. Campbell, Russia: market or menace? Longmans, 1932, p. 65.
7. See Walter S. Dunn, Jr., The Soviet economy and the Red Army 1930-1945, Praeger 1995, Table on p. 16.
8. Mark Tauger, pp. 109 and 112, Stalin, Soviet agriculture and collectivisation, in Frank Trentmann and Flemming Just, editors, Food and conflict in Europe in the age of the two world wars, Palgrave Macmillan, 2006, pp. 109-42.
9. Cited p. 56, E. H. Carr and R. W. Davies, Foundations of a planned economy, 1926-1929, Volume 1 Part 1, Macmillan, 1969.
10. Leon Trotsky, The real situation in Russia, International Publishers, 1928, p. 31.
11. Anna Louise Strong, I change worlds, Routledge, 1935, p. 331.
12. R. W. Davies, The Soviet economy in turmoil, 1929-1930, Macmillan, 1989, p. 486.
13. David Granick, Soviet metal-fabricating and economic development: practice versus policy, University of Wisconsin Press, 1967, pp. 26-7.
14. Cited p. 666, Sidney and Beatrice Webb, Soviet communism: a new

civilization, 3rd edition, Longmans, Green and Co., 1947.
15. Loren R. Graham, Science and philosophy in the Soviet Union, Alfred A. Knopf, 1972, p. 430.
16. Cited p. 455, Melvyn P. Leffler and Odd Arne Westad, editors, The Cambridge history of the Cold War, Volume I Origins, Cambridge University Press, 2010. See also Alexei Kojevnikov, Stalin's great science: the times and adventures of Russia's physicists, Imperial College Press, 2004.
17. Orest Subtelny, Ukraine: a history, 4th edition, University of Toronto Press, 2009, p. 388.
18. See for examples, Frederic Chaubin, CCCP: Cosmic communist constructions photographed, Benedikt Taschen Verlag, 2011.
19. Cited p. 37, Sidney and Beatrice Webb, Soviet communism: a new civilization, 3rd edition, Longmans, Green and Co., 1947.
20. All cited p. 189, Sarah Davies and James Harris, Stalin's world: dictating the Soviet order, Yale University Press, 2015.
21. Sheila Fitzpatrick, Education and social mobility in the Soviet Union, 1921-1934, Cambridge University Press, 1979, pp. 16-7, 205 and 254.
22. See Hiroaki Kuromiya, Stalin's industrial revolution: politics and workers, 1928-1932, Cambridge University Press, 1988, p. 116.
23. Cited p. 165, Edgar Snow, The pattern of Soviet power, Random House, 1945.
24. Robert W. Dunn, Soviet trade unions, New York: Vanguard Press, 1928, p. 45.
25. See Alexander Gerschenkron, Economic backwardness in historical perspective, Harvard University Press, 1962.
26. Isaac Mazepa, Ukrainia under Bolshevist rule, *Slavonic Review*, Vol. 12, 1933-34, pp. 342-3.
27. Stalin's letter to Sholokhov, 6 May 1933, cited p. 824, Michael Ellman, The role of leadership perceptions and of intent in the Soviet famine of 1931–1934, *Europe-Asia Studies*, 2005, Vol. 57, No. 6, pp. 823-41.
28. Michael Ellman, Footnote 9, p. 837, The role of leadership perceptions and of intent in the Soviet famine of 1931–1934, *Europe-Asia Studies*, 2005, Vol. 57, No. 6, pp. 823-41.
29. See Wolf Ladejinsky, Collectivisation of agriculture in the Soviet Union, *Political Science Quarterly*, June 1934, pp. 229 and 243.

30. See Mark B. Tauger, Le Livre Noire du Communisme on the Soviet Famine of 1932-1933, p. 4, available at *chss.montclair.edu/english/furr/taugerroterhol.pdf*.
31. See R. W. Davies and S. G. Wheatcroft, The years of hunger: Soviet agriculture, 1931-1933, Palgrave Macmillan, 2004, p. 214.
32. R. W. Davies and S. G. Wheatcroft, The years of hunger: Soviet agriculture, 1931-1933, Palgrave Macmillan, 2004, p. 221. For more details on the government's food aid, see their pp. 221-3, 424-5 and 440.
33. Terry Martin, The affirmative action empire: nations and nationalism in the Soviet Union, 1923-1939, Cornell University Press, 2001, p. 315.
34. David R. Shearer, p. 197, Stalinism, 1928-1940, Chapter 7, pp. 192-216, in Ronald Suny, editor, The Cambridge history of Russia, Volume III The twentieth century, Cambridge University Press, 2006.
35. Diane P. Koenker and Ronald D. Bachman, Revelations from the Russian archives: documents in English translation, Library of Congress, 1997, p. 401.
36. Barbara B. Green, p. 156, Stalinist terror and the question of genocide: the Great Famine, pp. 137-61, in Alan S. Rosenbaum, editor, Is the Holocaust Unique? Perspectives on comparative genocide, Westview Press, 1996.
37. Steven J. Katz, p. 31, The uniqueness of the Holocaust: the historical dimension, pp. 19-38, in Alan S. Rosenbaum, editor, Is the Holocaust Unique? Perspectives on comparative genocide, Westview Press, 1996.
38. Adam Ulam, Stalin: the man and his era, Viking, 1973, p. 349.
39. Michael Ellman, p. 833, The role of leadership perceptions and of intent in the Soviet famine of 1931–1934, *Europe-Asia Studies*, 2005, Vol. 57, No. 6, pp. 823-41.
40. Mark B. Tauger, What caused famine in Ukraine? A polemical response, *RFE/RL Poland, Belarus and Ukraine Report*, Prague, 25 June 2002, Vol. 4, No. 25.
41. Mark B. Tauger, p. 168, Grain crisis or famine? The Ukrainian State Commission for Aid to Crop-Failure Victims and the Ukraine famine of 1928-29, Chapter 7, pp. 146-70, in Donald J. Raleigh, editor, Provincial landscapes: local dimensions of Soviet power, 1917-1953, University of Pittsburgh Press, 2001.
42. *Globe and Mail*, 28 February 1984, cited p. 100, Douglas Tottle,

Fraud, famine and fascism: the Ukrainian genocide myth from Hitler to Harvard, Toronto: Progress Books, 1987.
43. Cited p. 267, R. W. Davies, The industrialisation of Soviet Russia, Volume 6: the years of progress: the Soviet economy, 1934-1936, Palgrave Macmillan, 2014.
44. Eugène Zaleski, Stalinist planning for economic growth, 1933-1952, Macmillan, 1980, p. 259.
45. N. Hans and S. Hessen, Educational policy in Soviet Russia, P. S. King & Son, 1930, p. 185.
46. Terry Martin, The affirmative action empire: nations and nationalism in the Soviet Union, 1923-1939, Cornell University Press, 2001, pp. 1-2 and 15.
47. Michael Ellman, Socialist planning, 2nd edition, Cambridge University Press, 1989, pp. 187-8.
48. Elena Shulman, Stalinism on the frontier of empire: women and state formation in the Soviet Far East, Cambridge University Press, 2008, p. 138. On the campaign, see her pp. 66-79, 130-9 and passim.
49. Cited p. 222, Edgar Snow, People on our side, Random House, 1944.
50. Cited p. 157, Edgar Snow, Glory and bondage, Gollancz, 1945.
51. See John Loftus and Mark Aarons, The secret war against the Jews: how western espionage betrayed the Jewish people, New York: St Martin's Griffin, 1994, p. 495.
52. Stephen F. Cohen, Sovieticus: American perceptions and Soviet realities, W. W. Norton, 1987, pp. 99-100.
53. Cited p. 491, Frederick L. Schuman, Soviet politics at home and abroad, Robert Hale Limited, 1948.
54. See R. W. Davies, The socialist offensive: the collectivisation of Soviet agriculture, 1929-1930, Macmillan, 1980, p. xiii.
55. See Ronald Suny, The Soviet experiment: Russia, the USSR, and the successor states, Oxford University Press, 1998, pp. 239-40.
56. See David L. Hoffmann, Cultivating the masses: modern state practices and Soviet socialism, 1914-1939, Cornell University Press, 2011, p. 312.
57. See Girsh Khanin, The 1950s – the triumph of the Soviet economy, *Europe-Asia Studies*, 2003, Vol. 55, No. 8, pp. 1187-212.
58. See Michael Kort, The Soviet colossus: history and aftermath, 7th edition, M. E. Sharpe, 2010, p. 212.

59. See David M. Kotz and Fred Weir, Revolution from above: the demise of the Soviet system, Routledge, 1997, p. 27.
60. See Tim Pringle and Simon Clarke, The challenge of transition: trade unions in Russia, China and Vietnam, Palgrave Macmillan, 2011, p. 46.
61. Kevin McDermott, p. 87, Stalin and Stalinism, Chapter 3, pp. 72-89, in Stephen A. Smith, editor, The Oxford handbook of the history of communism, Oxford University Press, 2014.

Chapter 3 Towards world war

1. J. V. Stalin, Problems of Leninism, Peking: Foreign Languages Press, 1976, p. 528.
2. See Sarah Davies and James Harris, Stalin's world: dictating the Soviet order, Yale University Press, 2015, p. 66. See also their pp. 60-7, 77 and 87-8.
3. David L. Hoffmann, p. 100, The conceptual and practical origins of Soviet state violence, Chapter 5, pp. 89-104, in James Harris, editor, The anatomy of terror: political violence under Stalin, Oxford University Press, 2013.
4. Oleg Khlevnyuk, p. 172, The objectives of the Great Terror, 1937-1938, Chapter 7, pp. 158-76, in Julian Cooper, Maureen Perrie and E. A. Rees, editors, Soviet history, 1917-53: essays in honour of R. W. Davies, St Martin's Press, 1995.
5. Edward Acton and Tom Stableford, editors, The Soviet Union: a documentary history, Volume 1 1917-1940, University of Exeter Press, 2005, p. 373.
6. Robert Thurston, Life and terror in Stalin's Russia, 1934-1941, Yale University Press, 1996, p. 26.
7. Mémoirs de Jules Humbert-Droz. De Lénine à Staline. Dix ans au service de l'internationale communiste 1921-1931, Neufchâtel: A la Baconnière, 1971, pp. 379-80.
8. Both cited p. 7, Grover Furr, The continuing revolution in Stalin-era Soviet history, http://lalkar.org/issues/contents/jul2014/grover.html, accessed 6 August 2014.
9. Cited p. 3, Grover Furr, The continuing revolution in Stalin-era Soviet

history, http://lalkar.org/issues/contents/jul2014/grover.html, accessed 6 August 2014.
10. J. Arch Getty and Oleg V. Naumov, Yezhov: the rise of Stalin's 'iron fist', Yale University Press, 2008, pp. 141-2.
11. J. Arch Getty and Oleg V. Naumov, Yezhov: the rise of Stalin's 'iron fist', Yale University Press, 2008, pp. 142-3.
12. See Grover Furr, The murder of Sergei Kirov: history, scholarship and the anti-Stalin paradigm, Erythros Press and Media, 2013.
13. Cited p. 229, Grover Furr, The murder of Sergei Kirov: history, scholarship and the anti-Stalin paradigm, Erythros Press and Media, 2013. See his pp. 229 and 233.
14. Grover Furr and Vladimir Bobrov, pp. 16-7, Nikolai Bukharin's first statement of confession in the Lubianka, *Cultural Logic*, 2007, 37 pp.
15. http://www.marxists.org/archive/bukharin/works/1938/trial/1.htm, accessed 19 March 2013.
16. Sarah Davies and James Harris, Stalin's world: dictating the Soviet order, Yale University Press, 2015, p. 91.
17. Genevieve Tabouis, They called me Cassandra, Charles Scribner's Sons, 1942, p. 257.
18. Winston S. Churchill, The Second World War, Volume 1, The gathering storm, Houghton Mifflin Harcourt, 1986, p. 258. For more on the Tukhachevsky plot, see Geoffrey Bailey, The conspirators, Harper & Brothers, 1960, pp. 135-40, 176-90 and 212-24; on Tukhachevsky's talks with the German High Command, see his p. 190.
19. See Grover Furr, Blood lies: the evidence that every accusation against Joseph Stalin and the Soviet Union in Timothy Snyder's 'Bloodlands' is false, Red Star Publishers, 2014, p. 193.
20. Louis P. Lochner, editor, The Goebbels diaries: 1942-1943, Hamish Hamilton, 1948, p. 277. On Tukhachevsky, see Grover Furr, Evidence of Leon Trotsky's collaboration with Germany and Japan, *Cultural Logic*, 2009, pp. 108-37.
21. *Socialist Appeal*, New York: Socialist Party of New York, Left Wing Branches, 20 November 1937, Vol. 1, No. 15, pp. 5 and 7. Quotation from first paragraph, p. 5. Reprinted in Leon Trotsky, Writings, 1937-1938, Pathfinder Press, 1970.
22. Cited p. 423, Adam Ulam, Stalin: the man and his era, Allen Lane,

1974.
23. See Grover Furr, The continuing revolution in Stalin-era Soviet history, http://lalkar.org/issues/contents/jul2014/grover.html, p. 7, accessed 6 August 2014.
24. Leon Trotsky, Transitional programme for socialist revolution, (1938), Pathfinder Press, 1971, p. 106.
25. *Bulletin of the Opposition*, October 1933.
26. Interview reported in the *New York Evening Journal*, 26 January 1937.
27. *American Mercury*, March 1937, reprinted in Leon Trotsky, The revolution betrayed: what is the Soviet Union and where is it going? Faber & Faber, 1937, p. 216.
28. See Grover Furr, Khrushchev lied: the evidence that every 'revelation' of Stalin's (and Beria's) 'crimes' in Nikita Khrushchev's infamous 'secret speech' to the 20th Party Congress of the Communist Party of the Soviet Union on February 25, 1956, is provably false, Erythrós Press & Media, corrected edition, July 2011, pp. 4 and 199. On Khrushchev's record of repression, see his pp. 201-5, 213 and 250-7.
29. Cited p. 115, Robert W. Thurston, Life and terror in Stalin's Russia, 1934-1941, Yale University Press, 1996.
30. Cited footnote 19, p. 674, Michael Ellman, Stalin and the Soviet famine of 1932-33 revisited, *Europe-Asia Studies*, June 2007, Vol. 59, No. 4, pp. 663-93.
31. Frederick Schuman, Soviet politics at home and abroad, Robert Hale Limited, 1948, p. 198.
32. Both cited p. 75, Stuart D. Goldman, Nomonhan, 1939: the Red Army's victory that shaped World War II, Naval Institute Press, 2012.
33. Official Report of Parliamentary Debates, 6 October 1938.
34. Anna L. Strong, The Soviets expected it, New York: The Dial Press, 1941, p. 147.
35. Louise Grace Shaw, The British political elite and the Soviet Union 1937-1939, Frank Cass, 2003, p. 127.
36. Paul Hehn, A low dishonest decade: the great powers, Eastern Europe, and the economic origins of World War Two, 1930-1941, New York: Continuum, 2002, p. 287.
37. Paul Hehn, A low dishonest decade: the great powers, Eastern Europe, and the economic origins of World War Two, 1930-1941, New York:

Continuum, 2002, p. 398.
38. Warren Kimball, Forged in war: Roosevelt, Churchill, and the Second World War, William Morrow and Company, 1997, p. 29.
39. Andrew Alexander, America and the imperialism of ignorance: US foreign policy since 1945, Biteback Publishing, 2012, p. 8.
40. Clement Leibovitz and Alvin Finkel, In our time: the Chamberlain-Hitler collusion, Monthly Review Press, 1998, pp. 21-2 and 32.
41. E. L. Woodward and Rohan Butler, editors, Documents on British Foreign Policy, 1919-1939, Third Series, Volume III, 1938-9, HMSO, 1950, p. 306.
42. E. L. Woodward and Rohan Butler, editors, Documents in British Foreign Policy, 1919-1939, Third Series, Volume III, 1938-9, HMSO, 1950, p. 307.
43. See Robert Service, Trotsky: a biography, Macmillan, 2009, pp. 459-60.
44. See Ronald Suny, The Soviet experiment: Russia, the USSR, and the successor states, Oxford University Press, 1998, p. 300.
45. Leon Trotsky, Problem of the Ukraine, *Socialist Appeal*, 9 May 1939, and, The independence of the Ukraine and sectarian muddleheads, 30 July 1939, Writings of Leon Trotsky 1939-40, New York, 1977, pp. 44-54.
46. Frederick Schuman, Soviet politics at home and abroad, Robert Hale Limited, 1948, p. 275.
47. Geoffrey Roberts, p. 73, The Soviet decision for a pact with Nazi Germany, *Soviet Studies*, 1992, Vol. 44, No. 1, pp. 57-78.
48. Richard Overy, Russia's war, Allen Lane, 1998, p. 5.
49. Samantha Carl, pp. 8 and 18, The buildup of the German war economy: the importance of the Nazi-Soviet economic agreements of 1939 and 1940, *Electronic Journal of Annual Holocaust Conference Papers*, 1999, http://www.millersville.edu/holocon/files/The%20Buildup%20of%20the%20German%20War%20Economy.pdf, accessed on 22 April 2013.
50. See Anthony Read and David Fisher, The deadly embrace, New York: Norton, 1988, p. 482.
51. Roy Medvedev, Let history judge, New York: Columbia University Press, 1989, p. 735.
52. Geoffrey Roberts, The unholy alliance: Stalin's pact with Hitler, I. B.

Tauris, 1989, p. 223.
53. Timothy Snyder, Bloodlands: Europe between Hitler and Stalin, The Bodley Head, 2010, p. 126.
54. Cited p. 18, Stephen G. Fritz, Ostkrieg: Hitler's war of extermination in the East, University Press of Kentucky, 2011.
55. George Ginsburgs, p. 73, A case study in the Soviet use of international law: eastern Poland in 1939, *American Journal of International Law*, 1958, Vol. 52, No. 1, pp. 69-84.
56. Cited p. 249, Edgar Snow, People on our side, Random House, 1944.
57. George Ginsburgs, p. 80, A case study in the Soviet use of international law: eastern Poland in 1939, *American Journal of International Law*, 1958, Vol. 52, No. 1, pp. 69-84.
58. W. S. Churchill, The Second World War, Volume 1, The gathering storm, Cassell & Co., 1949, p. 403.
59. Parliamentary Debates, 5th Series, Volume 351; House of Commons; London; 1939; Col. 996.
60. Cited p. 37, Gabriel Gorodetsky, Grand delusion: Stalin and the German invasion of Russia, Yale University Press, 1999.
61. Cabinet Papers, CAB 65-2, 85-10, 16 October 1939, The National Archives.
62. Cited p. 82, Anna Louise Strong, The Stalin era, New York: Mainstream Publishers, 1957.
63. See Caroline Kennedy-Pipe, Russia and the world 1917-1991, Arnold, 1998, p. 47.
64. See Mark Arnold-Forster, The world at war, Collins, 1973, p. 33; D. F. Fleming, The Cold War and its origins, Volume 2, Allen & Unwin, 1961, pp. 97-104; and I. Fleischhauer, 'Soviet foreign policy and the origins of the Hitler-Stalin pact', pp. 27-45, B. Wegner, editor, From peace to war: Germany, Soviet Russia and the world, 1939-1941, Oxford: Berghahn Books, 1997.
65. See William P. and Zelda K. Coates, The Soviet-Finnish campaign: military and political 1939-40, Eldon Press, 1942.
66. L. S. Amery, My political life, Volume 3, the unforgiving years 1929-1940, Hutchinson, 1955, pp. 347 and 345.
67. See Patrick R. Osborn, Operation *Pike*: Britain versus the Soviet Union, 1939-1941, Greenwood Press, 2000, pp. 91-2.

68. See L. S. Amery, My political life: Volume 3, the unforgiving years 1929-1940, Hutchinson, 1955, p. 346.
69. Cited p. 381, Ronald Steel, Walter Lippmann and the American century, Bodley Head, 1980.
70. See Chris Bellamy, Absolute war: Soviet Russia in the Second World War: a modern history, Macmillan, 2007, p. 71.
71. See Patrick R. Osborn, Operation *Pike*: Britain versus the Soviet Union, 1939-1941, Greenwood Press, 2000, p. x.
72. See Silvio Pons, Stalin and the inevitable war, 1936-1941, Frank Cass, 2002, pp. 205-10.
73. Cited p. 116, Chris Bellamy, Absolute war: Soviet Russia in the Second World War: a modern history, Macmillan, 2007.
74. Cited p. 292, Gabriel Gorodetsky, Grand delusion: Stalin and the German invasion of Russia, Yale University Press, 1999.
75. Cited p. 18, Susan Butler, editor, My dear Mr. Stalin: the complete correspondence between Franklin D. Roosevelt and Joseph V. Stalin, Yale University Press, 2005.

Chapter 4 World War Two

1. Chris Bellamy, Absolute war: Soviet Russia in the Second World War: a modern history, Macmillan, 2007, p. 208.
2. Stephen G. Fritz, Ostkrieg: Hitler's war of extermination in the East, University Press of Kentucky, 2011, p. 92.
3. Cited p. 155, Edgar Snow, People on our side, Random House, 1944.
4. Cited p. 156, Edgar Snow, Glory and bondage, Gollancz, 1945.
5. Cited p. 36, Karel C. Berkhoff, Harvest of despair: life and death in Ukraine under Nazi rule, Harvard University Press, 2004.
6. Cited p. 38, Karel C. Berkhoff, Harvest of despair: life and death in Ukraine under Nazi rule, Harvard University Press, 2004.
7. Cited p. 68, Stephen G. Fritz, Ostkrieg: Hitler's war of extermination in the East, University Press of Kentucky, 2011.
8. Richard Overy, p. 42, The Second World War: a barbarous conflict, pp. 39-57, in George Kassimeris, editor, The barbarisation of warfare, Hurst & Company, 2006.
9. Karel C. Berkhoff, Harvest of despair: life and death in Ukraine under

Nazi rule, Harvard University Press, 2004, p. 90.
10. Georgi Zhukov, Reminiscences and reflections, Volume 1, Progress Publishers, 1985, p. 297.
11. Cited p. 339, Grover Furr, Khrushchev lied: the evidence that every 'revelation' of Stalin's (and Beria's) 'crimes' in Nikita Khrushchev's infamous 'secret speech' to the 20th Party Congress of the Communist Party of the Soviet Union on February 25, 1956, is provably false, Erythrós Press & Media, corrected edition, July 2011.
12. Bryan Fugate and Lev Dvoretsky, Thunder on the Dnepr: Zhukov-Stalin and the defeat of Hitler's Blitzkrieg, Presidio Press, California, 1997, pp. xi-ii.
13. Richard Overy, Russia's war, Allen Lane, 1998, p. 64.
14. Evan Mawdsley, World War II: a new history, Cambridge University Press, 2009, p. 140.
15. Brian Fugate, Operation Barbarossa: strategy and tactics on the Eastern Front, 1941, Presidio Press, 1984, p. 58. For a full account, see his 'Prewar Soviet Defense Planning and Strategy', Chapter 1, pp. 13-59, especially pp. 33-59, 'The Strategy for the Defense of the Soviet Union in 1941'; see also his pp. 184-5.
16. Chris Bellamy, Absolute war: Soviet Russia in the Second World War: a modern history, Macmillan, 2007, p. 187.
17. Von Hardesty and Ilya Grinberg, Red Phoenix Rising: the Soviet air force in World War II, University Press of Kansas, 2012, p. 49.
18. David M. Glantz, Barbarossa derailed: the battle for Smolensk 10 July – 10 September 1941, Volume 2, Helion & Co. Ltd., 2012, pp. 504, 517 and 546.
19. Von Hardesty and Ilya Grinberg, Red Phoenix Rising: the Soviet air force in World War II, University Press of Kansas, 2012, p. 57.
20. Stephen Ambrose, Rise to globalism: American foreign policy since 1938, Pelican, 2nd edition, 1980, p. 51.
21. Walter S. Dunn, Jr., Stalin's keys to victory: the rebirth of the Red Army, Praeger Security International, 2006, pp. 4 and 5.
22. Richard Overy, Russia's war, Allen Lane, 1998, p. 214.
23. See Chris Bellamy, Absolute war: Soviet Russia in the Second World War: a modern history, Macmillan, 2007, pp. 220-1.
24. David M. Glantz, Barbarossa: Hitler's invasion of Russia 1941, Tempus,

2001, pp. 72-3.
25. Von Hardesty and Ilya Grinberg, Red Phoenix Rising: the Soviet air force in World War II, University Press of Kansas, 2012, p. 53.
26. Max Hastings, All hell let loose: the world at war 1939-1945, Harper Press, 2011, p. 141.
27. Stephen G. Fritz, Ostkrieg: Hitler's war of extermination in the East, University Press of Kentucky, 2011, p. 230.
28. David Glantz and Jonathan House, Armageddon in Stalingrad: The Stalingrad trilogy: Volume 2 September-November 1942, University Press of Kansas, 2009, p. 712.
29. Cited p. 550, George C. Herring, From colony to superpower: U.S. foreign relations since 1776, Oxford University Press, 2008.
30. Cited pp. 213-4, Edgar Snow, People on our side, Random House, 1944.
31. Cited p. 69, Susan Butler, editor, My dear Mr. Stalin: the complete correspondence between Franklin D. Roosevelt and Joseph V. Stalin, Yale University Press, 2005.
32. Cited p. 145, Susan Butler, editor, My dear Mr. Stalin: the complete correspondence between Franklin D. Roosevelt and Joseph V. Stalin, Yale University Press, 2005.
33. Evan Mawdsley, Thunder in the east: the Nazi-Soviet war 1941-1945, Hodder Arnold, 2007, p. 245.
34. Cited p. 156, Michael Schaller, The U.S. crusade in China, 1938-1945, Columbia University Press, 1979.
35. Cited pp. 75 and 76, Susan Butler, editor, My dear Mr. Stalin: the complete correspondence between Franklin D. Roosevelt and Joseph V. Stalin, Yale University Press, 2005.
36. Cited p. 389, Jan Triska and Robert Slusser, The theory, law, and policy of Soviet treaties, Stanford University Press, 1962.
37. John Barber and Mark Harrison, p. 226, Patriotic war, 1941-1945, Chapter 8, pp. 217-42, in Ronald Suny, editor, The Cambridge history of Russia, Volume III The twentieth century, Cambridge University Press, 2006.
38. Wendy Lower, Nazi empire-building and the Holocaust in Ukraine, University of North Carolina Press, 2005, p. 2.
39. Wendy Lower, Nazi empire-building and the Holocaust in Ukraine,

University of North Carolina Press, 2005, p. 202.
40. Karel Berkhoff, Harvest of despair: life and death in Ukraine under Nazi rule, Harvard University Press, 2004, pp. 306 and 308.
41. Cited p. 46, Alexander Statiev, The Soviet counterinsurgency in the Western borderlands, Cambridge University Press, 2010. On OUN terrorism, see his pp. 123-32.
42. Cited p. 289, Karel C. Berkhoff, Harvest of despair: life and death in Ukraine under Nazi rule, Harvard University Press, 2004.
43. Cited p. 286, Karel C. Berkhoff, Harvest of despair: life and death in Ukraine under Nazi rule, Harvard University Press, 2004.
44. Cited p. 126, Alexander Statiev, The Soviet counterinsurgency in the Western borderlands, Cambridge University Press, 2010.
45. See Alfred J. Reiber, Civil wars in the Soviet Union, *Kritika: explorations in Russian and Eurasian history*, 2003, Vol. 4, No. 1, pp. 147-8. See also Jeffrey Burds, The holocaust in Rovno: the massacre at Sosenski Forest, November 1941, Palgrave Macmillan, 2013.
46. Cited Daniel Lazare, Timothy Snyder's lies, *Jacobin*, 9 September 2014, http://www.jacobinmag.com/2014/09/timothy-snyders-lies/, accessed 14 September 2014.
47. Andrzej Paczkowski, The spring will be ours: Poland and the Poles from occupation to freedom, The Pennsylvania State University Press, 2003, p. 105.
48. Hubert P. van Tuyll, Review of Martin Dean's 'Collaboration in the Holocaust crimes of the local police in Belorussia and Ukraine, 1941-44', *The Russian Review*, 2001, Vol. 60, No. 3, pp. 448-9.
49. See Prit Buttar, Between giants: the battle for the Baltics in World War Two, Osprey Publishing, 2013, pp. 86-7 and 97-8.
50. See Prit Buttar, Between giants: the battle for the Baltics in World War Two, Osprey Publishing, 2013, pp. 139-41, 177-8, 205, 207-8 and 319.
51. See Prit Buttar, Between giants: the battle for the Baltics in World War Two, Osprey Publishing, 2013, pp. 182-3, 197, 201 and 319-20. See also Involvement of the Lettish SS Legion in War Crimes in 1941-1945 and the Attempts to Revise the Verdict of the Nuremberg Tribunal in Latvia, http://www.denmark.mid.ru/7e10.html, accessed 24 October 2014.
52. Prit Buttar, Between giants: the battle for the Baltics in World War Two, Osprey Publishing, 2013, The Baltic Holocaust, Chapter 4, pp.

103-32.
53. Andrejs Plakans, A concise history of the Baltic States, Cambridge University Press, 2011, pp. 351 and 353; see his pp. 351-4.
54. Alexander Statiev, The Soviet counterinsurgency in the Western borderlands, Cambridge University Press, 2010, pp. 69 and 71.
55. Alexander Statiev, The Soviet counterinsurgency in the Western borderlands, Cambridge University Press, 2010, p. 138. On Latvian, Lithuanian and Estonian terrorism, see his pp. 132-4.
56. See Involvement of the Estonian SS Legion in War Crimes in 1941-1945 and the Attempts to Revise the Verdict of the Nuremberg Tribunal in Estonia, 13 February 2004, URL: http://www.un.int/russia/other/eest1941.htm, accessed 25 April 2014.
57. Timothy Snyder, Bloodlands: Europe between Hitler and Stalin, The Bodley Head, 2010, p. 194. See also Involvement of the Estonian SS Legion in War Crimes in 1941-1945 and the Attempts to Revise the Verdict of the Nuremberg Tribunal in Estonia, 13 February 2004, URL: http://www.un.int/russia/other/eest1941.htm, accessed 25 April 2014.
58. Timothy Snyder, Bloodlands: Europe between Hitler and Stalin, The Bodley Head, 2010, p. 228.
59. Jeffrey Burds, Comments on Timothy Snyder's article, "To resolve the Ukrainian question once and for all: the ethnic cleansing of Ukrainians in Poland, 1943-1947", *Journal of Cold War Studies*, 1999, Vol. 1, No. 2, http://www.fas.harvard.edu/~hpcws/comments13.htm, accessed 9 August 2013.
60. See Charles Gati, Failed illusions: Moscow, Washington, Budapest, and the 1956 Hungarian revolt, Woodrow Wilson Center Press, 2006, p. 45.
61. See Keith Lowe, Savage continent: Europe in the aftermath of World War II, Penguin Books, 2012, pp. 246-7.
62. See Keith Lowe, Savage continent: Europe in the aftermath of World War II, Penguin Books, 2012, p. 144.

Chapter 5 Stalingrad and victory

1. Cited pp. 41-2, Michael K. Jones, Stalingrad: how the Red Army triumphed, Barnsley: Pen & Sword Military, 2007.
2. Cited p. 44, Michael K. Jones, Stalingrad: how the Red Army triumphed, Barnsley: Pen & Sword Military, 2007.
3. Cited p. 44, Michael K. Jones, Stalingrad: how the Red Army triumphed, Barnsley: Pen & Sword Military, 2007.
4. H. P. Willmott, The great crusade: a new complete history of the Second World War, Michael Joseph, 1989, p. 365.
5. Chris Bellamy, Absolute war: Soviet Russia in the Second World War: a modern history, Macmillan, 2007, p. 535.
6. Edward Acton and Tom Stableford, editors, The Soviet Union: a documentary history, Volume 2 1939-1991, University of Exeter Press, 2007, p. 137.
7. Louis P. Lochner, editor, The Goebbels diaries: 1942-43, Hamish Hamilton, 1948, p. 258.
8. See Mary Heimann, Czechoslovakia: the state that failed, Palgrave Macmillan, 2011, p. 135.
9. For a full account, see Grover Furr, The 'official' version of the Katyn massacre disproven? Discoveries at a German mass murder site in Ukraine, *Socialism and Democracy*, 2013, Vol. 27, No. 2, pp. 96-129.
10. David M. Glantz and Jonathan House, The battle of Kursk, University Press of Kansas, 1999, p. 280.
11. Stephen G. Fritz, Ostkrieg: Hitler's war of extermination in the East, University Press of Kentucky, 2011, p. 402.
12. Cited p. 158, William P. and Zelda K. Coates, Six centuries of Russo-Polish relations, Lawrence & Wishart, 1948.
13. Susan Butler, editor, My dear Mr. Stalin: the complete correspondence between Franklin D. Roosevelt and Joseph V. Stalin, Yale University Press, 2005, p. 221.
14. Forrest Pogue, Pogue's war, University of Kentucky Press, 2001, p. 190.
15. Williamson Murray and Allan Millett, A war to be won: fighting the Second World War, Harvard University Press, 2000, p. 451.
16. Mark Mazower, Hitler's empire: Nazi rule in occupied Europe, Allen Lane, 2008, p. 522.

17. Williamson Murray and Allan Millett, A war to be won: fighting the Second World War, Harvard University Press, 2000, p. 483.
18. Irina Mukhina, pp. 402 and 404, New revelations from the former Soviet archives: the Kremlin, the Warsaw uprising, and the coming of the Cold War, *Cold War History*, 2006, Vol. 6, No. 3, pp. 397–411.
19. Irina Mukhina, pp. 401 and 408, New revelations from the former Soviet archives: the Kremlin, the Warsaw uprising, and the coming of the Cold War, *Cold War History*, 2006, Vol. 6, No. 3, pp. 397–411.
20. Irina Mukhina, p. 405, New revelations from the former Soviet archives: the Kremlin, the Warsaw uprising, and the coming of the Cold War, *Cold War History*, 2006, Vol. 6, No. 3, pp. 397–411.
21. Irina Mukhina, p. 401, New revelations from the former Soviet archives: the Kremlin, the Warsaw uprising, and the coming of the Cold War, *Cold War History*, 2006, Vol. 6, No. 3, pp. 397–411.
22. See Edgar Snow, The pattern of Soviet power, Random House, 1945, pp. 54-6.
23. Cited p. 105, Anthony Tucker-Jones, Stalin's revenge: Operation Bagration and the annihilation of Army Group Centre, Pen and Sword Military, 2009.
24. Anthony Tucker-Jones, Stalin's revenge: Operation Bagration and the annihilation of Army Group Centre, Pen and Sword Military, 2009, p. 105.
25. Cited p. 122, Alexander Statiev, The Soviet counterinsurgency in the Western borderlands, Cambridge University Press, 2010.
26. Max Hastings, Armageddon: the battle for Germany 1944-45, corrected edition, Pan Books, 2005, p. 114.
27. Anthony Tucker-Jones, Stalin's revenge: Operation Bagration and the annihilation of Army Group Centre, Pen and Sword Military, 2009, pp. 100-5. See his Chapter 10, Rokossovsky: defeat at the gates of Warsaw, pp. 98-108.
28. Richard Overy, Russia's war, Allen Lane, 1998, pp. 248-9.
29. H. P. Willmott, The great crusade: a new complete history of the Second World War, Michael Joseph, 1989, p. 382.
30. Alan Bullock, Hitler and Stalin: parallel lives, 2nd edition, Fontana, 1998, p. 936.
31. Edward Acton and Tom Stableford, editors, The Soviet Union: a

documentary history, Volume 2 1939-1991, University of Exeter Press, 2007, p. 145.
32. Mark Mazower, Hitler's empire: Nazi rule in occupied Europe, Allen Lane, 2008, p. 512.
33. Stephen G. Fritz, Ostkrieg: Hitler's war of extermination in the East, University Press of Kentucky, 2011, pp. 419-20. See his pp. 418-20.
34. Robin Edmonds, The big three: Churchill, Roosevelt and Stalin in peace and war, Hamish Hamilton, 1991, p. 385.
35. Timothy Snyder, Bloodlands: Europe between Hitler and Stalin, The Bodley Head, 2010, p. 306.
36. Cited p. 183, William P. and Zelda K. Coates, Six centuries of Russo-Polish relations, Lawrence & Wishart, 1948.
37. Cited p. 183, William P. and Zelda K. Coates, Six centuries of Russo-Polish relations, Lawrence & Wishart, 1948.
38. Cited p. 178, William P. and Zelda K. Coates, Six centuries of Russo-Polish relations, Lawrence & Wishart, 1948.
39. Cited p. 455, Grover Furr, Blood lies: the evidence that every accusation against Joseph Stalin and the Soviet Union in Timothy Snyder's 'Bloodlands' is false, Red Star Publishers, 2014.
40. Stephen G. Fritz, Ostkrieg: Hitler's war of extermination in the East, University Press of Kentucky, 2011, p. 447. See his pp. 441-9.
41. R. L. Messer, The end of an alliance: James F. Byrnes, Roosevelt, Truman and the origins of the Cold War, Chapel Hill: University of North Carolina Press, 1982, p. 41.
42. H. P. Willmott, The great crusade: a new complete history of the Second World War, Michael Joseph, 1989, p. 382.
43. H. P. Willmott, The great crusade: a new complete history of the Second World War, Michael Joseph, 1989, p. 447.
44. Michael Schaller, The U.S. crusade in China, 1938-1945, Columbia University Press, 1979, p. 212.
45. Robert A. Nisbet, Roosevelt and Stalin, Washington, D.C.: Regnery Gateway, 1988, p. 69.
46. Cited p. 21, J. P. Morray, From Yalta to disarmament, New York: Monthly Review Press, 1961.
47. Cited p. 46, Frank Costigliola, Ambassador W. Averell Harriman and the shift in US policy toward Moscow after Roosevelt's death, Chapter

2, pp. 36-55, in Bevan Sewell and Scott Lucas, editors, Challenging US foreign policy: America and the world in the long twentieth century, Palgrave Macmillan, 2011.
48. Cited p. 33, Melvyn P. Leffler, A preponderance of power: national security, the Truman administration, and the Cold War, Stanford University Press, 1992.
49. Cited p. 20, J. P. Morray, From Yalta to disarmament, New York: Monthly Review Press, 1961.
50. Cited p. 170, William P. and Zelda K. Coates, Six centuries of Russo-Polish relations, Lawrence & Wishart, 1948.
51. See David M. Glantz, Soviet operational and tactical combat in Manchuria, 1945: August storm, Frank Cass, 2003, pp. 339-40.
52. David M. Glantz, The Soviet strategic offensive in Manchuria, 1945: August storm, Frank Cass, 2003, p. 1.
53. Cited p. 5, John L. Gaddis, The United States and the origins of the Cold War 1941-1947, New York: Columbia University Press, 1972.
54. Memoirs of Field Marshal the Viscount Montgomery of Alamein, London, 1958, p. 454.
55. Cited p. 119, William Mandel, A guide to the Soviet Union, New York: The Dial Press, 1946.
56. Cited pp. 432-3, Frederick L. Schuman, Soviet politics at home and abroad, Robert Hale Limited, 1948.
57. Cited p. 483, Frederick L. Schuman, Soviet politics at home and abroad, Robert Hale Limited, 1948.
58. Cited p. 119, Susan Butler, editor, My dear Mr. Stalin: the complete correspondence between Franklin D. Roosevelt and Joseph V. Stalin, Yale University Press, 2005.
59. Walter S. Dunn, Jr., Stalin's keys to victory: the rebirth of the Red Army, Praeger Security International, 2006, p. 94.
60. Andrew Roberts, Masters and commanders: the military geniuses who led the West to victory in World War Two, Penguin Books, 2009, p. 276.
61. Max Hastings, Armageddon: the battle for Germany 1944-45, corrected edition, Pan Books, 2005, p. 132.
62. Stephen G. Fritz, Ostkrieg: Hitler's war of extermination in the east, University Press of Kentucky, 2011, pp. xxi-ii.

63. H. P. Willmott, The great crusade: a new complete history of the Second World War, Michael Joseph, 1989, p. 146.
64. Geoffrey Roberts, Molotov: Stalin's cold warrior, Washington: Potomac Books, 2012, p. 91.
65. Frederick L. Schuman, Soviet politics, New York: A.A. Knopf, 1946, p. 419.
66. Evan Mawdsley, The Stalin years: the Soviet Union 1929-1953, Manchester University Press, 1998, p. 92.
67. Mark Harrison, Accounting for war: Soviet production, employment and the defence burden, 1940-1945, Cambridge University Press, p. 171.
68. Richard Overy, Russia's war, Allen Lane, 1998, p. 327.
69. Robert Rhodes James, editor, Winston S. Churchill, Complete Speeches, 1897-1963, Volume III, Macmillan, 1974, p. 2,664.
70. Chris Bellamy, Absolute war: Soviet Russia in the Second World War: a modern history, Macmillan, 2007, p. 424.
71. Cited p. 19, Jonathan Haslam, Russia's Cold War: from the October Revolution to the fall of the wall, Yale University Press, 2011.
72. All quotes cited p. 25, Stephen Dorril, MI6: fifty years of special operations, Fourth Estate, 2000.
73. See Keith Jeffery, MI6: the history of the Secret Intelligence Service, 1909-1949, Bloomsbury, 2010, pp. 436, 470, 472, 556 and 562.
74. See Max Hastings, Finest years: Churchill as warlord 1940-45, HarperPress, 2009, pp. 571-7.
75. Georgi Zhukov, Memoirs of Marshal Zhukov, London: Cape, 1971, p. 657.
76. Major General S. Woodburn Kirby, The War against Japan, Vol. 5: The surrender of Japan, HMSO, 1969, cited p. 646, Gar Alperovitz, The decision to drop the atomic bomb, HarperCollins, 1995.
77. See Tsuyoshi Hasegawa, Racing the enemy: Stalin, Truman, and the surrender of Japan, Harvard University Press, 2005, pp. 3-5.
78. Geoffrey Jukes, *Australian Slavonic and East European Studies*, 2008, Vol. 22 (1–2).

Chapter 6 The Soviet Union from 1945 to 1986

1. Stephen Ambrose, Eisenhower the soldier, 1890-1952, Allen & Unwin, 1984, p. 426.
2. Edward Crankshaw, Khrushchev: a career, Viking, 1966, p. 141.
3. Cited p. 353, Walter Isaacson and Evan Thomas, The wise men: six friends and the world they made: Acheson, Bohler, Harriman, Kennan, Lovett, McCloy, Faber and Faber, 1986.
4. Cited p. 106, Anna Louise Strong, The Stalin era, New York: Mainstream Publishers, 1957.
5. Cited p. 2, Andrew Alexander, America and the imperialism of ignorance: US foreign policy since 1945, Biteback Publishing, 2012.
6. Andrew Alexander, America and the imperialism of ignorance: US foreign policy since 1945, Biteback Publishing, 2012, p. 2.
7. Geoffrey Roberts, The Soviet Union in world politics: coexistence, revolution and Cold War, 1945-1991, Routledge, 1999, pp. 9-10.
8. Geoffrey Roberts, Molotov: Stalin's cold warrior, Washington: Potomac Books, 2012, p. 90.
9. Vladislav Zubok and Constantine Pleshakov, Inside the Kremlin's Cold War: from Stalin to Khrushchev, Harvard University Press, pp. 276-7.
10. Raymond L. Garthoff, A journey through the Cold War: a memoir of containment and coexistence, Brookings Institution Press, 2001, p. 223.
11. Warren Cohen, New Cambridge history of American foreign relations, Vol. 4, Challenges to American primacy, 1945 to the present, Cambridge University Press, 2013, pp. 31-2.
12. Raymond L. Garthoff, Détente and confrontation: American-Soviet relations from Nixon to Reagan, revised editon, Brookings Institution Press, 1994, p. 744.
13. Dimitri Volkogonov, Stalin: triumph and tragedy, Weidenfeld, 1991, p. 531.
14. Cited p. 119, Oliver Stone and Peter Kuznick, The untold history of the United States, Ebury Press, 2012.
15. Cited p. 186, Oliver Stone and Peter Kuznick, The untold history of the United States, Ebury Press, 2012.
16. Oliver Stone and Peter Kuznick, The untold history of the United

States, Ebury Press, 2012, p. 180.
17. Vladislav M. Zubok, A failed empire: the Soviet Union in the Cold War from Stalin to Gorbachev, University of North Carolina Press, 2009, pp. 49 and 71-2.
18. Frank Costigliola, p. 44, Ambassador W. Averell Harriman and the shift in US policy toward Moscow after Roosevelt's death, Chapter 2, pp. 36-55, in Bevan Sewell and Scott Lucas, editors, Challenging US foreign policy: America and the world in the long twentieth century, Palgrave Macmillan, 2011.
19. Cited p. 98, Peter Grose, Operation Rollback: America's secret war behind the Iron Curtain, Houghton Mifflin, 2000.
20. See Peter Grose, Operation Rollback: America's secret war behind the Iron Curtain, Houghton Mifflin, 2000, pp. 164-5.
21. See Stephen Dorril, MI6: fifty years of special operations, Fourth Estate, 2000, p. 243, 'Poland', Chapter 15, pp. 249-67, and pp. 501-2.
22. See Jeffrey Burds, The Early Cold War in Soviet West Ukraine, 1944–1948, *The Carl Beck Papers in Russian & East European Studies*, 2001, No. 1505, pp. 19 and 43-4.
23. Warren Cohen, New Cambridge history of American foreign relations, Vol. 4, Challenges to American primacy, 1945 to the present, Cambridge University Press, 2013, pp. 55 and 242.
24. Bernard Brodie, The absolute weapon, Harcourt, Brace, 1946, p. 75.
25. David Holloway, Stalin and the bomb: the Soviet Union and atomic energy 1939-1956, Yale University Press, 1994, p. 251.
26. Allan Millett and Peter Maslowski, For the common defense: a military history of the United States of America, Free Press, 1984, p. 524.
27. Cited p. 129, Geoffrey Roberts, Molotov: Stalin's cold warrior, Potomac Books, Washington, 2012.
28. Cited p. 136, Geoffrey Roberts, Molotov: Stalin's cold warrior, Potomac Books, Washington, 2012.
29. See Eugène Zaleski, Stalinist planning for economic growth, 1933-1952, Macmillan, 1980, pp. 400-1.
30. See Philip Hanson, The rise and fall of the Soviet economy: an economic history of the USSR from 1945, Pearson Education Limited, 2003, p. 25.
31. See R. W. Davies, The development of the Soviet budgetary system, Cambridge University Press, 1958, p. 322.

32. See Malcolm R. Hill and Richard McKay, Soviet product quality, Macmillan, 1988, especially pp. 1-16, 65-7, 90-1, 108-10, 123-5 and 126-35.
33. Girsh Khanin, p. 1193, The 1950s – the triumph of the Soviet economy, *Europe-Asia Studies*, 2003, Vol. 55, No. 8, pp. 1187-212.
34. For details, see J. Eric Duskin, Stalinist reconstruction and the confirmation of a new elite, 1945-1953, Palgrave 2001, Educating a new elite, Chapter 2, pp. 41-62.
35. Girsh Khanin, pp. 1196-9, The 1950s – the triumph of the Soviet economy, *Europe-Asia Studies*, 2003, Vol. 55, No. 8, pp. 1187-212.
36. Both quotations cited p. 150, Jonathan Haslam, Russia's Cold War: from the October Revolution to the fall of the wall, Yale University Press, 2011.
37. Joseph S. Berliner, Soviet industry from Stalin to Gorbachev: essays on management and innovation, Edward Elgar, 1988, p. 70, in his evidence to the Committee, reprinted as his Chapter 4, Managerial incentives and decision-making: a comparison of the United States and the Soviet Union, pp. 61-96.
38. Alexander Werth, Russia: hopes and fears, Barrie & Rockliff, 1969, pp. 14 and 16.
39. Michael Ellman, Socialist planning, 2nd edition, Cambridge University Press, 1989, p. 178.
40. David Stuckler and Sanjay Basu, The body economic: why austerity kills, Allen Lane, 2013, p. 159, note 18.
41. Cited p. 507, Ronald Suny, editor, The structure of Soviet history: essays and documents, 2nd edition, Oxford University Press, 2013.
42. E. H. Carr, Foundations of a planned economy, 1926-1929, Volume 2, Macmillan, 1969, p. 448.
43. E. H. Carr, Socialism in one country, 1924-1926, Volume 1, Macmillan, 1969, p. 185.
44. Cited p. 1206, Girsh Khanin, The 1950s – the triumph of the Soviet economy, *Europe-Asia Studies*, 2003, Vol. 55, No. 8, pp. 1187-212.
45. Cited p. 117, Anna Louise Strong, The Stalin era, New York: Mainstream Publishers, 1957.
46. Girsh Khanin, p. 1205, The 1950s – the triumph of the Soviet economy, *Europe-Asia Studies*, 2003, Vol. 55, No. 8, pp. 1187-212.

47. Nikolai Dronin and Edward Bellinger, Climate dependence and food problems in Russia, 1900-1990: the interaction of climate and agricultural policy and their effect on food problems, Central European University Press, 2006, pp. 337, 192 and 266.
48. See J. V. Stalin, Economic problems of socialism in the USSR, 1952, Peking: FLP, 1972, p. 95.
49. Philip Hanson, The rise and fall of the Soviet economy: an economic history of the USSR from 1945, Pearson Education Limited, 2003, p. 6.
50. Joseph Ball, The need for planning: the restoration of capitalism in the Soviet Union in the 1950s and the decline of the Soviet economy, *Cultural Logic*, 2010, pp. 1-2.
51. See Grover Furr, Khrushchev lied: the evidence that every 'revelation' of Stalin's (and Beria's) 'crimes' in Nikita Khrushchev's infamous 'secret speech' to the 20th Party Congress of the Communist Party of the Soviet Union on February 25, 1956, is provably false, Erythrós Press & Media, corrected edition, July 2011, pp. 4 and 199. On Khrushchev's record of repression, see his pp. 201-5, 213 and 250-7.
52. Mike Davidow, Perestroika: its rise and fall, International Publishers, 1993, p. 56.
53. Grover Furr, Khrushchev lied: the evidence that every 'revelation' of Stalin's (and Beria's) 'crimes' in Nikita Khrushchev's infamous 'secret speech' to the 20th Party Congress of the Communist Party of the Soviet Union on February 25, 1956, is provably false, Erythrós Press & Media, corrected edition, July 2011, p. 213.
54. John Lewis Gaddis, p. 10, Grand strategies in the Cold War, Chapter 1, pp. 1-21, in Melvyn P. Leffler and Odd Arne Westad, editors, The Cambridge history of the Cold War, Volume II Crises and détente, Cambridge University Press, 2010.
55. See Aleksandr Fursenko and Timothy Naftali, Khrushchev's Cold War: the inside story of an American adversary, W.W. Norton & Company, 2006, pp. 256-61 and 280-90.
56. Nikolai Dronin and Edward Bellinger, Climate dependence and food problems in Russia, 1900-1990: the interaction of climate and agricultural policy and their effect on food problems, Central European University Press, 2006, p. 223.
57. See David M. Kotz and Fred Weir, Revolution from above: the demise

of the Soviet system, Routledge, 1997, pp. 75-7.
58. See Stephen Handelman, Comrade criminal: Russia's new Mafiya, Yale University Press, 1995, p. 311.
59. See Michael Smith, New cloak, old dagger: how Britain's spies came in from the cold, Gollancz, 1996, p. 236.
60. Cited p. 5, Michel Chossudovsky, The globalization of poverty and the new world order, 2nd edition, Montreal: Global Research, 2003.

Chapter 7 Eastern Europe from 1945 to 1989

1. V. M. Molotov, Problems of foreign policy: speeches and statements, April 1945 – November 1948, Foreign Languages Publishing House, Moscow, 1949, pp. 213-4.
2. See Andrzej Paczkowski, The spring will be ours: Poland and the Poles from occupation to freedom, Pennsylvania State University Press, 2003, p. 190.
3. Ronald Suny, The Soviet experiment: Russia, the USSR, and the successor states, Oxford University Press, 1998, pp. 356-7.
4. Geoffrey Swain and Nigel Swain, Eastern Europe since 1945, Macmillan, 1993, p. 61.
5. See Victor Sebestyen, Twelve days - revolution 1956: how the Hungarians tried to topple their Soviet masters, Weidenfeld & Nicolson, 2006, pp. 56-7.
6. See Filip Slaveski, The Soviet occupation of Germany: hunger, mass violence, and the struggle for peace, 1945-1947, Cambridge University Press, 2013, pp. 88-102.
7. Filip Slaveski, The Soviet occupation of Germany: hunger, mass violence, and the struggle for peace, 1945-1947, Cambridge University Press, 2013, p. 150.
8. Anne Applebaum, Iron curtain: the crushing of Eastern Europe, Penguin, 2012, pp. 90-1.
9. Cited p. 207, William Blum, America's deadliest export: democracy - the truth about US foreign policy and everything else, Zed Books, 2013.
10. See Keith Jeffery, MI6: the history of the Secret Intelligence Service, 1909-1949, Bloomsbury, 2010, pp. 705-16; on Operation Valuable, see his pp. 712-6. For more detail, see Stephen Dorril, MI6: fifty years of

special operations, Fourth Estate, 2000, 'The Musketeers of Albania', Chapter 19, pp. 355-403.
11. Cited p. 77, James Klugmann, From Trotsky to Tito, Lawrence & Wishart, 1951.
12. Cited p. 331, David Carlton, Eden, Allen Lane, 1981.
13. *Newsweek*, December 1951.
14. Jan Gross, Fear: anti-semitism in Poland after Auschwitz: an essay in historical interpretation, Princeton University Press, 2006, p. 246.
15. See Andrzej Paczkowski, The spring will be ours: Poland and the Poles from occupation to freedom, Pennsylvania State University Press, 2003, p. 180.
16. Cited p. 106, Anne Applebaum, Iron curtain: the crushing of Eastern Europe, Penguin, 2012. For more on their activities, see her pp. 106-11.
17. Alexander Statiev, The Soviet counterinsurgency in the Western borderlands, Cambridge University Press, 2010, p. 312.
18. See Prit Buttar, Between giants: the battle for the Baltics in World War Two, Osprey Publishing, 2013, pp. 324-6.
19. See Prit Buttar, Between giants: the battle for the Baltics in World War Two, Osprey Publishing, 2013, pp. 326-7.
20. See Prit Buttar, Between giants: the battle for the Baltics in World War Two, Osprey Publishing, 2013, pp. 323-4.
21. Arvydas Anušauskas, editor, The Anti-Soviet resistance in the Baltic States, Vilnius: Genocide and Resistance Research Centre of Lithuania, 1999, p. 214.
22. Keith Lowe, Savage continent: Europe in the aftermath of World War II, Penguin Books, 2012, p. 352.
23. Andrzej Paczkowski, The spring will be ours: Poland and the Poles from occupation to freedom, Pennsylvania State University Press, 2003, p. 243.
24. Arvydas Anušauskas, editor, The Anti-Soviet resistance in the Baltic States, Vilnius: Genocide and Resistance Research Centre of Lithuania, 1999, p. 214.
25. Orest Subtelny, Ukraine: a history, 4th edition, University of Toronto Press, 2009, p. 489.
26. See Michael Ellman, Socialist planning, 2nd edition, Cambridge University Press, 1989, p. 59.

27. *The Times*, leader, 21 October 1947.
28. See Adi Schnytzer, Stalinist economic strategy in practice: the case of Albania, Oxford University Press, 1982, Table 1.1, on p. 1.
29. See Adi Schnytzer, Stalinist economic strategy in practice: the case of Albania, Oxford University Press, 1982, Table 5.5, on p. 110.
30. See Adi Schnytzer, Stalinist economic strategy in practice: the case of Albania, Oxford University Press, 1982, p. 88.
31. Adi Schnytzer, Stalinist economic strategy in practice: the case of Albania, Oxford University Press, 1982, pp. 18-9. For more on Albania's successful building of socialism, see William Ash, Pickaxe and rifle: the story of the Albanian people, Howard Baker Press, 1974.
32. Economic survey of Europe in 1956, United Nations, 1957, p. 2.
33. See Kalipada Deb, Soviet Union to Commonwealth: transformation and challenge, MD Publications PVT Ltd, Delhi, 1996, Table 8.6 on p. 203.
34. Pavel Kolář, p. 210, Communism in Eastern Europe, Chapter 11, pp. 203-19, in S. A. Smith, editor, The Oxford handbook of the history of communism, Oxford University Press, 2014.
35. Hugh Seton-Watson, The East European revolution, 2nd edition, Methuen, 1952, p. 254.
36. The UN Organization, Economic development in selected countries, cited p. 160, James Klugmann, From Trotsky to Tito, Lawrence & Wishart, 1951.
37. Cited p. 162, James Klugmann, From Trotsky to Tito, Lawrence & Wishart, 1951.
38. See Leonid Gibianski, p. 30, The 1948 Soviet-Yugoslav conflict and the formation of the 'socialist camp' model, Chapter 2, pp. 22-46, in Odd Arne Westad, Sven Holtsmark and Iver B. Neumann, editors, The Soviet Union in Eastern Europe, 1945-89, St Martin's Press, 1994.
39. Susan L. Woodward, Balkan tragedy: chaos and dissolution after the Cold War, The Brookings Institution, 1995, p. 25.
40. See Leonid Gibianski, pp. 34-43, The 1948 Soviet-Yugoslav conflict and the formation of the 'socialist camp' model, Chapter 2, pp. 22-46, in Odd Arne Westad, Sven Holtsmark and Iver B. Neumann, editors, The Soviet Union in Eastern Europe, 1945-89, St Martin's Press, 1994.
41. Cited p. 98, James Klugmann, From Trotsky to Tito, Lawrence &

Wishart, 1951.
42. Cited p. 85, Charles Gati, Failed illusions: Moscow, Washington, Budapest, and the 1956 Hungarian revolt, Woodrow Wilson Center Press, 2006.
43. Cited p. 175, James Klugmann, From Trotsky to Tito, Lawrence & Wishart, 1951.
44. Susan L. Woodward, Balkan tragedy: chaos and dissolution after the Cold War, The Brookings Institution, 1995, p. 25.
45. See Geoff Swain, Tito: a biography, I. B. Tauris, 2010, p. 102.
46. The *Economist*, 1 September 1951, cited p. 150, James Klugmann, From Trotsky to Tito, Lawrence & Wishart, 1951.
47. *Daily Mail*, 31 August 1951, cited p. 150, James Klugmann, From Trotsky to Tito, Lawrence & Wishart, 1951.
48. The *Economist*, 18 February 1950; see James Klugmann, From Trotsky to Tito, Lawrence & Wishart, 1951, p. 133. On these phoney collectives, see his pp. 131-4.
49. Reported in *The Times*, 25 October 1949, cited p. 115, James Klugmann, From Trotsky to Tito, Lawrence & Wishart, 1951.
50. *Daily Mail*, 25 October 1956.
51. Michael Smith, New cloak, old dagger: how Britain's spies came in from the cold, Gollancz, 1996, p. 122.
52. See M. C. Kaser, editor, The economic history of Eastern Europe 1919-1975, Volume 3, Institutional changes within a planned economy, Clarendon Press, 1986, p. 9.
53. See Richard Crampton, Bulgaria, Oxford University Press, 2007, p. 357.
54. Wilfried Loth, p. 514, The Cold War and social and economic history of the twentieth century, Chapter 24, pp. 503-23, in Melvyn P. Leffler and Odd Arne Westad, editors, The Cambridge history of the Cold War, Volume II Crises and détente, Cambridge University Press, 2010.
55. See Olav Njølstad, p. 151, The collapse of superpower détente, 1975-1980, Chapter 7, pp. 135-55, in Melvyn P. Leffler and Odd Arne Westad, editors, The Cambridge history of the Cold War, Volume III Endings, Cambridge University Press, 2010. See also Grover Furr, The AFT, the CIA, and Solidarnosc, *Comment* [Montclair State College, NJ], 1982, Vol. 1, No. 2, pp. 31-4.
56. See Charles Gati, editor, Zbig: the strategy and statecraft of Zbigniew

Brzezinski, The Johns Hopkins University Press, 2013, p. xviii.

Chapter 8 China

1. Lucien Bianco, Origins of the Chinese revolution, 1915-1949, Stanford University Press, 1971, p. 87.
2. Cited p. 370, Felix Greene, The wall has two sides: a portrait of China today, Jonathan Cape, 1964.
3. Albert Feuerwerker detailed the foreign presence in Republican China in the 1920s and 1930s in John K. Fairbank, editor, The Cambridge history of China, Volume 12, Republican China 1912-1949, Part 1, Cambridge University Press, 1983, Chapter 3, pp. 128-207.
4. Cited p. 32, Tom Buchanan, East wind: China and the British left, 1925-1976, Oxford University Press, 2012.
5. Cited p. 46, George Alexander Lensen, The damned inheritance: the Soviet Union and the Manchurian crises 1924-35, The Diplomatic Press, 1974.
6. See George Alexander Lensen, The damned inheritance: the Soviet Union and the Manchurian crises 1924-35, The Diplomatic Press, 1974, pp. 58-9 and 199-200.
7. For details of this campaign, see George Alexander Lensen, The damned inheritance: the Soviet Union and the Manchurian crises 1924-35, The Diplomatic Press, 1974, pp. 60-82.
8. See Angus Maddison, Chinese economic performance in the long run, Organisation for Economic Co-operation and Development, 1998, p. 15.
9. Andrew Roberts, The storm of war: a new history of the Second World War, Allen Lane, 2009, pp. 267-8.
10. See Odd Arne Westad, Decisive encounter: the Chinese civil war, 1946-1950, Stanford University Press, 2003, pp. 75-7 and 142-3; for the women workers' actions, see his pp. 90-1; for the students' actions, see his pp. 99-103 and 139-42.
11. Cited p. 274, Michael Schaller, The U.S. crusade in China, 1938-1945, Columbia University Press, 1979.
12. Michael Schaller, The U.S. crusade in China, 1938-1945, Columbia University Press, 1979, p. 212.

13. On the huge scale of the US intervention, see Michael Schaller, The U.S. crusade in China, 1938-1945, Columbia University Press, 1979, especially Chapter 11, SACO: the counter-revolution in action, pp. 231-50, and pp. 264-74.
14. Jack Belden, China shakes the world, (1949) Penguin Books, 1973, p. 602-3. On the crossing of the Yangtze, see his pp. 596-606.
15. Angus Maddison, Chinese economic performance in the long run, Organisation for Economic Co-operation and Development, 1998, p. 15.
16. Cited p. 97, Kenneth Neill Cameron, Stalin: man of contradiction, Toronto: NC Press, 1987.
17. Cited p. 258, Felix Greene, The wall has two sides: a portrait of China today, Jonathan Cape, 1964.
18. See Chris Bramall, The industrialization of rural China, Oxford University Press, 2007, p. 139.
19. Melvyn P. Leffler, The specter of communism: the United States and the origins of the Cold War, 1917-1953, Hill and Wang, 1994, p. 107.
20. Jack Gray, Rebellions and revolutions: China from the 1800s to the 1980s, Oxford University Press, 1990, p. 292.
21. Chun Lin, China and global capitalism: reflections on Marxism, history, and contemporary politics, Palgrave, 2013, pp. 49-50.
22. See Jack Belden, China shakes the world, (1949) Penguin Books, 1973, p. 664.
23. See Roderick MacFarquhar and John K. Fairbank, editors, The Cambridge history of China, Volume 15, The People's Republic, Part 2: revolutions within the Chinese revolution 1966-1982, Cambridge University Press, 1991, p. 677.
24. See Chun Lin, The transformation of Chinese socialism, Duke University Press, 2006, pp. 114-5.
25. See Chun Lin, The transformation of Chinese socialism, Duke University Press, 2006, p. 101.
26. Xizhe Peng, p. 644, in Demographic Consequences of the Great Leap Forward in China's Provinces, *Population and Development Review*, 1987, Vol. 13, No. 4, pp. 639-70.
27. Foreign Relations of the United States, 1943, China, US Government Printing Office, Washington, 1957, p. 630.

28. Cited p. 133, Jeremy Brown and Paul Pickowicz, editors, Dilemmas of victory: the early years of the People's Republic of China, Harvard University Press, 2007.
29. 2 September 1949, cited p. 133, Jeremy Brown and Paul Pickowicz, editors, Dilemmas of victory: the early years of the People's Republic of China, Harvard University Press, 2007.
30. Cited p. 157, Jeremy Brown and Paul Pickowicz, editors, Dilemmas of victory: the early years of the People's Republic of China, Harvard University Press, 2007.
31. George C. Herring, From colony to superpower: U.S. foreign relations since 1776, Oxford University Press, 2008, p. 692.
32. See Chun Lin, The transformation of Chinese socialism, Duke University Press, 2006, p. 103.
33. See Barry Sautman, p. 281, Tibet – myths and realities, *Current History*, September 2001, pp. 278-83.
34. Cited p. 467, George Alexander Lensen, The damned inheritance: the Soviet Union and the Manchurian crises 1924-35, The Diplomatic Press, 1974.
35. L. C. Reardon, The reluctant dragon, University of Washington Press, 2002, p. 55.
36. In Roderick MacFarquhar and John K. Fairbank, editors, The Cambridge history of China, Volume 14, The People's Republic, Part 1: the emergence of revolutionary China 1949-1965, Cambridge University Press, 1987, p. 178.
37. See Richard Aldrich, GCHQ: the uncensored story of Britain's most secret intelligence agency, Harper, 2010, p. 129.
38. Cited p. 512, Shu Guang Zhang, Constructing 'peaceful coexistence': China's diplomacy toward the Geneva and Bandung Conferences, 1954-55, *Cold War History*, 2007, Vol. 7, No. 4, pp. 509-28.
39. See Neville Maxwell, Renewed tension on the India-China border: who's to blame? http://www.eastasiaforum.org/2009/09/03, accessed 7 May 2013.
40. See Karl Meyer, The dust of empire: the race for supremacy in the Asian heartland, Abacus, 2004, p. 105.
41. See Lorenz M. Lüthi, The Sino-Soviet split: cold war in the communist world, Princeton University Press, 2008, pp. 115 and 150.

42. Cited p. 144, Lorenz M. Lüthi, The Sino-Soviet split: cold war in the communist world, Princeton University Press, 2008.
43. See Lorenz M. Lüthi, The Sino-Soviet split: cold war in the communist world, Princeton University Press, 2008, pp. 146-7.
44. Cited p. 147, Lorenz M. Lüthi, The Sino-Soviet split: cold war in the communist world, Princeton University Press, 2008.
45. See Lorenz M. Lüthi, The Sino-Soviet split: cold war in the communist world, Princeton University Press, 2008, p. 264.
46. On India's 'forward policy', see Allen S. Whiting, The Chinese calculus of deterrence: India and Indochina, Ann Arbor: University of Michigan Press, 1975, pp. 46-50, 55, 62 and 77.
47. See B. N. Pandey, Nehru, Macmillan, 1976, p. 419.
48. See Neville Maxwell, India's China war, Penguin, 1970, for a superb account of the war.
49. See Henry C. K. Liu, Mao and Lincoln Part 2: The Great Leap Forward not all bad, *Asia Times Online*, http://www.atimes.com/atimes/China/FD01Ad04.html, accessed 26 September 2012.
50. See Felix Greene, The wall has two sides: a portrait of China today, Jonathan Cape, 1964, p. 418. See also his Appendix 5, A postscript on China's economic problems, 1960-62, pp. 396-405, written in May 1963.
51. Robert Price, International Trade of Communist China 1950-1965: an economic profile of mainland China, Vol. II, US Joint Economic Committee, 1975, pp. 600-1.
52. Henry C. K. Liu, Mao and Lincoln Part 2: The Great Leap Forward not all bad, *Asia Times Online*, http://www.atimes.com/atimes/China/FD01Ad04.html
53. See Felix Greene, The wall has two sides: a portrait of China today, Jonathan Cape, 1964, p. 402.
54. Utsa Patnaik, The republic of hunger and other essays, Merlin, 2007, p. 118. For a fuller account, see her pp. 117-9.
55. Wim Wertheim, Wild swans and Mao's agrarian strategy, *Australia-China Review*, August 1995.
56. See Stanley Karnow, Mao and China: a legacy of turmoil, Penguin, 1990, p. 95.
57. Robert C. North, Chinese communism, Weidenfeld & Nicolson, 1966,

p. 191.
58. See Y. Y. Kueh, China's new industrialization strategy: was Chairman Mao really necessary? Edward Elgar, 2007, p. 41.
59. See Chris Bramall, Chinese economic development, Routledge, 2009, pp. 225-6.
60. Michael Dillon, Contemporary China: an introduction, Routledge, 2009, p. 32.
61. See Mark Selden, editor, The People's Republic of China: a documentary history of revolutionary change, Monthly Review Press, 1979, p. 134, note.
62. See Barry Naughton, The Chinese economy: transitions and growth, MIT Press, 2007, Chapter 11, Agriculture: output, inputs, and technology, pp. 251-70.
63. Y. Y. Kueh, p. 721, Mao and agriculture in China's industrialization: three antitheses in a 50-year perspective, *China Quarterly*, September 2006, No. 187, pp. 700-23.
64. See Jean Drèze and Amartya Sen, Hunger and public action, Clarendon Press, 1989, pp. 214-5.
65. Jean Drèze and Amartya Sen, Hunger and public action, Clarendon Press, 1989, pp. 204 and 205.
66. Gordon Chang, Friends and enemies: the United States, China, and the Soviet Union, 1948-1972, Stanford University Press, 1990, pp. 247 and 252. See his 'JFK, China, and the Bomb', Chapter 8, pp. 228-52.
67. See Gordon Chang, Friends and enemies: the United States, China, and the Soviet Union, 1948-1972, Stanford University Press, 1990, pp. 245, 275, note 30 on p. 348, notes 35 and 38 on p. 349, note 45 on p. 350 and note 2 on p. 355.
68. See Lorenz M. Lüthi, The Sino-Soviet split: cold war in the communist world, Princeton University Press, 2008, pp. 307-8 and 321-2.
69. See Lorenz M. Lüthi, The Sino-Soviet split: cold war in the communist world, Princeton University Press, 2008, p. 308.
70. See Lorenz M. Lüthi, The Sino-Soviet split: cold war in the communist world, Princeton University Press, 2008, p. 341-3.
71. Cited p. 342, Lorenz M. Lüthi, The Sino-Soviet split: cold war in the communist world, Princeton University Press, 2008.
72. See Lorenz M. Lüthi, The Sino-Soviet split: cold war in the communist

world, Princeton University Press, 2008, pp. 342 and 344.
73. See Michael Dillon, Contemporary China: an introduction, Routledge, 2009, pp. 40-1.
74. See John Gittings, The changing face of China: from Mao to market, Oxford University Press, 2006, pp. 99-100.
75. See Simon Kuznets, Economic growth of nations: total output and production structure, Harvard University Press, 1971, Table 4, pp. 38-9, and Gilbert Rozman, editor, The modernization of China, Free Press, 1981, Table 10.2, p. 350.
76. See Maurice Meisner, Mao's China and after: a history of the People's Republic, Free Press, 3rd edition, 1999, pp. 417-8.
77. World Bank, China: long term problems and countermeasures in the transition of health care patterns, New York: World Bank, 1994, pp. 1-17.
78. Chris Bramall, Chinese economic development, Routledge, 2009, p. 296.
79. World Bank, China: Socialist Economic Development, Vol. I, Washington: World Bank, 1983, I-94-5.
80. Joseph Ball, Did Mao really kill millions in the Great Leap Forward? http://www.maoists.org/mao.htm, p. 3.
81. Chris Bramall, Chinese economic development, Routledge, 2009, pp. 209-10.
82. Jack Gray, p. 676, Mao in perspective, *China Quarterly*, September 2006, No. 187, pp. 659-79.
83. Chris Bramall, The industrialization of rural China, Oxford University Press, 2007, pp. 142 and 146.
84. Chris Bramall, Chinese economic development, Routledge, 2009, p. 283.
85. Amartya Sen, Development as freedom, New York: Knopf, 2000, p. 17.
86. Delia Davin, p. 218, in Gendered Mao: Mao, Maoism, and women, Chapter 8, pp. 196-218, in Timothy Cheek, editor, A critical introduction to Mao, Cambridge University Press, 2010.
87. Chun Lin, China and global capitalism: reflections on Marxism, history, and contemporary politics, Palgrave, 2013, p. 51.
88. Cited p. 8, Gregor Benton and Chun Lin, Introduction, pp. 1-11, in Gregor Benton and Chun Lin, editors, Was Mao really a monster? The

academic response to Chang and Halliday's Mao: The Unknown Story, Routledge, 2010.
89. Amartya Sen, Development as freedom, Oxford University Press, 1999, p. 260.
90. Y. Y. Kueh, China's new industrialization strategy: was Chairman Mao really necessary? Edward Elgar, 2007, p. 32.
91. Maurice Meisner, 'The Significance of the Chinese Revolution in World History', London: LSE Asia Research Centre Working Papers 1, 1999, pp. 1 and 12.
92. See Michel Chossudovsky, Towards capitalist restoration? Chinese socialism after Mao, Macmillan, 1986, Chapter 1, The political transition, pp. 8-23.
93. See Michael Dillon, Contemporary China: an introduction, Routledge, 2009, p. 61.
94. See Michel Chossudovsky, Towards capitalist restoration? Chinese socialism after Mao, Macmillan, 1986, Chapter 3, The decollectivisation of agriculture, pp. 42-76. On the effects of these policies, see William Hinton, Through a glass darkly: U.S. views of the Chinese revolution, Monthly Review Press, 2006, pp. 192-202.
95. See Carl Riskin, China's political economy: the quest for development since 1949, New York: Oxford University Press, 1987, pp. 297-8.
96. See Michael Ellman, Socialist planning, 2nd edition, Cambridge University Press, 1989, p. 125.
97. See Barry Naughton, The Chinese economy: transitions and growth, MIT Press, 2007, pp. 202-6.
98. William Hinton, The privatization of China: the great reversal, Earthscan, 1991, p. 19.
99. See Chris Bramall, Chinese economic development, Routledge, 2009, p. 388, and Yasheng Huang, Capitalism with Chinese characteristics: entrepreneurship and the state, Cambridge University Press, 2008, p. 26.
100. See Michel Chossudovsky, Towards capitalist restoration? Chinese socialism after Mao, Macmillan, 1986, pp. 132-71.
101. See Chris Bramall, Chinese economic development, Routledge, 2009, p. 389.
102. See Lee Feigon, Mao: a reinterpretation, Ivan R. Dee, 2002, p. 143.

103. See Barry Naughton, The Chinese economy: transitions and growth, MIT Press, 2007, p. 197.
104. See Michael Dillon, Contemporary China: an introduction, Routledge, 2009, p. 72.
105. See William Hinton, Through a glass darkly: U.S. views of the Chinese revolution, Monthly Review Press, 2006, pp. 187, 195-7, 205-8, 231 and 250.
106. See Delia Davin, Gendered Mao: Mao, Maoism, and women, Chapter 8, pp. 196-218, in Timothy Cheek, editor, A critical introduction to Mao, Cambridge University Press, 2010.
107. See Ching Kwan Lee, Against the law: labor protests in China's rustbelt and sunbelt, University of California Press, 2007, p. 60.
108. See John Bellamy Foster and Robert W. McChesney, The endless crisis: how monopoly-finance capital produces stagnation and upheaval from the U.S.A. to China, Monthly Review Press, 2012, p. 163.
109. See Maurice Meisner, The Deng Xiaoping era: an inquiry into the fate of Chinese socialism, 1978-1994, Hill and Wang, 1996, pp. 485-6.
110. See John Bellamy Foster and Robert W. McChesney, The endless crisis: how monopoly-finance capital produces stagnation and upheaval from the U.S.A. to China, Monthly Review Press, 2012, pp. 170-6.

Chapter 9 Korea

1. See Sheila Miyoshi Jager, Brothers at war: the unending conflict in Korea, Profile Books, 2013, p. 19.
2. Melvyn P. Leffler, The specter of communism: the United States and the origins of the Cold War, 1917-1953, Hill and Wang, 1994, p. 97.
3. Melvyn P. Leffler, The specter of communism: the United States and the origins of the Cold War, 1917-1953, Hill and Wang, 1994, p. 100.
4. Cited p. 399, Bruce Cumings, The origins of the Korean War, Volume II, The roaring of the cataract 1947-1950, Princeton University Press, 1990.
5. Cited p. 713, Bruce Cumings, The origins of the Korean War, Volume II, The roaring of the cataract 1947-1950, Princeton University Press, 1990.
6. Allan Millett, The war for Korea 1945-50, University Press of Kansas,

2005, p. 144.
7. Sheila Miyoshi Jager, Brothers at war: the unending conflict in Korea, Profile Books, 2013, pp. 51-3 and 91-2.
8. See Bruce Cumings, The origins of the Korean War, Volume II, The roaring of the cataract 1947-1950, Princeton University Press, 1990, p. 283.
9. See Allan Millett, The war for Korea 1945-50, University Press of Kansas, 2005, p. 206.
10. See Bruce Cumings, War and television, Verso, 1992, p. 169.
11. See William Stueck, Rethinking the Korean War: a new diplomatic and strategic history, Princeton University Press, 2002, p. 71.
12. See Arnold A. Offner, Another such victory: President Truman and the Cold War, 1945-1953, Stanford University Press, 2002, pp. 355-7.
13. Bruce Cumings, War and television, Verso, 1992, pp. 169-70.
14. Cited pp. 5-6, Bruce Cumings, North Korea: another country, The New Press, 2004.
15. See Alex Carey, p. 79, 'The Bureaucratic Passport War: Wilfred Burchett and the Australian Government', in Ben Kiernan, editor, Burchett reporting the other side of the world 1939-1983, Quartet Books, 1986.
16. Cited p. 244, Oliver Stone and Peter Kuznick, The untold history of the United States, Ebury Press, 2012.
17. Cited p. 161, Allan R. Millett, Their war for Korea: American, Asian, and European combatants and civilians, 1945-53, Brassey's, 2002.
18. Cited p. 287, Max Hastings, The Korean war, Simon & Schuster, 1987.
19. Allan R. Millett, Their war for Korea: American, Asian, and European combatants and civilians, 1945-53, Brassey's, 2002, p. 169.
20. Robin Andersen, A century of media, a century of war, New York: Peter Lang Publishing, Inc., 2006, p. 43.
21. Warren Cohen, New Cambridge history of American foreign relations, Vol. 4, Challenges to American primacy, 1945 to the present, Cambridge University Press, 2013, p. 70.
22. Colonel Harry G. Summers, Foreword, Mark Moyar, Phoenix and the Birds of Prey: counterinsurgency and counterterrorism in Vietnam, Bison Books, 2008, p. xi.
23. Cited p. 138, Stan Goff, Full spectrum disorder: the military in the new American century, New York: Soft Skull Press, 2004.

24. Cited p. 40, Robin Andersen, A century of media, a century of war, New York: Peter Lang Publishing, Inc., 2006.
25. Cited p. 41, Robin Andersen, A century of media, a century of war, New York: Peter Lang Publishing, Inc., 2006.
26. Cited p. 41, Robin Andersen, A century of media, a century of war, New York: Peter Lang Publishing, Inc., 2006.
27. Cited p. 31, Bruce Cumings, North Korea: another country, The New Press, 2004.
28. Bruce Cumings, War and television, Verso, 1992, p. 158.
29. Bruce Cumings, War and television, Verso, 1992, p. 215.
30. William Stueck, The Korean War: an international history, Princeton: Princeton University Press, 1995, p. 6.
31. See Bruce Cumings, North Korea: another country, The New Press, 2004, p. 52.
32. Bruce Cumings, p. 287, You can't win for losing – at least in the third world, *Diplomatic History*, 2008, Vol. 32, No. 2, pp. 285-9.
33. Bruce Cumings, North Korea: another country, The New Press, 2004, pp. viii-ix. See also his Chapter 4, Daily life in North Korea, pp. 128-54.
34. See Bruce Cumings, North Korea: another country, The New Press, 2004, footnote 35, p. 240.
35. See Martin K. Dimitrov, editor, Why communism did not collapse: understanding authoritarian regime resilience in Asia and Europe, Cambridge University Press, 2013, p. 119.
36. Cited p. 199, Bruce Cumings, North Korea: another country, The New Press, 2004.
37. On the negotiations, see Bruce Cumings, North Korea: another country, The New Press, 2004, The nuclear crisis: first act and sequel, Chapter 2, pp. 43-102.
38. Cited p. 344, James Mann, The Obamians: the struggle inside the White House to redefine American power, Viking, 2012.

Chapter 10 Vietnam and South-East Asia

1. See Christopher Bayly and Tim Harper, Forgotten wars: the end of Britain's Asian empire, Allen Lane, 2007, pp. 158-89.

2. Cited p. 157, Charles Townshend, Britain's civil wars: counterinsurgency in the twentieth century, Faber, 1986; for a full account, see his pp. 155-65.
3. David French, Army, empire and the Cold War: British army and military policy 1945-71, Oxford University Press, 2012, pp. 115-6.
4. See Benjamin Grob-Fitzgibbon, Imperial endgame: Britain's dirty wars and the end of empire, Palgrave Macmillan, 2011, p. 327.
5. Cited p. 79, Stephen Dorril, The silent conspiracy: inside the intelligence services in the 1990s, Heinemann, 1993.
6. Cited p. 123, David French, Army, empire and the Cold War: British army and military policy 1945-71, Oxford University Press, 2012.
7. See Calder Walton, Empire of secrets: British intelligence, the Cold War and the twilight of empire, William Collins, 2014, p. 194.
8. Bruno C. Reis, p. 254, The myth of British minimum force in counterinsurgency campaigns during decolonisation (1945-1970), *Journal of Strategic Studies*, 2011, Vol. 34, No. 2, pp. 245-79.
9. Calder Walton, Empire of secrets: British intelligence, the Cold War and the twilight of empire, William Collins, 2014, p. 184.
10. Caroline Elkins, cited p. 419, Marilyn B. Young, Two, three, many Vietnams, *Cold War History*, 2006, Vol. 6, No. 4, pp. 413-24.
11. Christopher Hale, Massacre in Malaya: exposing Britain's My Lai, The History Press, 2013, pp. 284-5.
12. David French, Army, empire and the Cold War: British army and military policy 1945-71, Oxford University Press, 2012, p. 302.
13. Christopher Hale, Massacre in Malaya: exposing Britain's My Lai, The History Press, 2013, pp. 284-5.
14. Douglas Porch, Counter-insurgency: exposing the myths of the new way of war, Cambridge University Press, 2013, pp. 50, 71 and 125.
15. Douglas Porch, Counter-insurgency: exposing the myths of the new way of war, Cambridge University Press, 2013, pp. 130-1.
16. Fredrik Logevall, Embers of war: the fall of an empire and the making of America's Vietnam, Random House, 2014, p. 534.
17. See Fredrik Logevall, Embers of war: the fall of an empire and the making of America's Vietnam, Random House, 2014, p. 620.
18. Both cited p. 633, Fredrik Logevall, Embers of war: the fall of an empire and the making of America's Vietnam, Random House, 2014.

19. Cited p. 140, William Warbey, Vietnam: the truth, Merlin, 1965.
20. Article 14 (a), cited p. 546, Richard A. Falk, editor, The Vietnam War and international law, Volume 1, Princeton: Princeton University Press, 1968.
21. George C. Herring, From colony to superpower: U.S. foreign relations since 1776, Oxford University Press, 2008, p. 662.
22. Joseph Buttinger, Vietnam: the unforgettable tragedy, Horizon Press, 1977, p. 48.
23. Douglas Valentine, The Phoenix program, Backinprint.com, 2000, p. 33.
24. Cited p. 91, David Milne, America's Rasputin: Walt Rostow and the Vietnam War, Hill & Wang, 2008.
25. Cited p. 351, Fredrik Logevall, Choosing war: the lost chance for peace and the escalation of war in Vietnam, University of California Press, 1999.
26. See H. R. McMaster, Dereliction of duty: Lyndon Johnson, Robert McNamara, the Joint Chiefs of Staff, and the lies that led to Vietnam, HarperCollins, 1997, p. 36.
27. See H. R. McMaster, Dereliction of duty: Lyndon Johnson, Robert McNamara, the Joint Chiefs of Staff, and the lies that led to Vietnam, HarperCollins, 1997, p. 37.
28. See H. R. McMaster, Dereliction of duty: Lyndon Johnson, Robert McNamara, the Joint Chiefs of Staff, and the lies that led to Vietnam, HarperCollins, 1997, p. 37.
29. See Fredrik Logevall, Choosing war: the lost chance for peace and the escalation of war in Vietnam, University of California Press, 1999, pp. xxi, 4-5, 22, 27-33, 35, 37-9, 44-7, 51-3 and 67-73.
30. Fredrik Logevall, Choosing war: the lost chance for peace and the escalation of war in Vietnam, University of California Press, 1999, p. 22.
31. Fredrik Logevall, Choosing war: the lost chance for peace and the escalation of war in Vietnam, University of California Press, 1999, p. 258.
32. Cited p. 350, Fredrik Logevall, Choosing war: the lost chance for peace and the escalation of war in Vietnam, University of California Press, 1999.

33. Documents relating to British involvement in the Indo-China conflict, 1945-65, HMSO, 1967, p. 209.
34. Cited p. 76, Randall B. Woods, J. William Fulbright, Vietnam, and the search for a Cold War foreign policy, Cambridge University Press, 1998. For the context of the Gulf of Tonkin Resolution, see his pp. 71-8 and 164-70. For more on the incident, see Lloyd C. Gardner, Pay any price: Lyndon Johnson and the wars for Vietnam, Chicago: Dee, 1995, pp. 122, 134-9 and 142-3.
35. See Richard Aldrich, GCHQ: the uncensored story of Britain's most secret intelligence agency, Harper, 2010, p. 277.
36. See John Roosa, Pretext for mass murder: the September 30th Movement and Suharto's coup d'état in Indonesia, University of Wisconsin Press, 2006, p. 177.
37. See John Roosa, Pretext for mass murder: the September 30th Movement and Suharto's coup d'état in Indonesia, University of Wisconsin Press, 2006, p. 177.
38. CIA Memorandum of June 1962, cited p. 195, William Blum, Killing hope: U.S. military and CIA interventions since World War II, Black Rose Press, 1998. For more details of the British government's involvement, see Paul Lashmar and James Oliver, Britain's secret propaganda war, Sutton, 1998, pp. 4-10.
39. Cited p. 190, John Roosa, Pretext for mass murder: the September 30th Movement and Suharto's coup d'état in Indonesia, University of Wisconsin Press, 2006.
40. Cited p. 176, John Roosa, Pretext for mass murder: the September 30th Movement and Suharto's coup d'état in Indonesia, University of Wisconsin Press, 2006.
41. Cited p. 209, John Roosa, Pretext for mass murder: the September 30th Movement and Suharto's coup d'état in Indonesia, University of Wisconsin Press, 2006.
42. Cited p. 62, David Easter, 'Keep the Indonesian pot boiling': Western covert intervention in Indonesia, October 1965-March 1966, *Cold War History*, 2005, Vol. 5, No. 1, pp. 55-73.
43. All quotes cited from the *Observer*, 17 May 1998, p. 32. See John Dumbrell, A special relationship: Anglo-American relations in the Cold War and after, Macmillan, 2001, p. 69.

44. FO Telegram of 8 October, cited p. 63, David Easter, 'Keep the Indonesian pot boiling': Western covert intervention in Indonesia, October 1965-March 1966, *Cold War History*, 2005, Vol. 5, No. 1, pp. 55-73.
45. Cited p. 63, David Easter, 'Keep the Indonesian pot boiling': Western covert intervention in Indonesia, October 1965-March 1966, *Cold War History*, 2005, Vol. 5, No. 1, pp. 55-73.
46. See David Easter, p. 57, 'Keep the Indonesian pot boiling': Western covert intervention in Indonesia, October 1965-March 1966, *Cold War History*, 2005, Vol. 5, No. 1, pp. 55-73.
47. See David Easter, p. 63, 'Keep the Indonesian pot boiling': Western covert intervention in Indonesia, October 1965-March 1966, *Cold War History*, 2005, Vol. 5, No. 1, pp. 55-73.
48. See John Roosa, Pretext for mass murder: the September 30th Movement and Suharto's coup d'état in Indonesia, University of Wisconsin Press, 2006, p. 269.
49. See John Roosa, Pretext for mass murder: the September 30th Movement and Suharto's coup d'état in Indonesia, University of Wisconsin Press, 2006, p. 174.
50. Cited pp. 59-60, David Easter, 'Keep the Indonesian pot boiling': Western covert intervention in Indonesia, October 1965-March 1966, *Cold War History*, 2005, Vol. 5, No. 1, pp. 55-73.
51. Cited p. 181, Gabriel Kolko, Confronting the Third World: United States foreign policy 1945-1980, New York: Pantheon, 1988.
52. See John Prados, Lost crusader: the secret wars of CIA Director William Colby, Oxford University Press, 2003, pp. 155-6 and 356-7.
53. See Douglas Valentine, The Phoenix program, Backinprint.com, 2000, p. 414.
54. See John Dumbrell, A special relationship: Anglo-American relations in the Cold War and after, Macmillan, 2001, p. 69.
55. Cited p. 274, Lloyd C. Gardner, Imperial America: American foreign policy since 1898, New York: Harcourt, 1976.
56. Cited p. 79, Bernd Greiner, War without fronts: the USA in Vietnam, Vintage Books, 2009.
57. See Bernd Greiner, War without fronts: the USA in Vietnam, Vintage Books, 2009, p. 79.

58. Cited p. 332, Nicholas Turse, Kill anything that moves: the real American war in Vietnam, Metropolitan Books, 2013.
59. Cited p. 382, Douglas Valentine, The Phoenix program, Backinprint.com, 2000.
60. Cited p. 347, Douglas Valentine, The Phoenix program, Backinprint.com, 2000.
61. Cited p. 319, Douglas Valentine, The Phoenix program, Backinprint.com, 2000.
62. Cited p. 349, Douglas Valentine, The Phoenix program, Backinprint.com, 2000.
63. Thomas L. Ahern Jr., Vietnam declassified: the CIA and counterinsurgency, University Press of Kentucky, 2012, p. 360.
64. Cited p. 198, Ho Chi Minh, Down with colonialism! Verso, 2007.
65. Cited p. 19, Christian Appy, Patriots: the Vietnam war remembered from all sides, Viking, 2003.
66. Ziad Obermeyer, Christopher Murray and Emmanuela Gakidou, Fifty years of violent war deaths from Vietnam to Bosnia: analysis of data from the World Health Survey Programme, *British Medical Journal*, 2008, Vol. 226, pp. 1482-6.
67. Cited p. 22, James Blight, The fog of war: lessons from the life of Robert S. McNamara, Rowman & Littlefield, 2005.
68. Fredrik Logevall, Choosing war: the lost chance for peace and the escalation of war in Vietnam, University of California Press, 1999, p. 412.
69. Cited p. 81, Nicholas Turse, Kill anything that moves: the real American war in Vietnam, Metropolitan Books, 2013.
70. Douglas Valentine, The Phoenix program, Backinprint.com, 2000, p. 90.
71. Cited p. 192, David Milne, America's Rasputin: Walt Rostow and the Vietnam War, Hill & Wang, 2008.
72. William Shawcross, The quality of mercy: Cambodia, Holocaust and modern conscience, Andre Deutsch, 1984, p. 78; see also his p. 27.
73. *New York Times*, 3 July 1981.
74. For more on the British government's policies, see Stephen Dorril, The silent conspiracy: inside the intelligence services in the 1990s, Mandarin, 1994, pp. 393-4.

75. Cited p. 393, Stephen Dorril, The silent conspiracy: inside the intelligence services in the 1990s, Mandarin, 1994.
76. See Chris Bramall, Chinese economic development, Routledge, 2009, p. 396.
77. See Michel Chossudovsky, The globalization of poverty and the new world order, 2nd edition, Montreal: Global Research, 2003, Chapter 12, The post-war economic destruction of Vietnam, pp. 167-88.
78. Cited p. 35, Bill Hayton, Vietnam: rising dragon, Yale University Press, 2011.
79. See Bill Hayton, Vietnam: rising dragon, Yale University Press, 2011, pp. 164-6, 170-2 and 169-70.
80. See Bill Hayton, Vietnam: rising dragon, Yale University Press, 2011, pp. 48, 173-6, 179-80 and 227.
81. See Bill Hayton, Vietnam: rising dragon, Yale University Press, 2011, pp. xv, 3-4, 6-7 and 17-25. On the systemic corruption, see his pp. 33-4, 41-2 and 103-4. On the corruption of the party, see his pp. 3, 22, 24, 104, 106 and 108-10.
82. Quoted by Michael Peel, Cambodian Rolls-Royce elite highlights wealth gap, *Financial Times*, 19 July 2014, p. 5.

Chapter 11 Cuba, to 1990

1. Cited p. 60, Lars Schoultz, That infernal little Cuban republic: the United States and the Cuban revolution, University of North Carolina Press, 2009.
2. Cited p. 55, Lars Schoultz, That infernal little Cuban republic: the United States and the Cuban revolution, University of North Carolina Press, 2009.
3. See Lars Schoultz, That infernal little Cuban republic: the United States and the Cuban revolution, University of North Carolina Press, 2009, pp. 55-63, 71-8 and 85-6.
4. Both cited p. 36, Lars Schoultz, That infernal little Cuban republic: the United States and the Cuban revolution, University of North Carolina Press, 2009.
5. Cited p. 101, Arnold August, Cuba and its neighbours: democracy in motion, Zed Books, 2013.

6. Cited p. 61, Lars Schoultz, That infernal little Cuban republic: the United States and the Cuban revolution, University of North Carolina Press, 2009.
7. Cited p. 47, Keith Bolender, Cuba under siege: American policy, the revolution, and its people, Palgrave Macmillan, 2012.
8. See Lars Schoultz, That infernal little Cuban republic: the United States and the Cuban revolution, University of North Carolina Press, 2009, p. 53.
9. Cited pp. 53-4, Lars Schoultz, That infernal little Cuban republic: the United States and the Cuban revolution, University of North Carolina Press, 2009.
10. Cited p. 53, Lars Schoultz, That infernal little Cuban republic: the United States and the Cuban revolution, University of North Carolina Press, 2009.
11. Cited p. 47, Keith Bolender, Cuba under siege: American policy, the revolution, and its people, Palgrave Macmillan, 2012.
12. Cited p. 54, Lars Schoultz, That infernal little Cuban republic: the United States and the Cuban revolution, University of North Carolina Press, 2009.
13. See Salim Lamrani, The economic war against Cuba: a historical and legal perspective on the U.S. blockade, Monthly Review Press, 2013, p. 19.
14. *New York Times*, 19 April 1959.
15. Cited p. 70, Aviva Chomsky, A history of the Cuban revolution, Wiley-Blackwell, 2011.
16. Cited p. 3, Aviva Chomsky, A history of the Cuban revolution, Wiley-Blackwell, 2011.
17. Cited p. 19, Salim Lamrani, The economic war against Cuba: a historical and legal perspective on the U.S. blockade, Monthly Review Press, 2013.
18. Department of State, Foreign Relations of the United States, 1958-1960, Volume VI, Cuba (1991), p. 885.
19. Cited p. 144, Lars Schoultz, That infernal little Cuban republic: the United States and the Cuban revolution, University of North Carolina Press, 2009.
20. Department of State, Foreign Relations of the United States, Document

No. 499, 1960, cited p. 107, Arnold August, Cuba and its neighbours: democracy in motion, Zed Books, 2013.

21. Department of State, Foreign Relations of the United States, Document No. 607, 1960, cited p. 107, Arnold August, Cuba and its neighbours: democracy in motion, Zed Books, 2013.

22. Cited p. 58, Keith Bolender, Cuba under siege: American policy, the revolution, and its people, Palgrave Macmillan, 2012.

23. Cited p. 347, Aleksandr Fursenko and Timothy Naftali, Khrushchev's Cold War: the inside story of an American adversary, W.W. Norton & Company, 2006.

24. See Lars Schoultz, That infernal little Cuban republic: the United States and the Cuban revolution, University of North Carolina Press, 2009, p. 186.

25. See John Prados, Lost crusader: the secret wars of CIA Director William Colby, Oxford University Press, 2003, pp. 243-4 and 302.

26. Cited p. 299, John Prados, Lost crusader: the secret wars of CIA Director William Colby, Oxford University Press, 2003.

27. Cited p. 329, Piero Gleijeses, Cuba and the Cold War, 1959-1980, Chapter 16, pp. 327-48, in Melvyn P. Leffler and Odd Arne Westad, editors, The Cambridge history of the Cold War, Volume II Crises and détente, Cambridge University Press, 2010.

28. D. W. Greig, International law, Butterworth, 2nd ed., 1976, pp. 341 and 343. See his excellent discussion, pp. 339-43.

29. Quincy Wright, p. 553, 'The Cuban Quarantine', *American Journal of International Law*, 1963, Vol. 57, No. 3, pp. 546-65.

30. See Andrew Zimbalist, p. 91, Cuban industrial growth, 1965-84, pp. 83-93, in Andrew Zimbalist, editor, Cuba's socialist economy toward the 1990s, special issue of *World Development*, January 1987, Vol. 15, No. 1.

31. Cited pp. 193-4, Sandor Halebsky and John M. Kirk, editors, Cuba: twenty-five years of revolution, 1959-1984, Praeger, 1985.

32. See Andrew Zimbalist and Claes Brundenius, The Cuban economy: measurement and analysis of socialist performance, Johns Hopkins University Press, 1989, p. 5.

33. See Haleh Afshar and Carolyne Bennis, Women and adjustment policies in the Third World, Macmillan, 1992.

34. Steve Ludlam, p. 543, Cuban labour at 50: what about the workers? *Bulletin of Latin American Research*, 2009, Vol. 28, No. 4, pp. 542-57.
35. James K. Galbraith, Inequality and instability: a study of the world economy just before the great crisis, Oxford University Press, 2012, p. 287.
36. See José L. Rodríguez, p. 31, Agricultural policy and development in Cuba, pp. 23-39, in Andrew Zimbalist, editor, Cuba's socialist economy toward the 1990s, special issue of *World Development*, January 1987, Vol. 15, No. 1.
37. See Martin Carnoy, Amber Grove and Jeffrey Marshall, Cuba's academic advantage: why students in Cuba do better in school, Stanford University Press, 2007, p. 142 and passim.
38. Erwin H. Epstein, review of *Children Are the Revolution* by Jonathan Kozol, *Comparative Education Review*, October 1979, p. 456.
39. Medea Benjamin, Joseph Collins and Michael Scott, No free lunch: food and revolution in Cuba today, New York: Grove Press/Food First, 1986, pp. 189-90.
40. Piero Gleijeses, Visions of freedom: Havana, Washington, Pretoria, and the struggle for Southern Africa, 1976-1991, The University of Carolina Press, 2013, p. 29.
41. Cited p. 338, Piero Gleijeses, Cuba and the Cold War, 1959-1980, Chapter 16, pp. 327-48, in Melvyn P. Leffler and Odd Arne Westad, editors, The Cambridge history of the Cold War, Volume II Crises and détente, Cambridge University Press, 2010.
42. See Nancy Mitchell, The Cold War and Jimmy Carter, Chapter 4, pp. 66-88, in Melvyn P. Leffler and Odd Arne Westad, editors, The Cambridge history of the Cold War, Volume III Endings, Cambridge University Press, 2010.
43. Cited p. 345, Piero Gleijeses, Cuba and the Cold War, 1959-1980, Chapter 16, pp. 327-48, in Melvyn P. Leffler and Odd Arne Westad, editors, The Cambridge history of the Cold War, Volume II Crises and détente, Cambridge University Press, 2010.
44. Henry J. Richardson III, pp. 89-90, 'Constitutive Questions in the Negotiations for Namibian Independence', *American Journal of International Law*, 1984, Vol. 78, No. 1, pp. 76-120.
45. Piero Gleijeses, p. 290, Cuba and the independence of Namibia, *Cold*

46. Piero Gleijeses, Visions of freedom: Havana, Washington, Pretoria, and the struggle for Southern Africa, 1976-1991, The University of Carolina Press, 2013, p. 15.
47. Piero Gleijeses, pp. 296-7, Cuba and the independence of Namibia, *Cold War History*, 2007, Vol. 7, No. 2, pp. 285-303.
48. Cited p. 297, Piero Gleijeses, Cuba and the independence of Namibia, *Cold War History*, 2007, Vol. 7, No. 2, pp. 285-303.
49. Cited p. 526, Piero Gleijeses, Visions of freedom: Havana, Washington, Pretoria, and the struggle for Southern Africa, 1976-1991, The University of Carolina Press, 2013.
50. See Saul Landau, p. 42, July 26. History absolved him. Now what? pp. 41-4, Chapter 2, in Philip Brenner, Marguerite Rose Jiménez, John M. Kirk and William M. LeoGrande, editors, A contemporary Cuba reader: Reinventing the revolution, Rowman & Littlefield, 2008.
51. On Venezuela, see Arnold August, Cuba and its neighbours: democracy in motion, Zed Books, 2013, pp. 45-59, on Bolivia, see his pp. 59-66 and on Ecuador, see his pp. 66-72.

Chapter 12 The Soviet Union - counter-revolution and catastroika

1. Robert Fisk, The great war for civilisation: the conquest of the Middle East, Fourth Estate, 2005, pp. 100 and 69.
2. US Department of the Army, Afghanistan, A Country Study, 1986, cited p. 86, William Blum, America's deadliest export democracy: the truth about US foreign policy and everything else, Zed Books, 2013.
3. Interview in *Le Nouvel Observateur* (France), 15-21 January 1998, p. 76. For more on the CIA operation in Afghanistan, see pp. 688-91, Douglas Little, 'Mission Impossible: The CIA and the Cult of Covert Action in the Middle East', *Diplomatic History*, 2004, Vol. 28, No. 5, pp. 663-701.
4. Cited p. 461, Oliver Stone and Peter Kuznick, The untold history of the United States, Ebury Press, 2012.
5. *New York Times*, 1 February 1980.
6. D. W. Greig, International law, Butterworth, 2nd ed., 1976, p. 914.
7. Raymond L. Garthoff, Détente and confrontation: American-Soviet

relations from Nixon to Reagan, revised edition, the Brookings Institution, 1994, pp. 1037 and 1074.
8. See Mike Davidow, Perestroika: its rise and fall, International Publishers, 1993, pp. 21-2 and 62.
9. See Roger Keeran and Thomas Kenny, Socialism betrayed: behind the collapse of the Soviet Union, New York: International Publishers, 2004, pp. 141-2.
10. See Irene Brennan, 'Dialogue with Janus: the political economy of European Union-Russia relations', Chapter 5, pp. 93-125, in Vassiliki Koutrakou, editor, The European Union and Britain: debating the challenges ahead, Macmillan, 2000.
11. Ernest Mandel, *Temps Nouveaux*, 1990, No. 38, pp. 41-2. My translation.
12. *De Financieel Ekonomische Tijd*, 21 March 1990.
13. See Stephen Cohen, Soviet fates and lost alternatives: from Stalinism to the new Cold War, Columbia University Press, 2009, p. 90.
14. Cited p. 109, Stephen Cohen, Soviet fates and lost alternatives: from Stalinism to the new Cold War, Columbia University Press, 2009.
15. Yeltsin supporter Yegor Yakovlev, cited p. 133, Stephen Cohen, Soviet fates and lost alternatives: from Stalinism to the new Cold War, Columbia University Press, 2009.
16. John B. Dunlop, The rise of Russia and the fall of the Soviet empire, Princeton University Press, p. 267.
17. David M. Kotz and Fred Weir, Revolution from above: the demise of the Soviet system, Routledge, 1997, pp. x and 129.
18. Roger Keeran and Thomas Kenny, Socialism betrayed: behind the collapse of the Soviet Union, New York: International Publishers, 2004, p. 143.
19. Peter Nolan, China's rise, Russia's fall: politics, economics and planning in the transition from Stalinism, Macmillan, 1995, p. 309.
20. See Stephen F. Cohen, Failed crusade: America and the tragedy of post-communist Russia, W. W. Norton, 2001, note 89, on p. 325.
21. Cited p. 37, David Stuckler and Sanjay Basu, The body economic: why austerity kills, Allen Lane, 2013.
22. Michael Kort, The Soviet colossus: history and aftermath, 7th edition, M. E. Sharpe, 2010, p. xii.
23. Jerry F. Hough, The logic of economic reform in Russia, Brookings

Institution Press, 2001, p. 231.
24. Stephen F. Cohen, Failed crusade: America and the tragedy of post-communist Russia, W. W. Norton, 2001, pp. 45 and 172.
25. Cited p. 32, David Stuckler and Sanjay Basu, The body economic: why austerity kills, Allen Lane, 2013.
26. For details, see for example Irene Brennan's section, 'The implosion of the Russian economy', pp. 97-100 of her 'Dialogue with Janus: the political economy of European Union-Russia relations', Chapter 5, pp. 93-125, in Vassiliki Koutrakou, editor, The European Union and Britain: debating the challenges ahead, Macmillan, 2000. See also David Satter, Darkness at dawn: the rise of the Russian criminal state, Yale University Press, 2004, and Marshall I. Goldman, The piratisation of Russia: Russian reform goes awry, Routledge, 2003.
27. Cited p. 23, David Stuckler and Sanjay Basu, The body economic: why austerity kills, Allen Lane, 2013.
28. David Stuckler and Sanjay Basu, The body economic: why austerity kills, Allen Lane, 2013, pp. 21 and 40.
29. Cited pp. 150-1, Mike Davidow, Perestroika: its rise and fall, International Publishers, 1993.
30. The challenge of slums, Global Report on Human Settlements 2003, published by Earthscan Publications Ltd on behalf of the UN Human Settlements Programme, p. 30.
31. Cited p. 178, Tim Pringle and Simon Clarke, The challenge of transition: trade unions in Russia, China and Vietnam, Palgrave Macmillan, 2011.
32. See David Stuckler and Sanjay Basu, The body economic: why austerity kills, Allen Lane, 2013, pp. 38-9.
33. Cited p. 235, Stephen F. Cohen, Failed crusade: America and the tragedy of post-communist Russia, W. W. Norton, 2001.
34. Cited note 86, on p. 324, Stephen F. Cohen, Failed crusade: America and the tragedy of post-communist Russia, W. W. Norton, 2001.
35. See Stephen F. Cohen, Failed crusade: America and the tragedy of post-communist Russia, W. W. Norton, 2001, pp. 234-5.
36. Sally Cummings, Understanding Central Asia, politics and contested transformations, Routledge, 2011, pp. 123 and 175.
37. Cited p. 63, Philip Shishkin, Restless valley: revolution, murder, and intrigue in the heart of Central Asia, Yale University Press, 2013.

38. See Mark Curtis, Secret affairs: Britain's collusion with radical Islam, Serpent's Tail, 2010, and Robert Dreyfuss, Devil's game: how the United States helped unleash fundamentalist Islam, Henry Holt & Company, 2005.
39. Cited p. 84, Sally Cummings, Understanding Central Asia, politics and contested transformations, Routledge, 2011.
40. Craig Janes and Oyuntsetseg Chuluundorj, pp. 233-4, Free markets and dead mothers: the social ecology of maternal mortality in post-socialist Mongolia, *Medical Anthropology Quarterly*, 2004, Vol. 18, No. 2, pp. 230-57.
41. Cited p. 105, Mary Elise Sarotte, 1989: the struggle to create post-Cold War Europe, Princeton University Press, 2009.
42. See Mary Elise Sarotte, Not One Inch Eastward? Bush, Baker, Kohl, Genscher, Gorbachev, and the origin of Russian resentment toward NATO enlargement in February 1990, *Diplomatic History*, 2010, Vol. 34, No. 1, pp. 119-40.
43. Karl Lieber and Daryl Press, p. 51, The rise of US nuclear primacy, *Foreign Affairs*, March/April 2006, Vol. 85, No. 2, pp. 42-54.
44. Robert Gates, Duty: memoirs of a secretary at war, W. H. Allen, 2014, p. 97.
45. Zbigniew Brzezinski, The geostrategic triad: living with China, Europe, and Russia, Center for Strategic and International Studies, 2001, p. 68, Point 8 in his 'Decalogue of Strategic Guidelines'.
46. *Wall Street Journal*, 10 January 2003.
47. *Washington Post*, 3 December 2004.

Chapter 13 Eastern Europe – counter-revolution and war

1. Cited p. 168, Geoffrey Swain, Tito: a biography, I.B. Tauris, 2010.
2. See Geoffrey Swain, Tito: a biography, I.B. Tauris, 2010, p. 168.
3. See Michael Ellman, Socialist planning, 2nd edition, Cambridge University Press, 1989, p. 56.
4. Pavel Kolář, p. 207, Communism in Eastern Europe, Chapter 11, pp. 203-19, in S. A. Smith, editor, The Oxford handbook of the history of communism, Oxford University Press, 2014.
5. Cited p. 189, Nafeez Mosaddeq Ahmed, The London bombings: an

independent inquiry, Duckworth, 2006.
6. See Susan L. Woodward, Balkan tragedy: chaos and dissolution after the Cold War, The Brookings Institution, 1995, pp. 336 and 381.
7. See Susan L. Woodward, Does Kosovo's status matter? On the international management of statehood, *Südosteuropa*, 2007, Vol. 55, No. 1, S. 1-25, especially p. 5.
8. Rosalyn Higgins, p. 468, The new United Nations and former Yugoslavia, *International Affairs*, 1993, Vol. 69, No. 3, pp. 465-83.
9. See Rosalyn Higgins, The new United Nations and former Yugoslavia, *International Affairs*, 1993, Vol. 69, No. 3, pp. 465-83.
10. Cited p. 184, Susan L. Woodward, Balkan tragedy: chaos and dissolution after the Cold War, The Brookings Institution, 1995.
11. Rosalyn Higgins, p. 470, The new United Nations and former Yugoslavia, *International Affairs*, 1993, Vol. 69, No. 3, pp. 465-83.
12. Susan L. Woodward, Balkan tragedy: chaos and dissolution after the Cold War, The Brookings Institution, 1995, p. 388.
13. See Barry Eichengreen and Andrea Boltho, The economic impact of European integration, Centre for Economic Policy and Research, 2008, p. 43.
14. Cited p. 234, John R. Schindler, Unholy terror: Bosnia, Al-Qa'ida and the rise of global jihad, Zenith Press, 2007.
15. Cited p. 235, John R. Schindler, Unholy terror: Bosnia, Al-Qa'ida and the rise of global jihad, Zenith Press, 2007.
16. See *New York Times*, 28 March 2000.
17. UN Security Council resolution 1160 (1998).
18. 'Private U.S. firm training both sides in Balkans', *The Scotsman*, 2 March 2001.
19. Cited p. 90, Michel Collon, Media lies and the conquest of Kosovo: NATO's prototype for the next wars of globalization, Unwritten History, Inc., New York, 2007.
20. *New York Times*, 18 July 1996.
21. *Washington Post*, 4 August 1996.
22. Wesley Clark, Waging modern war, Westview Press, 2001, p. 418.
23. Jonathan Charney, p. 834, 'Anticipatory Humanitarian Intervention in Kosovo', *American Journal of International Law*, 1999, Vol. 93, No. 4, pp. 834-40.

24. John Murphy, The United States and the rule of law in international affairs, Cambridge University Press, 2004, pp. 154 and 157. See his discussion, pp. 154-61.
25. Cited p. 184, Michel Collon, Media lies and the conquest of Kosovo: NATO's prototype for the next wars of globalization, Unwritten History, Inc., New York, 2007.
26. 1 April 1999, cited p. 117, David R. Willcox, Propaganda, the press and conflict: the Gulf War and Kosovo, Routledge, 2005.
27. See David R. Willcox, Propaganda, the press and conflict: the Gulf War and Kosovo, Routledge, 2005, p. 116.
28. 24 April 1999, cited p. 136, David R. Willcox, Propaganda, the press and conflict: the Gulf War and Kosovo, Routledge, 2005.
29. See Victor Malarek, The Natashas: the new global sex trade, Vision Paperbacks, 2004, pp. 228-55.
30. *Washington Post*, 24 April 2000.
31. *BBC World News*, 29 January 2001.
32. Cited p. 225, Michel Collon, Media lies and the conquest of Kosovo: NATO's prototype for the next wars of globalization, Unwritten History, Inc., New York, 2007.
33. See Vesna Peric Zimonjic, How did we become so poor? Belgrade, 18 May 2010, Inter Press Service.
34. Cited Vesna Peric Zimonjic, How did we become so poor? Belgrade, 18 May 2010, Inter Press Service.
35. See Susan L. Woodward, Does Kosovo's status matter? On the international management of statehood, *Südosteuropa*, 2007, Vol. 55, No. 1, p. 13.
36. See Victor Malarek, The Natashas: the new global sex trade, Vision Paperbacks, 2004, pp. 157-82. See also Stephen Holden, 'American in Bosnia discovers the horrors of human trafficking', *New York Times*, 4 August 2011.
37. See Nauro F. Campos and Fabrizio Coricelli, Growth in transition: what we know, what we don't, and what we should, Centre for Economic Policy Research, 2000, pp. 36-7.
38. See Nauro F. Campos and Fabrizio Coricelli, Growth in transition: what we know, what we don't, and what we should, Centre for Economic Policy Research, 2000, p. 35.

39. Public policy and social conditions, United Nations International Children's Emergency Fund, Geneva, 1993.
40. For more detail on how the IMF, along with the EU, helped to wreck Yugoslavia, see Michel Chossudovsky, The globalization of poverty and the new world order, 2nd edition, Montreal: Global Research, 2003, Chapter 17, Dismantling former Yugoslavia, recolonizing Bosnia, pp. 257-77. For more on the IMF's destruction of Albania's economy, see his Chapter 18, Albania's IMF sponsored financial disaster, pp. 279-98.
41. See Martin Myant and Jan Drahokoupil, Transition economies: political economy in Russia, Eastern Europe, and Central Asia, John Wiley & Sons, Inc., 2011, p. 116.
42. See Jeffrey Sommers, Flashpoint in Ukraine: how the US drive for hegemony risks World War III, edited by Stephen Lendman, Clarity Press, 2014, p. 145.
43. The European Commission's 2000 Enlargement Strategy Paper, cited p. 22, Ambrose Evans-Pritchard, 2003 deadline call for larger EU, *Daily Telegraph*, 9 November 2000.
44. Andrzej Paczkowski, The spring will be ours: Poland and the Poles from occupation to freedom, Pennsylvania State University Press, 2003, p. 527.
45. See L. C. Bresser Pereira, J. M. Maravall and A. Przeworski, editors, Economic reforms in new democracies, Cambridge University Press, 1993, p. 199.
46. Cited p. 26, Japhy Wilson, Jeffrey Sachs: the strange case of Dr Shock and Mr Aid, Counterblast Series, Verso Books, 2014.
47. David Ost, The defeat of Solidarity: anger and politics in postcommunist Europe, Cornell University Press, 2005, p. 8.
48. See Rita O. Koyame-Marsh, The complexities of economic transition: lessons from the Czech Republic and Slovakia, *International Journal of Business and Social Science*, 2011, Vol. 2, No. 19, pp. 71-85.
49. Robert Bideleux and Ian Jeffries, A history of Eastern Europe: crisis and change, Routledge, 2006, p. 612.
50. See Martin Myant and Jan Drahokoupil, Transition economies: political economy in Russia, Eastern Europe, and Central Asia, John Wiley & Sons, Inc., 2011, p. 330.
51. See, for example, Guglielmo Meardi, Social failures of EU enlargement:

a case of workers voting with their feet, Routledge, 2012, p. 184.
52. See Christian Dustmann et al, The labour market impact of immigration, *Oxford Review of Economic Policy*, 2008, Vol. 24, No. 3, pp. 477-94.
53. Stephen Nickell and Jumana Saleheen, The impact of immigration on occupational wages: Evidence from Britain, Spatial Economics Research Centre, Discussion Paper 34, October 2009.
54. Cited pp. 101-2, Stewart Parker, The last Soviet republic: Alexander Lukashenko's Belarus, Trafford Publishing, 2007.
55. Both cited p. 177, Stewart Parker, The last Soviet republic: Alexander Lukashenko's Belarus, Trafford Publishing, 2007.
56. Cited p. 110, Stewart Parker, The last Soviet republic: Alexander Lukashenko's Belarus, Trafford Publishing, 2007.
57. Both cited p. 144, Stewart Parker, The last Soviet republic: Alexander Lukashenko's Belarus, Trafford Publishing, 2007.
58. See *New York Times*, 26 February 2006.
59. See Jeffrey Burds, Ethnic conflict and minority refugee flight from post-Soviet Ukraine, 1991-2001, *International Journal of Human Rights*, 2008, Vol. 12, No. 5, pp. 689-723.
60. See Orest Subtelny, Ukraine: a history, 4th edition, University of Toronto Press, 2009, p. 598.

Chapter 14 Cuba, the Special Period – workers in control

1. See Emily Morris, p. 8, Unexpected Cuba, *New Left Review*, 2014, No. 88, 27 pages.
2. Cited pp. 87-8, Keith Bolender, Cuba under siege: American policy, the revolution, and its people, Palgrave Macmillan, 2012.
3. Cited p. 13, Salim Lamrani, The economic war against Cuba: a historical and legal perspective on the U.S. blockade, Monthly Review Press, 2013.
4. See Philip Brenner, Marguerite Rose Jiménez, John M. Kirk and William M. LeoGrande, editors, A contemporary Cuba reader: Reinventing the revolution, Rowman & Littlefield, 2008, p. 21.
5. See Steve Ludlam, Cuban labour at 50: what about the workers? *Bulletin of Latin American Research*, 2009, Vol. 28, No. 4, pp. 542–57.

6. On Cuba's sustainable development, see Pamela Stricker, Towards a culture of nature: environmental policy and sustainable development in Cuba, Lexington Books, 2007, pp. 1-13; on its farming, see her pp. 15-44; on its renewable energy sources – biomass, biogas, solar, hydroelectric and wind, see her pp. 45-50 and 56-7; and on its efforts to cut energy use, see her pp. 50-2.
7. See John M. Kirk and H. Michael Erisman, Cuban medical internationalism: origins, evolution, and goals, Palgrave Macmillan, 2009, pp. 13, 107-8, 137-9, 141-6 and 156.
8. For more on CELAC, see Arnold August, Cuba and its neighbours: democracy in motion, Zed Books, 2013, pp. 72-4.
9. See Steve Brouwer, Revolutionary doctors: how Venezuela and Cuba are changing the world's conception of health care, Monthly Review Press, 2011, p. 38.
10. See Julie Feinsilver, Cuba's health politics: at home and abroad, Report prepared for the Council on Hemispheric Studies, March 2010. http://www.coha.org/cuba/%2%/80%99s-health-politics-at-home-and/abroad. Accessed 20 September 2010.
11. On this programme, see John M. Kirk and H. Michael Erisman, Cuban medical internationalism: origins, evolution, and goals, Palgrave Macmillan, 2009, pp. 13-4, 49, 135-7, 139, 141-2, 144-5, 148-52 and 159. The most recent account is John M. Kirk, Medical internationalism in Cuba, *Counterpunch* 14-16 December 2012, accessed 25 January 2013 at www.counterpunch.org/2012/12/14/medical-internationalism-in-cuba/print.
12. See John M. Kirk and H. Michael Erisman, Cuban medical internationalism: origins, evolution, and goals, Palgrave Macmillan, 2009, pp. 51-5, 57, 128, 132, 135-7, 139-42, 152, 169, 182 and 213.
13. See Steve Ludlam, Cuban labour at 50: what about the workers? *Bulletin of Latin American Research*, 2009, Vol. 28, No. 4, pp. 542–57.
14. Cited p. 542, Steve Ludlam, Cuban labour at 50: what about the workers? *Bulletin of Latin American Research*, 2009, Vol. 28, No. 4, pp. 542–57.
15. See *Cuba Sí*, Autumn 2013, p. 24.
16. Oficina Nacional de Estadísticas, 2008.
17. See Duncan Green, From poverty to power, Oxfam, 2008, p. 251.

18. See Steve Ludlam, p. 51, Aspects of Cuba's strategy to revive socialist development, *Science & Society*, 2012, Vol. 76, No. 1, pp. 41–65.
19. For more on Cuba's system of local democracy, see Peter Latham, The state and local government: towards a new basis for 'local democracy' and the defeat of big business control, Manifesto, 2011, pp. 305-22. On People's Power, see Arnold August, Cuba and its neighbours: democracy in motion, Zed Books, 2013, pp. 112-4. On the 1997-98 elections, see his Democracy in Cuba and the 1997-98 elections, Editorial José Marti, 1999.
20. On Cuba's elections, see Arnold August, Cuba and its neighbours: democracy in motion, Zed Books, 2013, Chapter 7, Elections in contemporary Cuba, pp. 146-94.
21. See Carollee Bengelsdorf, The problem of democracy in Cuba: between vision and reality, Oxford University Press, 1984, pp. 122-31.
22. For more on the workings of the National Assembly, see Arnold August, Cuba and its neighbours: democracy in motion, Zed Books, 2013, Chapter 8, The ANPP and the municipality: functioning between elections, pp. 195-227.
23. Sergio Díaz-Briquets and Jorge Pérez-López, Corruption in Cuba: Castro and beyond, University of Texas Press, 2006.
24. See Lois M. Smith and Alfred Padula, Sex and revolution: women in socialist Cuba, Oxford University Press, 1996, pp. 142 and 182.
25. See Aleksandr Fursenko and Timothy Naftali, Khrushchev's Cold War: the inside story of an American adversary, W.W. Norton & Company, 2006, p. 314. See also their pp. 318-9 and 321.
26. See Michael Parenti, The face of imperialism, Paradigm Publishers, 2011, p. 97.
27. See Arnold August, Cuba and its neighbours: democracy in motion, Zed Books, 2013, p. 138.
28. See Deisy Francis Mexidor, Cuba's reasons: There will always be an Emilio, *Granma International*, 1 March 2011, http:///www.granma.cu/ingles/ cuba-i/1march-emilio.html, accessed 4.11.2013.
29. See Margo Kirk, Early childhood education in revolutionary Cuba during the Special Period, Chapter 32, pp. 302-8, in Philip Brenner, Marguerite Rose Jiménez, John M. Kirk and William M. LeoGrande, editors, A contemporary Cuba reader: Reinventing the revolution,

Rowman & Littlefield, 2008.
30. http://www.savethechildren.org/publications/state-of-the-worlds-mothersreport/SOWM-2010-Index-Rankings.pdf
31. Isaac Risco, Homosexuals, too revolutionary for Cuba? *Havana Times*, 21 September 2012.
32. See John M. Kirk and H. Michael Erisman, Cuban medical internationalism: origins, evolution, and goals, Palgrave Macmillan, 2009, pp. 143, 160 and 177.
33. See Monty Don, Around the world in 80 gardens, Weidenfeld & Nicolson, 2008, p. 97. See his accounts of Organoponico Vivero Alamar, pp. 90- 2, Huerto Alberto Rojas, pp. 93-4, and Huerto Angelito, pp. 95-7.
34. See Pamela Stricker, Towards a culture of nature: environmental policy and sustainable development in Cuba, Lexington Books, 2007, pp. 95-104; on Cubans' understanding of sustainable development, pp. 105-19.
35. See Duncan Green, From poverty to power, Oxfam, 2008, p. 114.
36. See Richard Wilkinson and Kate Pickett, The spirit level: why equality is better for everyone, Penguin, 2010, p. 220.

Bibliography

Select bibliography

Ash, William, Pickaxe and rifle: the story of the Albanian people, Howard Baker, 1974

Belden, Jack, China shakes the world, (1949), Pelican Books, 1973

Bellamy, Chris, Absolute war: Soviet Russia in the Second World War: a modern history, Pan, 2008

Bramall, Chris, Chinese economic development, Routledge, 2009

Bramall, Chris, In defence of Maoist economic planning: living standards and economic development in Sichuan since 1931, Clarendon Press, 1993

Carr, E. H., History of Soviet Russia, 10 volumes, Macmillan, 1950-78

Carr, E. H., The Soviet impact on the western world, Macmillan, 1973

Chossudovsky, Michel, The globalization of poverty and the new world order, 2nd edition, Montreal: Global Research, 2003

Chossudovsky, Michel, Towards capitalist restoration? Chinese socialism after Mao, Macmillan, 1986

Coates, W. P. and Zelda K., Six centuries of Russo-Polish relations, Lawrence & Wishart, 1948

Collon, Michel, Liar's poker: the great powers, Yugoslavia and the wars of the future, International Action Center, New York, 2002

Collon, Michel, Media lies and the conquest of Kosovo: NATO's prototype for the next wars of globalization, Unwritten History, Inc., New York, 2007

Davies, R. W., Crisis and progress in the Soviet economy, 1931-33, Palgrave Macmillan, 1996

Davies, R. W., The Soviet collective farm, 1929-1930, Macmillan, 1980

Davies, R. W., Harrison, Mark, & Wheatcroft, S. G., editors, The economic transformation of the Soviet Union, 1913-1945, Cambridge University Press, 1994

Dorril, Stephen, The silent conspiracy: inside the intelligence services in the 1990s, Mandarin, 1994

Dunn, Walter S., Stalin's keys to victory: the rebirth of the Red Army, Praeger, 2006

Fleming, D. F., The Cold War and its origins, 2 volumes, New York: Doubleday, 1961

Furr, Grover, Blood lies: the evidence that every accusation against Joseph Stalin and the Soviet Union in Timothy Snyder's 'Bloodlands' is false, Red Star Publishers, 2014

Furr, Grover, Khrushchev lied: the evidence that every 'revelation' of Stalin's (and Beria's) 'crimes' in Nikita Khrushchev's infamous 'secret speech' to the 20th Party Congress of the Communist Party of the Soviet Union on February 25, 1956, is provably false, Erythrós Press & Media, 2011

Furr, Grover, The murder of Sergei Kirov: history, scholarship and the anti-Stalin paradigm, Erythros Press & Media, 2013

Garthoff, Raymond L., Détente and confrontation: American-Soviet relations from Nixon to Reagan, New York: Brookings Institution, 1994

Garthoff, Raymond L., The great transition: American-Soviet relations and the end of the Cold War, New York: Brookings Institution, 1994

Getty, J. Arch, Trotsky in exile: the founding of the Fourth International, *Soviet Studies*, 1986, Vol. 38, No. 1, pp. 24-35

Glantz, David, Barbarossa: Hitler's invasion of Russia 1941, Tempus, 2001

Glantz, David, and House, Jonathan M., When titans clashed: how the Red Army stopped Hitler, University Press of Kansas, 1995

Gleijeses, Piero, Visions of freedom: Havana, Washington, Pretoria, and the struggle for Southern Africa, 1976-1991, The University of Carolina Press, 2013

Hill, Christopher, Lenin and the Russian Revolution, (1947) Penguin, 1971

Hinton, William, Fanshen: a documentary of revolution in a Chinese village, New York: Vintage Books, 1966

Hinton, William, The privatization of China: the great reversal, Earthscan, 1991

Hinton, William, Through a glass darkly: U.S. views of the Chinese revolution, Monthly Review Press, 2006

Jones, Michael, The retreat: Hitler's first defeat, John Murray, 2009

Jones, Michael, Stalingrad: how the Red Army triumphed, Casemate, 2007

Keeran, Roger and Kenny, Thomas, Socialism betrayed: behind the collapse of the Soviet Union, New York: International Publishers, 2004

Kirk, John M. and Erisman, H. Michael, Cuban medical internationalism: origins, evolution, and goals, Palgrave Macmillan, 2009

Klugmann, James, From Trotsky to Tito, Lawrence & Wishart, 1951

Kojevnikov, Alexei, Stalin's great science: the times and adventures of Russia's physicists, Imperial College Press, 2004

Lee, Ching Kwan, Against the law: labor protests in China's rustbelt and sunbelt, University of California Press, 2007

Leffler, Melvyn P., For the soul of mankind: the United States, the Soviet Union and the cold war, Hill & Wang, 2007

Leibovitz, Clement, and Finkel, Alvin, In our time: the Chamberlain-Hitler collusion, Monthly Review Press, 1998

Macdonald, Théodore H., The education revolution: Cuba's alternative to neoliberalism, Manifesto Press (in association with the National Union of Teachers), 2009

Macdonald, Théodore H., Hippocrates in Havana: analytical and expository account of the development of the Cuban system of healthcare from the revolution to the present day, Able Publishing, 1995

Maddison, Angus, Chinese economic performance in the long run, Organisation for Economic Co-operation and Development, 1998

Mandel, William, A guide to the Soviet Union, New York: The Dial Press, 1946

Mawdsley, Evan, The Russian civil war, Allen & Unwin, 1987

Mawdsley, Evan, The Stalin years: the Soviet Union 1929-53, Manchester University Press, 2nd edition, 2003

Mawdsley, Evan, Thunder in the east: the Nazi-Soviet war 1941-1945, Hodder, 2007

Mawdsley, Evan, World War II: a new history, Cambridge University Press, 2009

Maxwell, Neville, India's China war, Penguin, 1970

Nettl, J. P., The Soviet achievement, Thames & Hudson, 1976

Sayers, Michael and Kahn, Albert E., The great conspiracy against Russia, Boni & Gaer, 1947

Schoultz, Lars, That infernal little Cuban republic: the United States and the Cuban revolution, University of North Carolina Press, 2009

Schuman, Frederick L., Soviet politics at home and abroad, Robert Hale Limited, 1948

Sen, Amartya, Development as freedom, Oxford University Press, 1999

Smelser, Ronald, and Davies, Edward J. II, The myth of the eastern front: the Nazi-Soviet war in American popular culture, Cambridge University Press, 2008

Snow, Edgar, Red China today: The other side of the river, Penguin Books, 1970

Snow, Edgar, Red star over China, Penguin Books, revised edition, 1972

Stout, Nancy, One day in December: Celia Sanchez and the Cuban revolution, Monthly Review Press, 2013

Stricker, Pamela, Towards a culture of nature: environmental policy and sustainable development in Cuba, Lexington Books, 2007

Suny, Ronald, The Soviet experiment: Russia, the USSR, and the successor states, Oxford University Press, 1998

Suny, Ronald, editor, The Cambridge history of Russia, Volume III The twentieth century, Cambridge University Press, 2006

Swain, Geoffrey, Russia's civil war, The History Press, 2000

Van Ree, Erik, The political thought of Joseph Stalin: a study in 20th-century revolutionary patriotism, RoutledgeCurzon, 2002

Werth, Alex, Russia at war 1941-1945, Barrie & Rockliff, 1964

Wheatcroft, Stephen G., editor, Challenging traditional views of Russian history, Palgrave Macmillan, 2002

Wheeler-Bennett, John W., Brest-Litovsk: the forgotten peace, March 1918, (1938) Macmillan, 1963

White, Theodore H., and Jacoby, Annalee, Thunder out of China, (1946), Da Capo Press, 1980

Zaleski, Eugène, Stalinist planning for economic growth, 1933-1952, Macmillan, 1980

Index

Abhazia, 212
Abramovitch, Roman, 184
Abzug, Bella, 157
Acheson, Dean, 145
Acton, Edward, 13, 43, 71, 78
Afghanistan, 11, 19, 123, 177-9, 190, 212
Africa, 65, 83, 165, 172, 173-6, 217, 222, 223, 233
Agreed Framework, 146
Agriculture, 1, 17-8, 20-4, 31, 34, 38, 42, 94, 98, 102, 110, 120, 126-7, 133-4, 170, 208, 225
Ahern Jr. Thomas L., 158
Al-Qaeda, 190, 197
Alanbrooke, Viscount, 86
Albania, viii, 106, 109, 111, 191, 198, 204-5, 206
Albertson, Ralph, 14
Alexander, Andrew, 50, 89
Alibabic, Munir, 201
Alksnis, Colonel Viktor, 46
Alternativa Bolivariania para las Américas (ALBA), 192, 220, 225
Ambrose, Stephen, 62

American Documentary Films, 230
American Enterprise Institute, 145
Amery, Leo, 56
Anders, General Wladyslaw, 73
Angola, 173-5, 178
Apartheid, 175-6
Apple, 137
Applebaum, Anne, 106
ARCOS, 18-9
Aristides, President Jean-Bertrand, 222
Armed Resistance League, 108
Arms, 10-11, 56, 63-4, 78-9, 92, 101, 156, 173, 204-5
Army, British, 149
Army Intelligence School (US), 157
Ashdown, Lord, 201
Asia, 41, 83, 118, 124, 151, 171, 192-3, 200, 223, 233
Asian Development Bank, 162
Asian Infrastructure and Investment Bank, 193
Asquith, Henry, 12
Association of Central and Eastern European Election Officials, 208

309

Association of South East Asian Nations (ASEAN), 192-3
Attlee, Clement, 86
Austerity policy, 161, 171, 188, 201-2, 206, 210
Austria, 8, 86, 111
Austria-Hungary, 3
Axis, see Rome-Berlin Axis
Azerbaijan, 9, 12, 23, 26

Bachman, Ronald, 33
Baldwin, Stanley, 18-9, 50
Balkans, 55, 80, 108, 109
Ball, Joseph, 99
Baltic states, 8, 9, 19, 52, 55-7, 67-8, 76, 80, 92, 107, 109, 110, 205, 211
Bandera, Stepan, 209
Bartolome Maso, 235
Basu, Sanjay, 96-7, 186
Batista, Fulgencio, 164-6
Battle of Ideas, 219-20, 234-7
Battle of the Bulge (1944), 79
Bay of Pigs, 167-8
Beijing, 133, 137, 138
Belarus, 53, 66, 107, 108, 207-9
Belarus Democracy Act (2004), 208-9
Belgium, 56, 61
Bellamy, Chris, 61-2, 63, 71, 84
Bellinger, Edward, 98-9
Benard, Cheryl, 178-9
Beneš, Eduard, 46, 106
Benjamin, Medea, 172-3
Berezovsky, Boris, 184
Berkhoff, Karel, 6, 61, 66

Berlin, 18, 46, 49, 75, 88, 106, 194
Berlin Wall, 192, 198, 206
Berliner, Joseph, 96
Bihac, 202
Biological weapons, 169
Biotechnology, 218, 220, 224, 234
Birch, Reg, vii-viii
Birobidzhan, 37
Black Hundreds, 2
Black Sea, 12, 56, 211
Blockades, viii, 9-10, 16, 21, 97, 105, 145, 167, 169, 216-7, 218, 230, 234, 235
Blumenfeld, Hans, 34
Bolivia, 222
Bombing, 86, 144, 150, 151, 154, 159, 198-9
Bondarchuk, Sergei, 29
Bonnet, Georges, 50-1
Bonsal, Philip W., 166
Boothby, Robert, 55
Bor-Komorowski, General Tadeusz, 76-7, 79
Bosnia, 194, 195, 196-7, 199, 200, 201-2
Boutros-Ghali, Boutros, 196
Braden, Spruille, 164
Bramall, Chris, 129-30, 131-2
Brandel, Peter, 231-2
Breedlove, General Philip, 214
Brest-Litovsk, Treaty of (1918), 7-8
Brezhnev, Leonid, 103, 128
Bridges, General, 11
British Broadcasting Corporation (BBC), 92, 200
British Empire, 3, 58, 82, 117, 123

Brodie, Bernard, 93
Brzezinski, Zbigniew, 178, 191, 192, 212
Budberg, General, 14
Budko, Vitaly, 181
Bug, River, 53
Bukharin, Nikolai, 23-4, 43-5
Bulgaria, 16, 41, 57, 59, 60, 104, 191, 204, 206, 213
Bullock, Alan, 78
Burds, Jeffrey, 92
Burma, 123, 125
Burton, John, 141
Bush, President George W., 146, 147, 209, 222, 231
Business Week, 111
Buttar, Prit, 67
Buttinger, Joseph, 153
Byrnes, James, 80

Cairo Conference, 139
Cambodia, 152, 154, 159-61, 162-3
Cameron, David, 215
Campbell, Thomas, 23
Canada, 125, 193
Capital export, see Investment, foreign
Carl, Samantha, 52
Carr, E. H., 15, 17-8, 97-8
Carriles, Luis Posada, 169
Carrington, Lord Peter, 178, 196
Cason, James, 230
Castro, President Fidel, 166-8, 173-6, 182, 222, 230, 232
Castro, President Raul, 232
Castro Espin, Mariela, 232

Catholic University Association, 165-6
Central Asia, 9, 15, 36-7, 63, 98, 182, 187, 189-90, 191-2
Central Intelligence Agency (CIA), 92, 106, 107, 119, 121, 123, 145, 154, 156, 157-8, 165, 167, 168, 169, 178, 181-2, 191, 205, 232
Chamberlain, Neville, 49-52, 56
Chang, Gordon, 127
Changkufeng, battle of (1938), 48-9
Charney, Jonathan, 199
Che Guevara, Ernesto, 222
Chechens, 68-9, 190, 192
Cheju-do, 140
Chelsea Football Club, 184
Chemical weapons, 11
Cheney, Dick, 191
Chiefs of Staff, British, 85
Chiefs of Staff, US, 81, 107, 168
Child care, 26, 204, 228-9
Children, 26-7, 33, 120, 128, 130-1, 132, 140, 143, 145, 159, 162, 165, 169, 170, 187, 204, 219, 221, 229, 232
Chile, 97, 156
China, viii, 18, 19, 48, 49, 80, 81, 82, 83, 101, 115-38, 142, 143, 145, 147, 161, 163, 191, 192-3
Chinese Eastern Railway, 116, 122
Chinese revolution, 18, 115, 117-9, 120, 126, 130, 133
Chubais, Anatoly, 185
Church, Roman Catholic, 109
Church, Russian Orthodox, 2, 5, 67
Churchill, Winston, 9-11, 46, 51, 55, 56, 65-6, 74, 78-80, 82, 84, 85-6, 89, 90, 97, 151

City of London, 84
Clark, General Mark, 145
Clark, General Wesley, 198
Clarke, Simon, 40
Class consciousness, 195
Co-ordinating Committee for Multilateral Trade Controls (COCOM), 105
Coal, 8, 35, 110, 128-9, 180, 181
Cohen, Stephen, 37-8
Cohen, Warren, 90, 93, 143
Collins, Joseph, 172-3
Colonialism, 36, 38, 120, 148-51, 152, 165, 173
Commerce, see Trade
Committees for the Defence of the Revolution, 166, 218
Commonwealth Brigade, 143
Communist Party of Britain Marxist-Leninist, vii-viii
Communist Party of the Soviet Union, 179, 182
Comunidad de Estados Latinoamericanos y Caribeños (CELAC), 220
Concentration camps, 72, 149, 153
Conservative Party, 55, 56
Conyers, John, 157
Corruption, 114, 115, 135, 179-80, 183, 185, 189, 201-2, 203, 219, 228
Cotonou Agreement, 217
Counter-revolutions, 44-5, 177-85, 189-90, 195, 202-7, 209-15, 231
Covert operations, 16, 113, 121, 153
Crankshaw, Edward, 88
Crimea, 12, 68-9, 211, 212

Crimean War (1854-56), 41, 56,
Croatia, 191, 194, 196, 199, 200, 201, 202
Cuba, viii, 25, 101, 161, 164-76, 216-37
Cuba Encuentro, 231
Cuba Fund for a Democratic Future, 231
Cuban American National Foundation, 230
Cuban Civil Defence Authority, 226
Cuban Communist Party, 218
CubaSolar, 235
Cuito Cuanevale, battle of (1988), 175
Cumings, Bruce, 141, 144, 145
Cummings, Sally, 189
Curzon, George Nathaniel, 9, 16
Curzon line, 53, 55, 74
Cyprus, 150
Czech Legion, 7, 9, 14
Czech Republic, 191, 203, 204, 230, 231
Czechoslovakia, 10, 16, 46, 49, 50, 69, 105-6, 110, 202

D-Day, 74, 83
Dagestan, 23, 192
Daily Mail, 112, 113
Daily Mirror, 199
Daily Telegraph, 2
Daladier, Edouard, 56
Dalai Lama, 121
Davidow, Mike, 100-1
Davies, Joseph, 65
Davies, R. W., 25, 38
Davies, Sarah, 45
Davin, Delia, 132

Debts, 57, 99, 113-4, 161, 189, 202, 203

Democracy, vii, 3, 6, 7, 14-5, 31, 49, 51, 91, 101, 133, 145, 164, 179, 180, 181, 208, 210-11, 223-9

Denikin, General Anton, 9, 10-11

Depression, Great (1929), 186, 203

Deutscher, Isaac, 7-8

Development, vii, 3-4, 17-8, 21, 38-9, 95-6, 109, 120, 122-5, 128-32, 135, 170-3, 210, 224, 234, 235

Dictatorship of the proletariat, 223-4, 227-9

Diem, President Ngo Dinh, 152-4

Dien Bien Phu, battle of (1954), 151

'Divide and rule', 150, 151, 209

Dnieperstroy dam, 25

Doenitz, Admiral Karl, 85

Don, Monty, 234

Doo-hwan, General Chun, 145

Dorril, Stephen, 16

Drèze, Jean, 127

Dronin, Nikolai, 98-9

Dukes, Sir Paul, 13

Dulles, Allen, 165

Dulles, John Foster, 96

Dunn, Robert, 31

Dunn, Walter, 62-3, 83

Dvoretsky, Lev, 61

Dynocorp, 202

Eastern Europe, 25, 38, 66, 76, 79-80, 89, 90, 101, 104-14, 122-3, 182, 187, 191, 194-215, 216

Eberstadt, Nicholas, 145-6

Ebola, 222

Eco-tourism, 235

Economist, 112

Eden, Anthony, 151

Edmonds, Robin, 78

Education, 2, 15, 22, 25, 26, 27-9, 30, 36, 38, 39, 95-6, 102-3, 118, 120, 128, 130-1, 132, 135, 136, 160, 162, 170-2, 177-8, 181, 189, 203, 206, 207, 208, 218, 223, 224-5, 228, 231-2, 233, 235-6

Eisenhower, President Dwight, 88, 89, 144-5, 151, 152, 167

Eisenstein, Sergei, 29

Ekaterinburg, 9

El Alamein, battle of (1942), 65

Elkins, Caroline, 150

Ellman, Michael, 32, 33, 37, 96

Emigration, 195, 205, 206

Emmons, Terence, 5

Engineering, 25, 29, 95

Enlai, Zhou, 123-4

Environment, 234-6

Epstein, Erwin, 172

Ernesto Che Guevara Cuban Medical Brigade, 220-1

Espionage, 19, 92, 106

Estonia, 57, 67-8, 108, 110, 191, 205-6, 213

Ethiopia, 173-4

European Commission, 193, 203

European Parliament, 210

European Union (EU), 190, 191-3, 195-203, 206, 209-12, 213, 215, 217

Eurosolar, 235

Exploitation, viii, 137, 165

Exports, 2, 19, 20, 21, 34, 35, 109, 111, 134, 137, 156, 166, 170, 184, 186, 201

Family planning, 130
Famines, 1, 10, 16, 20, 21, 23, 31, 33-4, 115, 125-6, 145, 162
Farkas, Mihály, 113
Federal Bureau of Investigation (FBI), 103
Federation of Cuban Women, 166, 218
Federation of Independent Trade Unions of Russia (FNPR), 180-1
Fergana, 23
Finance, 17, 20, 26-7, 34-5, 37, 49, 112, 116, 134, 162, 184, 188, 195, 203
Finkel, Alvin, 50
Finland, 9, 19, 53, 56-7, 211
Finnish-Soviet War (1939), 56-7
First New York Festival of Cuban Cinema, 230
First World War, 2-4, 71, 81, 83, 84, 87, 104
Fischer, Louis, 8
Fitzpatrick, Sheila, 30
Five-Year Plans, 24-6, 30, 34-6, 95, 110, 122
Food, 8, 12, 16, 21, 23, 32-4, 38, 60, 78-9, 95, 102, 104-5, 106, 119, 123, 127, 128, 130, 144, 149, 160, 162, 167, 172, 180, 186, 189, 195, 207, 210, 218-9, 223, 225, 234
Forest, 28, 137, 159, 162, 163, 235
Foreign Office, Australian, 141
Foreign Office, British, 4, 17, 85, 92, 116, 140, 155-6

Fort Holabird, 157
Foshan, 137
Foster-Carter, Aidan, 146
Fourth International, 180
Foxconn, 137
France, viii, 3, 4, 7, 8, 9, 12, 16, 18, 19, 34, 42, 46, 49, 50-1, 54, 56, 58, 59, 61, 69, 74, 76, 82, 83, 125, 142, 148, 151-2, 161, 210, 214
Franco, General Francisco, 7
Free Trade Agreements, 193, 210-1
French, David, 150
French Revolution (1789), viii
Fritz, Stephen, 64, 74, 78, 79, 83
Fugate, Brian, 61
Furr, Grover, 101

G8 countries, 223
Gaddis, John Lewis, 101
Gagarin, Yuri, 95
Gaidar, Egor, 98, 183
Galbraith, James K., 171
Galicia, 54, 69
Gandhi, Indira, 124
Garthoff, Raymond, 16, 90, 179
Gas, 35, 114, 186, 189, 193, 210
Gas warfare, 11
Gates, Robert, 191
Gati, Charles, 114
Geco bullets, 73
General Staff, British, 58
General Staff, German, 7, 8
Genetics, 218
Geneva Conference (1954), 152-3, 158

Genocide, 59-61, 66, 104, 144, 156, 186
Georgia, 9, 12, 19, 192, 205, 210, 212, 214
German Democratic Republic (GDR), 93, 94, 106, 109, 110
German Social-Democratic Party, 3
Germany, 2, 3, 7-8, 10, 19, 37-8, 41, 42-3, 45-7, 49, 50-94, 106, 108, 129, 191, 196, 197-8, 202, 206-7, 210, 214, 231
Ghana, 222
Giap, General Vo Nguyen, 151
Gilchrist, Sir Andrew, 155
Ginsburgs, George, 54, 55
Glantz, David M., 62, 63, 64, 73, 81
Gleijeses, Piero, 173, 174-5
Goebbels, Josef, 46, 71-2
Goering, Hermann, 53-4, 60
Gorbachev, Mikhail, 103, 114, 133, 174, 179-80, 182, 191
Gorodetsky, Gabriel, 16
Gosbank, 17
Gottwald, Klement, 105
Gracey, General Douglas, 151
Graham, Loren, 28
Grand Alliance, 64, 76
Granick, David, 25-6
Granma, 235
Graves, General William, 13
Gray, Colin, 93
Gray, Jack, 131
Greece, 111, 140, 200, 202
Green, Barbara, 33
Greig, D. W., 169, 179
Grinberg, Ilya, 62, 63

Gromyko, Andrei, 127
Guama, 235
Guangdong, 136, 137
Guantanamo Bay, 168, 200
Guardian, 199
Guatemala, 156, 168
Guderian, General Heinz, 64
Guevara, Che, 222
Guillain, Robert, 115
Guinea-Bissau, 173
Gulf of Tonkin, 128, 154

Haeju, 141
Hague Conventions, 60
Haiti, 220-2, 226
Halder, General Franz, 53-4, 58
Hale, Christopher, 150
Halifax, Lord Edward, 50
Hans, N., 36
Hanson, Philip, 99
Harbin, 116
Hardesty, Von, 62, 63
Harris, James, 45
Harrison, Mark, 84
Harvard Medical School, 158-9
Hasegawa, Tsuyoshi, 86-7
Hastings, Sir Max, 77, 83
Havana, 175, 217, 230, 234
Hawk jets, 156
Health, 22, 26-7, 36, 38-9, 96-7, 121, 128, 129-30, 132, 134, 135, 137, 145, 160, 162, 170-2, 181, 187, 188, 189, 190, 204, 205, 206, 207, 208, 216-7, 218, 220-3, 224-5, 226, 228, 229, 233-4, 236

Health care, 26, 38, 39, 121, 128, 130, 132, 133, 135, 145, 160, 162, 170, 171, 172, 181, 187, 189, 204, 205, 206, 207, 208, 216-7, 220-3, 224, 225, 226, 229, 231-2, 235
Hearst, Randolph, 47
Hehn, Paul, 49-50
Helms-Burton Act (1996), 216
Hensel, Struve, 91
Henze, Paul, 173, 174
Herring, George, 152-3
Herteleer, General, 199
Hessen, S., 36
Higgins, Rosalyn, 195-6
Hitler, Adolf, 34, 43, 46, 47, 49, 50-5, 57, 58-60, 74, 79, 83, 86, 89, 104, 197
Ho Chi Minh City, 162
Hoffmann, David, 38, 43
Hoffmann, General Max, 7, 8
Holidays, 26, 103, 187
Holloway, David, 93
Home, Lord Alec, 127
Honda, 137
Hong Kong, 123
Horrocks, General Sir Brian, 13
Hospitals, 26, 88, 102, 130, 152, 159, 160, 162, 165, 171, 178, 222
Hough, Jerry, 185
House, Jonathan, 64, 73
House of Commons, 10, 55, 179
Household Responsibility System, 133-4
Housing, 26, 38, 95, 97, 128, 145, 181, 186, 187, 203, 227-8
Howard, Sir Michael, 89

Hughes, Michael, 13
Human Development Index, 235-6
Humbert-Droz, Jules, 44
Humphrey, George, 164
Hungary, 3, 57, 69, 104, 106, 108, 109, 110, 111, 113, 186, 191, 203-4, 206, 213
Hunger, 12, 60, 115, 167, 172, 216
Hunger Plan, 60
Hurricanes, 146, 220, 226
Hyundai, 137

Immigration, 195, 205, 206
Imperialism, 3, 47, 66, 87, 97, 111, 118, 152
Imports, see Trade
Independent Union of Coal Industry Employees, 180-1
India, 11, 12, 16, 18, 28, 123-4, 125, 126, 127, 128, 129, 130, 131, 135, 192, 193
Indochina, 151, 159
Indonesia, 126, 148, 154, 155-7
Industrialisation, 17, 20, 21, 24, 34-5, 42-3, 109-10, 123, 145
Industry, 17-8, 20-1, 23-5, 28, 34-6, 39, 42, 52, 60, 63, 94, 98, 101, 104, 108, 113, 117, 119, 122-3, 128-9, 131, 133, 140, 160, 170, 180, 181, 199, 201, 206, 207, 225, 226
Ingush, 23, 68-9
Ingushieta, 23
Institute for Food and Development Policy, 172-3

Institute for Health Metrics and Evaluation at the University of Washington, 158-9
Institute of Innovators and Rationalisers, 218
International Civil Aviation Organization (ICAO), 211-2
International Criminal Tribunal for the Former Yugoslavia, 197, 200
International Day Against Homophobia and Transphobia, 233
International debts, 113-4, 161, 189
International Institute for Strategic Studies, 188
International law, 54, 60, 125, 169, 174, 181, 195-6, 198-9
International Military Tribunal, Nuremberg, 43, 68
International Monetary Fund (IMF), 112, 161, 162, 171, 178, 189, 193, 195, 200, 201-2, 206, 207, 208
International Police Task Force, 202
International Republican Institute, 231
International Trading Corporation of Seattle, 125
Internationalism, 173-6, 195, 220-3, 236-7
Internment, 150
Interrogation, 44, 157-8, 230
Investment, domestic, 17-8, 20, 23-5, 35, 36, 52, 95-6, 108, 112, 119, 122, 134, 170, 183, 186, 189, 194, 203, 224
Investment, foreign, 20, 49, 129, 134, 161, 163, 186, 203, 216, 219
Inzko, Valentin, 202
Iran, 57, 147, 192, 193

Ireland, 16
Iron and steel, 2, 122
Ironsides, General, 13
Islamic Movement of Uzbekistan (IMU), 190
Italy, 47, 59, 86, 111, 197-8
Izetbegovic, Alija, 196, 197

Jager, Sheila Miyoshi, 140
Jamaica, 168
Jane's Defense Weekly, 198
Japan, 9, 10, 39, 41, 42, 43, 47, 48-9, 52, 81, 86-7, 92, 94, 97, 116-7, 118, 122, 129, 132, 139, 140, 147, 148, 161, 193
Jews, 15, 37-8, 67-8, 69, 71-2, 107, 113, 199, 209, 210
Johnson, Harold K., 157
Johnson, President Lyndon, 127-8, 154, 158, 159
Johnston, Eric, 38
Joint Chiefs of Staff, 81, 107, 168
Joint Economic Committee of the US Congress, 96, 170
Joint Intelligence Committee, 58, 77, 85
Joint Intelligence Committee, Australian, 156
Jones, Howard P., 155
Jong-il, Kim, 147
Jukes, Geoffrey, 86-7

Kaganovich, Lazar, 48
Kai-Shek, Chiang, 18, 116-7, 118, 119, 123, 124, 142
Kalashnikov, 64

Kalinykov, Mikhail, 70-1
Kamenev, Lev, 43-5
Kampong Sam, 160
Kaplan, Fanny, 9
Karachi-Cherkesa, 23
Karshi-Khanabad Air Base, 190
Katyn, 71-3
Katyusha, 64
Katz, Steve, 33
Kazakhstan, 23, 32-3, 38, 98-9, 123, 189, 192
Keeran, Roger, 182
Keitel, Field Marshal Wilhelm, 60
Kennan, George, 89, 91-2, 111, 179
Kennedy, President John, 127, 153, 154, 155, 164-5, 167-9
Kennedy, Robert, 168
Kenny, Thomas, 182
Kenya, 150
Kerensky, Alexander, 4
Kerry, John, 236
Khanin, Girsh, 38-9, 95, 98
Khlevnyuk, Oleg, 43
Khmer Rouge, 160-1
Khrushchev, Nikita, 47-8, 98-102, 113, 124, 125, 211
Khyber Pass, 18
Kiev, 41, 86, 212, 213
Kimball, Warren, 50
Kingston, Dr J. A., 26-7
Kinvig, Clifford, 13
Kirov, Serge, 44-5
Kissinger, Henry, 168
Kleist, General Paul von, 64

Knox, General Alfred, 10
Koch, Erich, 60
Koenker, Diane, 33
Kohl, Chancellor Helmut, 191
Kokh, Alfred, 188-9
Kolář, Pavel, 195
Kolchak, Admiral Aleksandr, 9, 10, 13-4
Korea, 25, 123, 129, 132, 145-7, 151
Korean War (1950-53), 108, 123, 139-45, 159
Kornilov, General Lavr, 4, 7, 14
Kort, Michael, 39, 185
Kosovo, 15, 197-200, 202, 211
Kosovo Force (KFOR), 202
Kosovo Liberation Army (KLA), 197-8, 200
Kostunica, Vojislav, 199-200
Kotz, David, 39-40, 182
Kozak Memorandum, 192
Krauthammer, Charles, 188
Kueh, Y. Y., 127, 133
Kulaks, 1, 17-8, 21-22, 23, 31-2, 112
Kuomintang, 117, 119
Kursk, battle of (1943), 73-4
Kuznick, Peter, 91
Kwangju, 145
Kwantung Army, 81
Kyrgyzstan, 123, 189, 190, 192

Laar, Mart, 108
Ladies in White, 232
Land reform, 5, 13-4, 107-9, 117, 119-20, 121, 133, 152
Laos, 123, 148, 152, 159, 160, 161, 163

Latin America, 169, 171, 172, 192, 193, 217, 220, 222, 223, 228, 231-2, 233, 234

Latin American School of Medicine, 223

Latvia, 57, 67, 68, 92, 108, 110, 191, 205, 206, 213

Latvian Central Council, 108

League of Nations, 9, 16, 54

League of Nations Covenant, 54

Leakey, Major General David, 201

Lech Walesa Institute, 231

Leffler, Melvyn, 139, 140

Leibovitz, Clement, 50

LeMay, General Curtis, 144

Lend-lease, 64, 89

Lenin, Vladimir, 3-4, 5, 8, 9, 11, 15, 100

Leningrad, 56-7, 60, 62

Lewin, Moshe, 21-2

Liberalisation, 99

Libraries, 22, 28, 88, 159

Libya, 147

Life, 42

Life expectancy, 26, 95, 96-7, 115, 121-2, 123, 130, 132, 135, 145, 171, 187, 204, 208, 221, 232

Lin, Chun, 120, 132

Lippmann, Walter, 11, 12, 56, 153

Literacy, 27-8, 131, 132, 133, 160, 170, 171, 172, 177, 203, 208, 233

Literacy Campaign, 166

Lithuania, 11, 12, 41, 42, 57, 67, 68, 108, 109, 110, 191, 205-6, 213

Lithuanian Activists' Front, 67

Lithuanian Defense Force, 108

Living standards, 99, 102, 161, 207

Lloyd George, David, 9, 10, 54-5

Lockhart, Robert Bruce, 9, 85

Logevall, Fredrik, 151, 154

London, 72, 75, 76, 78, 84, 104, 193

London Ambulance Unison, 217

London Olympics (2012), 232

Loth, Wilfried, 113

Lower, Wendy, 66

Luce, Don, 158

Ludlam, Steve, 171

Lukashenko, President Alexander, 207-8

Lysenko, Trofim, 28

MacArthur, General Douglas, 82, 144

Macedonia, 194, 199, 200

Machine Tractor Stations, 22, 99

Macmillan, Harold, 155

Malacca Straits, 156

Malaya, 148-51

Malaysia, 154, 156

Malenkov, Georgy, 94, 113

Mallory, Lester, 167

Manchuria, 41, 116, 119

Mandel, Ernest, 180

Mandela, Nelson, 174-6

Mannerheim, General Carl, 56

Mannerheim line, 56

Manufacturing, see Industry

'Market socialism', 98, 112, 179

Marshall, General George C., 82, 90

Marshall Islands, 234

Marshall Plan (1947), 90-1, 105

Martial law, 8, 151

Martin, Terry, 33, 36-7

Martinez, Yamil Eduardo, 225
Marxism, 101, 112
Maslowski, Peter, 93
Mason-Dixon Line, 142
Matanzas, 227
Mawdsley, Evan, 5, 61, 65, 83-4
Mazepa, Isaac, 31-2
Mazower, Mark, 74, 78
McCain, Senator John, 208
McCloskey, Pete, 157
McDermott, Kevin, 40
McGee, Senator Gale, 154
McGovern, John, 49
McMahon Line, 124
McNamara, Robert, 159, 169
McNeil, Hector, 112-3
Médecins Sans Frontières, 223
Media, 136, 156, 199, 209, 222, 225, 231
Medical schools, 26, 221, 223
Medvedev, Roy, 52-3
Meisner, Maurice, 133
Mercenaries, 167-8, 178, 214, 215
Mereshko, Lieutenant Anatoly, 70
Merz, Charles, 11, 12
Messer, Robert L., 79
Messersmith, George, 164
MI6, 16, 92, 106, 113, 121, 178
Miami, 168
Micronesia, 234
Microsoft, 137
Migration, 195, 205, 206
Milinkevich, Alexander, 209
Military spending, viii

Millett, Allan, 93
Milosevic, Slobodan, 197-200
Mindszenty, Cardinal, 109
Minh, Ho Chi, 151, 152, 158
Minsk, 11, 77, 214
Modric, Zarko, 201
Moldova, 192, 205, 212, 214
Molotov, Vyacheslav, 54, 59, 65, 94, 105
Mongolia, 49, 123, 190
Montenegro, 194, 195, 200, 201, 202
Montgomery, Field Marshal Bernard, 82, 85
Moo-hyun, President Roh, 147
Moody, Jim, 103
Morality, 114, 137, 219, 233, 235, 236-7
Moscow, 5, 9, 14, 26, 29, 41, 45, 48, 57, 59, 60, 62-3, 66-7, 75, 78, 81, 86, 88, 100, 113, 182, 190
Moscow Conference, 139
Moscow Federation of Trade Unions, 182
Moscow Metro, 29
Mostar, 201
Movimento Popular de Libertacao de Angola (MPLA), 173, 174
Mozambique, 173
Muhammad, Khalid Sheikh, 197
Mujehadin, 178, 201
Mukhina, Irina, 75-6
Munich Agreement (1938), 49-50
Munich Security Conference (2014), 214
Murmansk, 9
Murom, 9
Murphy, John, 199

Murray, Williamson, 74-5
Mussolini, Benito, 51
Mustard gas, 11

Nagy, Imre, 113
Namibia, 174-5
Napalm, 144
National Armed Forces, 107
National Centre for Sex Education, 232
National Endowment for Democracy, 231
National liberation movements, 158, 160, 173
National Security Strategy, 146
National United Front for the Salvation of Kampuchea, 160
National unity, 80, 108-9, 195-6, 236-7
NATO (North Atlantic Treaty Organization), 90, 93-4, 112, 114, 160, 161, 190-3, 195-200, 208, 210-15
Navy, Royal, 116, 148
Nehru, Jawaharlal, 124
Netherlands, 148
New Economic Policy, 15, 17-8, 20, 24
New York Times, 11-2, 198
Newsday, 169
Newsholme, Sir Arthur, 26-7
Newsweek, 107
Nikolaev, Leonid, 44
Nisbet, Robert, 80
Nixon, President Richard, 157, 160
Nizhny Novgorod, 9
NKVD, 16, 47-8, 72
No Gun Ri, 143

Non-Aggression Pact (1939), 51-3
Non-Governmental Organisations (NGOs), 190, 210, 231
Non-Proliferation Treaty, 146
Norilsk Nickel, 184
Novorossisk, 11
Nuclear Posture Review, 146
Nuclear weapons, 86-7, 92-3, 97, 101, 123, 128, 129, 145, 146
Nuland, Victoria, 210
Nuremberg Trials (1945-49), 43, 68
Nurseries, 15, 26, 102-3, 187

Obama, President Barack, 213, 231, 236
Observer, 19
Office for Democratic Institutions and Human Rights, 208
Official Secrets Act, 18
Oil, 104, 108, 110, 114, 129, 145, 147, 184, 186, 189, 193
Olympics, London (2012), 232
Oman, 178
Open Door policy, 150
Operation Bagration, 74-5, 77
Operation Milagro, 222
Operation *Pike*, 57
Operation Rollback, 91-2
Operation UNTHINKABLE, 85
Opium smoking, 129
Opium trade, 190, 205
Opium Wars, 115
'Orange Revolution' (2004), 210
Organization for Security and Co-operation in Europe [OSCE], 208

Organisation of Ukrainian Nationalists (OUN), 66-7, 108, 209
Osborn, Corporal Bart, 157
Osh, 190
Ottoman Empire, 41
Overy, Richard, 52, 60-1, 63, 77-8, 84

Pact of Steel, 51
Paczkowski, Andrejez, 67, 108
Padee, Jacek, 230
Pakistan, 123, 126, 178, 222
Pakistan Aid Consortium, 178
Palau, 234
Palestine, 150
Panama, 168, 229
Partition, 52; see also Divide and rule
Patriotism, 37, 75, 82-3, 110, 221, 236-7
Patten, Chris, 217
Peck, Edward, 155
Peking, see Beijing
Pellet, Volker, 231
Pensions, 26, 96, 128, 134, 136, 186, 187, 189, 204, 205, 206, 207, 208, 225, 226, 227
Penza, 9
People's Power, 227-9
Perestroika, 179-80
Pétric, Boris-Mathieu, 190
Petrograd, 5, 6, 11-2, 56
Phay, Siphan, 163
Phillips, Hugh, 5-6
Phoenix program, 153, 157-8
Pilsudski, Marshal Josef, 18
Plakans, Andrejs, 67-8

Planning, viii, 24-6, 39, 84, 97-100, 112, 113, 125, 127, 170
Pleshakov, Constantine, 90
Pogue, Forrest, 74
Pol Pot, 160-1
Poland, 9, 11, 12, 18, 19, 38, 41, 51-6, 59, 65-7, 69, 72, 75-81, 82, 84-5, 89, 91, 92, 107, 108-9, 110, 113-4, 191, 203-4, 206, 211, 213, 231
Polish Home Army, 67, 78, 107
Pollution, 137-8, 162, 193
Porch, Douglas, 150-1
Poroshenko, Petro, 211
Potanin, Vladimir, 184
Potsdam Agreement (1945), 86, 91, 99
Potsdam Conference (1945), 69, 91
Poverty, 99, 110, 115, 120-1, 122, 130, 132, 134, 137, 163, 171, 187-8, 189, 190, 195, 200, 201, 203-4, 205, 207-8, 210
Powell, Colin, 192
Poznan, 85
Pravy Sektor, 210
Pringle, Tim, 40
Prisoners of War (POWs), 7, 60-1, 91, 157
Productivity, 1, 21, 30, 35-6, 94, 126-7, 135, 170, 224, 225
Project Censored, 222
Propaganda, 8, 18, 34, 67, 72, 105, 112, 156, 199, 212, 213
Public services, 26, 188, 201, 236
Pudovkin, Vsevolod, 29
Putin, President Vladimir, 212, 214
Putna, Vitovt, 47

Racism, 37-8, 66, 83, 150, 172, 175, 210, 228-9, 233

Radek, Karl, 44, 47

Radio Martí, 231

RadioTV Serbia, 199

RAF, 11, 149, 150, 213

Railways, 25, 35, 88, 117

Rakosi, Matyas, 113

Raleigh, Donald, 5, 6

Rambouillet Accords (1999), 198

Rasmussen, Anders Fogh, 211

Raw materials, 34, 39, 102, 104, 183, 186, 189

Reagan, President Ronald, 174, 192

Red Army, 13, 32, 42, 45, 46, 48-9, 53, 56, 61-4, 68, 69, 71, 74-84, 86, 92

Red Cross, 60-1, 72

Reich, Otto, 222

Reichstag, 3

Reis, Bruno, 149

Reitemeyer, Lieutenant Francis, 157

Religion, 185

Renewables, 218-9, 235

Repression, 100, 107, 149

Republican Party, 209

Revai, József, 113

Revolutionary National Militias, 166

Rhee, Syngman, 140, 141

Rhineland, 49

Richardson III, Henry J., 174

Roberts, Andrew, 83, 117

Roberts, General William, 141

Roberts, Geoffrey, 52, 53, 83, 90-1

Rokossovsky, General Konstantin, 76, 77

Romania, 9, 18, 19, 53, 54, 55, 57, 59, 104, 105, 110, 111, 187-8, 191, 206, 213, 231

Rome-Berlin Axis, 43, 57-8, 59, 64, 82, 117

Rommel, General Erwin, 65

Roosevelt, President Franklin D., 65, 80, 82, 83, 89, 91

Rosenthal, Ben, 157

Rostov region, 62

Rostov-on-Don, 25

Rostow, Walt, 153

Royal Navy, 116, 148

Rozanov, General, 14

Rubottom, Roy, 166

Rusk, Dean, 124, 127, 144

Russia, viii, 1-19, 20-40, 41-2; see also Soviet Union

Russian Orthodox Church, 2, 15

Russian Revolution (1917), vii-viii, 1, 3-8, 12, 15, 26, 30, 41, 48, 60, 100, 182

Russian Union of Industrialists and Entrepreneurs, 183

Rutskoy, Alexander, 186

Rydz-Smigly, Marshal Edward, 53

Saar, 49

Sachs, Jeffrey, 204

Saetia Cay, 235

Saigon, 151

Samara, 188

Sanchez, Yoanni, 231

Sanctions, 54, 97, 118, 145, 147, 161, 167, 196, 199, 209, 212, 216-7

Santiago de Cuba, 235

Sarajevo, 202

Saratov, 5

Sargent, Orme, 85

SAS, 197-8

Save the Children, 232

Savimbi, Jonas, 174

Savinkov, Boris, 9

Sberbank, 184

Scarselleta, Mario, 143

Schaller, Michael, 80, 117

Schnytzer, Adi, 109

Schools, 25, 27, 36, 88, 130-1, 135, 159, 160, 172, 178, 218, 219, 233, 235, 236

Schuman, Frederick, 6-7, 14-5, 48, 51, 83

Science, 21, 24, 27-8, 29, 38, 39, 95-6, 98, 124-5, 129, 172, 177, 186, 189, 218, 220, 233

Scott, Michael, 172-3

Second Front, 65

Second International, 3

Second World War, 27, 39, 42, 48-87, 104, 117, 144, 148, 197, 204, 217

Secret Intelligence Service (SIS), 13, 17, 85, 154

Sedov, Sergei, 44

Self-Defence Commando, 68

Self-determination, see Sovereignty

Sen, Amartya, 127

Separatism, 50-1, 91, 122, 179-80, 194, 195, 212

Serbia, 194, 195, 196, 198, 199-201, 211

Serpa, Carlos Manuel, 231

Service, Robert, 6

Seton-Watson, Hugh, 110

Settlers, 37

Shackleton, Lieutenant Robert, 143

Shanghai, 18, 48, 116, 117, 118, 119

Shaw, Louise, 49

Shawcross, William, 160

Shearer, David, 33

Shenyang, 136

Shenzhen, 137

Sholokhov, Mikhail, 32

Shukhevych, Roman, 67, 209

Shulman, Elena, 37

Siberia, 63, 98-9

Siberian Ore, 188

Sibneft, 184

Sierra del Rosario, 235

Sirovy, General Jan, 46

Skoropadsky, General, 8

Slavery, vii

Slaveski, Filip, 106

Slovenia, 191, 194, 196, 201, 206

Smetona, President Antanas, 57

Smith, Howard K., 98

Smith, Michael, 113

Smolensk, 62, 71-2

Snyder, Timothy, 53, 69, 78

So-lin, Chang, 115

Social Revolutionary party, 9

Socialism, vii, viii, 3-4, 7, 15-8, 22, 24, 27, 28, 30, 39-40, 48, 84, 96-7,

99-100, 105, 109, 113, 179, 181-2, 190, 223-4, 225, 235, 236-7
Sokolnikov, Grigori, 44
Solana, Javier, 192
Solidarity (Solidarnosc), 114, 204, 206
Solidarity with Cuba, 231
Somalia, 173-4
South Africa, 96-7, 173-5, 192
South African Defence Force, 175
South Ossetia, 192, 212
South-East Asia, 148-63
Sovereignty, 16, 21, 80, 81, 121, 152, 158, 175, 178, 195-6, 212, 236-7
Soviet Union, vii-viii, 16-9, 20-40, 41-58, 59-69, 70-87, 88-103, 107-8, 109, 110-1, 112-3, 114, 116, 118, 122, 124, 127-8, 129, 139-40, 142, 145, 150, 169, 173, 177-93, 195, 197, 203, 207, 209, 212, 213, 217, 219, 223
Soviet-Polish Treaty of Friendship (1945), 80-1
Soviet-Yugoslav Treaty of Friendship (1945), 110-1
Soviets, 5, 6, 7
Spain, 7, 106, 231
Special Forces, 154, 161, 198
Special Period, Cuba's, 216-37
Sputnik, 95
Srebrenica, 197
Stahlecker, Franz, 68
Stalin, Joseph, 19, 21, 28, 29, 30, 32, 33, 35, 37, 40, 41-2, 43, 44, 45, 46-7, 52, 58, 61, 62, 64, 65-6, 74, 75-6, 77, 78, 80-1, 83-4, 85-6, 89-91, 92, 93-4, 97-8, 99-101, 102, 109, 111, 113, 118, 122, 139

Stalingrad, battle of (1942), 70-1
Stalingrad tractor factory, 25
Standley, William, 64
State Privatization Committee, 185
Statiev, Alexander, 5, 13, 68, 107-8
Steel, 2, 122
Stets'ko, Iaroslav, 67
Stettin, 85
Stettinius, Edward, 71
Stiglitz, Joseph, 189
Stilwell, General Joseph, 49
Stokes, Richard, 142
Stone, Oliver, 91
Stoudmann, Gerard, 208
'Strategic hamlets', 149
Strategy, 11, 13, 61-3, 71, 75, 101, 109, 130, 133, 159, 170, 191-2, 212, 213-4, 219, 220
Strong, Anna Louise, 25, 49
Structural Adjustment Programs (SAPs), 203-4
Stuckler, David, 96-7, 186
Subtelny, Orest, 28
Süddeutsche Zeitung, 212
Sudetenland, 49, 50, 51
Sudoplatov, Pavel, 92
Suharto, General, 156
Sukarno, President Dewi, 155-6
Summers, Colonel Harry, 144
Suny, Ronald, 5, 38, 105-6
Sustainable development, 218-9, 234-6
Svoboda party, 210
Swain, Geoffrey, 106
Swain, Nigel, 106

SWAPO (South West Africa People's Organisation), 174, 175
Sweden, 41, 211, 231
Syria, 193, 212

T-34 tank, 64
Tabouis, Genevieve, 45-6
Tactica riot-control vehicles, 156
Taiwan, province of China, 123, 137, 142
Taiwan Strait, 142
Tajikistan, 123, 189, 190, 192, 205
Tatars, 41, 68-9
Tauger, Mark, 23, 33-4
Teheran Conference (1943), 74
Templer, Field Marshal Gerald, 148-9
Temps Nouveaux, 180
Terms of trade, 193
Terrorism, viii, 2, 16, 18, 19, 23, 44-5, 46-7, 94, 107-8, 109, 119, 169, 190, 191, 197-8, 200, 209, 211, 217, 222, 236
Thailand, 154, 161
Thatcher, Margaret, 161, 196
Tibet, province of China, 121-2, 142
Tientsin, 18
Times, The, 11, 72, 109
Tito, President Josip, 110-3
Tobruk, 65
Tonkin Gulf incident (1964), 128, 154
Topes de Collantes Hills, 235
Torricelli-Graham Act (1992), 216
Torture, 14, 107, 150, 157, 200
Trade, 2, 10, 18, 21, 34, 45, 64, 97, 98, 110, 112, 118, 134, 160, 161, 162, 166, 185, 189, 190, 192-3, 200, 201, 202, 208, 210-1, 216-7, 234
Trade schools, 28
Trade unions, 2, 31, 57, 103, 114, 157, 180-1, 182, 185, 187, 188, 204, 206, 217, 218, 219, 224-7
Trafficking, 120, 200, 204-5, 208
Transnistria, 192, 212
Transparency International, 228
Transport, 28, 35-6, 39, 59, 95-6, 170, 187, 188, 206, 218, 234
Treblinka, 67
Trotsky, Leon, 7-8, 24, 40, 43-5, 46-7, 51, 180
Trotskyism, 49, 180
Truman, President Harry, 86, 91, 92, 118-9, 142, 144-5
Truman Doctrine, 90
Tse-Tung, Mao, 121, 122, 127, 132-3, 137
Tucker-Jones, Anthony, 76, 77
Tudjman, President Franjo, 201
Tukhachevsky, Marshal Mikhail, 45-6
Tung, Tran Thi, 158
Turkestan, 11
Turquino National Park, 235
Turrino, Enrico, 235
Tuyll, Hubert van, 67
Tuzla, 202
Typhoon jets, 213

Ukraine, 8, 12, 18, 19, 25, 28, 31-4, 48, 50-1, 53, 54, 55, 60, 66-7, 69, 73, 92, 100, 107-8, 187, 192, 209-15
Ukrainian Insurgent Army, 67

Ukrainian Landowners' Party, 8
Ulam, Adam, 33
Uneksimbank, 185
Unemployment, 39, 96, 117, 136, 167, 171, 186, 201-6, 209-10
UNESCO, 172, 233, 235
UNICEF, 160
Union of Communist Youth, 218
Union of Works Collective Councils and Workers' Committees, 180
Unison, 217
United Nations, 48, 82, 121, 141, 142, 143, 160, 173-4, 178, 195-6, 198-9, 214
United Nations Charter, 198-9
United Nations Definition of Aggression, 178
United Nations Development Program (UNDP), 202
United Nations Global Fund to Fight AIDS, Tuberculosis and Malaria, 232
United Nations Human Settlements Programme, 187-8
United Nations Legal Bureau, 161
United Nations' Millennium Goals, 172
United Nations Security Council, 142, 174, 195, 199, 214
United Nations World Development Report, 136
United States Agency for International Development, 231
United States Air Force (USAF), 117, 143, 144, 159, 168
United States bases overseas, 167-8

United States Interests Section (USIS), 230
United States Navy, 222
United States of America, 9, 16, 39, 63, 64-5, 68, 76, 80, 81, 83, 84-5, 86, 89-91, 93, 96, 97, 101, 104-5, 106-7, 111, 113, 114, 117-8, 119, 121, 123, 125, 128, 139-47, 148, 151-61, 162, 164, 166-9, 172, 173-4, 178, 190, 191, 192, 193, 198, 199-200, 201, 202, 208, 209-15, 216-7, 222, 229, 230, 231, 232, 233, 234, 236
United Tariff Scale (UTS), 188
US Department of Commerce, viii
US Department of Defense, 168
US News and World Report, 106-7
US Treasury, 164, 201-2, 231
USA Today, 206-7
Ustashe, 194
Uzbekistan, 189, 190, 192

Valentine, Douglas, 153, 159
Vance, Cyrus, 173
Vatican, 57, 196
Venezuela, 168, 193, 220, 222
Vershbow, Alexander, 213-4
Vietnam, viii, 123, 124, 128, 139, 142, 144, 148, 151-4, 157-63, 219
Vilna, 11, 57, 76
Viñalas Valley, 235
Vistula, River, 53, 77, 78, 79
Vladivostok, 9, 10, 116, 143
Vojvodina, 195
Volkogonov, Dimitri, 90-1
Volodymyr-Volyns'kiy, 73

Voronin, Vladimir, 192
Vyatka, 9
Vyshinsky, Andrey, 46

Wade, Rex, 6
Waffen SS, 67, 76
Wages, 2, 31, 94, 102-3, 112, 123, 128, 136, 137, 161, 163, 167, 171, 180, 181, 186, 188, 189, 195, 203, 204, 205, 206, 207, 209, 210, 224, 225, 226, 227
Walker, General Walton, 144
Wall Street Journal, 145-6, 191-2
Wallace, Henry, 91
Walton, Calder, 150
Wanhsien, 116
War crimes, 68, 144, 157-8, 198
War of Intervention against Russia (1918-22), 9-15, 41, 89
Warsaw, 53, 67, 75-9
Warsaw Pact, 90, 124, 196-7
Water, 138, 160, 162, 165, 221, 235
Wedemeyer, General Albert, 65, 117
Weir, Fred, 39-40, 182
Welfare services, 26-7, 38, 96, 120, 135, 136, 189, 204, 217, 227, 232, 236
Welles, Sumner, 64, 82-3
Werth, Alexander, 96
Wertheim, Wim, 126
West Germany, 91, 93-4, 106, 129
Western Europe, 1, 2, 60, 93-4, 97, 104-5, 113, 200
Westing, Arthur, 159
Wheeler-Bennett, John, 6
White Legion, 209

Wiebes, Cees, 197
Wilson, Harold, 156
Wilson, Sir Henry, 9
Wolfowitz, Paul, 146
Women, 2, 15, 26, 27, 28, 37, 97, 117, 120, 132, 135, 136, 139, 140, 143, 145, 152, 171, 177-8, 187, 200, 205, 208, 219, 221, 223, 228-9, 233
Woodrow Wilson International Center for Scholars, 106
Woodward, Susan, 112, 196
Workers' Central Union of Cuba, 166
Working class, vii-ix, 2, 3, 4, 6, 15, 21, 27, 29-31, 38, 60, 100, 103, 104, 117, 129, 134, 136, 166, 180-2, 183, 186, 188, 194, 195, 202, 217, 219, 220, 223, 224-30, 236-7
World Bank, 112, 119, 128, 129, 130, 161-2, 165, 171, 178, 180, 185, 189, 201-2, 207-8, 228
World economic crisis, 172
World Health Organisation (WHO), 135, 137-8, 223
World Wildlife Fund, 235-6
Wright, Quincy, 169

Xiao-Ping, Deng, 133-4, 137
Xinhua News Agency, 121
Xinjiang, 122

Yalta Agreement (1945), 79-80
Yalta Conference (1945), 79-80, 89, 91
Yalu River, 144
Yangtze River, 118
Yanukovych, Viktor, 210

Yaroslavl, 9
Yatsenuk, Arseniy, 211
Yellow River, 125
Yeltsin, President Boris, 179-84, 186-7, 217
Yezhov, Nikolai, 47-8
Yo, sí puedo, 233
Yudenich, General, 9
Yugoslavia, 82, 98, 105, 110-3, 194-202
Yushchenko, President Viktor, 209

Zambia, 223
Zapata swamp, 235
Zenica, 202
Zhukov, Marshal Georgi, 58, 61, 76
Zimmerman, Warren, 195
Zinoviev, Grigory, 43-5
'Zinoviev letter', 16-7
Zubok, Vladislav, 90, 91

Printed in the United States
By Bookmasters